Dreamers Before the Mast,
The History of the Tall Ship *Regina Maris*

By John Kerr

Carol Lew Simons, Contributing Editor

Cover photo by Shep Root

Preface and a Tribute to *Regina*

Steven Katona

Somehow wood, steel, cable, rope, and scores of other inanimate materials and parts create a living thing when they are fastened together to make a ship. I have often wondered why ships have souls but cars, trucks, and skyscrapers don't. I think the explanation is the intensity of bonding between people and ships, starting with the slow handwork required for their construction and continuing with the round-the-clock involvement necessary for sailing them. I think their souls grow each night. As each watch ends, people sleep the strange shipsleep, so far away, so full of dreams. And as they do, pieces of their souls slip away and stick to the ship, while fragments of accumulated shipsoul fall off and stick to the people. All this happens easily in the small, dark bunk, and the ship's gentle rocking stirs everything together so that pretty soon peoplesoul and shipsoul are all tangled up and neither party feels complete without the other, ever. But no matter how alive and ensouled ships are, they have not yet learned to speak in words, so their stories must be told by the people they carry over the sea.

Steven Katona is managing director of the Ocean Health Index for Conservation International. He wrote a Tribute to Regina Maris *to introduce the summer 1988 edition of* Whalewatcher, *the journal of the American Cetacean Society, from which the above excerpt is reprinted with permission. That entire issue is dedicated to* Regina's *years as a whale research vessel, and more excerpts from it appear in Chapters 16 through 20.*

Acknowledgements

As Steve Katona says, ships … have not yet learned to speak in words, so their stories must be told by the people they carry over the sea." I have tried to do just that, allow those involved with the ship do the speaking. This is easy to say but hard to do. I contacted hundreds of people for help and gave them the opportunity to give feedback, and at times the book was being written by committee. I have quoted very many and paraphrased many more. I hope I have done them justice. You all have my sincerest thanks for all you have given to the project.

Additional thanks must go to Evan Ginsburg for starting *Friends and Crew of the Regina Maris* on Facebook. The page can be found at https://www.facebook.com/reginamaris1908/. Without that connection, many of the memories and much history would have been lost. Readers should view this site for many additional photos and historical information. Many thanks also go to Steve Nelson, who had the vision and fortitude to organize and develop three ways for *Regina* friends and crew to keep in contact. He was responsible for three reunions — two formal and one informal — that brought old shipmates together to keep connections and memories alive. He started *The Jolly Boat* newsletter, which can be subscribed to at http://eepurl.com/rmcQv. And he started the *Regina Maris* Society, the website for which can be found at: *www/reginamsociety.org*.

To Penny Kerr, for her love, patience, and forbearing as the other woman in my life, for all the years we have been together, thank you.

Photo Quality

Unfortunately, through the ravages of time and flood many of the original photos have been lost or damaged. Moreover, many were taken before the advent of digital enhancement and DPIs above 200. A coffee table book this is not. Many wonderful photos can be found in the photos section on the Facebook page, *Friends and Crew of the Regina Maris,* https://www.facebook.com/reginamaris1908/.

Table of Contents

CHAPTER ONE — 7
In the Beginning
1908 – 1932

CHAPTER TWO — 14
Trade and Fish
1932 – 1963

CHAPTER THREE — 22
Queen of the Sea
1963 – 1966

CHAPTER FOUR — 33
Voyage of a Barkentine
1966

CHAPTER FIVE — 41
The Horn
1967

CHAPTER SIX — 50
Australia Bound, Plymouth England to Funchal, on the Island of Madeira
1968 – 1969

CHAPTER SEVEN — 59
Dismasted
October 1969 – February 1970

CHAPTER EIGHT — 69
Australia Bound Once More
February – August 1970

CHAPTER NINE — 77
Mutiny?
August 9 – September 7, 1970

CHAPTER TEN — 87
End of the Glory Days
Late 1970

— 92

CHAPTER ELEVEN
Scheveningen Harbor to Long Beach, California
1970 – 1971

CHAPTER TWELVE 101
Long Beach to Papeete
June – August 1971

CHAPTER THIRTEEN 110
One Queen vs. Two Typhoons
1971-1973

120

CHAPTER FOURTEEN
New Owners and Passages
September 1973 – April 1974

133

CHAPTER FIFTEEN
Southampton to the Black Sea
1974 – 1976

144

CHAPTER SIXTEEN
The ORES Years Begin
1976

150

CHAPTER SEVENTEEN
R/V *Regina Maris* Heads to the Caribbean
January 1977

159

CHAPTER EIGHTEEN
Voyages 1978 Through 1980

172

CHAPTER NINETEEN
Voyages 1981 Through 1983

CHAPTER TWENTY 187
Regina's Last ORES Years
1983 – 1986

198

CHAPTER TWENTY-ONE
In Marina Bay, Massachusetts
1986 – 1991

203

CHAPTER TWENTY-TWO
To Greenport, New York
February – September 1991

214

CHAPTER TWENTY-THREE
Fairhaven, Massachusetts
September 1 – October 22, 1991

CHAPTER TWENTY-FOUR
Greenport, New York
October 24, 1991 – August 25, 1998   224

CHAPTER TWENTY-FIVE
Glen Cove, New York
August 1998 – February 2002   239

Epilogue   250

Regina Maris Lives On   251

Appendix A   255

Appendix B   256

Appendix C   257

Appendix D   259

Appendix E   269

Appendix F   276

Appendix G   281

Appendix H   283
Index   287

CHAPTER 1
IN THE BEGINNING
1908 – 1932

The history of any ship is difficult to separate from stories of the people who were involved with her. The story of *Regina Maris* begins with a dreamer, Olof Bengtsson, born in 1866 in Raa, Sweden. [1]

In 1895 Olof was in the Australian Outback searching for gold with a friend and 3,000 other "panners." From the end of the rail line they had to walk thirty miles to the gold fields. Water was at a premium and they saw many dehydrated men. Olof and his friend Olof Paulsson bought their claims, two 100-foot triangles, side by side. They came prepared to pan with water but there was none, so sifting the sand became their method. It was backbreaking work under nearly intolerable conditions. On their first day of operating, they obtained seven pounds of gold. Their "strike" made the other panners wild. All worked themselves into a feverish state. The two friends had to sleep with guns under their pillows.

Much of the gold they found had to be used to purchase food and water. The food was very simple—— canned fish and bread baked on the coals of a fire. Water had to be boiled for it was infected with the typhoid bacteria. The Aborigines were the only people who could drink the water, but they kept their distance from the miners. Dingoes posed a major problem, for these wild dogs were always ready to attack the unwary.

One day the two Olofs sifted 30 pounds of gold, but that was a rarity in that inhospitable place. The hard work went on for 10 months until the rush was over and the two friends returned to the civilization offered by Fremantle, a port on Australia's west coast, Olof Bengtsson stayed on in west Australia for two years, fishing for snappers and sharks, then headed east to Melbourne, where he found employment taking guests from the hotels out sailing. He decided to go home for some "vacation" as he called it and obtained passage on a ship bound for Southampton, England, and then on to Hamburg, Germany. By the summer of 1899 he was back in Raa.

Jakob from Being from a seafaring family, he went right to work as skipper of *Blenda,* a small yacht he had purchased on his return with some of his Australian gold. He sold her before the end of the year 1900. In 1901, he became first mate under Captain L. Bose on *Betty,* a large schooner. In 1902, Olof took over command of the schooner A.R. Rawall and sailed her until 1908.

During a major storm on Christmas Day 1902, the tall ship *Direkter* stranded on the rocks outside Raa. Olof stood at the end of a chain of men, up to his chest in the raging sea, and rescued the passengers and crew. The King of Sweden awarded them all medals for heroism.In 1904, Olof married Maria Reinhold and the newlyweds settled into a new house at #8 Matrasgatan Street in Raa. They had one son, Bertil, who also became a sea captain.In 1907, Olof was planning to build a ship and start a shipping company. Interest in the project was considerable, for Olof Bengtsson was well liked and respected. There were 77 shares in the company, each at 510 kr (kronor). Olof held 10; his father-in-law, Per Reinhold, held eight; and there were 36 other shareholders. *(See Appendix A for a list of shareholders and their share amounts.)* Per Reinhold, also a licensed captain, was thus the company's other operating partner, and at times over the years he captained *Regina*.

To get his ship built, Olof traveled to Svendborg, Denmark, where he contracted with the famous ship builder Jorgen Ring-Andersen to build a three-masted schooner. This ship was the 100th hull that Ring-Andersen was to produce. The two men walked the woods of Denmark selecting the white oak trees to be used in the construction. [2] Jorgen Ring-Andersen believed that for a ship to be strong, all her curved lines and timbers should have grown into that shape. To this day, they do not steam timbers at the Ring-Andersen Shipyard. [3]

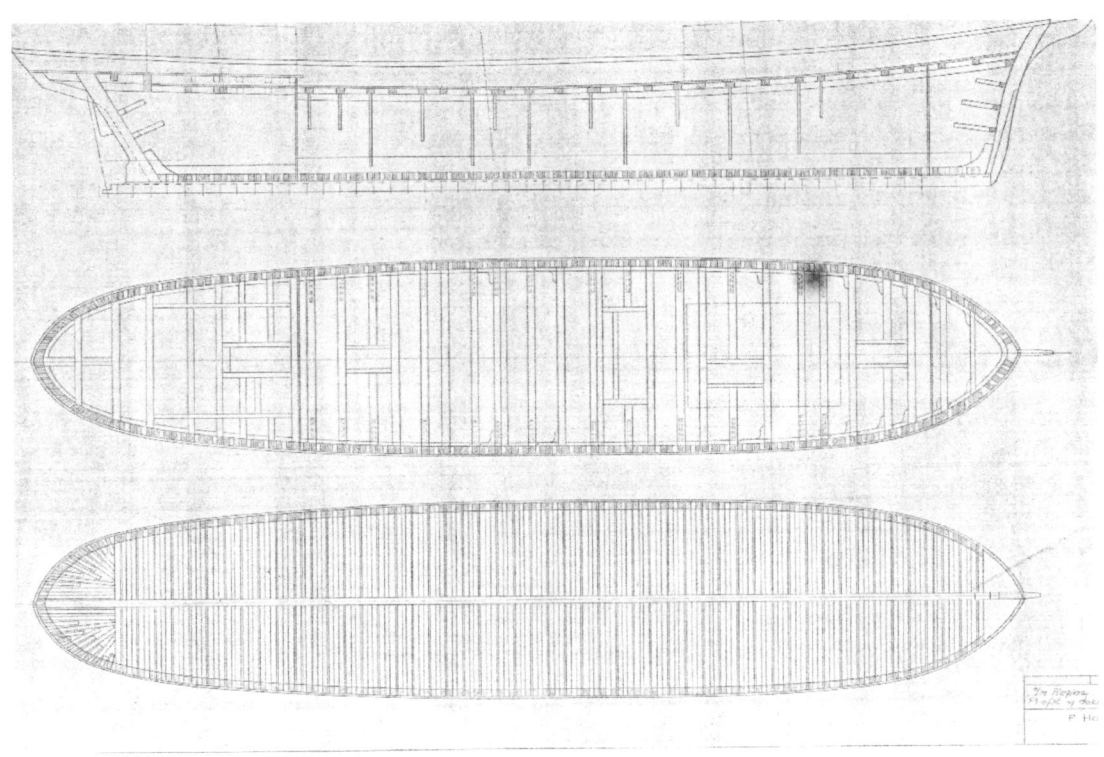

This drawing from a 1963 restoration and rebuild of *Regina* shows the timber framing plan for the "sistered" ribs that were part of the ship's original architecture and remained unchanged in the rebuild. [4] *Drawing courtesy of Holger Nestorson of the Skarhamns Sjofartsmuseum.*

The ship's keel was laid March 15, 1907, the shipyard's 40th birthday. The new ship was named for Jorgen's wife, Regina Ring-Andersen, and was called *Regina* until 1964, when she became *Regina Maris (see chapter 3, page 28)*. *Regina* was caravel-built, meaning that the beechwood hull planks were laid edge to edge to form a smooth surface. The oak ribs were set in pairs with 100 feet between perpendiculars. An additional hull was laid on the inner surface of the ribs for greater strength in the ice of the Baltic and North Atlantic. Her breadth was 25 feet and her draft 10 feet, 10 inches, for 166.86 gross tons. She had only an aft cabin on the raised poop half deck in the stern. Her sail plan as a three-masted schooner was to have 12 fore- and aft-rigged sails plus two square sails mounted on the yardarms of the foremast.

Regina was launched March 28, 1908. The photo shows her painted white with her masts stepped and flags flying as she slips into the sea. The launching cradle collapsed as she started down the ways, throwing her on her side. She landed upright and undamaged. *Photo from the Ring-Anderson Shipyard Centennial volume.* [2]

When the time came for delivery, Olof paid for the vessel in full — 38,534.52 kr. Four days later *Regina* arrived in her homeport of Raa, and shareholders and friends went onboard to inspect her. At the shareholders meeting on April 10, 1908, it was decided that Captain Olof would be paid 70 kr. per month for every voyage plus 5 percent of the profits from the cargo. Each crewmember would be paid .90 kr. per day. She was sailed with a crew of six: the Captain, the cook, the first mate, an ordinary seaman, and two deck boys. The first three slept in the deckhouse and the others slept in the forecastle below deck.

The aft cabin had a salon with plush furniture, oak parquet flooring, and beautifully carved woodwork lit by brass lamps. On the port side were the galley and cabins for the cook and first mate. On the starboard side were the captain's cabin, a head, and a storeroom for code flags and charts. The cabin house had ventilators and a skylight. The lifeboat hung from davits in the stern, which was decorated with a beautifully carved shield-shaped nameboard surrounded by two carved dragons with their tails reaching forward along the sides of the quarter deck rail. The windlass, or capstan, was a new type, self-tailing with a brake system. Two years after her launch another deckhouse was built around the foremast to be used as a forecastle. This gave more space below decks for cargo and moved the crew up on deck for better access to the ship's activities.

Regina's maiden voyage commenced April 22, 1908, from Raa, sailing south around the southern tip of Sweden and into the Baltic Sea to the island of Gotland and the village of Hellvi Hide, for 404 nautical miles. (Sailing ships, because of wind and weather, may actually travel more than double the rhumb line course to a given destination.) From there they sailed north and into the Gulf of Bothnia and on up to its halfway point, to the town of Hornefors, Sweden, a total of 498 nm. From there the ship sailed back south 852 nm through the Gulf of Bothnia and across the Baltic Sea to the mouth of the Warnow River (Germany) and eight miles up the channel to Rostock, Germany. Then it was back north across the Baltic to Stockholm, a distance of 438 nm. Stockholm is over 60 miles inland through very narrow fiords and channels. Sailing those miles would have been very challenging — and Captain Bengtsson was not one to pay for a tug to tow the ship to port.

The next port of call was Sundsvall, Sweden, 233 nm north of Stockholm in the Gulf of Bothnia. From there they sailed back to the south and around the southern tip of Sweden to Malmo, Sweden, a distance of 710 nm. The ship then sailed back north through the Baltic Sea and up into the very northern shore of the Gulf of Bothnia and the remote port of Batskarsnas, Sweden, covering 1,020 nm. The next leg of the voyage was to sail 966 nm back south to Rostock, Germany. They went back north 453 nm to Stockholm for the next voyage. Then with another new cargo the ship sailed north, to the southern end of the Gulf of Bothnia, docking at the port of Gavle, Sweden, covering 503 nm. The next leg of the trip was to sail 761 nm south to Copenhagen, Denmark. From there they sailed 22 nm to Raa, their home port, arriving December 1. Her first season of carrying cargo covered 6,560 nautical miles. It is unknown what her cargo was for all these voyages at this time but she usually carried general trade goods, fuel oil in metal tins, fish products, and lumber.

In early spring 1909, *Regina*, was brought to a shipyard to have her sails checked and adjusted by sailmaker J.P. Jonsson. There was some additional welding to do by a master smith named P. Siversson. An insurance underwriter's certificate was purchased and membership dues were paid to join the Sailing Ships Association and the Sailors House in Halsingborg. Additional costs for provisions and for towing all amounted to 500 kr.

Regina loaded with a cargo of lumber. *Photo courtesy of Holger Nestorson of the Skarhamns Sjofartsmuseum.* [5]

Olof Bengtsson was an excellent bookkeeper, and his records that survive *(see Appendix B)* show excellent profits. *Regina's* worst year, 1914, was due to the start of World War I and a collision with a Norwegian steamboat that necessitated an early haul-out and layup. She only made 9,249.48 kr. that year. However, demand for freight shipping rose in wartime, and the profits were very good despite the risks. The ship owners in 1915 gave Olof a bonus of 100 kr. for the increased risk he incurred. As the war went on his bonus increased, as did the tonnage. The ship was put up in Raa for winter at nearly the same time each year, during which time Olof enjoyed many days fishing in the Oresund, a sound near Raa, where he would saw a hole in the ice and hand line for cod.

During the 20-year period that Olof Bengtsson commanded *Regina,* she visited 94 different harbors, mostly in Sweden, Denmark, and Finland. She called at two-thirds of these ports only once or twice. Calls at harbors visited more frequently from 1908 to 1927 are detailed in the table below. This is proof that *Regina* was a Baltic trader for the first 19 years of her working life. The stories that she was a nitrate carrier plying the world's oceans are not true.

Copenhagen, DK	16	Rafso, FI	6	Kemi, FI	3
Limhamm, SE	15	Malmo, SE	5	Kristiania, DK	3
Sundsvall SE	10	Horsens, DK	5	Koge, DK	3
Raa, SE	10	Odense, DK	5	Landskrona, SE	3
Gavle, SE	9	Halmstad, SE	4	Norrwundet, SE	3
Holbaek, DK	9	Harnosand, SE	4	Presto, SE	3
Arhus, DK	8	Randers, DK	4	Uleaborg, FI	3
Alborg, DK	7	Stettin, DE	4	Umea, SE	3
Halsingborg, SE	7	Stockholm, SE	4	Visby, SE	3
Hoganas, SE	7	Flensborg, DE	3		

In 1910, Olof asked the ship owners for permission to trade with the city of St. Petersburg, Russia, and permission was granted. On the way to St. Petersburg, however, the ship stopped at the port of Reval, Estonia (now called Tallin). While in port, it was discovered that a very valuable cargo destined for Copenhagen was looking for a ship. Olof changed plans, loaded the cargo, and set sail for Copenhagen.

In 1926, sea captain Per Reinhold, Olof's partner and father-in-law, died and Olof was appointed head ship owner. He was 60 years old and did not operate the ship as rigorously as he had as a young man. In 1929, at the age of 63, he retired from command of *Regina* and stayed on shore as CEO of the shipping company. Another shareholder, Olof Andersson, took command of the ship.

Over the 20 years Olaf Bengtsson was involved, the costs of operating the ship increased considerably. The chart below compares the 1909 shipping season to the 1929 season, when Olof Andersson took over *Regina's* operation.

	1909	**1929**
Gross Freight income	13,660.51 kr.	19,265.97 kr.
Monthly rents, warehousing	1,958.34 kr.	4,488.61 kr.
Provisions	1,320.30 kr.	2,463.61 kr.
Fees and docking costs	2,851.80 kr	4,526.60 kr.
5% tax surcharge	467.80 kr.	963.30 kr.`
Total costs	6598.24 kr.	12442.12 kr.
Net profit	7062.27 kr.	6823.85kr.

In 1908, the costs for provisioning one man per day were .90 kr. Twenty years later it was 1.71 kr. per man per day. The skippers during those times were considered thrifty and cheap. There is a Swedish saying that goes, "They had to turn their pockets inside out, once or twice, before money was given out."

At the ship owners meeting in November 1931, Olof Bengtsson proposed that *Regina* be put up for sale. For the first time in her history she had turned a loss. It was only 593 kr. but Olof wanted to retire. Her sale price was 22,000.00 kr. Buyers came to inspect but none wanted to pay the price. She eventually sold, however, for 16,000.00 kr. on February 19, 1932. At the time of the sale, the owners paid a bonus of 177 kr. to every shareholder. A smaller amount was donated to the Swedish Society for Saving the Shipwrecked.

Upon his retirement, Captain Olof Bengtsson received many awards from Swedish shipping and sailing organizations. From the Insurance Underwriters Association he received a silver cup, to honor *Regina,* her owner and commander, with this inscription: "For dutiful efficiency and for successful commandership of the schooner *Regina."*

Because of the *Regina's* excellent safety record, (never a loss or a death) the King of Sweden gave Olof an award, and for many years he was a member of the board of Sweden's Sailing Ships Association and Sweden's Sea Captains' Association. Olof was also the chairman of the Raa division of Sweden's Sailing Ship Association and a member of the board of Raa Trading Association, founded by his father-in-law, Per Reinhold. Captain Olof Bengtsson died in 1963 at the age of 97. In his obituary it stated, "Raa has lost a prominent figure, a man tough as nails, with a boyish mind, a sailor of unusual stature." [6]

CHAPTER 1
IN THE BEGINNING

1. Jan Davidsson, *Skeppoch Sjoman* (Killbergs [publisher], 1930). This book provided much of the history and tables included in the text. It was translated by Lotta Clark and Susie Lange, both of Shelter Island, New York.

2. Jorgen Ring-Andersen Shipbuilders provided the documents reproduced in the appendix, as well as photos and other helpful information. The shipyard provided a copy of the original contract for construction signed by O.B. Bengtsson and Jorgen Ring Andersen, dated 31 January, 1907. Also sent were a list of specifications and the launching schedule.

3. David Moodie, "A doorway to the Past, Denmark's Ring-Andersen yard has an unbroken lineage dating back to 1867," *WoodenBoat* #150, September/October 1999. This article includes many historical photographs of the yard and shipbuilding, courtesy of Svenborg Og Omegns Museum.

4. John Aage Wilson and his daughter Marianne Wilson provided the drawings of the hull timbers, drawn by the staff at Hoivold Mekaniske Verksted shipyard in Kristiansand, Norway.

5. Holger Nestorson of the Skarhamns Sjofartsmuseum provided photos of *Regina* and information on the Edvardsson and Nilsson families. The Museum and Holger also operate a sail-training, two-masted schooner, *MS Atene*, built by J. Ring-Andersen in 1909. Holger's letters were translated by Lotta Clark.

6. Eric Bjorck, of both the Raa Musiforenin and the Raa Museum for Fiske Och Sjofart, provided history notes and information on the Per Reinhold-Olof Bengtsson families.

CHAPTER 2
TRADE AND FISH
1932 – 1963

During her first 24 years, *Regina's* homeport had been Raa. For the next 31 years, it was Sarkhamn, up Sweden's west coast on the Island of Tjorn, just north of the city of Goteborg. Sarkhamn was the home of Captain Gustaf N. Edvardsson, her new owner as of February 19, 1932. [1]

Captain Gustaf Edvardsson, owner of *Regina*, 1932 to 1960.
Photo courtesy of Holger Nestorson of the Skarhamns Sjofartsmuseum.

Gustaf Edvardsson owned *Regina* in partnership with his brother-in-law, Ernst Nilsson, of Ronnang, Sweden, although Ernst was captain and owner of *Folke* and did not sail *Regina.* In Ronnang, a "help" engine was installed in *Regina*, just to move the ship in and around the harbors and for emergency power, not for motoring long distances. The ship's rig was also changed at this time: The two foremast yards were removed and the foremast shortened so that all three masts were the same height. On deck two "donkey engines" were installed to facilitate the loading and unloading of cargo. Many of *Regina's* activities, her cargo, and the ports of call, remained similar to her first 24 years. What did change was the politics of Sweden and the world. [2]

Regina unloading wood in a Danish harbor. The child is Ola Thuvik, a relative of future owner Sigurd Thuvik. The two donkey engines can also be seen. *Photo courtesy of Holger Nestorson of the Skarhamns Sjofartsmuseum.*

In the mid 1930s, with the rise in power of Germany, Sweden and her Scandinavian neighbors followed a strictly neutral course, in close collaboration with the Netherlands, Belgium, and Switzerland. During World War I, Sweden had maintained her neutral standing and traded with both sides, making *Regina's* owners very wealthy. In 1935, Hitler started the rearming of Germany, and many products were needed for his military buildup, putting great demands on the Baltic shipping industry and *Regina's* owners. When the U.S.S.R. attacked Finland in November 1939, Sweden helped Finland with supplies and a volunteer corps. *Regina,* temporarily based in Stockholm, was used to ferry materials and members of the volunteer corps across to Finland. On one of her trips to Finland, she ran aground on the Oregrund archipelago and suffered severe keel damage. Repaired quickly, she went back to work, for there was cargo waiting all over the Baltic to be transported to Finland and Germany.

In 1942, on her way from Sarkhamn to Lubeck, Germany, *Regina* collided with an unknown object, sprang a leak, and sustained propeller damage. According to surviving family members of Gustaf Edvardsson, he always believed that *Regina* had hit a German submarine. While no official confirmation of this information exists, there were German sub bases in the area. [2]

As the persecution of "undesirables" increased in Germany, many people fled through Denmark hoping to find freedom in Sweden and Norway. Maria Theander, grand-niece of Gustaf Edvardsson, claimed that *Regina* was involved in "saving Jews from Hitler." [3] One account has *Regina* embarking 60 Jewish men, women, and children for a night voyage from Dragor, Denmark, in October 1943 and sailing to Limhamn, Sweden. Hanne Ekman was a small child when she fled with her uncle Herman Ekman, owner of the Danish newspaper *Politiken*. She stated that "she will never forget *Regina Maris*, nor will she forget the man who commanded it, Captain Finn Jensen of Esbjerg, Denmark."[4]

According to Lloyd's Register of Shipping, Captain Edvardsson was the only captain/owner listed for *Regina*, and Lloyd's listed no ship named *Regina Maris* during the years 1938 to 1945. Lloyd's, of course, does not insure and register every ship in existence at a given time, but *Regina's* name did not change to *Regina Maris* until 1964. Finn Jensen could have been hired for the above-described nighttime voyage. There was no central registration for captains at that time, as many earned their title through experience, not schooling.

When Janet Blatt of Glen Cove, N.Y., (*Regina Maris's* final resting place) went to Sweden and Denmark in 1999 to research the possible participation of the ship in rescuing Jews from Hitler's Germany, she found the family of Gustaf Edvardsson "very tight-lipped about their involvement." [5] Even to this day people, are very reluctant to talk of their involvement in the war, as anti-Semitism is alive and well in many hearts.

Janet Blatt met with Professor Leo Goldberger, of New York University's department of psychology and editor of *The Rescue of the Danish Jews: Moral Courage Under Stress*, published in 1987 by New York University Press. In her interview with him, he stated that he had "left Dragor, Denmark, on a sailing ship with Herman Ekman. He said that, "he walked into the water 100' up to his neck carrying young children and their belongings." He and Janet felt that *Regina* had been involved in this humanitarian effort, but since the family whose members may have been directly involved refuses to talk about it, there can be no special recognition for *Regina*, and more documentation would be needed to prove that the ship was involved in rescuing Jews from Germany. [6]

During the war, *Regina* suffered one other collision. In 1944, near Lysekil, just north of Sarkhamn, the Swedish Coast Guard vessel *Skagerack* ran into *Regina*, and she suffered extensive damage and many leaks. Although she was repaired, after the war many surplus steam and diesel ships were available to carry cargo, and a wooden schooner had a difficult time paying her way. Gustaf Edvardsson decided to take up Grand Banks cod fishing off the coast of Newfoundland and herring fishing off Iceland.

Every April, from 1945 until 1960, Captain Edvardsson and *Regina* would leave Sweden with tons of salt for preserving her catch and a deck-load of lumber. The lumber would be sold in Iceland. Dories were stacked in nests of five on deck, and *Regina* would sail the 2,500 miles to the fishing grounds. Waters on the Grand Banks are between 10 and 30 fathoms deep. In the shallow waters, codfish congregate in large numbers to feed on the schools of herring coming inshore to spawn. *Regina* would anchor in the shallows as a mother ship for her flock of dories.

Regina during her fishing years, with her fishing registration number painted on her bow, in her home port of Sarkhamn, Sweden. *Photo courtesy of Holger Nestorson of the Skarhamns Sjofartsmuseum.*

Each dory was about 13 feet long and manned by one fisherman. This was very demanding work for the dory men, who had to have an excellent sense of direction and knowledge of sea and weather. Using a small sail, they would venture out of sight of the mother ship to a likely spot, then throw out a 1,300-foot line on which were 400 hooks baited with herring. Two to three hours later they would haul the line in by hand, and if successful, remove their catch. Then they would repeat the process until nearly dark. During bad weather, *Regina* sailed to Labrador and Greenland for safety and supplies. The ship would stay on the banks until September or October, depending on the weather, then return by way of Iceland to offload some of their catch. They would also pick up other trade goods for sale in their home port of Sarkhamn. The ship would then be laid up for the winter.

As a point of interest, the tall ship *Gazela,* (*Gazela Primeiro* was her name for 83 years) was also fishing on the Grand Banks during this time. The two ships were to meet twice in the years to come, once in Lisbon in 1971 and once, many years later — July 7 to July 10, 1993 — when *Gazela* and *Regina* shared dock space in Greenport, New York. At that time, they were the world's only wooden barkentines.

Captain Edvardsson made this museum model of *Regina,* which was presented to the Skarhamn Sjofartsmuseum. *Photo courtesy of Holger Nestorson of the Skarhamns Sjofartsmuseum.*

In the winter of 1960-61, *Regina* was sold to Sigurd Thuvik of Sarkhamn, and the ship went back to carrying cargo in the Baltic Sea. On May 4, 1963, off the island of Bornholm in the Baltic, she had a fire in the engine room. All efforts to extinguish it were in vain, so the crew abandoned ship. The Russian tanker *Edward Wilde* arrived on the scene, put out the fire, rescued the crew, and towed *Regina* to a wharf in Yastad, Sweden. [7] She was so badly burned from the engine room aft that her ribs were half burned off, and she was condemned. All the valuable equipment was removed, and a local farmer was planning to store his harvest for the winter in what remained of her hold. However, later in 1963, the Ocean Wide Steamship Company, of Monrovia, Liberia, and Ocean Transport Lines of Arendal, Norway, purchased her for 6,000 kr. The double sale was made for tax reasons, for the new owners, John Aage Wilson and his brother, Sigfried, were the principals of both shipping companies. Though badly damaged, *Regina* had escaped an un-nautical end and had a chance for new life.

Gustaf Edvardsson with the sailing model of *Regina* he made when he was 75 years old. Notice the change in cargo hold openings from the deck plan of 1963, shown in Chapter 1, page 8. *Photo courtesy of Holger Nestorson of the Skarhamns Sjofartsmuseum.*

CHAPTER 2
TRADE AND FISH

1. Jan Davidsson, *Skeppoch Sjoman* (Killbergs [publisher], 1970.) Translated by Lotta Clark and Susie Lange, both of Shelter Island, New York.
2. Holger Nestorson of the Skarhamns Sjofartsmuseum provided photos of *Regina* and information on the Edvardsson and Nilsson families. The Museum and Holger also operate a sail-training, two-masted schooner, *MS Atene*, built by J. Ring-Andersen in 1909. Holger's letters were translated by Lotta Clark.
3. Christina Theander, interview by the author, in Greenport, New York, July 11, 1993. A great niece of Gustaf N. Edvardsson, Ms. Theander, of Billdal, Sweden, was a cadet apprentice on the Danish school ship *Georg Stage*, which was visiting Greenport.
4. Dan Rattiner, "Fleeing the Nazis," *Dan's Papers* (Southampton, New York), July 31, 1998.
5. Janet Blatt, telephone interview by the author, December 1998. The interview was conducted after Ms. Blatt's trip to Sweden and Denmark that month, searching for the Jewish connection to the *Regina* story.
6. Annika Thuvik, daughter of *Regina's* last Swedish owner, and Arne Edvardsson, son of Gustaf, telephone interview by author, September 1998. Both were visiting Janet Blatt in Glen Cove.
7. Sunny Seitler, "From the Crows Nest" (a column), *Gold Coast Gazette*, Glen Cove, New York, October-November 1998.

CHAPTER 3
QUEEN OF THE SEA
1963 – 1966

Author's note: Personal letters from John A. Wilson and Marianne Wilson, John Wilson's daughter, provided background material and the names of contacts who could provide answers to my questions on Chapters 3-8. They also graciously provided copies of the three full-length movies about Regina Maris *and her voyages.*

The Wilson brothers, John and Sigfried, had their economic roots and their dreams in the 19th century. They came from a long line of sea captains and ship owners going back to the days of the Vikings.

Their father, John Wilson II, and his partner started the shipping company Wilson and Morland in 1916. Their grandfather, John Wilson I, a master of sail, had been lost with his tall ship in the Atlantic in 1880. John Aage Wilson III, new owner and captain of *Regina,* was born in 1916. Upon completing his education in Norway, he joined the Norwegian Mercantile Marine and went to sea for five months, learning the trade with his hands and body as an ordinary seaman. With this practical experience, he was able to join the Norwegian Merchant Marine Academy and graduated in two and a half years with excellent marks. Further experience in various capacities as an officer entitled him to be licensed as a Ship Master. He then worked with his father in their shipping business and took it over upon his father's death in 1940.

John and Sigfried owned two ships that carried nitrate, used for gunpowder and fertilizer, which were sunk early in World War II. With their ships lost, both brothers became more involved in the Norwegian resistance, hiding weapons during the German occupation, and were arrested by the Gestapo, John having been betrayed by a business associate whom he had discovered embezzling. John was sentenced to two years in a German concentration camp and was later decorated by the King of Norway for his active service in the underground resistance and for his imprisonment at hard labor. He also received the Royal Yugoslav Commemorative War Cross 1941-45 for his war efforts. [1]

After the war, however, as a result of government mismanagement, the brothers received no compensation for their lost ships. This left John very bitter, and he eventually left the country, emigrating to Panama. The brothers had to go deeply into debt to reassemble their shipping company, slowly, one ship at a time. The first of these was a 29-year-old coal burner. John named her *Penelope,* after a vessel in his grandfather's Swansea, Wales, fleet in the 1870s. For many years, the brothers struggled close to bankruptcy as they bought and sold many ships and built others. Those they bought were old and held together with patches on patches and could not pass any safety inspections.

The brothers dangerously overloaded their ships and, to increase profits, started smuggling liquor, cigarettes, and silk stockings, under cover of darkness, into small ports along the coast of Chile. One such scheme went very badly, or as John described it, "a Grand Style smuggling venture went sour and people were killed" — two policemen and two soldiers, to be precise, and the Wilson brothers became wanted men in Chile.

To buy time for John to escape to New York, a grand luncheon with much alcohol was held in the town where the killings had taken place and the ship was impounded. Some bribe money exchanged hands with the chief of customs so that John could leave the country for New York. Unfortunately his brother, Sigfried, master of the vessel involved in the ill-fated scheme, and the chief officer were arrested and held for two months. John hired some high-powered lawyers from New York, who managed to get the ship, his brother, and the chief officer released. [2]

Penelope was sold in 1949. *Nortuna,* an older but larger ship, was found. John Wilson put $50,000 down, borrowed another $45,000, and paid it off in three years with the profits from the nitrate trade and smuggling. *Nortuna* was sold in 1958 for scrap.

In 1954, John went to Japan to supervise the building of two new ships for his fleet after negotiating for long-term charters that would cover their cost. John's and Sigfried's mother christened the ships in 1956. The Wilsons eventually owned a lucrative fleet of cargo vessels plying the seas of the world, amassing a fortune that provided them with a lifestyle that included socializing with the world's royalty. In Arendal, Norway, there is a pub named "Herr Wilson" for John A. Wilson, and T-shirts with his profile can be bought there. [3]

In 1963, one of John's nitrate ships had been impounded in Yastad, Sweden, and he went there to deal with the red tape of releasing it. There he found *Regina,* and he and John purchased what was left of her. Despite her appearance, the brothers felt that one day *Regina* could play a key role in fulfilling their lifelong ambition to be the fourth generation in their family to sail around Cape Horn. John jury-rigged the ship and managed to sail her to the Hoivold Mekshipyard, in Kristiansand, Norway.

The Association Amicale Internationale des Capitaines au Long Cours Cap Horniers (AICH) had been founded in Saint Malo, France, in 1937. Membership in this very exclusive organization of Cape Horn captains and sailors became the brothers' goal. At the time *Regina* was purchased, the organization had two main levels, or titles. Albatross was the highest, awarded a captain of a square-rigged cargo ship that has rounded Cape Horn. Mollymawks were sailors who had rounded the Horn as crewmembers on square-rigged cargo ships. The captains Wilson had to command a sailing cargo vessel to qualify for the highest honor and achieve their ambitious goal. Their national pride in the Norse explorers, their own adventurous spirits, and their love of clipper ships led them on this adventure. They planned to sail around the world and round the Horn on the final leg back home.

The brothers traveled to England to study *Cutty Sark* — the last surviving tea clipper and the fastest and greatest of her time — and to Mystic Seaport in Connecticut to gather information on clipper ships. The task of converting a burned-out hulk into a sailing cargo vessel capable of crossing oceans and rounding the Horn was monumental and costly. At the Hoivold Mekaniske Verksted shipyard in Kristiansand, the brothers used their research to make plans for a tall ship, and a clipper with a "cloud of sail" in her masts was conjured up.

When *Regina's* previous owner, Sigurd Thuvik, heard of the Wilsons' plans to rebuild the ship, much of her original equipment that had been removed for storing grain was returned before she sailed to Norway. Until recently, a collection of artifacts, carvings, and rigging details from the *Regina* of 1908 was carefully preserved and on display at the Ruffen Restaurant in the Tyholmen Hotel in the Wilson brothers' ancestral hometown of Arendal. [4]

Regina was to be rebuilt as a barkentine, combing the advantages of square sails with those of fore-and-aft sails. She was designed to carry all the fancy sails of her famous sisters, with a skysail and moonsail above the course, double topsails, single topgallant, and royal, plus four studding sails on each side of the foremast. She would also carry a "Mae West" jib above the bowsprit but under the six other jibs and "Jamie Greens" (a type of staysail), hanging below the bowsprit, figurehead, and dolphin striker. And there would also be "save alls," a flying studding sail, a flying mizzen topsail, and, finally, water sails laced onto and below the main and mizzen booms. Thirty-eight sails in all.

According to Henk Ahrens, a former crewman, "She had 7 [yard arms] up the foremast and Stu'nsails as well as water sails. This was done by the Wilsons to earn the name of 'Tallest Tall Ship in the World' according to Lloyd's of London classification. The designation was based on the relative height compared to the length. In *Regina's* case, 132' high 144' long, the ratio is 1 to 1.09; or if you compare height to length on deck (125') that was also occasionally used, it equals 1 to 0.95." [5] *(See Appendix C for sail plan and rigging plans.)*

Operating all these flax sails would require fifteen miles of Terylene (Dacron, synthetic polyester) running rigging (the ropes that run through blocks or pulleys). The sails would be sewn by a family of sailmakers who had been in the trade for seven generations.

Finding the skilled shipwrights required for the project took an extensive search, for wooden sailing ships were not common in 1964. Many of the craftsmen recruited were old men, and the shipyard obtained the services of several elderly sea captains to help rig the ship. Among these was a Captain Aralt, who became the lead rigger and held definite opinions about how a sailing ship should work. [6]

Much of the necessary equipment was not available and only existed as artifacts in museums. Hand fabrication from antique models was time-consuming and costly. Only the best materials were used and no expense was spared. It took 60 tons of Danish oak to rebuild the rib frames and hull. To counteract the new, taller masts and acres of sail, a 20-ton reinforced concrete slab was poured into the hull and a 10-ton, 3-inch thick, 98-foot-long steel shoe was attached around the keel below the hull planks. *(See diagram below.)* Caulking went on for weeks, and then, with layers of tar and felt, two and a half tons of copper plates were added to cover her hull from keel to deep load line to protect her from shipworms. The new masts, yardarms, and booms, made from Norwegian pitch pine, were held in place by stainless steel standing rigging. A 250-horsepower G.M. 8-71 diesel engine was added, with its exhaust leading up to a hollow steel mizzenmast. Her new decks were made of Douglas fir from Oregon.

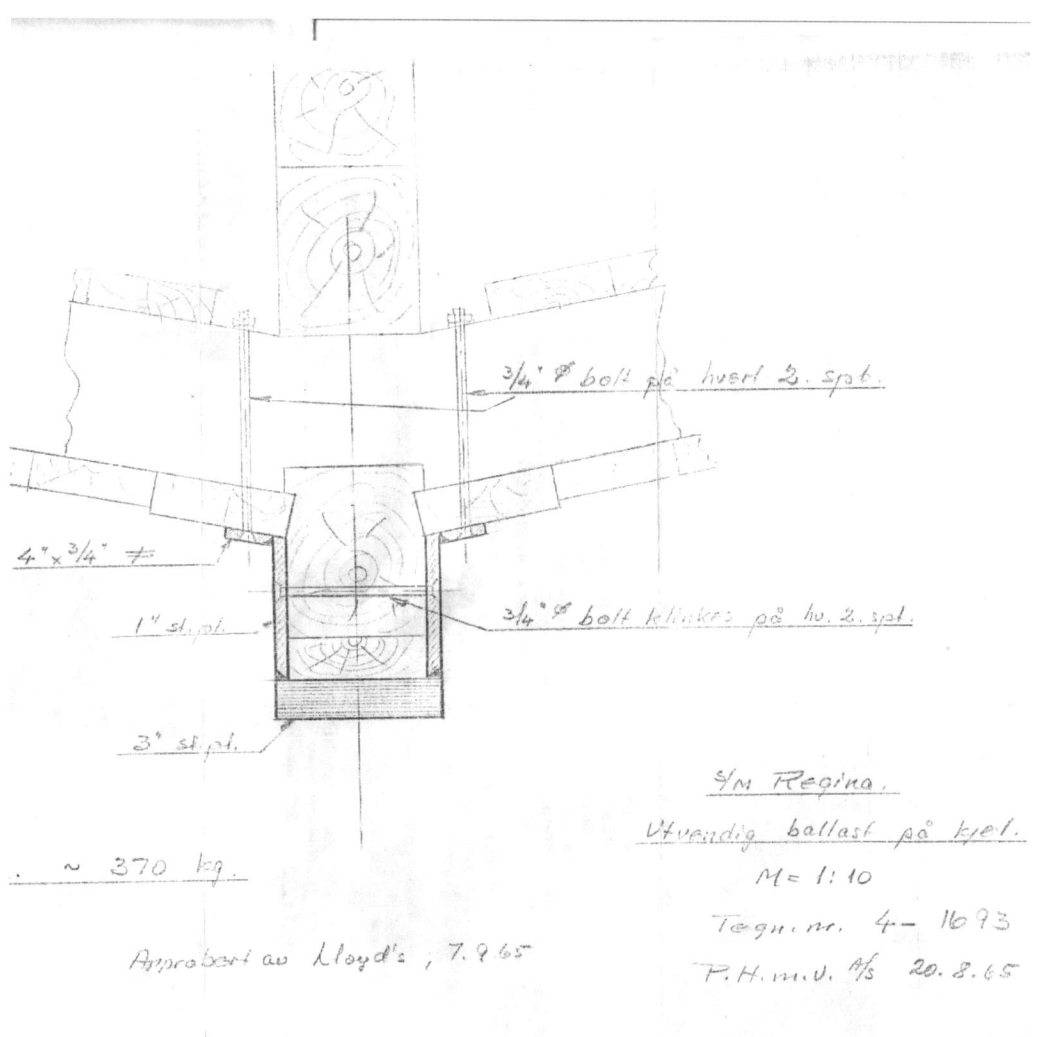

Diagram of the steel-wrapped keel installed for ballast, which also improved windward performance.

Lloyd's of London was to insure this ship, and they had very strict requirements for their A1-A Winter North Atlantic load rating. Their team of experts inspected each bolt, nail, and plank; each weld was x-rayed for flaws.

Every effort was made to create the look of a ship from the clipper era. A carved figurehead of a queen was added under her bowsprit. The catheads (timbers that hold the antique stocked anchors) were adorned with cast bronze snarling cat faces. The ship carried two cannons on the aft cabin top. The interior of the salon was paneled in mahogany with intricate hand-carved borders and contained a large dining table with velvet-covered seats, a navigation table with built-in gimbaled chronometer, a wet bar, and a passageway leading below to the captain's stateroom. Hanging crystal chandeliers illuminated the entire salon.

Up on deck, all *Regina's* brightwork had seven coats of varnish, and the yards and masts were given coat after coat of linseed oil until they shone. Her hull was painted a deep royal blue. An ornate octagonal binnacle held the ship's compass in front of a six-foot diameter wheel attached to a raised steering station amidships.

The Wilson brothers believed in the old methods of seafaring. Even though *Regina* had all the modern navigational equipment housed in the aft raised pilothouse, the brothers insisted that she also carry time-honored equipment. She had both kerosene and electric running lights, an ancient chip log (an instrument for determining the speed of the ship) with14- and 21-second sandglasses, and a traverse board for recording the courses; and she carried hand deep-sea lead lines for depth sounding.

The galley could cater for up to 45 people. There were huge freezers and a spirits locker for cases of wine and beer. The crew of 16 berthed in the fo'c'sle. There were storerooms, sail lockers, and a chart room containing 3,500 charts of the world. *Regina* kept her cargo hold, for she had to be registered as a cargo vessel to meet the requirements for membership in the Amicale Internationale des Capitaines au Long Cours Cap Horniers.

The end result was a ship of 188 gross registered tons, a total dead weight of 260 tons, and a displacement of 490 tons. She was 144 feet long, 25 feet wide with a 12-foot draft. Her foremast was 150 feet off the water. She was a first-rate tall ship and private yacht. The re-build overall cost 3,500,000 Norwegian kronor and took approximately two and a half years to complete. [7]

In 1966, finding a crew for a 58-year-old wooden ship was a difficult task for the Wilson brothers. The old salts were just that, too old. Most everyone was busy being modern, and old ships did not fit into their plans. Ads were placed in newspapers and magazines all over Europe. In these ads, the plans to sail around the world got attention until it was mentioned that they would also be rounding the Horn. Most prospective crewmembers walked away shaking their heads and saying, "That's a crazy idea." But young men and teenage boys from Norway, Germany, Sweden, England, Spain and Portugal responded. Some had sailing experience, others were new to the sea.

One young Englishman, Terrance (Terry) Leggett, was a friend of recently hired first mate Peter Wilson, also English, and no relation to the owners. Terry recalled in a 2011 email to the author, "I knew Peter Wilson from the Ocean Youth Club in Plymouth [England] when it first started up. I had worked as an apprentice shipwright at Her Majesty's Royal Dockyard. I was trained to build and repair any naval vessel belonging to the Royal Navy. Pete arranged an interview for me in London with Captain Wilson and his German wife. She was in fact to be the radio officer. My interview was at the beginning of January, 1966. I was told a few days later that I had been selected to serve as carpenter/deckhand for the trip to sail around the world. I joined *Regina* with Peter Wilson and Roger Callan on May 5th. Roger Callan was from England and was hired as cook." [8]

Paul Maskell, a former London civil servant, was hired as third mate. A crew of 16 was eventually assembled.

In the spring of 1966, as the crew slowly arrived in Kristiansand, they were put to work at the Hoivold Mekaniske Shipyard. The jobs were, as Terry Leggett remembered, "mostly mundane, like filling the space between the outer and inner hull between the frames with salt. Wilson said it was for the preservation of the wood. " [8]

On July 1, 1966, the last day at the shipyard before sailing up to Arendal, the Wilson brothers' home, Terry Leggett recalled the following incident: "Hoivold, the old man who owned the shipyard, met with John Wilson and he said to Wilson, 'I think the time has come for you to pay me.' Wilson's reply was, 'How do you want it, sterling, dollars, marks, or kroner?' I think Hoivold said, 'Sterling will do.' Wilson sat down and we stood around and the cheque was written and left on the table, a sum of over 150,000 pounds sterling." [8] This must have been a final payment as over two million pounds sterling had actually been spent in the two years of rebuilding.

The ship then left for sea trials and the short voyage to Arendal. Terry remembered the several sea trials as disasters. "There was water in the diesel tanks and diesel in the water tanks." [8]

This problem was due to human error, and the guilty party was not determined. "I was very seasick," Terry recalled, "and afraid pretty useless. I think Roger had a hard time with the galley also. In Arendal we anchored off the Wilsons' home and we cleaned the tanks, crawling in and mopping them out. We reeked of fuel oil."[8]

Captain John Wilson was master mariner and his brother, Captain Sigfried Wilson, was chief officer. Sigfried, who was living in, Santiago, Chile, had returned to Norway for the round-the-world voyage. Also sailing were John's second wife, Anne-Luise, as radio officer, and as passengers, his daughter, Anne Margrethe, and her Chilean fiancé, Fernando Fuenzalida. A film crew under the direction of Klaus P. Hanusa, from Ocean Wide Productions, was on board to document the voyage. [9] The film company, owned by the Wilson brothers, had offices in Berlin, Germany, and Santiago and would eventually produce three full-length movies about *Regina's* voyages

On July 13, 1966, with tons of equipment, spare parts, food, and water, *Regina* set sail on the Wilson brothers' dream quest. Since *Regina* was registered as a cargo vessel, to qualify her crew for the Cape Horn Society, she needed a cargo. On the fishing grounds just west of Denmark, the ship stopped and the crew caught 400 pounds of codfish, which was then salted and stored in the cargo hold. The token cargo of fish joined *Regina's* 58-year legacy of cargo — lumber, oil, freedom fighters to Finland, and, possibly, Jews fleeing Hitler's Germany. Only one problem remained. Because of her age, no country wanted her on its register of ships. However, LaValetta, the capital city of Malta, agreed to register her, but it already had a ship named *Regina.* So while the ship was at sea on her maiden voyage as a barkentine, *Regina,* The Queen, became *Regina Maris,* "Queen of the Sea," at the suggestion of the first mate, Peter Wilson.

Soon after the ship left Arendal, workmanship flaws began showing up, as Terry remembered. He recounted this example: "We were sweating up the topsail gaff and bang! The eye plate taking the block shot passed our heads. It had pulled straight out of the deck. Instead of it being through-bolted with a plate under the deck, the yard had only used coach screws. John Wilson was helping at the time so he could have been severely injured or even killed, as we all could have been." [8]

Problems also surfaced in the engine room. A locking plate of the "screw-up pad" bent. The screw-up pad allowed the engineer to stop the prop shaft from turning so that the two-bladed propeller remained in a vertical orientation relative to the keel (causing less drag). The ship could then, under sail, achieve her best speed. To get the needed repairs, the ship's course was changed to sail up the Elbe River to Hamburg. They put in at the Blohm and Voss Shipyard for three weeks to correct, as John Wilson said, "an endless number of flaws from waterline to truck [the circular piece of wood placed at the head (top) of the masts] from stern to jib boom." [1]

With all the rigging repairs going on and other shipyard problems, Captain Wilson began to show the first signs of being "edgy, and short on temper," as Terry recalled. For example, he noted, "We were coiling ropes to put back on the belaying pins and I, being left-handed, did not do it his way. So words were exchanged." [8]

A new member of the crew was acquired — a ship's dog named Grief, a German shepherd variation peculiar to that area of Germany. He was always biting the crew and had received several kicks from the men. He bit like the dog on the *Joseph Conrad* that Alan Villiers made famous in his silent documentary movie in 1933 "Around the Horn in a Square Rigger."

Terry Leggett added the following anecdote: "In Hamburg I was on watch/gangway duty. This little old man came along in a blazer and grey flannels with a Breton type cap. His cap badge and blazer badge showed he was a full member of the Cape Horn Society. It appears that as he had been around the Horn so many times he was the only crew member to be granted full membership. I showed him around and learned he had sailed with Villiers in the last great grain race. He of course loved the ship, but now something strange — he went on about the damage the *Regina* could suffer if she went round the Horn. It was unsettling. I gave him a drink in the forward deck mess room and he looked at the book shelf. He said, 'You got no cowboy story books. You will want to read them in the Southern Oceans. I will go and get you some.' Sure enough he did return with the said books. I secretly pooh-poohed the idea or need for them. But during a very severe storm before Montevideo I actually picked one up and read it right through. If you knew me, then you would know reading is not a priority with me. But the book took me right out of my environment and I could not put it down and I was oblivious to the powerful storm and all bangs and crashes that were going on about me." [8]

Another crew member, Tim Nossiter, remembered a story told to him by film director Klaus Hanusa about the brothers Wilson and their corporate operating style. All the documents, contracts, and such for their shipping company were kept in a briefcase. Sigfried appeared to run the company, and this briefcase would go everywhere with them whenever they left the ship; it was extremely important to them. "Klaus tells the story of the time they came to visit him, before the ship had finished her refit, in Hamburg. [The two brothers] arrived at the hotel they were staying at, in a taxi with Klaus. When they got to the reception desk they noticed they had left the briefcase in the taxi. John apparently grabbed the person behind the desk, threw some money down and said, 'Find that taxi.' John Wilson believed in the 'greenback' and always had a pile of it on him or in the safe on board. Eventually the taxi driver noticed the bag in the taxi and drove straight back to the hotel. He walked into the foyer with it. John gave him a big hug, pulled out his wallet and put $4,000 U.S. in his hand, the equivalent of a year's pay for the man. This was in the '60s' and I think it demonstrates the value of the briefcase to them. I was very fond of Sigfried, he was a kind, normal guy. The two brothers were so different it was hard to imagine they were brothers." [10]

All the corrections and repairs at Blohm and Voss cost $90,000. Something to remember is that a ship of this type had not been constructed for years and skilled craftsmen were hard to find. The shipyard staff was forced to learn the old ways of rigging sailing ships as they worked.

The newly repaired ship left the shipyard on August 7, bound for Saint Malo, France. On August 11, with *Regina Maris* back at sea and off the coast of France, Captain Wilson married his youngest daughter, Anne Margrethe, to Fernando H. Fuenzalida. This was the first marriage at sea on a tall ship in 50 years. At the time it was not certain if the wedding would be legitimized by any country. John Wilson had anticipated that problem, so he planned for another wedding to take place in Spain later in the voyage.

The ship sailed on to St. Malo, to check in with the officers of AICH and let them know of the brothers' plan to sail around the Horn in a wooden tall ship. When entering the harbor basin, the ship had to pass under a drawbridge. The harbor pilot made a huge mistake by not bracing the yards to their minimum width. The topgallant yard hit the bridge, was sprung, and cracked. "After this row, Wilson was in quite a strop," Terry said. [8]

There was no shipyard there to fix the damage. Where to go? The captain called for a conference to discuss options. Terry suggested that, "across the channel, in England, there were two yards: Uphams of Brixham in Devon, which had built the replica *Mayflower*; and in Plymouth, there was Mashfords Yard, also very capable yacht and boat builders." Terry had had experience with both in the past. However, John Wilson decided to put off repairs and sail on to Santander, Spain. [8]

When the ship was off the Ile d'Ouessant, Brittany, on a fine day for sailing, the main boom collapsed, snapping in half, dropping the clew with a bang, and landing in the walkway between the aft deckhouse and the rail on the port side. The center, or heart, of the timber was full of powder dry rot. With the damaged yardarm and the main boom broken, as well as other "flaws in workmanship," John Wilson decided to find a shipyard when they arrived in Lisbon. The newlyweds were seasick and did not enjoy the sail across the Bay of Biscay to Santander — not the best way to start their life together, nor much of a honeymoon experience.

The ship arrived in Santander on August 16. The newlywed couple's vows were legitimized in the Gothic Cathedral of the Assumption of the Virgin Mary. The reception was held in a hotel high above the city next to the royal summer palace. After the meal, Wilson opened the dance floor to all the hotel guests since the wedding party, family, and crew made up a small group. Terry Leggett had an interesting recollection of the party: "Wilson was what I would call upper crust, and a little arrogant at times. The money made him that way I suppose. So for the crew, a card table was set up with six or eight bottles of Johnny Walker Black Label whisky for us to drink. We thought it strange that he assumed we would party with a fancy drink like that. How many youngsters would party on whisky? We would have liked beer or wine, especially for the ladies we treated. He was put right by the crew about how they felt; we refused to drink at the party and left early."

After the newlyweds left for their honeymoon, John Wilson took his crew on a tour of the area, including a stop in the village of Cantabria to see the famous paintings in Altamira Cave. This rich archaeological site dates from 16000 to 9000 BC and is now a World Heritage Site.

The ship left Santander August 19 bound for Lisbon, Portugal. She arrived August 23 and was moored alongside the shipyard's pier. While the ship was docked in Lisbon, Sigfried Wilson was called back to Norway to manage the brothers' shipping company.

Seven weeks were spent in Lisbon on rigging repairs, and the ship was totally repainted and varnished. After one of the days of varnishing, "a wind blew strong that night and she got covered in dust, sand and dirt from the quay," Terry remembered. [8]

The crew took a day trip up the coast to visit a small village. While there, the film director, Klaus Hanusa, wanted footage of the crew attempting to dance with a local group of folk dancers. Terry recalled, "We were pitiful and the locals did not appreciate our efforts either." [8]

When the galley was being worked on, John Wilson's agent at the shipyard made arrangements for the crew to go to a local restaurant for all their meals. At lunch the first day, the crew ate heartily and left. When they arrived back that evening, the police were called and threatened to arrest them. John's agent had evidently neglected to tell the restaurant's management that they were to send the bill to him. It was an uncomfortable situation but fortunately the crew didn't end up at a police station. [8]

After the yard work was done, the ship was moved out into the river Taqus and anchored above the April 25th Bridge. Workers came from the shipyard daily and the crew continued their work duties as well. While there, the mechanic, Mike Uver, had a birthday. Terry remembered "that the crew spent too much money on beer celebrating with Mike and the police made us get down off the famous navigation monument, as a couple of us decided to clean Henry the Navigator's shoes. Fortunately our boat arrived and took us back to the *R.M.*"[8]

Captain John Wilson would occasionally take a small number of crew out to dinner in a good restaurant. Terry went once, "with Wilson's wife and Klaus Hanusa to the older part of town. We had wine, beer, lobster, steak and crepes. It was brilliant. Wilson could certainly pack it away. Whatever the bill came to, he gave a big tip, which pleased the restaurant staff." [8]

The ship was moved and anchored down the river off Casscias, Portugal. There was not much to do, so the crew started jumping off the bow or cathead, floating in the river current, and surfacing in time to grab a rope streamed from the stern, pulling themselves back up to the deck. "Wilson got a bit funny with us. Whether the time and worry in Lisbon got to him, or he didn't like us playing in the water, I don't know, but he was very short tempered. He had us make miles of baggywrinkle. He was obsessed with it. Some dissatisfied crew left and were replaced by two Portuguese." [8]

The shipyard work in Lisbon and on the river Taqus to make *Regina* ready for the voyage around the world and the Horn cost an additional $60,000.00. The ship left Casscias on October 11 and proceeded out to sea, bound for Las Palmas, in the Canary Islands.

CHAPTER 3
QUEEN OF THE SEA

1.   Captain John Aage Wilson, *Wooden Walls to Distant Shores, A Maritime Concoction and the* Regina Maris *Saga* (Sussex, England: The Book Guild, 1992).
2.   Captain J. A. Wilson, *Under Steam and Sail, Reminiscences of a Sea Captain* (Sussex, England: The Book Guild, 1990).

3. "*Regina Maris* The Sail Ship with Eternal Life," *Faederlandvenneil* (Norway), March 13, 1993. Translated by Peter Wilson.

4. Peter Wilson, letters to the author, received August 9, 1992.

5. Henk Ahrens, email to the author, February 6, 2011. Henk Ahrens stated, "I have seen papers from Lloyd's that were in Captain Paul H. Nelson's possession with the Lloyd's letter- head that referred to *Regina Maris* as the 'Tallest Tall Ship' in the world. To the best of my recollection they were sent to him in Papeete, Tahiti, in care of the local paper, *Les Nouvelles* that had just published an article about the arrival of the "Oldest Three master in the Pacific."

6. Retter Hoivold, of Hoivold Mekaniske Shipyard, letters to the author, dated December 19, 1991, including the keel drawing #4-1693.

7. Erling Brunborg, "Around the World with *Regina Maris*," *Faederlandvenneil*, translated by Ottar and Barbara Kirkbak of St. James, New York.

8. Terry Leggett, emails to the author, April 18-22, 2011.

9. John Aage Wilson, letter to the author, dated December 19, 1991.

10. Tim Nossiter, email to the author, May 23, 2011.

CHAPTER 4
VOYAGE OF A BARKENTINE
1966

The *Queen of the Sea* crossing the Atlantic. *Photo Courtesy of Marianne Wilson and Ocean Wide Film Production, Santiago and Berlin.*

"On October 11, the *Regina Maris,* 'The Queen of the Sea,' left Lisbon, Portugal, and set sail for Rio de Janeiro. 1 to 3 November stopped in Praia, Cape Verde Islands to re-fill freshwater tanks. 10 November, Passed Equator. King Neptune on board and usual ceremony performed. 20 November 1500 hrs Pilot embarked. 1600 hrs in anchorage outside Rio de Janeiro. [1]

The above paragraph is how John Wilson recorded the first leg of their voyage around the world. A more complete description of happenings on board the ship during that Atlantic passage is found in the email comments of crewman Terry Leggett and the diary of first mate Peter Wilson.

In a 2011 email to the author, Terry stated, "After sailing from Lisbon things were good and we settled down to being at sea again and getting to know the *Regina Maris* properly. The trip to Las Palmas was uneventful with good sailing weather. Relations were good all round. Wilson also I think was better tempered and he worked with us during the day." [2]

Arriving in Las Palmas, the Canary Islands, on October 18, the ship took on stores and water. Captain Wilson arranged for a tour of the island for the crew and they all had lunch together at an elegant hotel. When they left Las Palmas on October 21, the ship ended up drifting for most of the day waiting for the trade winds to blow. Finally they motored until they found a breeze to take them to the Cape Verde Islands.

While awaiting clearance to go ashore in the Cape Verde Islands on November 1, the crew bartered with a group of children who had paddled out to the ship with some lobsters to sell. The cook, Roger Callan, cooked them up and a great feast was held in the forecastle cabin. After the meal, a young agent who had been hired to show the crew the sites took some of the crew ashore for a beer. Terry recalled, "It was my first real experience of poverty. I was very aware of men and boys with bits or all of some limbs missing. Apparently these injuries were shark bites suffered when diving for lobsters in the nooks and crannies around the island. I lost a bit of the enjoyment of the visit and our meal from then on. Guilt I suppose, as we only paid for the lobsters with old clothes, soap and a few dollars." [2]

After leaving the Cape Verde Islands on November 3, and when the ship was well into the trade winds, John Wilson wanted to rig the studding sails. He had brought along two books, one by Harold Underhill, *Masting and Rigging: The Clipper Ship & Ocean Carrier Sailing,* one by R. C. Anderson, *The Rigging of Ships*. The books were the only guide he had, as there were no other actively sailing ships that carried studding sails. The landbound *Cutty Sark* was the only other ship that had the sliding yard extensions and the standing rigging to support the studding sails. The books were only very rough guides and caused more problems than they solved. But John Wilson insisted that the books be used and that "Underhill couldn't be wrong." [2]

The crew spent days running lines, adjusting blocks, and lashing the sails to the yard extensions of the course and upper topsail yards. Taking all the sails down and trying another idea to make them work became very tedious, and tempers flared.

Terry wrote, "Those bloody stun sails, as I recall, things got fraught again because rigging did not go according to plan. Wilson got a bit timid about leaving the studding sails up. She did carry too much canvas and was only a converted topsail schooner, not a three masted square rigger. Still they were up a couple of days I think and soon got blown down with no damage." [2]

The group photo is off Gran Canarias, before our arrival at Las Palmas. From right to left is Earnest Fault, Uver Helm, the mechanic, and Arnfinn. Then is Amorie, who was one of two Portuguese sailors who joined in Lisbon and had experienced cod fishing by long line from a dory on the Grand Banks. Then it`s Hanis Schroybler, who played the part of King Neptune at the crossing of the line. *Photo and caption from Terry Leggett.*

At the Equator on November 10, King Neptune came on board and the usual ceremony was performed. Later that day, John Wilson shot a dolphin with a shotgun that had a harpoon attachment. It was hauled in and the two Portuguese crewmen set about cutting it up. The ship was rolling badly and there was blood everywhere. The innards were thrown overboard. Roger cooked the meat that night, and it reminded Terry of fish-flavored beef. He didn't remember seeing many dolphins after that. A few days later, Captain Wilson shot a very big dorado with which Roger fed the crew.

On Sundays, if calm, the ship would hove to and all who wanted could swim, as it was very warm in the tropics. On one occasion, the captain asked if anyone could look at the copper bottom to see how it was doing. Terry dove down to look and saw a silver and black striped pilot fish swimming toward him. Pilot fish often leave their host shark just before the shark attacks. Terry got back on board as fast as he could and just then one of the crew saw a hammerhead swim under the rudder. It stayed off the port quarter, just out of range of the captain's shotgun, until it got dark. There was no more swimming that day, and after that the gun was always left loaded but broken down in a deck locker and a lookout always sat on the crosstrees platform of the main mast during the swim time, watching for sharks.

Terry and Peter both remembered that one night the captain had the crew all aft because he wanted Klaus to record them singing chanteys. Mike White and Peter Wilson had guitars and beer was provided. Most of the crew knew the melodies but many had learned different lyrics. Some chanteys mention a port's name, and in them, the Germans would sing "Hamburg," the English, "London," and the Americans, "Boston." It was a recipe for disaster — no agreement could be found, and the recording was unsuccessful. John Wilson loved the chanteys, wanted it to work out, and became frustrated with his crew. After that attempt, Peter Wilson over the course of the voyage conducted many rehearsal sessions and a successful recording was eventually made. [3]

When the ship arrived in Rio de Janeiro December 2, Klaus left for Germany to do some film editing, and Sigfried Wilson arrived from Chile, where he had been running the brothers' shipping interests. Upon Sigfried's arrival, John's demeanor changed. He became brusque, and one night he failed to order a late shore boat to pick up crew members visiting town. Some of the crew had to spend the night on the quay, which caused some strife. Another day, John and his brother took some of the crew to a fancy dinner, but a row broke out when John did not receive the meal he had ordered. When he and Sigfried settled the bill they did not leave a tip. He was not his usual generous self. [2]

Sigfried had planned to sail with his brother around the Horn, but pressing issues in the shipping business required his attention, and he had to return to Santiago before *Regina* left Rio. John was greatly saddened by this necessary change in their shared dream.

Upon leaving Rio, the ship headed for Montevideo, Uruguay. This was an unexpected course change that presented a problem for many of the crew. They had signed on for what they had assumed would be an eastward trip round the world, going east from Rio toward Africa and the Cape of Good Hope and then around the Horn, the easier and safer route. But John Wilson had changed the route, shortened the trip, and embarked on the foolhardy westward rounding of the Horn. This was a frightening prospect for many of the crew, as the prevailing winds and seas would be against them all the way.

Some of the crew were wondering what they had gotten themselves into by signing on to the voyage. John's behavior ever since Sigfried arrived had them questioning their captain's sanity. In the following excerpt from his diary, as emailed to the author, Terry Leggett recalled a significant event that helped lead to a near mutiny.

"We were hit by one hell of a gale; I think they are called pompanos. All hands were on deck and we shortened down to the bare minimum sail. I was not present but a huge row/argument took place by the mainmast between the two senior Germans, Harold and Earnest, [and John Wilson.] Wilson disappeared below when I came on the scene. Harold told me Wilson wanted all sail off. This would be very dangerous as you must keep some sail up to steady her and keep her up wind. A broach would be the end of us. In hindsight I now believe Wilson got scared and his lack of sailing experience showed up that evening. I backed the Germans; one or two of the others were unable to decide what to do or how to react. One thing for sure I knew they were aware of the consequences if all sail was taken off. Sometime later the Captain appeared with a head bandage. I later learned his wife, Anne, had hit him with a candle stick when he went to get a gun to make us do as he wanted." [2]

Christmas 1966 was a non-event as the tension aboard the ship was great. The crew sailed her and the captain commanded, but they did not see a lot of one another as he spoke little and issued commands through the mates.

Of the trip from Rio to Montevideo, first mate Peter Wilson stated in a 1993 personal letter to the author, "It was a troubled voyage. Dissension was smoldering for most of the voyage with fears that they would all be lost, because the captain was 'MAD.' The Captain's plan to sail west around the Horn was a point of disagreement." [4]

Some of the unhappy crew members used the story of the tall ship *Pamir* to incite their colleagues. *Pamir* was a German grain ship that had been caught in Hurricane Carrie off the Azores and sank September 21, 1957. Only six survivors were recovered after an extensive rescue effort; 80 were lost.

There was more to the troubles than just the itinerary. John Wilson was a tough man, hardened by the sea. His idiosyncrasies caused much of the discontent. To him the right ways of doing things aboard ship were the old ways. These were often the hard ways. He rationed water, gave more work, and allowed less free time. In this type of ship the captain, good or bad, runs God a very close second in dictating what shall happen to the ship. [4]

First mate Peter Wilson often tried to smooth things over between crew and captain, and in one statement to the crew, he summed up his position: "I joined the *Regina Maris* for only one thing. I am going around Cape Horn, and this is the only chance I'll get in a short, miserably wasted life. Nothing is going to stop me, absolutely nothing! And when she breaks up on the Horn, I'll sit on the nearest piece and paddle it round." [1]

With determination like that, Peter kept the crew from a full-blown mutiny, and by December 28, 1966, they safely made it to Montevideo, where six of the crew left the ship. Mrs. Anne Wilson also left the ship as planned, leaving only six on board besides the captain. It seems possible that the crew's twentieth-century attitudes were causing friction on a nineteenth-century rigged ship with a captain trying to fulfill an eighteenth-century dream.

The following indented material, from Terry Leggett's emails to the author, is included because it tells the story of sailors in strange lands, operating under unfamiliar maritime rules, and provides additional insight into the character of John Wilson.

> Whilst going up the River Plate [the Rio de la Plata, a large estuary between Argentina and Uruguay] *Regina* sailed then motored right up the middle and did not see land for some time. I was up the foremast with Harold securing sails and talking about the *Graff Spee* and the battle of the River Plate. It was then that he told me the four Germans were going to get off and he said he would like me to join them. He was like an older brother to me and I needed little convincing. They were to leave a day or two after our arrival. I did not have any money to get home so I told him I would visit U.K. ships to try and work a passage but stay on board until I got a ship.
>
> The four Germans, Harold Selbach, Ernst Fault, Hanis Schroybler, and the Mike Uver who was not the mechanic and Mike White left the ship and moved into the Salvation Army hostel in the red light district.
>
> Life on board was very strange for me as Wilson wanted me to stay, but knew I was very unhappy being there. Klaus returned from Germany but he come back to a different ship. I enjoyed his friendship but he was not working crew and therefore favored the Captain's methods and style. We started to receive drums of fuel which were to be lashed on deck. John Wilson told us that we were not going to go to Australia after all, but round the Horn the hard way and then head for home. This finished me completely as that was not the trip I signed on for. I think he wanted to do the Horn from the very beginning. I searched for a ship at every opportunity but did not meet with much success.
>
> To replace the crew who left he signed on Uruguayans but they would not work aloft. I challenged Wilson on this, who said they would be alright on deck while we had experience aloft. I said, at night I do not want them letting go of the wrong rope and a yard dropping with me on it. I also learned that they were going to be paid more.
>
> Not giving a damn for that, I spent the day visiting ships to look for work and passage home. On my return to the ship that evening, he sent for me and I said I wanted off, he offered more pay but I said the Royal Dockyard gave me time off to sail around the world, not a short trip for glory. Wilson said he would sign me off but not pay my fare home. I left, and moved into the hostel with the others.
>
> Most mornings Major Smart, the Salvation Army hostel boss, would shout to us that we were required at the ship agent's office. We knew Wilson would be

there, so we would amble up to a cafe at the top of our road. The cafe was run by two brothers who had day-old ham finger rolls. We ate these at half price with a cappuccino. We would then walk to the agent's office some way away.

When we arrived Wilson would be fuming, shouting at us, and then trying to get us back, then offering to pay our way to go to Buenos Aires. Saying we stood a much better chance of getting a ship. He would often get so mad at us he would shout at me in German and in English to the Germans. All of which only made us laugh. He would then tell the agent to reason with us to get back on board as he would not pay our repatriation.

The agent, who was English, would then lecture us but whilst doing so would wink at us. We then of course realized something was up. Then Wilson stormed off, saying if we did not come back onboard and if he ever saw us again he'd shoot us.

We were told by the agent to stay where we were and hold on. So we did exactly that and learned about Wilson's big mistake. The maritime law states that if a person or persons had a dispute with a ship's captain and refused to sail, then the captain's company was responsible for providing passage out of the country. Within 17 days of the vessel sailing those persons would be deported on the next available ship no matter where it was going. Under an agreement with other South American countries that company's ship or vessel would be held until the money for the sailor's passage home was paid. Wilson ran things like a commercial business so we had entered Uruguay on the manifest; our passports were never stamped, so we came under the maritime law and were not tourists. All we had to do was sit tight. If we left Montevideo to go to Buenos Aires as Wilson suggested then the game was up — we were stuck and he had no liability.

So we enjoyed town. In a local bar run by a Polish chap who was stationed in Honiton Devon during the war, we had a friend. We sold him our oilskins as he had a BSA motorbike with a sidecar. It was bloody funny to see this guy in yellow oilskins going up the road on his bike.

We were well known in the locality. The street girls in the bar had more money than us so, if we had two beers and no more money, they would, when the boss turned his back, slip us another beer. Even the police who often raided knew all about us and became friends whilst others got frisked. We had immunity. They were looking for locals buying foreign currency.

When the *Regina Maris* sailed, we all went to the hotel where Mrs. Anne Wilson was staying, where we watched from her room as the ship sailed out. She provided us with champagne cocktails. After the ship had sailed, Anne flew home and Harold and Ernst left on the ferry to Argentina. They were good mates who stuck by me. I met them once again, two years later when they, with Anne, Wilson's now ex-wife, visited my cargo ship in Hamburg. Hanis decided to hitchhike to the U.S.A. I heard he met the *Regina Maris* in Panama and signed on to get to New York.

Mike and I continued to look for a ship to take us home, but knowing really we had to wait for the seventeen-day limit to expire. We found out the sailing times of passenger ships from the royal mail line office and made our inquiries. Just before the 17 days were up, the *S.S.Aragon* was to sail. The morning she sailed, the ship's agent and the immigration police escorted Mike Uver and me to the ship and we were on our way back to England. [2]

CHAPTER 4

VOYAGE OF A BARKENTINE

1. Captain John Aage Wilson, *Wooden Walls to Distant Shores, A Maritime Concoction and the* Regina Maris *Saga* (Sussex, England: The Book Guild, 1   992).
2. Terry Leggett, emails to the author, April 18-22, 2011
3. Peter Wilson, letter to the author, received November 30, 1993.
4. Peter Wilson, letter to the author, received April 11, 1993.

Chapter 5
The Horn
1967

Captain John Wilson's efforts to replace the lost crew members were always met with interest until it was mentioned that the ship was headed around the Horn; then many would say, "Captain Loco!"

Five new crew members of dubious ability were eventually assembled in Montevideo. A sixth was recruited from one of the Wilson's cargo ships that happened to be in that harbor. A green Parrot named Pepe also joined the crew and became a mascot to all but Captain John's dog. Pepe terrorized the dog, but, as the dog often bit some crew members, most of the crew enjoyed the show.

On January 3, 1967, with all water tanks full, the needed stores all aboard, and the ship in every way seaworthy, *Regina Maris* set sail for Cape Horn and, if successful, Callao, Peru.

Some background on this most fearsome objective and goal is necessary at this time. In 1616, a Dutchman named William Schouten in the vessel *Unity* discovered the southernmost tip of South America and named it Cape Hoorn after his homeport in Holland. This last tip of land lies 1,300 nautical miles farther south than the Cape of Good Hope on the African continent. A barren jagged rock, the end of the continent sits at the juncture of the world's mightiest oceans. It is where the South Atlantic and the South Pacific collide, awash with storms, boiling seas, icebergs, and the many thousands of souls who have perished over the centuries. Between 1900 and 1914, 53 windjammers were claimed by the Horn's fury, in most cases with all hands lost. The ships and men that fought and survived the sleet, squalls, and mountainous seas left with awed relief. This fearsome cape has a hellish reputation found nowhere else.

The monument unveiled at Cape Horn in 1992. *Photo taken by an unknown photographer and provided to the author by Peter Wilson.*

Captain John Wilson recorded *Regina's* rounding of the Horn in his book *Wooden Walls to Distant Shores* as follows: "*25 January to 27 February:* 25 January passed through Strait le Maire and on 26 January at 1300 hrs Cape Horn bearing True 061 degrees, dist. two and a half miles. At 1600 hrs started to blow and soon reached storm force. Under trysail on mainmast and foremast staysail only. On 13 February at 0320 hrs — wind about force 6 — in a sudden squall the fore topgallant mast parted. All the wreckage was taken down by daylight. Otherwise a usual, average voyage — maybe better than average, that was very lucky, as the new crewmembers were not very good. 0900 hrs Pilot embarked outside Callao, Peru. 1000 hrs moored alongside. Pilot disembarked." [1]

John Wilson's comments are oddly short and to the point at the completion of a lifelong dream — typical of this determined sea captain. A much fuller account of the story comes, again, from first mate Peter Wilson's journal, in the indented material below, which was quoted in *Wooden Walls to Distant Shores*.

At daylight we were in sight of the awful pinnacle. Approaching it from the east, the profile is that of a closed fist lying on a table, rising sheer to 1400 feet at the 'knuckles' then sloping much less steeply back and leveling out towards the mainland. Throughout the morning it loomed ever larger as we approached under full sail. The dark silhouette became a green-tinged mountain towering above us. Now we were directly beneath the citadel of the storm-kings, where the south face with its vertical fissures made me think of organ pipes. The clear cold air and weak sunshine did nothing to dispel the feeling of desolation and remoteness that wild place gave me. I could only think of countless bones lying deep in that cold water; I never see fronds of seaweed without thinking of supplicating hands.

A celebration group photo of the crew taken at Cape Horn. Captain John Aage Wilson is in the center with the black hat. Peter Wilson is on the far right, wearing glasses. Roger Callan is to the left and behind the captain. *Photo by Klaus P. Hanusa, Ocean-Wide Film Production Berlin-Santiago.*

It was an exciting point in the voyage. The pictures would be remarkable, taken as they were at a distance of less than a mile. Few ships of old were foolhardy enough to venture as close and many Cape Horners have never set eyes on this monument to the cruelty of nature. "Let's get the hell out of here; we've been lucky so far!" I said with a slight shudder.

We continued into the afternoon, getting well past the Cape until at 2 p.m. we were being sent in toward the coast to leeward.

The current here probably had much to do with it. I went below to rouse the captain. While studying the chart a deep moan, like a siren, started up. The sea turned completely black, and white horses (in the waves) were being whipped in from the South. The wind was rising so fast that there was hardly time to think. Leaving the captain to the wheel, we rushed forward to reduce the headsails so that she might be more easily luffed and put about. With the wind rising like a dynamo the task of coming about was proving hopeless, and the captain decided to wear ship, paying off towards the land, and come up onto the new tack. As she gathered speed towards the all-too-near rocks I remember thinking: only God can help us now! Slowly she came up again, the wind heeling us right over as the pressure now hit her from starboard. The buntlines required every available hand — a group of men on deck and another group on the galley roof all hauling the same rope — yet we could only sweat them in an inch at a time.

And how we pulled up! We pulled our hearts out, our lives depended upon it. At 3:30 p.m. the wind was a full gale force 10, and nothing could be heard above it. Getting the mainsail in was almost too much for us. When we finally got the brails into the mast the belly of the sail was flagging so badly I thought the mast might break. It took five men an hour to finally get the mainsail snug. After some time we had her down to just three sails; two fishermen's stay-sails and lower topsail. With the onslaught we were sliding eastwards at a fast rate. Soon Cape Horn itself passed up to weather and we were back in the Atlantic again but, at least, there were no more lee shores. The seas were now very high and we had big waves coming in on the beam. Beside the green water flowing aboard, foam would come off the waves in sheets and be flung over us at terrific speed. This water, although atomized by the wind, felt like lead shot for the men working at the rails knee-deep in spaghetti of ropes

The morning revealed that the topgallant mast had parted and the mizzen topmast sprung. The wreckage was cleared away, and we continued on 'bald-headed.' In the evening the barometer began rising again but it continued to blow even harder. It finally eased around midnight and the high seas took a day or two to settle. Apart from the bad moments by the lee shore, I had little real fear except that unknown quantity, how much can the rigging stand? After three days of being blown east we were able to turn and head west around the Horn again, back into the Pacific. But this time 200 miles further south of the Cape.

The sea was fairly lumpy for the most of the time and the deck was constantly awash with icy water. Rain and hail were ever present. We slept in everything we could lay our hands on as the temperature was around 2 Celsius. We were on constant watch for icebergs during this re-rounding of the Horn. We were eventually able to set a course to the north, keeping well off the coast of Chile. [1]

Roger Callan, the bo'sun, remembered a relatively calm day south of Cape Horn. In his journal, quoted in John Wilson's *Wooden Walls to Distant Shores,* he stated, "On the 59th parallel, Captain Wilson shot four albatrosses. The biggest of which measured 11 feet, 8 inches wing tip to wing tip. All were perfectly shot without being damaged, and immediately wrapped and carefully placed in the deep-freeze to await preparation and stuffing by the taxidermist in New York. The stuffed birds were later distributed as gifts to the Cape Horn Museum in Saint Malo, France, the Maritime Museum in Oslo, the Maritime Museum in Arendal, and the biggest one was presented to the Senior Officers' Club in Arendal, Norway." [1]

One of the albatrosses shot by Captain John Wilson, in the center with a hand on a wing. Roger Callan is in the center background with a camera. *Photo by Klaus P. Hanusa, Ocean-Wide Film Production Berlin-Santiago.*

In 1993 interview by the author, Roger Callan recalled, "The *Regina Maris* rounded on January 26, 1967, and was the first wooden cargo vessel to round the Horn, east to west, in nearly 60 years. The next rounding of Cape Horn by a tall ship, I believe was the *Soren Larsen* (built of oak in Denmark in 1948, 148'x25'6" 350 tons) on September 9, 1991. The Iron Bark, *Eye of the Wind,* also accomplished the challenge of the Horn a month later, on October 12, 1991." [2]

Chris Roche, editor of *The Cape Horner Journal*, published three times a year, cannot confirm or deny Callan's statement concerning *Regina's* 60-year-record-breaking rounding. On record for the last rounding before *Regina Maris* by a commercial square rigger is *Pamir,* in 1949. She was of steel construction.

You may be wondering why the captain proceeded all the way up to Callao, Peru, bypassing many ports in Chile. After all, his ship, with two broken masts and a beleaguered crew, had been at sea for 54 days. The captain did arrange for a ship to bring fresh stores from Chile to offset the canned food. The fact is, John Wilson never planned to go to Chile because it was not a safe place for him. A warrant for his arrest was outstanding related to the cigarette smuggling scheme recounted in Chapter 3, in which two policemen and two soldiers had been killed and from which Wilson escaped to New York with a million dollar profit. [3]

From Callao, Peru, *Regina* headed toward the Panama Canal and then Florida. Two days out, an interesting event took place. The following is first mate Peter Wilson's account, quoted in John Wilson's *Wooden Walls to Distant Shores*: "At 4:00 p.m. off Isla La Plata, a motor ship loomed up. It was the *John Wilson* — one of the captain's own vessels. This was a chance meeting in the Pacific. After a variety of salutes with guns, flags, and sirens we put over our pitifully small boat (16') and not without difficulty due to the running swell at the time. We now hove to and the *John Wilson* had stopped her motor and also put down a boat. After this lifeboat had circled us with enthusiastic greeting and camera popping, the captain went into our little dinghy with two crewmen to row. At 11:30 p.m. the captain returned and the two ships, new and the old, slowly went their separate ways." [1]

Sailing on, the voyagers passed through the Panama Canal and meandered through the Caribbean. The ship and crew wound up in a Jacksonville, Florida, shipyard for six weeks for repairs. The ship was hauled out and repainted. The engine was overhauled. A new, taller fore-topgallant mast with two additional yards replaced the one broken at the Horn, and the mizzen topmast was enlarged. Sails for the new sky- and moonsail yards were delivered from Kristiansand, Norway.

When the ship was ready to leave, the dry dock manager told first mate Peter Wilson, "Captain Wilson paid the bill in cash; they were at their yard for about a month so you can imagine the size of the account. John Wilson believed in the power of cash and always had a lot on him." [4]

After the refit, their northerly course took them to Nassau, Bahamas; Norfolk, Virginia; and Greenport, New York. No one then could have guessed what a major role that small Long Island village about 100 miles east of New York City would play much later in *Regina's* life.

The indented material below, included in a letter to the author, is from Peter Wilson's personal log recounting his visit to Greenport and, later, the ship's entry into New York Harbor.

The Regina Maris, *Greenport, N.Y., May 1967*

> I was greeted by the mournful sound of our own foghorn as I woke this morning, while on deck a thick mist blankets everything. The whole crew is on lookout and Ivar is on the end of the bowsprit, while I steer. There had been a big scare in the previous watch when we missed a light buoy by a few feet. We are inching our way (we think) towards the coast of Long Island. A sudden shout from Ivar and three small fishing boats scatter in the gloom. Something tells us we are very close to the land. We are maneuvering among what I guess to be lobster pots. The fog lightens a little and all eyes are straining. It could be a trick of the sunlight, but ahead I can see a bar of light.
>
> "There's something there, sir," I said to the Captain.
>
> Then unmistakably, we catch the glint of the white breakers, it's a beach. We steer parallel to it and the fog returns thicker than ever. Right around the Montauk Light we sailed, without seeing it, guided only by the sound of its fog-horn. Later, in clearing fog we let go the anchor off the old whaling town called Greenport. It is a fine place with gleaming white wooden houses and jetties, and set in as English a countryside as can be found anywhere away from the British Isles. It is also a beautiful setting for the *Regina Maris* which stirs up much interest and reminiscing from the old salts here who jumped ship many years previously to enjoy the peace of this quiet countryside.
>
> The Captain has gone to New York City leaving the ship in my care. I had a visitor today, Ted Schmidt, who was a counselor with me at a boys summer camp in the Adirondacks in 1965. His girlfriend's family lives on Shelter Island in sight of our anchored vessel. It is the merest coincidence that we should meet again. Ted and his girlfriend, Virginia [Clark] came on board and I later joined them at her parents' house on Shelter Island.
>
> From the [Greenport- Shelter Island] ferry we drove through real Kentish countryside, but which is full of wildlife. Fox and deer crossed our headlights as we made our way to the house. After an enormous steak, done over an open fire and washed down with red wine, I left six children [Virginia's siblings], Keith, Patty, Heather, Wendy, John and Andy, pondering many sea stories and the intricacies of the Turk's head knot. I took the last ferry, 12:30 a.m., back to Greenport and the *Regina Maris*. [5]

Robert ("Bucky") and Barbara Clark were Peter Wilson's hosts on Shelter Island at the Mashomack Manor House, now the Nature Conservancy's Mashomack Preserve. The Clarks are the aunt and uncle of the author's wife, their children her cousins. All but Virginia and Patty still live on Shelter Island.

July 12, *Regina* left Greenport, headed for New York City. Peter Wilson's log for that day, in the indented materials below, recorded the following dialogue between himself, operating *Regina's* radio, and the New York Port Authority, as they entered the approach to the city:

> "Calling N.Y. Marine Operator, *Regina Maris* calling N.Y., over."
> "Come in RETAINER MORIS. What kind of vessel are you?"
> "REGINA MARIS to N.Y. We are a barquentine."
> "Do I read you right? A bargentine?"
> "No. A sailing ship!"
> "A selling ship?"
> At this point several enormous tankers were creeping up on us as the river narrowed. A burly voice broke in:
> "This is the tanker TEXAN calling N.Y. — "
> "Stand by TEXAN. What do you require, REGINA MARIS?"
> "Wind speed and direction, a.m. tomorrow — "
> "Bulk carrier VAMOSE calling N.Y. — "
> "Hold on, VAMOSE. New York back to REGINA . . ."
> So New York was holding up the world's commerce to tell us which way the wind could be blowing in the morning!" [4]

Upon entering New York Harbor on June 12, 1967, *Regina Maris* received an overwhelming reception. The captain had decided to set 36 sails, and the breeze kept them filled. The following is Roger Callan's account, quoted in John Wilson's *Wooden Walls to Distant Shores*: "We were escorted by Coast Guard cruisers; helicopters were buzzing around overhead and astern came Fire boats shooting jets of water into the air. Everywhere sounded ships' whistles and sirens. Both our cannons were fired on passing the Statue of Liberty. We tied up to the Battery. This was a really gracious reception to the 'Queen of the Sea' and was followed up by invitations, excursions, and parties ashore. Flying the Maltese colors, the two Norwegian owners, Captain John A. Wilson and Sigfried Wilson, who had rejoined the ship in New York, were made Knights of Malta and the Order was bestowed upon them by His Majesty King Peter 2nd of Yugoslavia, who had sought asylum during the Russian takeover of Yugoslavia and was living in New York. After a very full and exciting week during which we had time to see Mystic Seaport, we again put to sea, homeward bound." [1]

After some fishing on the grand banks and a fast passage, *Regina Maris* called at Saint Malo, France, where the Amical Internationale des Capitaines au Long Cours enthusiastically received them. The ship was inspected; logbooks and charts were checked and stamped. The owners were given the title of Albatross, the crew were named Mollymawks, and all were given active membership in the Cape Horners, with the right to fly the flag of the association. The brothers' quest had been achieved.

CHAPTER 5

THE HORN

1. Captain John Aage Wilson, *Wooden Walls to Distant Shores, A Maritime Concoction and the* Regina Maris *Saga* (Sussex, England: The Book Guild, 1992).
2. Roger Callan, interview by the author at his home on Shelter Island, New York, September 1993.
3. Captain JA Wilson, *Under Steam and Sail, Reminiscences of a Sea Captain (*Sussex, England: The Book Guild, 1990).
4. Peter Wilson, personal letter, received November 30, 1993.
5. Peter Wilson, personal letter, received April 11, 1993.

CHAPTER 6
AUSTRALIA BOUND
Plymouth, England, to Funchal, on the Island of Madeira
1968 – 1969

After triumphal receptions in Oslo and in her home port of Arendal, *Regina Maris* was laid up there for the winter. This winter work entailed the lowering of her seven yardarms and all 15 miles of running rigging (ropes). All the blocks (pulleys) were brought down, checked for wear, and rebuilt if necessary. The sails, all 70 of them, were washed, dried, and stored ashore in a warehouse. A false deck was built over the vessel to protect the deck and cabins from snow. The ship had a central hot water heating system that kept the interior cozy and warm. Bo'sun Roger Callan stayed on board throughout the winter as watchman. It was his job to knock the ice off the rigging so the ship would not become top-heavy. Although the fjord froze solid, *Regina's* double-planked hull was more than a match for the icy onslaught. [1]

During the summer of 1968, the ship was chartered to Radio-Televisione-Luxembourg (RTL). The forward deckhouse was converted into a radio station that broadcast every day on a promotional trip that followed the coast of France.

The crew for this trip was recruited from towns in the south of Norway. In France, the ship would anchor off a bathing beach and broadcast the daily show while bathers would swim and boaters row out to visit the ship. (At that time, *Regina Maris* had a large following in Europe. A full-length feature movie of her rounding the Horn had been released in the spring of 1968 and was shown all across Europe.)

After the radio broadcast, the ship would up anchor and sail, in the company of many small local yachts, to the next resort town for the next day's broadcast. The ship would have to be clean and presentable for the next group of tourists to explore. First mate Peter Wilson remembered, "The time schedule was grueling for sailors who generally go to sea to be away from the maddening crowd — and this trip brought them into the thick of it." [2]

By autumn, Peter recalled, the ship was back in Arendal for a repeat of the winter layup, a welcome change for the crew after the summer's experience. [2]

By mid-summer 1969, the ship had been completely overhauled, made ready for sea, and fully stocked with enough equipment and supplies for a year-long voyage, for she had been chosen for a special mission — re-creating the first voyage of Captain James Cook from England to Australia via Cape Horn (1768-1771). *Regina Maris* was to represent the Royal Norwegian Yacht Club (KNS), to which John Wilson belonged, in Sydney during the Cook Bicentenary Celebrations in April, 1970.

With her she was to carry the Challenge Cup that would be presented to the Royal Sydney Yacht Squadron on behalf of the KNS for the then-new Olympic Soling Yacht class. Designed by the Norwegian yacht designer Jan H. Linge, the Soling had won the

International Yacht Racing Union's competition for a new, three-man Olympic boat that was to be used in the 1972 Olympics at Kiel, Germany. Along with the Challenge Cup, *Regina* would carry a dispatch signed by Norway's Crown Prince Harald, Commodore of the KNS, requesting that the Royal Sydney Yacht Club lay down the rules for the Soling race. Setting sail for Plymouth, England on September 1, the ship made her way across the North Sea to receive yet another Royal commission.

Queen Elizabeth II of England had also authorized John Wilson and his ship to carry a packet containing many official dispatches and proclamations to the festivities in Sydney. All aspects of the Cook voyage were to be duplicated as closely as possible by *Regina*. That meant *Regina's* captain would be given the same official command that the First Sea Lord had given Captain Cook in 1768. Delivered to Captain John Wilson with much pomp and ceremony, the command read as follows:

"Whereas you are to receive herewith a pacquet for Vice-Admiral Sir A.L. Smith, Chief of Australian Naval Staff which pacquet contains Dispatches of very great importance to the Public Service, you are hereby required and directed to put to sea in the Ship you command at the very first opportunity of Wind and Weather and to proceed without a moments loss of time to Australia.

"You are to keep a proper weight constantly affixed to the pacquet and in case you shall meet with an enemy of superior force, and find it impossible to avoid being taken, you are to throw said pacquet overboard." [3]

With the very important cargo of dispatches and documents properly weighted as in the original voyage, *Regina Maris* made ready to sail from Plymouth, England. Marianne was accompanying her father, Captain John Wilson, 53, and mother, John's third wife, Alice, 19, who was from China. Her Chinese name was Tsui-yuk or "green jewel." On board were a year's supply of baby food, diapers, and other necessities for baby Marianne. John had hopes of his daughter's becoming the youngest member of the Cape Horn Society. [4]

Also on the ship was an additional, very important bundle: Six-week-old For September 13, 1969, a grand send-off from Plymouth was planned, including a mock battle with the replica of *Nonsuch,* a 1650 ketch. A BBC film crew was aboard *Regina Maris,* and other members of the press were in helicopters and the many small boats milling around the two combatants. With all sail set on both ships, the shots began, first one from *Regina's* cannon, then one from *Nonsuch.* When *Regina's* cannon fell silent, all the cameras turned to see a member of her crew being lowered into a waiting press boat with a cloth over his face. On the television world news that night it was announced that "*Regina's* bo'sun, Roger Callan, had been killed in a freak accident during the battle.[1]

The press did not have the facts straight. Roger, who is alive and well today, told the author and his wife, Penny, the entire story in a conversation in September 1993.

Roger had been loading and firing the cannons. He got the first round off perfectly. In the excitement of the moment, however, he did not swab the barrel effectively and left some burning embers inside. When he rammed a new powder charge down the barrel with the ramrod, the force of air inflamed the remaining sparks and ignited the charge, blowing the ramrod out through his hand and burning his face, temporarily blinding him. Roger was concerned about infection so he asked John Wilson for his handkerchief to protect his face. He was rushed to the hospital and spent four hours on the operating table having his hand reconstructed and his burns dressed. He still has some of the black powder imbedded in the skin of his face. [1]

Unfortunately, Roger's parents learned of his accident from the news report, as did his aunt and uncle in Australia, who were looking forward to welcoming him in Australia. Two phone calls from the captain set things straight, and everyone was much relieved. Roger rejoined the ship in Funchal, Madeira Island, on September 24. [1]

When the accident occurred, the ship canceled its leave-taking, and John Wilson went ashore to check on Roger. Upon learning that, although Roger was to be in the hospital for 10 days, he was expected to make a full recovery, John Wilson brought five cases of beer back to the ship, and an enjoyable evening was spent singing sea chanteys. John Wilson's favorite was "Rolling Home," which he planned to teach to the crew so they could sing it perfectly by the time they reached Australia. The evening of revelry ended when one of the crew climbed to the skysail yard to play "When the Saints Come Marching In" on his trumpet.

Early the next morning, September 14, *Regina Maris* set sail, without Roger, to keep with the Cook re-creation timetable. The following indented material is the personal log of third mate Paul Maskell, recounting eight days on *Regina Maris* at sea, as quoted in John Wilson's book *Wooden Walls to Distant Shores*. This log is included here because his words portray life at sea and the necessary functions of the ship and also convey an awe of sailing and the sea. His narrative also allows a glimpse into the heart and soul of Captain John A. Wilson.

15 September 1969. Monday.

Our voyage in the wake of Captain Cook had at last begun. In contrast to yesterday's escort of boatloads of keen photographers and film units our departure today was witnessed by only a few weekend yachtsmen and fishermen. Our first day at sea, after leaving Plymouth Sound, and not a very memorable one, weather still calm and overcast wind very light from the north-east. We sailed past Lizard Head lighthouse abeam about seven miles distant. In the afternoon porpoises start to escort the ship, at times they break surface to reveal their white bellies, before diving again, a brief distraction from life on board the ship.

16 September 1969. Tuesday.

Position approx. Lat. 46 20' N. Long. 8 40' W.

I spent some time on the 12 to 4 a.m. watch last night watching the porpoises as they rush towards the bow looking like glowing torpedoes. Their whole body was outlined, being lit up by the phosphorescence in the water.

1130 hrs. Owing to missing wind from southwest, brailed and seized all fore and aft sails. Also lowered yards and seized all square sails. Wind gradually increased during the remainder of the morning and there was every indication from the sky appearance that we were in for a blow.

At 1300 hrs. It was gusting gale force 7 to 8 [approx. 40 mph] from southwest, the wind, as the old sailormen would say, a "dead muzzler."

1500 hrs. Heavy rainsqualls struck the ship, and as they were passing over the wind suddenly veered more to the west than to the northwest.

1600 hrs. When the wind still at gale force from the northwest the Captain gave orders to set the three inner jibs, two lower staysails, and mainsail. By now we had begun to ship water along the lee-rail and over the fo'c's'le head, the ship also took up a definite heel to port, working on deck without a good hand or foot hold became more difficult, many of us ended up sliding into the scuppers when she rolled, sea sickness also began to make its presence felt amongst the crew.

1630 hrs. Captain's orders were that we were to set the course and lower topsail. There was not an immediate rush of hands to go aloft I remember. It was the roughest weather and sea that many of us had ever had to go aloft on the yardarm and we all knew that a good handhold was essential. As soon as the sails were sheeted home we braced hard up on the starboard tack.

2230 hrs. Wind blowing as hard as ever — have to go aloft to take in lower topsail and the course. Heavy rainsquall struck at the time to make the job more difficult. Also took in upper and top staysail and flying jib that had been set. Gale continues all night, lot of water on deck, with ship rolling and crashing her way through the seas, at times the clinometer measures 40 degrees angle of heel. On a course 210 compass but making quite a bit of leeway speed, patent log 6 knots.

Working aloft. *Photo by Klaus P. Hanusa, Ocean-Wide Film Production Berlin-Santiago.*

17 September 1969. Wednesday.

Position Lat. 44 15' N. Long. 9 30' W. approx.

In second day of this gale, the Bay of Biscay is certainly living up to its reputation. Wind has been at force 7 to 8 all day, NW occasional rain showers and also periods of sunshine. The ship has been heeled over now for the last thirty-six hours, still a lot of water on deck, seas at times breaking over the port bulwarks. Have not had to lay a hand on the braces or sheets all day, still driving along under three headsails, two lower staysails main and main topsail doing a good 6 knots, one gets the impression the Captain intends driving the ship to the limit. At times the bows and fo'c's'le head are briefly hidden from sight by the sea and flying spray only to reappear seconds later looking as strong and powerful as ever. Most of the cabins are now in quite a mess being littered up with drying clothes and oilskins and upturned drying sea boots and socks, we all look forward to the warmer more southern latitudes and the chance to dry out everything.

18 September 1969. Thursday.

Position approx. Lat. 41 40' N. Long. 11 W.

At 0400 hrs. approx. 45 miles due west from Cape Finisterre and approx. 630 miles from Plymouth. A wonderful day's sailing, the best I have experienced in the *Regina Maris*. Wind having eased to force 5 from the northwest it enabled us to set the square sails braced around hard on the starboard tack, so now bowling along doing 8 knots. Early this morning the main topsail split, so we had to go aloft, unbend it and lower it down to the deck, this is our first sail damage and no doubt it will not be our last. Re-stowing and securing the boxes of provisions and ships-gear in the cargo hold all afternoon, some of it had slipped and moved in Tuesday's gale. The Captain measured our speed using the old fashioned knotted line and sand-glass method, over the stern; it caught the interest and attention of the crew members on board who all rushed aft to see what the Captain's new game was. In all have had fourteen sails up today, the Captain decides to keep all of them set during the night and hope that the wind does not change or increase.

Australia bound. *Photo by Ben Klein* (*taken from a press boat*).

19 September 1969. Friday.
   Position approx. lat. 39 36' N. long. 13 52' W.

Wind holds steady all night and we reel off another thirty-four miles in the 12 midnight to 4 a.m. watch, a good 8 and ½ knots. Barometer now 30.2 and rising. Temperature 18 C. Wind about force 5 from the north, has been sunny all day with cumulus cloud about. Have had four more extra fancy sails set today, the sky and moon sail, flying staysail and upper flying jib, so eighteen sails set in all now. The *Regina Maris* must really have looked a cloud of sail to anyone on a passing steamer they probably would not have believed their eyes at such a sight — a clipper ship sailing the seas in this day and age. Has not been so much water on deck today; although the seas have gone considerably down there is still the occasional swell rolling up from the west and catching the ship, the aftermath of our gale no doubt. The wind has held steady coming from a point just abaft the starboard beam, one cannot help feeling that the *Regina Maris* really excels herself in these conditions of sea and wind for the last two days now we have not had to lay a hand on the braces or sheets, the ship has really sailed herself. I have spent some time today wistfully standing on the after deck, gazing up at the mass of billowing canvas, moved by the sight of it all and the thought of the fact that we are really reenacting Cook's historic voyage of 200 years ago. The silence of the occasion is broken only by the sounds which are peculiar to a ship under sail, rush of water past the bows, the noise of the wind past the leeches, the sudden jerking and chucking of the clew cringles and the swilling coughing of water in the port scuppers.

20 September 1969. Saturday.

    Position approx. Lat. 36 56' N. Long. 16 24' W.

    Approx. 250 sea miles to Madeira. The weather is somewhat warmer today the thermometers on the side of the wheelhouse record air temp. as 20 C a 4 to 5 rise from two days ago. The sea has now turned a deep blue in color and appears to have a friendly sparkle about it, the wind has held steady from the north-north-east, this morning brailed the mizzen out and came about so we now have the ship sailing on a broad reach. We have been logging 6 and ½ knots all day. The warm weather has allowed us to dry our damp clothes and bed linen. Our more even keel allowed the galley boy, Dave, to bake a cake. As the weather seems fairly settled the Captain decides to keep all the fancy sails set tonight, barometer is on 30.30 inches and steady.

21 September 1969. Sunday.

    Position approx. Lat. 34 15' N. Long. 16 30' W.

    Saw the first ship last night on the 12 to 4 a.m. watch, it crossed astern of us going fast — appeared to be on course for Gibraltar. Another warm sunny day, and the ship is still sailing well. Captain now says we will arrive off Madeira at daybreak tomorrow, so we are all looking forward to seeing land. Have been a week at sea now and have covered well over 1,000 sea miles. Re-stowing and re-marking the spare sails today which is quite a job, it is important that we know exactly where any particular replacement sail is so that it can be brought out quickly in an emergency. 1930 hrs. clewed up the moon, sky, royal, and topgallant sails, also let down the flying jibs, the three uppermost staysails and brailed in the mizzen, although it was then dark, the moonlight enabled us to see, to work out on the yards. Having taken in the sails we all retired to the mess below and were given a ration of rum and blackcurrant from the Captain. At 2245 hrs lookout called that he had sighted the lighthouse on Pta. do Pargo, Madeira, bearing on the starboard bow. 2345 hrs took in all remaining sails except forestaysail and main sail. With the breeze now light from the north-east and with nearly all way off the ship we closed very slowly with the Island of Madeira.

22 September 1969. Monday.

0400 hrs proceeded around the eastern tip of the island then towards Funchal. As the dawn broke the cliffs and highland of the island became more discernible. 0900 hrs with pilot on board entered the harbor of Funchal, eight days out from Plymouth, and with the first leg of our voyage now completed. The sun now very hot with no breeze inside the harbor, we were soon all sweating like pigs as we heaved and pulled on the mooring lines to draw the ship alongside the pier. Roger Callan rejoined the ship, his right hand and wrist still bandaged, a bloodshot left eye and eyelashes burned away, but otherwise none the worse for his accident in Plymouth when gunpowder in one of the cannons exploded as he was reloading. He was eager to continue in the re-creation of Captain Cook's voyage of discovery. Our biggest surprise was the presence of a big German cruise ship from Lübeck moored just astern of us with the name of none other than the *Regina Maris*. A strange coincidence that the two ships each signifying a different era in the history of sea travel should meet in this small harbor. Customs, harbor officials and ships agents all swarm onboard, the crew soon engrossed in their letters from home. It is not long before the ship is surrounded by street traders both up on the pier and in boats around the ship, trying to sell us souvenirs and trinkets. In the evening together with the Captain we pay a visit to the dining room of the German cruise ship for a screening of the *Regina Maris* film; it is well enjoyed and appreciated by the passengers as well as the crew of the ship; afterwards we sampled some of their cool German beer. [3]

During their visit in Funchal, it was discovered that a tree planted by Captain James Cook in 1769, two hundred years before, was now dead. John Wilson and his crew took the initiative, and planted a new Tulip Poplar, *Tulipeiro de Virginie,* on the same site. This event attracted the highest military and civil authorities and was blessed by the Archbishop. A commemorative bronze plaque, donated by the ship's crew, was placed at the base of the new tree. When the ship was provisioned in early October, *Regina Maris* left Funchal and headed once again for Cape Horn. [4 p. 12, 3 p. 350]

CHAPTER 6
AUSTRALIA BOUND

1. Roger Callan, interview by the author and his wife, Penny Kerr, September 5, 1993.
2. Peter Wilson, letter to the author, dated May 3, 1996.
3. Captain John Aage Wilson, *Wooden Walls to Distant Shores, A Maritime Concoction and the* Regina Maris *Saga* (Sussex, England: The Book Guild, 1992).
4. "The Tiniest Sailor in the Wake of Captain Cook," *The Independent Newspaper* (United Kingdom), September 14, 1969. Courtesy of Roger Callan.

CHAPTER 7
DISMASTED
October 1969 – February 1970

A dismasting at sea is a potential hazard all sailors face when venturing offshore. The strength of your rigging, masts, and stays are all tested during a blow. As technology and materials improve, new innovations adopted by marine designers and yacht builders improve safety. *Regina* did have stainless steel standing rigging, the best you could buy in 1964, but the rest of her was 18th- and 19th-century technology. That mix of different technologies, plus the human factor, probably played a role in what happened October 13, 1969, as the ship sailed southwest, some 1400 nm from Funchal bound for the Horn and the South Pacific. The personal logs of first mate Peter Wilson and third mate Paul Maskell for October 13, 1969, are nearly identical in their description of what happened next. The following indented material is from Paul Maskell's personal log, published in *Dog Watch,* an Australian annual, and also, with some slight differences, in Captain John Aage Wilson's book, *Wooden Walls to Distant Shores.*

October 13, 1969
   Sailing along steadily all night, wind remains a gentle breeze from the east-north-east. We have the wind over the port quarter, fore and aft sails sheeted and square sails braced around hard to starboard. All working canvas set, 24 sails in all. Lightning flashes which became visible yesterday at dusk, again light up the sky to the east during the early morning. At about eight a.m. as we were setting the portside water sail it started raining and was soon a steady warm downpour. Most of the crew assembled on deck dressed only in swimming trunks and with soap and towel started washing themselves down in the rain; also many take the opportunity to launder their dirty clothes. During the heavier periods of rainfall the wind drops down to a dead calm and the surface of the sea becomes smooth and glass-like. I took three boys aft [some crew members were only 14 to 16 years old] to assist me in setting the mizzen topsail. We had just completed setting the sail as the rain started falling much heavier again. There was also an increase in wind from the north-east. All the sails then started filling and stretching and we started picking up speed.
   I made my way down the lee and starboard side of the mizzen rigging keeping a good hand and foothold and was just about halfway down and making the topsail downhaul fast to the shrouds, when suddenly a terrific and violent gust of wind with torrential driving sheets of rain hit the ship. I had to grip and cling on to the shrouds and rigging with both hands more tightly than ever to save myself from being blown away to leeward off the

rigging. As the sudden wind and rain pressure hit the ship and her massive area of canvas set aloft, she began to heel over more to starboard, the shrouds and battens on the leeward side of the ship and on which I was standing suddenly became loose and started to shake.

At this second I heard a terrible, loud and sharp cracking sound, similar to the noise made by a thunderclap, come from the area of the forward part of the ship. I looked up and through the driving rain saw sails, some of which were torn, yards and broken pieces of masts come crashing down. It was such an unbelievable and frightening sight that for a brief instant I was gripped with fear and thought the whole ship was going over. I then looked up directly above me and saw the main and mizzen topmasts come crashing downwards, the mizzen topmast hung suspended vertically in mid-air swinging a foot or so from where I was still standing. I thought, "Hell, I've gotta get down from here before all the lot comes down." For at that moment the other masts and rigging could quite easily have fallen also. Although seemingly paralyzed by the sight of what I had just witnessed I quickly made my way back down to deck, half jumping half falling the last few feet and landing on the poop deck near the salon door.

The captain was just coming on deck from the salon. I said to him with near panic in my voice, "Everything's gone over captain." He looked forward in amazement, not believing what he saw, trying to keep in the shelter of the after deckhouse, as pieces of rigging and masts were still falling down onto the deck on the starboard side of the deck. I was sure and feared in my mind that someone must be lying injured under all the masts, spars and wires that lay across the deck and forward starboard rail.

Strangely enough, the wind had already started to drop and was by this time just a normal breeze again from the north-east, but there was still heavy pouring rain. The sea was not rough; there was swell which caused the ship to roll.

Looking forward I then saw the true extent of the damage: the complete foremast together with all the yards, the seven square sails, the foremast stays and the five headsails, the upper Jamie Green [a type of staysail] and the main topmast stays and the five staysails were down lying over the starboard bow in the sea. All the square sails and yards lay flat in the clear blue water, some appeared to be perfectly set and the sails still sheeted out as they were when aloft and they looked apparently undamaged. The huge, two-ton, Norwegian pine course yard lay horizontal in the water close to the ship's starboard side just outside the channels. The foremast appeared to be broken in about four places. The shrouds and backstays of the foremast from the port side leading up from the channel had been pulled down flat and lay tight over the galley house roof, supporting most of the weight of the foremast as it lay in the water. The main topmast was broken off in two places below the platform and halfway up the mast. The two pieces were hanging up in the shrouds vertically towards the deck and were swinging precariously and banging together and against the mainmast with the rolling of the ship. The mizzen topmast was hanging down against the shrouds. All the other crew who had either been sitting in the mess in the forward deckhouse or who had been below then came running out on deck.

Where the foremast should have been. *Photo by Roger Callan.*

There was difficulty opening the port side door of the deckhouse as the shrouds were pinning it shut, the starboard door was blocked by the broken mast and other debris. Some of the boys who had still been on the foredeck washing when the disaster struck came hurrying aft. All hands on board were accounted for; no one had even been injured. By a fantastic piece of luck none of the crew had been aloft working or on the starboard side of the ship; if they had been they would undoubtedly have been killed. I will never forget those first moments after the dismasting, the rain still pouring down we just stood there on the midship deck, all of us dressed only in swim trunks, looking up where the foremast used to be and then at each other, shaking our heads in disbelief. Some of the boys had their hands clasped over their ears, others covered their heads, some were quite pale with fear and shock, unable to speak but just looked in amazement at the sight of it all. The few words spoken were, "What the hell happened," and "The ship's finished now." We all in fact had the same expression of utter astonishment on our faces. "How could it happen?" One minute we had been sailing along so well, doing about four or five knots, with all 24 sails set, in a normal breeze, and then a sudden onslaught of the elements hits us and the next moment all our sails and foremast have been knocked flat into the sea. In a second that great area of sail had disappeared.

It was beyond comprehension how the *Regina Maris* could, within seconds, be transformed from a beautiful sailing ship into a wallowing, helpless "wreck." We were all filled with intense sorrow, disappointment and shock. Our dreams of the last few months of sailing to Australia, the ship we had learnt how to sail and to love now lay in such a pitiful and forlorn state. Then the Captain came on deck, dressed in green oilskins and hat, he showed no emotion on his face and acted as if everything was normal. He said in a cold, calm voice, "We had better start cutting away the masts and rigging." I expected him to say something of regret or sorrow but he did not, perhaps he was still not accepting the reality of it all or maybe he was suffering from shock at seeing his brainchild and life-long dream dismasted and in ruins.

The broken top mast of the mizzen. *Photo by Roger Callan.*

We then started the miserable task of cutting away at the foremast rigging; it was decided that no attempt would be made to save any of the yards or sails on the foremast, for as well as being nearly an impossible task, it would also have been very dangerous to have attempted to salvage anything alongside the ship. It was still too dangerous to walk on the starboard side of the ship, there was a lot of loose gear up aloft liable to come crashing down at any minute, the main and the mizzen topmasts were still swinging and banging about and lines were swishing across the deck every time the ship rolled. Some of the main and mizzen backstays that had fallen down and were trailing in the sea around the stern of the ship were then cleared away and heaved on deck, we were then able to go ahead on the auxiliary and turn so that we were "bows on" to the swell and so reduce the rolling motion of the ship. All available knives, axes, hacksaws, wrenches and all other cutting tools were brought out on deck and we set to cutting away at the foremast rig; we also assembled the cutting equipment. The foremast stays were first cut through with hacksaws; this was much easier than trying to undo seized shackles and bottle-screws sitting on the bowsprit. Then the shrouds and backstays on the port side channel and rail were released. Many of the shackles and bottle-screws were unscrewed with wrenches and grips, the others were cut with hacksaws and cold chisels. The lines of the running rigging of the foremast were cut away with knives and cast off from the pins; very little was of any useful length to save for future use.

It was a heartbreaking and callous job to have to cut at all the cordage, sheets, braces, buntlines, clew lines, downhauls and halyards that we had become so familiar with and which we had pulled and sweated on so much during the last few months. We worked like hell hacking away at that foremast rigging, some finding strength in their bodies that they did not know they had. So concerned were we in our task that no one had noticed a number of sharks swimming around the ship; it was as if they knew we were in some sort of trouble and were waiting to see the outcome. We hooked one of the sharks and soon the massive beast was fighting for his life. To make his end quicker the captain brought his shotgun out and fired one barrel into him, he was then hauled on board and his belly slit open.

We then all went back to more serious work at hand. As it was apparent that the mainmast was now in a considerably dangerous and un-stayed condition, (the stays having fallen with the foremast), a four-inch nylon hawser was therefore rigged from just below the mainmast platform down to the bowsprit to give the mast some forward support; a similar stay was set up from the mizzenmast platform to the foot of the mainmast. Eventually by late afternoon the final foremast shrouds were cut away from the starboard channel using the oxyacetylene gear and the complete foremast together with all the square sails slid beneath the surface, and could be seen for several moments sinking slowly down, deeper into the clear blue water; it was a sad sight indeed. The forepart of the ship now appeared bare and exposed on deck, cut and frayed lines and wires were all over the place and trailed into the water over the starboard side where the foremast had just sunk.

The mainsail and mizzen which had been brailed in soon after the storm were then cut down and stowed on deck. We were unable to cut the two pieces of the main topmast down before nightfall, they were still held by the shrouds below the main platform, and we lashed them together and to the mainmast so as to prevent them swinging about across the deck during the night. Midship deck now in chaos, pieces of wood that had fallen from the broken platform of the mainmast were littered everywhere, lines, wires, blocks, tackles and baggywrinkle lay in tangled heaps. We stopped work at dusk, 7 p.m., having done as much as possible to make everything secure, we were now exhausted, miserable and saddened by it all, still not believing it has all happened.

Many of the crew on board are of the opinion that it was a thunderbolt that hit the mast. The helmsman at the time, said he saw the flash the instant the mast began to fall. Maybe we will never know the truth of the matter, or whether it was a violent wind gust or a flash of lightning. At about 7:15 p.m. the auxiliary engine was started and the ship turned and headed on a course of 045 degrees for Las Palmas, the captain having already decided that this would be the nearest and most suitable port to try and make for. Being well in the northeast trade wind belt we now have the wind and the sea from dead ahead; this affects the movement of the ship much more, now there is so much less weight forward, she takes on a stiffer attitude and pitches more violently into the sea."[1, also 2]

Roger Callan, the bo'sun, remembered, "I had a safety belt on, and I was cutting the turnbuckles with the torch standing on the starboard channel. One minute my feet in the water the next minute 8' above the water as the ship rolled with all the rigging and everything. I was stretching down trying to cut away the rigging under tremendous tension so that every time I cut the last bit of turnbuckle it went, 'BING' and shot away. I had to keep my head out of the way it was so dangerous!" [3]

Roger with the torch watching his head. *Photo by Roger Callan.*

John Wilson contacted his brother back in Norway via radio to make arrangements, as he planned to have the ship re-rigged immediately. This determined man was not going to give up.

Later that night, the captain's salon filled with smoke. The paneling around the hollow steel mizzen mast that served as the exhaust stack for the engine had caught fire. With the fire out and the interior a shambles, it was determined that a part of the wooden mizzen top mast had fallen into the stack and created back pressure and the heat had ignited the wooden paneling.

Alice Wilson and four-week-old baby Marianne remained calm throughout the ordeal. John Wilson did remark in his personal log, "My wife did not for a second think of anything but washing and feeding her little treasure. Extraordinary!" He goes on to say, "The reason for bringing my wife and baby was obvious, viz. that I wanted them to qualify for membership in the A.I.C.H. (Association International Cape Horn) as 'Cape Pigeons.' " [4]

John Wilson felt the damage had been caused by a lightning strike. He stated that he "was the only one who knew that when the new, taller, topgallant mast had been stepped in Jacksonville, Florida, in 1967, the lightning conductor was too short, and a piece had been added. The conductivity of the joint was inadequate." [4]

After the dismasting wreckage was cleared, the ship, under engine power, motored to Las Palmas, 1100 nautical miles away, arriving October 19. Las Palmas is a substantial port on a major shipping route, with the finding of a tow vessel a good probability. There, as the ship waited for a tow to Kristiansand, Norway, where she would be re-rigged, John, with his wife and baby, flew to Norway to start the fabrication of all the metal parts, sails, and running rigging. He also organized the shipment of 35 tons of Douglas fir (for the new masts and spars) from Vancouver, Washington, to be air-freighted to Norway. John then returned to Las Palmas and the ship for the tow to Kristiansand.

While waiting for the tow, John Wilson made an interesting statement in his personal log of October 26 concerning his plans for bringing *Regina Maris* from Las Palmas to Kristiansand. The following was written after the auxiliary motor's exhaust had caught the ship on fire in mid ocean, after the dismasting.

"I do not consider the auxiliary motor (GM 8-71) to be sufficient propulsion power or safe enough for this sailing vessel. The ship would have to be provisionally re-rigged with sufficient sails to take care of an emergency and to steady the vessel which otherwise is un-maneuverable, being too stiff. Even such temporary rig would not be sufficient and also other measures would have to be taken, first instance proceed with the barest minimum of fuel and fresh water in bottom tanks and have supplies stowed on deck in drums. The broken steel mizzen-mast with the four exhaust pipes inside would have to be taken down and provisional exhaust pipes provided. Also for towing, all tanks emptied and weights placed on deck to make the ship softer and avoid excessive rolling. Weights in the bottom of the ship (that had to be compensated for on deck) consist of:

16 steel tanks, empty weight	16 tons
Fixed iron and cement ballast weight	40 tons
Steel outside keel with fastenings	20 tons
	About 76 tons

Bowsprit and jib boom would probably be broken down by a towline and would have to be removed." [2]

On November 20, 1969, the freighter *Paniutos*, bound for North Germany, took *Regina Maris* in tow from Las Palmas, bound for Kristiansand. Some of John's well-thought-out plans did not come to fruition, for the movie of the tow and re-masting clearly shows the bowsprit and the mizzen mast intact. In interviews, the crew who participated in the tow back to Norway agreed unanimously that it was a terrible trip. *Regina* did pitch and roll. It took two men on the wheel to try to keep her following the freighter. To decrease the "tugging" motion, the two anchor chains were led through the hawse pipes out toward the freighter and attached to the tow cable 500 feet from *Regina's* bow. That tonnage on the tow cable helped control the ship's unwanted movements.

On December 1, the freighter cast off *Regina* five miles from the shipyard in Kristiansand, where work for her re-rigging was already well underway, and the actual re-rigging started on December 3. For just over two months, the work crews labored far into the night in below zero temperatures. The Wilson brothers documented *Regina's* re-rigging in a movie that was to be used as a teaching film for future tall-ship builders. The filming is excellent, but the narration is all in Norwegian, unfortunately limiting its usefulness.

Concerning the new masts *Regina* was to receive, first mate Peter Wilson, in a 1994 phone call with the author, shared some interesting information he had obtained from a logger he had met years later in Norway:

"A rugged British Columbian mountainside was the home of the Douglas firs (*Tsugatsuga taxifolia*) that were cut for *Regina Maris's* new masts. To meet the size requirements for the masts, the largest trees had to be cut. For the loggers, it was an unusual order, three 70-foot-long log sections of specific diameters. The trees had to be climbed, diameters taken at the given length, and the tree topped. Then the tree had to be felled uphill, landing on thick piles of foliage stacked to cushion the fall, so that there would be less chance of breakage or splitting. The trucks were designed to carry 10- and 15-foot-long logs, so they had to be modified to handle the weight and length. The mountain road was treacherous with the over-long loads. Back at the New Westminster lumber mill, the logs' bark was peeled by hand, for the mill's machine peeler was too small for the gigantic logs. Other shorter and various diameter logs were also peeled and added to the order. The 35 tons of logs were then loaded onto trucks and taken to the

Vancouver Airport, then loaded onto a chartered, specially configured Globemaster cargo plane, bound for Norway." [5]

In an interview with the author in 1993, Roger Callan contributed more information about the journey of the masts: "The Globemaster took off on its route over the North Pole. Hours later, bad weather was encountered and they could not land in Norway, for the airports were closed. The plane was diverted to the only available airport, Paris, France. Several days went by waiting for the weather to pass and the airport in Oslo to open up. The forecast was for a series of storms to hit Northern Europe for the next several weeks. Sigfried Wilson, who was coordinating the log shipment, ordered the logs be unloaded from the Globemaster in Paris. The logs were then loaded onto two stretched lo-boy trailers that made up a convoy with a police escort. From Paris the convoy traveled 1,850k (1,150 miles) to Kristiansand, Norway. The route took them 300 kilometers north on highway 17 through Lille, France, and on to Brussels. They traveled through many small towns in Holland, where they caused a great deal of interest. The convoy passed through Bremen, then Hamburg, and just past Flensburg, Germany, they passed into Denmark. The road conditions worsened due to the storms, as they drove northward to Alborg. The last 68 kilometers were the worst. A snowstorm raged as the trucks slowly made their way onto the ferry in Hitshals, for the five-hour trip to Kristiansand, Norway." [3]

As soon as the logs arrived, the team of woodworkers started turning them by hand into masts and spars. On January 28-29, 1970, the fore, main, and mizzen lower and top masts and fore topgallant masts were stepped. Under each mast, on the keelson, is a Norwegian one-kroner coin placed there by John Wilson. Below, and in the forward companion way, are two more Norwegian coins nailed to the foremast. All crew members were taught to be sure to touch them as they passed, for good luck.

All the new standing rigging was stainless steel and had been air-freighted from the United States. The documentary film shows in great detail the splicing of the cable and the forging of the countless metal parts by the blacksmiths. Thirty-eight new flax sails had to be made since the entire original set was lost over the side into the Atlantic. The 15 miles of sail-controlling lines and the blocks the lines run through had to be assembled. Soon the pieces of the puzzle were in place and ready to install when *Regina* arrived at the shipyard.

All during the reconstruction, a great deal of controversy raged concerning the cause of the dismasting. Pages of testimony in the ship's log from the entire crew and the captain's wife detail where they were and what they experienced on the day of the dismasting.

The insurance issue was very complicated. After earlier and costly repairs to fix damage sustained during the voyage around the Horn, replacement insurance costs had been so high that the Wilsons had decided only to carry hull insurance. After the dismasting, the underwriter, Lloyd's of London, looking to cut their potential losses, blamed the Wilson brothers for being foolhardy and irresponsible, feeling John had been at fault for carrying too much sail. They also questioned the cause of the fire in the main salon the evening of the dismasting. The media, which covered the entire event, complicated the insurance issue even further. Lacking facts, they reported hearsay and garbled details, and the public, wanting to place blame, focused on John Wilson. Lloyd's considered the ship a total loss, but the case was settled eventually and the insurance company paid for the re-rigging. [2]

At first, John Wilson feared the dismasting would put a halt to *Regina's* mission to replicate Captain Cook's voyage to Australia and that all her historic dispatches and the Royal Norwegian Yacht Club silver cup would have to be returned. It is hoped this narrative has conveyed John Wilson's vision and fortitude. He was determined that Norway would be represented at the Captain Cook Bicentenary if humanly possible. One hundred and twenty-one sailing days had been lost between October 13, 1969, the day of the dismasting, and the day she set sail for Australia again. Could she get there in time?

Captain Wilson chose a shorter course for his second attempt, following the route Captain Cook took on his second and third voyages to Australia, going by way of the Cape of Good Hope and across the Indian Ocean. This would mean *Regina Maris* would cross the south Indian Ocean in early winter. That was not the best season for safety, but there would always be a lot of wind to power the ship. He was concerned about the danger and in his log states that he could not afford insurance for the trip. He says, "I comforted myself by the philosophy that I would receive no benefit of insurance anyway, once in Davy Jones's locker." [2]

Nevertheless, on February 13, 1970, with an icebreaker leading her out of the harbor, *Regina Maris* once again set sail for Australia.

CHAPTER 7

DISMASTED AT LATITUDE 11.13' N, LONGITUDE 26.34" W

1. "Dismasted," *Dog Watch* (annual published by The Shiplovers' Societies of Australia, Melbourne), 1970. Contains the personal log of Paul Maskell, which was used in the insurance case testimony, and was also included, with some slight differences, in reference 2, below.
2. Captain John Aage Wilson, *Wooden Walls to Distant Shores, A Maritime Concoction and the* Regina Maris *Saga* (Sussex, England: The Book Guild, 1992).
3. Roger Callan, interview by the author, September 5, 1993.
4. Captain J. A. Wilson, *Under Steam and Sail, Reminiscences of a Sea Captain* (Sussex, England: The Book Guild, 1990).
5. Peter Wilson, phone call with the author, June 10, 1994.

CHAPTER 8
AUSTRALIA BOUND ONCE MORE
February – August, 1970

To speed the departure from the cold Norway winter and avoid the risk of becoming icebound, *Regina Maris* left the Hoivold Mekaniske shipyard with only 12 of her 38 sails operational. John Wilson took three of the shipyard's best riggers with him to complete the work on the running rigging at sea. For this voyage, the ship had an enlarged sail plan. The foremast was made taller than before — it now reached 150 feet above the water. Two royal studding sails were added, along with a flying main staysail and a mizzen top staysail. John was fond of saying "she had all the fancy kites." [1]

Three days after setting sail, the standing rigging of the fore- and mizzen masts had to be tightened one revolution on the turnbuckles due to the stress of the wind load. The ship encountered high winds on the fourth day, and the upper bobstay chain connecting link below the bowsprit broke, as did the fore-topmast forestay. These two events potentially endangered all the masts because the bobstay chain pulls down on the bowsprit to counter the force of the three masts that pull it up and toward the stern. Disconnected from the bowsprit, the topmast could break and cause considerable damage. These problems could not be repaired at sea, so the ship proceeded to Southampton, England, arriving February 18, 1970.

For 10 precious days, the ship stood still in the shipyard, no bow wave, no wake, no progress toward Australia. Workers scurried to repair the damaged bowsprit and topmast. The Norwegian riggers were grateful for the circumstances for they were able to rig several more sails. Between sightseeing trips, the crew re-caulked the deck. The movie *Regina Maris Around Cape Horn* was shown at the Norwegian Seaman's Church to a packed crowd. The Lord Mayor of Southampton, Kathie Johnses, paid a visit and delivered a dispatch for the Lord Mayor of Sidney. At last, on February 28, with the pilot and compass adjuster put ashore, *Regina Maris* passed The Needles, on the western most tip of the Isle of Wight, and set a course for Las Palmas, in the Canary Islands.

The winds were favorable, for they traveled the 2,100 miles in just nine days. In Las Palmas, they took on supplies for the long haul (John Wilson estimated five weeks) to Cape Town. On March 11, two tugs came alongside to help the ship out of the Las Palmas harbor. The forward tug broke one of the bowsprit stays and tore out a bolt for the cathead (the timber that the anchor hangs from) back stay. The captain sent the tugs away and went back to the dock for repairs. The ship left at midnight, without the help of tugs. On leaving Las Palmas, freshwater rationing began, for this would be a longer open ocean run than on previous voyages. Each person was allotted four liters a day; the pump was locked and the cook had charge of the key.

On March 16, they passed 20 miles east of the Cape Verde Islands. The riggers were still working. As soon as they finished a new sail, it was bent to the yard or boom. Every square foot of sail meant more power and more speed, and more time made up.

The riggers hoped to fly home from Cape Town, so they had to work fast to complete their task. Each day's entry in the log book is filled with the tasks at hand and the work accomplished. For example, all the new wooden masts, spars, yards, and ratlines were bare wood and had to have their seasoning cracks filled with beeswax and then given coat after coat of linseed oil.

The captain's log mentions two occasions of complaints against the cook being lodged by two crew members. It seems that they wanted fresh-baked bread but all they were getting was canned German brown bread (Volkornbrot). The captain warned them all "to behave." Being at sea, away from shoreside amenities, it's often the little things that cause tension among crew members.

The crew was kept busy making baggywrinkle, which was necessary to protect the flax sails from chafing on the standing rigging. Old hemp lines would be separated into their individual strands and then cut into six-inch lengths. These would be looped around and down through two long strands of line, as shown in the photo. These long baggywrinkle sections would be wound around the standing rigging, providing a cushion for the sails. Hemp does not last long in the sea air, so baggywrinkle had to be replaced regularly and the crew could be kept busy for long hours at this task.

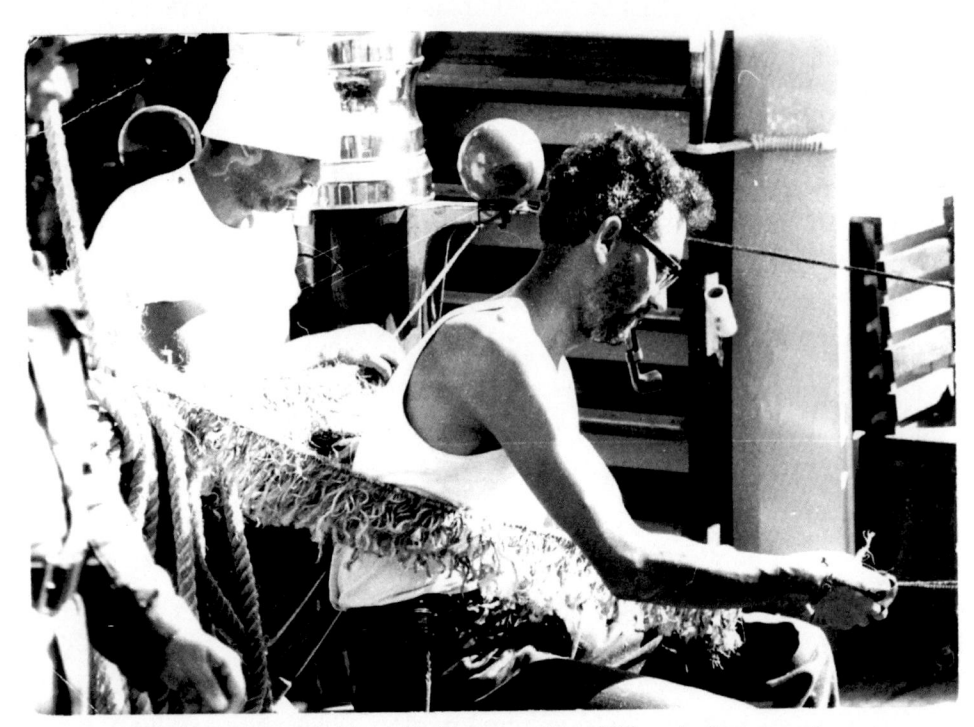

Making baggywrinkle, with first mate Peter Wilson in foreground.
Photo by Klaus P. Hanusa, Ocean-Wide Film Production Berlin-Santiago.

By April 1, all the running rigging had been completed. *Regina Maris* now had all 38 sails powering her through the sea and was making up the many lost days.

On April 6, the light-weather sails were dried and stowed and the heavy winter sails were bent onto the masts and yards. Remember, as *Regina* crossed the Equator, off the coast of Liberia, the seasons switched from spring in the north to fall in the southern hemisphere. Using the heavy, winter sails meant a loss in speed, but changing them now, before winter weather set in, was much safer.

On April 11, 1970, 30 days and 5,000 nautical miles from Las Palmas, *Regina* arrived at Cape Town, and the pilot embarked at 8 o'clock in the morning. In Cape Town for nine days, the ship was put in dry dock for a bottom inspection and cleaning and to install two iron bands around the stem for extra reinforcement of the bobstay fittings. Also while the ship was in the dry dock, an earthquake, 5.7 on the Richter scale, caused damage inland, but *Regina* was unharmed.

Tremors of another sort, however, continued to rattle the crew. The cook complained again about the same two crewmen making trouble concerning the quality of the bread. When admonished by the captain on the contested issue, the two still refused to get along with the cook and were consequently asked to leave the ship. Both signed off and were sent home. Food quality and quantity often cause problems at sea because a sailor frequently works all day with only the hope of a good meal keeping him going. Small issues can become large on a 100-by-25-foot ship at sea.

As the Norwegian riggers disembarked and headed home, preparations continued for the two-month crossing of the Indian Ocean. With winter approaching, this crossing could be very dangerous, and the crew did a great deal to prepare. The hawseholes and chain pipes were cemented down, the anchors secured with extra lashings, and the anchor windlass greased and covered. The storm sails, with gear and spares and a sea anchor, were made ready and available for instant use. The lifeboats received extra lashings and lifelines were placed where needed. An emergency rudder was designed and lashed on deck with its tackle. The ship and crew had to be prepared for any emergency, for they would be on their own in one of the most unforgiving oceans on the planet.

On April 19, 1970, *Regina Maris* left Cape Town, South Africa, on a course due east to Australia for the bicentennial celebration of Captain Cook's discovery. When it came time for the evening meal, it was discovered that the cook had deserted the ship with all of his possessions. "Supper was a make-do affair that night," said Roger Callan, the second mate. [2] He took over culinary duties for a few days until one of the other crew members could be trained.

Captain Wilson planned for a two-month voyage across the Indian Ocean. The ship and crew were still trying to make up the days lost to the dismasting and re-rigging in Norway. They were going to be late, that they knew, but the question was, how late.

Captain Cook's ship *Endeavour* may also have arrived late in a sense, for the first European to land and map the Australian shore may have been Christovao de Mendonca in 1521. (De Mendonca's claim is questioned in some academic circles.) The Portuguese had explored and colonized much of Indonesia when de Mendonca, with his fleet of three caravels, wandered southward looking for the fabled "Island of Gold." He lost one ship on the north coast of Australia and headed back to Portugal to make his discovery known.

At that time there was intense rivalry between Spain and Portugal over claimed territories, and the Treaty of Tordesillas specified the areas each country could explore and claim. To claim the "Island of Gold" for Portugal, on his newly drawn charts de Mendonca moved Australia into Portugal's territory as specified in the treaty. This movement was to be only temporary until Portugal could send more ships and fully explore the new discovery

In 1536 the Portuguese completed their chart of the known world, with Australia in its proper position. Now called the *Dauphin Map,* (since it was given by King Francis I of France to his son, the Dauphin), this map was lost for 200 years. Then for awhile it was the property of the Earl of Oxford, Edward Harley, Lord of the Admiralty. (At that time the map was called *The Harleian* map.) It was stolen and turned up in 1770 in the hands of Sir Joseph Banks, who accompanied James Cook on his voyage of discovery to Australia, but it is not known if the 1536 map was taken on board *Endeavour* for that journey. Most assuredly the accuracy of de Mendonca's drawings of 1521 helped Cook make his "discovery" of the continent in 1770.

On *Regina Maris* on April 25, John Wilson decided to hunt some seabirds. The weather was calm, and the ship was hardly moving. With his double-barreled shotgun he brought down yet another albatross. For many sailors this beautiful and largest of seabirds is a good luck omen. By killing one, the captain had sealed their fate, for the weather deteriorated and it was apparent they were being overtaken from the west by a cyclonic storm.

For the next six days the wind never dropped below 60 mph and there were many gusts to 85 mph. It took three men on the wheel to keep her on course in a high following sea. The deck was constantly flooded. The crew went on a two-watch system, eight men on each watch, three on the helm, one in the bow as a lookout, and three standing by in the crew's mess. Only two of the 38 sails were set, the course and the lower topsail, both square sails on the foremast. The center of the storm eventually passed to the south of the ship and by May 3 the crew had most of the sails up again. They made good time — for two days they had log entries of 250 nautical miles in 24 hours. The next storm hit on May 5.

No log entries exist for the next 10 days. Through interviews with the crewmen, what happened during that time has been pieced together. The wind was above force 12 on the Beaufort scale (hurricane force). The crew fought for their lives and the ship with everything they had. *Regina* ran before the storm with no sails up, for they would have been ripped to shreds in an instant. The sea anchor (an underwater parachute) was set. Also, 120 fathoms (720 feet) of six-inch nylon hawser was let over the side to slow the ship. Wave oil bags (bags of fuel oil that release oil into the sea, increasing the water's surface tension) were used to calm the seas in hopes of controlling the ship's movements. The crew lived in constant fear while on deck, for the wind and sea were beyond words. "Awesome" was the most often-used adjective in their narratives. [3]

The storm finally passed, and by May 17, Norway's National Day, the crew was able to celebrate by flying the flags of their respective countries. They held competitions on deck and enjoyed wine for lunch and dinner, with many toasts. John Wilson loved to teach the old sea chanteys and held an instructive chorus session until after dark.

The ship made good speed, with fair winds and weather during the remaining six days to their first port of call, Albany, West Australia. Their three days in port included many parties and festivities. All media arrangements had to be made for the coming grand entrance into Sydney Harbor, and the crew had to prepare room for camera crews and all their equipment. Thirty-eight bright new sails were bent onto the yards. The signal flags and the flags of every nation were flown. The cannons were loaded and large loudspeakers were put on deck so the Norwegian National Anthem could be played. The ship bid farewell to all the good people of Albany and departed on May 26 for the journey around Australia's southern shores and up the east coast.

On June 6, 1970, *Regina Maris* entered grandly into Sydney Harbor. Every sail was set. On each end of the seven yardarms stood a crew member, dressed in red and waving an Australian flag. All the ships in the harbor started saluting with cannon, horn, and whistle. The aircraft carrier USS *Coral Sea* provided a flyover. *Regina Maris* sailed past the Queen of England on her royal yacht and saluted her with the cannons. [4] At the end of *Regina's* entry parade, she tied up at Circular Quay. The ship was crawling with newspaper reporters, movie cameras were rolling, and bottles of champagne were everywhere. It was difficult for the crew to operate the ship with all the celebrating going on all around them. [3]

So ended an incredible voyage of 15,000 miles in 116 days and began a month-long celebration. The activities involving the crew and ship during this time are too numerous to list, but here are some especially noteworthy ones. *Regina's* longboat and crew reenacted Captain Cook's landing. All the special documents that had been handed over to Captain John Wilson in Plymouth so long ago to keep safe were presented to the Queen and the Admiralty. The Queen inspected the ship and had tea with captain and crew. There were parades, parties and much time for the crew to explore and relax. [5]

Officially *Regina Maris* had arrived 37 days late, since James Cook had arrived in Botany Bay on April 28, 1770. No one seemed to notice, however, or if they did, they were overcome with the effort John Aage Wilson and the crew of *Regina Maris* had made. As terrible as the dismasting, re-rigging, and severe storms had been, all were thankfully dimmed by the welcome the ship and her crew received from the people of Sydney.

While in Australia, John Wilson decided to produce a fictional film sequence based on the romance of his daughter and son-in-law, who had met the ship in Sydney. The footage was included in the documentary film of the entire voyage and is a confusing segment, with no relation to the rest of the film. But filming it provided an interesting diversion for the ship's crew and a challenge for the film company's staff.

All the festivities in Australia came to an end when *Regina Maris* set sail for Papeete, Tahiti, on June 30, 1970. John Wilson's brother and co-captain, Sigfried Wilson, and some new crew members had joined the ship in Sydney, and their presence affected the shipboard camaraderie and loyalty to the captain that had developed during the very challenging voyage to Australia. The effects of this change would be felt later. Once *Regina* was at sea, shipboard life settled down to the daily watches and occasional storms found in the tropics. One of these was very severe, with heavy pitching and rolling, requiring bare poles (no sails up), and straining the bodies of the crew members trying to maintain their balance. The film footage of this leg of the voyage is incredible. After 22 days at sea, the tall ship tied up to the pier in front of Quinn's Bar in Papeete.

Newspaper reporters and TV people swarmed all over the ship. Crowds assembled to take tours and see this apparition from the past. The crew all headed to the bar, for it is the most fabled watering hole in the South Pacific, its yellow front walls shining like a beacon to all thirsty seafarers. The tables and walls are carved with the names of ships, crew, the famous and infamous, the lost and forgotten.

Regina's crew took excursions around the island, including a visit to the museum devoted to Paul Gauguin. It was to French Polynesia that the Impressionist had fled from France in 1891, hoping to find the peace he had always longed for. *Regina's* crew was greeted by the painter's son and given a tour of the collection of Gauguin's work.

The crew also visited Venus Point, the site of Captain James Cook's astronomical observations, which had been sponsored by the Royal Astronomical Society, a fact that gave this island group its name, the Society Islands. Captain Cook's ship *Endeavour* had set out for the South Pacific in August 1768 and arrived in Tahiti on April 11, 1769, in time to observe the eclipse of the first moon of Jupiter on April 17. *Endeavor* stayed on in Tahiti, where everyone collected flora and fauna, to observe the passage of the planet Venus over the disk of the sun, which was predicted to occur on June 3, 1769. The Royal Astronomical Society was expecting to use the information gained in Tahiti to determine more accurately the distance of the Earth from the sun.

Having gathered the required astronomical and biological data, Captain Cook left Tahiti July 13, but not before having a lasting impact on the island. He had established a population of poultry and pigs and planted in the island's rich volcanic soil watermelons, oranges, limes, and other plants, all of which forever changed the lives of the inhabitants. Theirs had been a sea-based culture of fishing, gathering, and some taro and breadfruit farming. The chicken and pork, as well as the flavors provided by limes, oranges, and melons, forever changed the Tahitians' diet and palates.

Captain Cook's days in Tahiti also changed forever the life of fellow officer Captain William Bligh, of mutiny fame. In the course of gathering biological data, Captain Cook had realized the potential value of Tahiti's breadfruit trees as a food source for slaves in Britain's West Indies. His report concerning this nutritious food, delivered to the Royal Astronomical Society upon his return to England, the society was inspired to sponsor an expedition to gather breadfruit plants in Tahiti and deliver them for an experiment to the West Indies. The ship chosen for the expedition was *HMS Bounty,* captained by William Bligh. Many books and movies have told the story of the *Bounty* mutiny. The following is a brief summary.

The mutineers seized *HMS Bounty* April 28, 1789, off the island of Tofua, near the Fiji Islands. They set Captain Bligh and 17 men into a 23-foot open boat and cast them adrift. In one of the most incredible sailing feats ever, Bligh sailed 3,618 nautical miles in 41 days to the island of Timor, and safety.

Fletcher Christian, leader of the mutiny, after dumping the cargo of breadfruit trees into the sea, searched for a remote island to escape the avenging British Admiralty. First sailing to Tubuai and then to Tahiti, the eight mutineers, six Tahitian men, twelve Tahitian women, and a little girl finally settled on uninhabited Pitcairn Island, where they stripped and burned the *Bounty*. Eighteen years later, the ship *Topaz,* captained by Mayhew Folger, out of Boston, visited Pitcairn Island and discovered a "flock of women and children and one lone aging Englishman — sole survivor of Christian's band." [6]

Fighting over the women and against the Tahitian men had caused the deaths of all the other mutineers. Fletcher Christian had been shot while working his fields, according to the only survivor, John Adams. [6]

Regina Maris was scheduled to stop at Pitcairn Island, and while the ship was in Papeete, two sisters and native Pitcairn Islanders, Lettie Maistui and Jane Tuahu (maiden name Young), paid a visit. Their father was magistrate of Pitcairn and a great-grandson of a mutineer. Having heard that the ship was going to call on the lonely island, the two women brought presents and supplies to send to their family.

As *Regina* was readied for the next leg of the voyage, another cook resigned due to some crew members' complaints. The crew was warned to stop complaining, and a new cook was found. With that issue resolved, Captain John Wilson went to the French Navy Headquarters to show the Cape Horn film, and the next day, July 25, 1970, the ship cast off all lines, bound for Pitcairn Island, a voyage of some 1275 nautical miles.

That island is only two square miles in area and does not have a protected anchorage, so *Regina* anchored offshore on August 7th. The visit was long enough for all to go ashore in a longboat through the breakers of Bounty Bay and see the sights of Adamstown, the island's only town.

On August 9, *Regina Maris* set sail, heading for Montevideo, Uruguay, by way of Cape Horn, and the crew fired off many rockets as a farewell to the islanders. "It was quite sad and very moving when we left," third mate Paul Maskell told a Sydney newspaper. "A longboat with about 30 or 40 islanders rowed out to the ship and sang original songs, still waving as the wind caught our sails and drove us on." [7]

The brothers Wilson estimated the voyage would take two months, so the ship was fully stocked with fresh food from the Pitcairn islanders. There were rough seas ahead for the ship, and, for the Wilson brothers, a possible mutiny of their own to face.

CHAPTER 8

AUSTRALIA BOUND ONCE MORE

1. Captain John Aage Wilson, *Wooden Walls to Distant shores, A Maritime Concoction and the Regina Maris Saga* (Sussex, England: The Book Guild, 1992.)
2. Roger Callan, interview by the author, September 5, 1993.
3. Peter Wilson, letter to the author, dated November 30, 1993.
4. "Better Late than Never," *The Sidney Daily Mirror*, June 6, 1970.
5. "Haven for a Tall Ship," *The Sidney Sun*, June 6, 1970.
6. Captain Amasa Delano, *A Narrative of Voyages and Travels* (1817.) Captain Folger related an account of the discovery to his friend Captain Amasa Delano. The account is included in the book *Pitcairn Island*, by Charles Nordoff and James Hall (Boston: Little, Brown and Company, 1934).
7. Paul Maskell, telephone interview by the author, December 20, 2010, and email to the author, January 18, 2011.

CHAPTER 9
MUTINY?
August 9 – September 7, 1970

The unique circumstances of shipboard living require a great amount of trust and teamwork on the part of the crew. There is no escaping interaction with others. There is no place to go to be alone except aloft, which can be a dangerous place. The young and inexperienced are easily swayed by the older members of the crew. As previous chapters have shown, the Wilson brothers had a difficult time keeping cooks and crew. This is not atypical. Often a sailor's loyalty is to his world-hopping adventure, not to the ship or a captain.

This reality of life at sea was reflected in events on *Regina Maris* between August 9 and September 7, 1970, events some characterized as a mutiny. These events were precipitated by the fact that, just as with the first time John Wilson rounded the horn, he never planned to go to Chile on this trip, where he was still wanted in connection with smuggling and the deaths of two policemen and two soldiers . He recounts the smuggling escapade in his first book written after he retired from the sea, *Under Steam and Sail, Reminiscences of a Sea Captain.* [1] In his second book, *Wooden Walls to Distant Shores,* he admits to not having planned to go to Chile on the 1970 trip. [2]

The following indented material, quoted directly from Captain John Aage Wilson's log books, recounts this difficult time. This composite of logs and diaries appears in *Wooden Walls to Distant Shores* [2] and includes diary notes of his second mate, Paul Maskell, and first mate, Roger Callan. John Wilson attributed these excerpts only by the writer's last initials, according to Paul and Roger. However, in the following material, when full names are known, they are included in brackets, as are other notes by the author. (Note that Roger's and Paul's diary excerpts are not individually cited in endnotes here.)

It is for the reader to decide: Was there actually a mutiny?

August 9 [the day the ship left Pitcairn Island]
About 2000 hrs Deckhand T [Joe Tyrrell] appeared in the owner's salon asking explanation for proceeding to Cape Horn rather than Chile. At 2030 hrs Cook S [Larry Stouffer], appeared on the poop deck asking the same question and both were protesting, claiming they were promised to proceed to Chile first. Master informed them this assumption was entirely wrong. [John Wilson refers to himself as Master throughout the logs.]

August 10
1100 hrs All crew on foredeck. Informed them of the new route direct to Montevideo via Cape Horn. Crew X and Y protested and tried to stir up

mutiny and disobedience to the Master's orders. Otherwise no comments aside from a few questions by various crew-members which were answered to everyone's satisfaction but there are continued mutterings. X and Y partly supported by a few, in the formers' attempts to organize disobedience and lead the crew. The Master ordered an inventory of provisions to be taken by three crew-members. A summary signed by all crew-members is being prepared.

Seven crew-members started brewing up a mutiny because an alleged call at Valparaiso had been cancelled and the three crew members assigned to the task made a false inventory of stores and provisions, refusing ship's work etc. *(See Appendix D for a copy of the "false inventory.")* The loyal crew-members in majority and Master fully prepared for maintaining order and discipline.

[Note: John Wilson's use of the words "new route" above seems to add credence to the crew's concerns about a change in plans. As captain, John may have thought the route was at his option and communicating that opinion to the crew unnecessary. He seems to have lived by the old adage, "This is my ship and I will do as I damn well please." To some, John Wilson was a man to follow anywhere, with ultimate trust. For others, his brusque, demanding manner was more than they could endure.]

August 11

0800 hrs First mate Roger Callan reported to Master that crew flatly refused to use hand pumps for bilges ten minutes each every two hours from 0600 hrs to 1800 hrs as ordered by Master. Master went to crew's mess room and explained the simple reason and all but X and Y and a few others were satisfied. Working schedule worked out for ten men. Attempt to promote disobedience amounts to attempted mutiny under the circumstances, endangering ship and complement and was supported by X and Y. Master observed water level to be reduced in bilges during a few cooperating crew-member's ordinary pumping efforts, and also observed X and Y's slow down action, which in turn influenced everyone. Hand pumping was discontinued at 1700 hrs and never resumed.

[Later, John Wilson wrote of this incident, "For me, when underway to Cape Horn and with no possibility of contacting a rescue vessel, the hand pumps would have made the difference of 'to be or not to be' or 'dead men tell no tales.' " [2]]

August 12

1415 hrs Master was presented provision summary and requests signed by all crew-members. On request Master signed a copy with his remarks. *[See Appendix D for this document.]*

August 13

The Master, during his inventory, found an ample supply of baking flour has been omitted from the provision summary.

August 16

About 2000 hrs Cook S [Larry Stouffer], Deckhand T [Joe Tyrrell] expressed doubts about quantities of provision supplies being sufficient, and that they felt that I should change the itinerary.

August 18

At 1600 hrs a Ships Council was called. Present: Master John Wilson, Capt. Sigfried Wilson, First mate Roger Callan, and second mate Paul Maskell. Considering condition and sentiment on board because of the three mutinous crew-members and S [Larry Stouffer], and T's [Joe Tyrrell] threats of legal action and possible sabotage, it was decided to sail to Callao, Peru, to disembark the above mentioned — a deviation of some 2600 miles. At 1800 hrs, the entire crew informed.

[Note: For the next eight days, ship and crew struggled through a tropical hurricane. It was a very dangerous time, with some dissatisfied crew questioning the ability of the ship, and the captain unsure of his crew. During the "mutiny" hearings conducted by and in the press, Captain John Wilson stated that "the ship was built for such conditions." [2] Upon the ship's return to Norway on November 27, in order to quell the "unsafe ship" rumors, he had a complete survey done by Lloyd's of London at the Hoivold Shipyard. The ship was given an excellent rating at that time.] [2]

August 28

Considering prevailing wind and current decided to call at Talara rather than Callao, Peru. 1900 hrs the following six crew-members: J [Tore Jongensen], B [Thor Bie], N [Jan Eric Nestande], S [Larry Stouffer], Z [Eovald Zogbaum], O [Arne Ostgaard], appeared in salon canceling contracts and wishing to disembark at first port of call. No reason given. Master informed them of the new port of call and the reason above.

2000 hrs called Ships Council in salon. Present all loyal crew-members: Master, S. Wilson, Roger Callan, Paul Maskell, Tim Pickthall, Joachim Bliese, Klaus Hanusa [cameraman], Tim Nossiter, Henk Manussen and Morten Bruenech. Master explained situation and final itinerary: Talara, Peru — Panama Canal — Madeira — Kristiansand, Norway, possibly via London, which was unanimously accepted.

August 29

During the day received letters from J [Tore Jongensen], S [Larry Stouffer], N [Jan Eric Nestande], Z [Evivald Zogbaum], and O [Arne

Ostgaard], with reasons for cancelling contracts. B [Thor Bie], refused to cancel in writing, which was accepted by Master.

September 3

0700 hrs Jan Eric Nestande appeared in wheelhouse asking if possible to cancel his notice to leave ship.

September 4

1750 hrs Called Jan Eric Nestande to Wheelhouse and informed him that his request to cancel his notice to leave in first port of arrival was granted.

September 6

0900 hrs In checking provision inventory for preparing "Custom Stores List" for clearance in Talara revealed quantities which shows the previous inventory to be quite incomplete both with regard to quantities and assortment and with a very good safety margin for the intended voyage around the Horn.

September 7

0100 hrs Pilot embarked outside Talara, Peru. 1900 hrs Moored alongside pier. Filled all fresh water tanks, and took on provisions, five crew disembarked. [2]

So ends John Wilson's log book account, which included the diary notes of Roger Callan and Paul Maskell. The captain and his loyal first officers provide strong evidence that a mutiny was close or underway.

Additional evidence of a mutiny comes from the Kristiansand, Norway, newspaper, *Faedrelandsrennen,* which ran an interview with Thor Bie and Tore Jorgensen, two of the supposed mutineers, on their return. Tore was quoted as saying, "Captain Wilson engaged in heated arguments with the ring-leaders and used the words, mutiny and mutineers." Both men also said that "they did not want to sail around Cape Horn in mid winter." [3]

Crewmember Tim Nossiter, under the mistaken impression that Tore Jorgensen had written the article, commented in an email to the author, "This article written by Jorgensen tells the story about the whole trip and nothing left out. Only one thing wrong with the article, Jorgensen forgot to mention all the trouble he caused on-board." [4]

Tim Pickthall, another crew member, recalled this period as being very unsettling. In an email to the author, he wrote, "The crew was divided, and working together became very difficult. It was hard to know who to trust." [5]

He remembered that "the Wilson brothers locked themselves in their cabins and the crew passed notes [to them] back and forth under the door. I felt that it was a schism and if it were not for the mates' and seven loyal crew-members' skills at keeping order, the situation could have ended very badly." [5]

Tim Nossiter wrote the author a very detailed account of the events, and his opinion of the mutiny issue is included in its entirety in the following indented material.

> I don't think you could actually say it was a mutiny but more correctly a *"near mutiny,"* but you could definitely say some crew members were mutinous although they never mutinied. Maybe I'm becoming too technical but I can guarantee one thing, if Wilson had persisted with The Horn there would have been a mutiny.
>
> After Pitcairn, (and how ironic is it that it happened after leaving Pitcairn Island, the home of the infamous Mutineers), we were due to sail to Valparaiso, Chile, and wait for the summer before doubling the Horn and it was here we were going to buy all our winter woollies, gloves etc, before heading south. All our families and friends knew this to be the case and had sent letters to us there. It was a total shock to us all when only half an hour after our departure from Pitcairn a notice from Captain John Wilson was posted in the mess stating the following, *"We are now bound for Montevideo via Cape Horn,"* or words to that effect.
>
> None of us knew the reason why our voyage had been cut so short but the biggest speculation by the crew who had been on board for a year or more was the following: It was rumored that Wilson had tried smuggling a large amount of cigarettes into Chile in one of his ships some years previously and had been caught and was banned from entering Chile for some time. They now speculated that he thought he would now [1970] be allowed back in the country but reckon he received word in Tahiti that he was still banned.
>
> The main reason, as far as I was aware, for us to do the Cape Horn thing was to enable his brother Sigfried to become an Albatross in the Cape Horn Club. Master of a vessel doubling the Horn becomes this while the crew become Stormy Petrels within the Club; well this is what I was told at the time.
>
> After the above notice from Captain John Wilson was posted in the mess, it naturally made a big difference on board, and eventually divided the crew into three separate groups:
>
> Group 1. Those that were not prepared to follow the Captain's orders and would not sail around Cape Horn no matter what and consisted of nearly half the crew (approximately 7). As I stated earlier, they would have mutinied if the Captain had persisted and I don't think they would have had much opposition.
>
> Group 2. Those that didn't want to sail around the Horn at that particular time but would follow the Captain's orders and were not

prepared to be part of a mutiny. The other half of the crew, approximately 8, and myself included.

Group 3. Those that were prepared to follow Captain's orders and were quite willing to go (Captains John and Sigfried Wilson and Henk Manussen Jr.)

Most people on board respected the views of each other but Jorgensen in particular was totally one-eyed and did become a worry. He seemed to lose control and became irrational with a lot of yelling and abuse towards the Captain. I remember thinking at the time that he could have been capable of anything; I didn't like it or him. I was never very close to him before this compared to most of the other crew, like his close ally, Thor Bie, who I had a lot of fun with and was very fond of.

Henk Manussen was unfairly ostracized a fair bit due to his stand to support the Captain. Henk had been a fisherman, he was a bit on the wild side and wasn't afraid of a fight and had done things he said he couldn't talk about. I think he had seen a pretty rough side of life. He also was not afraid to follow the Captain and fully supported him. I did not agree with Henk's stand but respected his resolve. Henk was the type if you were his friend he would defend you to the end. At some time he became very upset with things that were said to him by someone (I'm pretty sure it was Klaus) and pulled a knife on him. This was down below at the door of one of the cabins and I think it was Tim who quickly put a thick book between the knife and Klaus.

I didn't witness this and I don't think Henk actually went to stab him but was just threatening. I'm pretty sure Henk was actually in tears at the time as he was very upset. Henk also picked a fight with Paul, a long time after all this, it may have been in Curacao, but we managed to talk Henk out of it. I never witnessed any other fisticuffs during my whole time aboard.

The following was my point of view then: It was the second worst time of year to attempt rounding the Horn. We were not prepared for it particularly as regards warm clothing, etc., and we were not provisioned for it. The ship was leaky, like any timber ship of that age but could potentially get a lot worse in conditions we were bound to encounter. I was personally frightened of what would lie ahead at this time of year sailing the most dangerous passage in the world. I did not want to go, for my own safety, but felt to mutiny was a very serious offence. I didn't want to end up in jail so reluctantly was prepared to follow the Captain's orders. The mutinous crew was talking of locking him up.

Thank God for the storm we hit where we were hove to with huge seas and winds up to 80 knots for three days. I'm sure this had a big bearing on his decision not to continue as it was a small taste of what we could encounter further south.

My point of view today, particularly with the sailing I have done in *Eye of the Wind*, is that it was a ridiculous, dangerous whim by the Captain; I very much doubt if I would be here today if we had gone. I was greatly looking forward to doubling this icon but at the right time of year. In hindsight even going at the right time, late December, *Regina Maris* was not rigged for the Horn. She was then ridiculously over-rigged with a high centre of gravity, little freeboard and could be easily overwhelmed in the conditions experienced down there. I am well aware to sail the Horn in any square-rigged vessel there is always an element of real danger but in that ship and particularly that time of year it was just foolhardy.

To more or less prove my point, we very nearly foundered on a lee shore in the English Channel just off the White Cliffs of Dover. We were in a storm carrying too much sail and got caught in a strong gust braced hard up. I was windward, amidships standing right next to Sigfried. She heeled over with the sea pouring aboard to leeward, more than I had ever witnessed before and she went dead. You could feel her on the point of hovering, either going to go one way or the other but she slowly righted herself. Sigfried turned to me and said, *'That was close,'* he didn't need to say it, I knew.

To me John Wilson was quite eccentric and I think if he wasn't we wouldn't have had the ship. He ran the ship in a very traditional way; no one allowed on the Poop unless you had a reason to be there, it was his domain. You would be fined a dollar if you appeared on deck without your knife (and rightly so, I guess you could say). He never ate with the crew on-board; all his meals were delivered to him by Joachim, his steward. Sigfried would occasionally try to eat breakfast with us but if John caught him he would order him back aft. We were paid a dollar a day. He was very generous when we were in port, taking us out to the best restaurants. His favorite tipple was Bols Genever in the stone bottles. He always kept the empty bottles and said he had hundreds of them at home that he was going to sell back to them one day. On occasions, but only in port, he would iron himself out and be totally legless but then again who wouldn't. He only ate one meal a day, at teatime and would be starving by then and sometimes eats two portions." [4]

The above account by Tim Nossiter is similar to that in fellow crew member Tim Pickthall's diary, a copy of which is included in Appendix D. Tim Pickthall also includes additional information concerning food quality and the force 11 storm encountered during the schism and documents the damage and fuel problems caused by the storm. He also wrote in a 2013 email to the author, "I don't really have a statement to make about the mutiny, other than to say it was not really a mutiny, or a near mutiny, but more of a 'schism.' It was a very difficult, divisive time which one could not get away from by going for a walk. The knife incident in the main hold, between Henk and Klaus, amplified the prevailing tensions. We were also all aware that in September, winds are 80% of the time above force 8, which was of concern as she leaked quite badly when caught in the very fierce storm out of Pitcairn, which is discussed in my diary. All said and done, Captain John gave a large bunch of guys a wonderful opportunity and adventure, paying us a $1.00 a day. Doing something similar now, if it was possible, would cost thousands of dollars." [5]

Was there a mutiny? Well, a captain's will was tested and members of the crew got their way. With their actions, the "mutineers," as well as other crew members lost their opportunity to join the Cape Horn Society. It may have been a rude awakening for John Wilson, bringing him back into the twentieth century. His romance with the sea could enthuse many, but when conditions became difficult, the romance conflicted with the attitudes of the crew he was able to hire.

The discontented crew members left the ship in Talara, Peru, on September 7, 1970. Tim Nossiter remembered, "When the 'mutinous' group departed in Talara, Peru, we were all still friends but I was glad to see the last of Jorgensen." [4]

The remaining crew filled the water tanks and brought fresh provisions on board, and the next morning *Regina Maris* set sail for Panama. It was a very relaxed cruise all the way to Curacao after the disgruntled men left. The nine crew managed quite easily as they were quite close to the equator, with very little wind, and they mainly motored or motor sailed. King Neptune embarked and treated the crew members from the southern hemisphere to their proper induction at the equator. Four days after leaving Talara the ship moored alongside the pier in Balboa, the Pacific entrance to the Panama Canal. The crew went ashore to play tourist and met the ship again three days later in Cristobal on the shores of the Caribbean.

September 17 found the ship at sea and bound for Willemstad, Curacao, for a haul out and painting. It was hurricane season and a winter crossing of the Atlantic required considerable preparation. The winter sails with their stronger canvas had to be bent onto the yards. During this stopover, Morten Bruenech and Jan Eric Nestande left the ship for adventures in the islands and berths on a tanker.

By October 24, the ship was ready, stocked with fresh food and seven islanders as additional crew, plus a new Dutch cook. Tim Pickthall remembered, "There was a little friction for a while between the new and old crew, but eventually all became good shipmates and very much respected each other." [5]

"The above photo and Christmas card was staged on Santa Barbara, Curacao. We were posing in such a way because we conceitedly called ourselves *The Magnificent Seven*. From left to right are Joachim Bliese, John Wilson's steward and a lovely gentleman; Henk Manussen Jr.; Klaus Peter Hanusa, ship's photographer and the first person the Wilsons employed for *Regina*; Roger Callan, first mate (his mother went to school with my mother in the UK, hence the way I became crew); me, Paul Maskell (Second Mate), and Tim Pickthall." *Photo, on timed delay, by Klaus P. Hanusa, Ocean-Wide Film Production Berlin-Santiago. Caption supplied by Tim Nossiter.*

It was a great crossing, smooth and uneventful, until November 18, when in the English Channel the ship was hit by a force 11 storm. Tim Pickthall remembered "sailing through the English Channel, freezing cold, terrible weather with the odd bit of snow and incredible traffic. Because of the traffic in the Channel and visibility we kept watch from the forward deckhouse roof. One of the young Curacan boys was crying while on lookout, he was so cold, they had never been out of the tropics." [5]

The ship and crew fought for their lives and were nearly forced on the rocks of the lee shore. The visit to London had to be canceled due to the weather. A new course was set, out into the North Sea, bound for Kristiansand, Norway.

On November 27, the pilot embarked outside Kristiansand and moored the ship at the pier. *Regina Maris* had brought her owner and crew home safe from a voyage around the world in 288 eventful days.

CHAPTER 9
MUTINY?

1. Captain John Aage Wilson, *Under Steam and Sail, Reminiscences of a Sea Captain* (Sussex, England: The Book Guild, 1990), pages 335-339.
2. Captain John Aage Wilson, *Wooden Walls to Distant Shores, A Maritime Concoction and the Regina Maris Saga* (Sussex, England: The Book Guild, 1992).
3. "The Mutiny on Regina Maris," *Faedrelandsrennen* (Kristiansand, Norway). The article presents Thor Bie's and Tore Jongensen's side of the mutiny story. The article was translated for the author by Ottar and Barbara Kirkbak of St. James, New York.
4. Tim Nossiter, email to the author, May 23, 2011.
5. Tim Pickthall, email to the author, February 13, 2013.

CHAPTER 10
THE END OF THE WILSON ERA
Late 1970

On the day after *Regina Maris* arrived in her home port of Arendal, Norway, Neil Davis, a California businessman, came on board to inspect the ship as a prospective buyer. A deal was struck, and as part of the purchase agreement, the ship was made shipshape and the Wilson brothers delivered her to the Pronk Shipyard in Den Haag, the Netherlands. On December 15, 1970, John and Sigfried disembarked and returned to Norway. They had used the ship to make their dreams come true. It was now up to other dreamers to take *Regina Maris* on to new adventures.

In his book *Under Steam and Sail,* John Wilson goes into great detail about all the recognition and honor he received upon *Regina's* return to Norway, from being knighted by the King of Yugoslavia to being honored with membership in the Explorers Club in New York. The list is lengthy. But he also had had to endure one more slight at the hands of the Norwegian government. Soon after he returned home in late November 1970, he was arrested for tax evasion. In a court hearing, he was sentenced to five weeks in custody in Arendal. After the hearing, he was released so he could deliver the ship but he eventually served his sentence. After the lawyers and accountants were appeased, he was released, as he says, "with his honor still bright." [1]

Despite the incarceration, the recognition from his homeland was most important to him, for the treatment he had received after World War II was still a raw subject. After the war, as a result of the government's mismanaging of reimbursement funds, he and his brother had received no compensation for their lost ships. This had left John very bitter and led eventually to his emigration to Panama in 1947.

As a side note, John was proud to say that three of the original *Regina Maris* crew included "Regina" in their daughters' names. Peter Wilson named his daughter Silvia Regina. Another crew member named his daughter Hedda Regina, and a third, Katherine Regina. Not to be outdone, John Wilson had a granddaughter named Astrid Regina.

In 1971 the brothers' shipping company closed its Santiago, Chile, office. Sigfried, who had been living there and managing the office, moved and established himself in Skagen, Denmark. The company's two remaining cargo ships were sold in 1972. John continued as president of the holding company, Oceanwide Steamship Company Inc., with Sigfried as vice president. (Sigfried was president and John was vice president of their other company, Ocean Transport Lines, Inc.) They held the loan in common for *Regina Maris* when it was sold to the new owners.

In 1972 John was designated *charge' d'affaires* in Norway for his adopted country, the Republic of Panama. He served until retirement in 1983, at the age of 67.

Concerning retirement, he stated, "I was now bored, and felt like a racing engine shaking itself to pieces because it is no longer connected up with the work for which it was built. Audacity and romance passed forever like a comet in its eccentric orbit." [1]

To channel his boundless energy, John, with the help of Peter Wilson (no relation), his former first mate, wrote two books about his life and life at sea. Peter had moved to Arendal, and writing the books was a rewarding pastime for both men. Peter said, "John had some interesting usages of the English language. So he needed my help in the translations." [2]

John also entered the academic field of historical archeology. He had long been curious about the Phoenician seafarers and the location of ancient Thule. The more he studied the subject, the more he became convinced that the Phoenicians had traveled to the Telemark, a district in southeast Norway. In his readings, he came across references to an ancient sea cave named after St. Michael. He visited it, but the tide filled the entrance throughout the tide cycle, allowing no access. John became convinced that the cave had been used by the Phoenicians, and he was sure there was a hidden entrance from the top of the bluff.

Using dynamite, illegally procured, he blew away the rocks and exposed a hidden entrance. Enough dynamite was used to move a 300-kilo rock 500 meters, and another blast moved a 30-ton boulder six meters. The authorities stepped in when the farmer whose land the cave was on complained. But John had entered the cave and claimed to have found many artifacts, including coins, jewelry, and lamps.

The archeologist John referred to as "The Antiquarian of the Realm in Oslo" demanded John cease and desist, hit him with a 15,800-pound sterling claim for damages and a 500-pound fine, and vowed to confiscate any antiquities found. The news media and courts took over and John was eventually forced to hand over some artifacts. The government's numismatics expert inspected the find and concluded that the coins were from Phoenicia, Carthage, Egypt, and Rome, dating from 300 BC to 117 AD. The jewelry was reported to date from several hundred years BC. The lamps, the antiquarian said, were from Iceland, dating from the 16th century.

Through the courts, John's penalty was reduced and he paid a total of 500 pounds. But John Wilson had done much more than get his penalties reduced. It seems he had set a trap for the antiquarian by giving him some old coins and oil lamps he had bought while in Tunis in 1948. These items had been collected at the ruins of the Tunis amphitheatre. He also gave the Norwegian authorities broken jewelry bought from a shop in the Frankfurt airport, and an unpolished piece of amber jewelry bought in Copenhagen, which had been found on a local beach.

From his school days onward, John had claimed he "was always a Dennis the Menace, sorely troubling the female teachers as well as the male ones, to say nothing of my parents, brother and sister, and this continued with some variation in degree until I retired in Arendal at the sage age of sixty-seven." [1]

Scamp and "menace" that he was, however, John Wilson divulged his archeological truth six years later in his book *Under Steam and Sail, Reminiscences of a Sea Captain*, published in 1990. [1]

In 1986, when *Regina Maris* was again in the news, (as detailed in Chapter 21), John made inquiries into repurchasing the ship, planning to restore her to glory. Chris Roche, of the International Association of Cape Horners, remembers talking to John about restoring *Regina,* after John had moved to live in London with his youngest daughter, Marianne, in a flat just off Leicester Square. The topic was also discussed at one of the Cape Horner reunions, according to Peter Wilson. Wise friends counseled John to rethink this idea, as he was 71 at the time, and eventually he came to feel himself too old to start that project.

Ever interested in ships and the sea, however, John became involved in another maritime project when he moved in with Marianne, a law student. Roald Amundsen's Norwegian polar vessel was called *Gjoa.* Amundsen had sailed her through the Northwest Passage in 1903. John, always a dreamer, planned, at age 75, to build a replica of that ship for use as a personal yacht. Marianne sent the author the nearly completed plans for this project, which he was working on at the time of his death. *Gjoa* looks to be a sturdy, gaff-rigged cutter with two square sail yards on the single mast.

John, born in 1915, and Sigfried, born in 1919, were throughout their lives very close, sharing each other's adventures and dreams. When Sigfried passed away in 1983 at only 64 years of age, it was a blow to John. Sigfried is buried in the family burial place, a grassy clearing at Faervik, the brothers' home town, on Tromoy Island, across the bay from Arendal, Norway. After his brother's death, John placed a clipper ship anchor on the grave, with bronze plaques on each of its flukes, one for Sigfried, one for himself. On the crown of the anchor is another bronze plaque inscribed, in English, "Faervik for Orders," probably meaning "Home for Orders." [1]

In early spring 1992, John Aage Wilson died, at the age of 77, and he joined his brother under the anchor in the family plot. The story and lyrics presented in the indented material below are a eulogy to John Wilson written by his former first mate and writing partner on the voyages of *Regina Maris*, Peter Wilson. This material was included in a 1993 letter to the author. [2]

> It never failed. It was the oldest trick in the world: find a man's soft spot and you've got him. The man in this case was our own irascible, uncompromising and apparently unfeeling Captain John. A man who held the utmost admiration for the old-time sailors, and for whom history had produced only one figure worthy of his unlimited admiration, Captain William Bligh of *H.M.S. Bounty.*
>
> But he did have a soft spot. Though Captain John was not a musical man by any means (he boasted to have slept through most of the great

operas either in La Scala, Covent Garden, or the Metropolitan in N.Y.) he could be deeply touched by sea shanties. The tenderest touch of them all to him was the moving shanty, *"Rolling Home."*

The shanties are beautiful and evocative, and though many of them are sentimentally embroidered concerning their text, the melodies have stood the test of time and made a small though rich contribution to the world of music, especially for the seafaring nations.

Picture now if you can, a glassy sea in the vicinity of the equator with the ship rolling gently; very little forward motion — a knot or two perhaps, and generally in the wrong direction. The wind is never going to blow again, the refuse from the galley has been accumulating around the stern for days, the pitch bubbles between the deck planks until the sun at last plummets below the horizon leaving a hot afterglow.

What price a cool beer?

The Captain is snoozing in his salon with the door wide open. I steal aft, guitar in hand, and sit on the steering case after gathering the boys who now sit in a semi-circle on the taffrail.

We are crawling over a carpet of stars....

A soft chord, and we begin, only a humming at first. After a couple of numbers we smell cigarette smoke from within. He has woken; he is listening. Now is our chance:

"ROLLING HOME, ROLLING HOME,
"ROLLING HOME ACROSS THE SEA,
"ROLLING HOME TO DEAR OLD ENGLAND
"ROLLING HOME DEAR LAND TO THEE."

He emerges quietly on the poop deck. Braces his shoulders, a deep breath, feigning nonchalance. Was it a tear in his eye? He focuses his attention on the dim horizon:

"I think we'll have a case of beer brought up on deck, Mr. Wilson."

"Aye aye, sir."

As I said, it never failed. [2]

The following additional verses to the captain's favorite chantey were written by Peter Wilson in memory of John Aage Wilson:

Are you listening, Captain John,
Is your hearing aid switched on?
Tonight in Hilo, with your glass of Cote du Rhone
A shanty echoes back to me
'Cross the dark and lonely sea

Can you hear? The boys are singing *Rolling Home*.
The girls of Callao
Are much older now, you know,
But so are we, and how the time has flown!
And so well you played the part
But the dream was in your heart
And the boys were always singing *Rolling Home*.
The dreams of youth today
Are all dead, and sad to say
Data, Discotheque and cars are all that's known.
But for us who heard the call
The horizon was too small
When the boys were gently singing *Rolling Home*.
My eye, it fills alas!
While I'm emptying my glass
To the girl who "dressed her hair with a codfish bone,"
Tommy's Gone, Lowlands and more
Rio, Farewell, Shenandoah
Haul Away Joe and the good old Rolling Home.
Oh, I'd do the same today
If a ship should sail that way,
But men with dreams no longer wish to roam.
You put something in our lives
That you cannot get from wives
And the boys, they are still singing *Rolling Home*.
Rolling home to dear old England
Norway, Hamburg and the rest,
Or to Hilo, where we know you're not alone.
There beyond the tropic sky
We'll all be with you bye and bye
And we'll sing again together *Rolling Home*. [2]

CHAPTER 10
END OF THE GLORY DAYS

1. Captain John Aage Wilson, *Under Steam and Sail, Reminiscences of a Sea Captain* (Sussex, England: The Book Guild, 1990).
2. Peter Wilson, letter to the author, received December 17, 1993.

CHAPTER 11
SCHEVENINGEN HARBOR, NETHERLANDS, TO LONG BEACH, CALIFORNIA
1970 – 1971

Neil Davis had bought *Regina Maris* on December 15, 1970, for $250,000, through the yacht brokerage firm of Southern Yacht and Charter Company of Bexhill-on-Sea, England. Bexhill's broker, John Stapley, handled the sale for the Wilson brothers, who carried the financing, with $100,000 down and the rest in quarterly payments.

Now the 63-year-old *Queen of the Sea* was going through yet another transformation: She was now to become a cruising tall ship, fulfilling the dreams of paying voyagers seeking to make memories.

For tax benefits, the ship kept her registry in Valletta, Malta, and the Wilson brothers' Oceanwide Sailing Company Ltd. maintained title to the ship. [1] *Regina*'s sale came at a great financial loss to the Wilsons. Their original investment to convert the burned-out hulk into a barkentine had been $300,000. The re-masting and new sails in 1970 had cost $250,000. Crew wages, provisions, regular maintenance, and insurance had cost $250,000 a year for the five years they sailed her. [2]

Neil Davis was a businessman from Los Angeles, California, and his partner in this venture was his sister, Joyce Kerin. Together they formed Oceanwide Adventure Cruises of Palos Verdes Estates, California. Needing more funds to finance this new company, Neil brought in Greg Cook, a social studies teacher in Los Angeles, and Greg's friend David Wiseman. The four were equal partners in the company's only asset, *Regina Maris*. Their plan was to cruise to the South Pacific during the summer months and the coast of Mexico during the winter.

To fill her cabins with passengers, the four also formed Trade Wind Cruises (TWC), a travel agency with offices in Palos Verdes, California. Greg Cook acted as an agent, using the pseudonyms Eric Nord or Eric North when representing the agency. When asked about this, Greg said, "The names sounded more nautical and I hoped would be appealing to adventurous travelers." [1]

In the advertising campaign he developed to promote the ship, brochures were sent to other travel agencies and to college campuses on the West Coast. He hired Tom Ince, a photographer, to produce "great travel shots" to be used in the advertising.

Neil hired Captain Paul H. Nelson to be *Regina's* master. Captain Nelson had spent nearly 12 years in the British Merchant Navy and had previously sailed as mate on the four masted barque *Patria*, renamed *Sea Cloud*, which at the time was one of the largest sailing vessels in the world. Roger Callan and Paul Maskell stayed on through the change in ownership and became first and second mate, respectively. Tim Pickthall, a South African, and Tim Nossiter also stayed on from the Wilsons' crew.

Tom Clawson (Tommy) was hired by Neil to be his representative and find additional crew members. Henk Ahrens, one of those he hired, wrote in a 2011 email to the author, "We — Ari Pronk, Fred Leeflang, Willi Prestin and I — first heard about the *Regina Maris* at our 'hang-out,' The King's Cellar, an old bar under the royal Palace 'Noord Einde' in the Hague, Holland. It was there we met Tom Clawson. When we went to visit the ship in Scheveningen Harbor, Tommy was the only one on board. The ship had been delivered there by a skeleton crew that sailed with the Wilson brothers, but they had left for England to visit family and planned to return in mid-January. At that time the newly hired captain was also to arrive." [3]

In a 2011 email to the author Fred Leeflang recalled, "I got on board just before Christmas as a crewmember because I knew how to sail with 2- and 3-masted ships. On a night between Christmas and New Year's Eve, the ship was rather low in the water and I helped Tommy down in the engine room to start the Lister pump. The pump was nearly underwater but it saved the ship from sinking. We had a Dutch cook on board named Jan and his assistant was his younger brother George. Sometime in January, late at night, Jan was working in the galley and he ran out of water. He had to switch water tanks. But he and his brother were drunk and they took an axe and started to chop on the deck to find the next water tank. Luckily, we could stop them very quickly and saved the deck and moved them to their bunk for a good night's sleep. In January a group of carpenters came on board and started to make some new cabins and bunks in the cargo space and also in the paint locker. These changes were finished in Lisbon." [4]

So a crew of adventurous young men and boys from Holland, Germany, France, England, South Africa, and the U.S. made the ship ready for her voyage to Lisbon where some alterations were to be made to the ship and the first passengers were to be picked up for the voyage to California. The newly assembled crew, Henk remembered, "was a motley crew alright; Paul Maskell had been a river Thames policeman, Fred an accountant, Ari worked as a mathematical wizard, I believe the term is "actuary," and I had been a high school teacher, ceramic artist, and aspiring photographer. I am not sure what Willy used to do, he did not seem to know himself most of the time." [4]

Regina Maris as Fred Leeflang first saw her in Scheveningen Harbor, Holland.
Photo by Fred Leeflang.

They finally got underway February 3, 1971, before ice and storms could trap *Regina Maris* for the rest of the winter. Going out of the locks and through the canals to get to sea caused some damage to the course yardarm. *Regina* sailed on to Newhaven, near Brighton, England, where a shipyard repaired the damage and the ship was docked next to the Customs House on the landing of the ferry to Dieppe, France.

A series of storms with 30- to 40-knot winds hammered Newhaven for three days. The ship could not be turned around to leave the dock, even with the help of a tug. However being tied to the Customs House dock turned out to be the crew's good fortune, for many cases of Mateus found their way into their hands. There was a party every night.

When the weather broke at last, the ship set sail for Portugal on February 15th. Ward Murphy, one of the new able bodied (AB) seamen hired, remembered this voyage very well in a 1994 interview with the author. "We had only the fore and aft sails set, no squares. The lee rail was buried constantly in the force 8 tossed seas. It was very bad weather. It took a week to get around Brest." [5]

Ward remembers seeing rocks on the coast of France on his watch every night as the ship tacked, trying to make headway. The lighthouse at St. Mathieu, blinking its constant warning, was the night watch's companion.

Seasickness took its toll. Ward said, "The Dutch kids, Fred Leeflang, Adriaan Pronk, and Henk Ahrens, were the only ones that were not sick having been to sea many times before on the local fishing trawlers." [5]

Henk recalled "we ate T-bone steaks for breakfast, lunch and dinner every day, for days at a time, being that it was one of the few items that was on board in abundance and that it was one of the few things that our 'cook' knew how to cook without burning it up. You have to remember that such steaks were a virtual unknown to us Dutchmen and a luxury we rarely encountered." [3]

Ward's friend the photographer Tom Ince was so sick that "the army fatigues he wore matched the color of his face." Tom drank orange juice during his sickness because, "It tasted good going down and just as good coming back up." [5] This ordeal of a passage took eight days.

They finally reached Lisbon on February 23, and the ship went into dry dock for two full weeks of hull repairs at the shipyard of Parry & Sons. *Regina* had been leaking badly on the way from England to Lisbon because of a serious leak below the waterline. To address this problem, the yard brought in an old man in his 80s who climbed about on the scaffolding around the hull for days, tapping on it with a little brass hammer. He found the exact spot; one copper sheet was removed and a weak and rotted spot about the size of a football was found and repaired. [3] The ship was also re-caulked and new electrodes were fixed to her keel. Henk Ahrens, who was a professional artist, painted the queen figurehead and her stern nameboard in bright new colors. [4]

While the ship was in dry dock, extensive modifications were also made below decks to accommodate more passengers. The six spacious single-berth cabins were each given an additional berth. The dining area was turned into a four-berth cabin and the hold was converted into two four-berth cabins. Each cabin had a sink and a vertical locker for each occupant. Daylight came in through round prism lights mounted in the deck above. A third head, with a shower, was added. The owners' cabins were physically unchanged, only their designation was altered. The starboard cabin was to be shared by the hired captain and the cruise director. The portside cabin, which had a bathtub and private access to the main salon and bar, was to be occupied by passengers who wanted those amenities and had the additional money to pay for them.

With these modifications, the ship could carry 25 passengers, who paid $2,000 each for the Lisbon-to-Los Angeles sail, along with 20 officers and crew. On later voyages that year, the number of paid crew was reduced by five, and the next year the crew was reduced by 10, and their berths were filled with eager paying passengers. Many passengers were willing to work, and their hands made it easier for the remaining crew members. In fact, on later voyages, realizing many passengers wanted to help with the work of sailing, Craig Cook instituted crew-trainee tickets for a reduced fee.

Changes were also made topside, including the addition of four 12- person, self-contained life rafts mounted on the exterior forward and aft cabin bulkheads. An additional 16-foot jolly boat was lashed next to the existing 18-foot boat on a new rack built over the top of the old hold entrance. The space under the rack was used for the ship's tools and a paint locker. All this work, topside and below decks, was done by skilled craftsmen using only hand tools.

On the forward deck, wine and rum casks were placed and filled in Lisbon with Portuguese wine and "raw" rum. It got stronger by the day, Henk Ahrens recalled. [3] Fred remembered, "On the bow there were two barrels installed, one for wine and one for rum. I filled them both out of five-liter bottles. Some people who helped me opening the bottles did taste some of the wine and got drunk. Some other people who helped me fill the rum barrel got drunk just from the fumes." [4]

Captain Paul Nelson then instituted the rum ration, which became a daily ritual in port or at sea. At four o'clock, he would gather the ship's crew and passengers in the ship's bow and hand out the ration from the locked casks, which were otherwise opened only if spirits were required for cooking.

While the ship was in Lisbon, a crew from Philadelphia arrived to bring the wooden barkentine *Gazela Primeiro* to the United States. In a 2011 email to the author, Henk Ahrens recalled, "We donated some of the *Regina's* extra rigging, a couple of yard arms, blocks, and tackle and several of our spare sails to her for her voyage to America." [3] *Regina* was re-provisioned and weeks went by while they waited for all 25 passengers to board. (This was a new venture, and the departure date for this first voyage was flexible.) Neil Davis rejoined the ship in Lisbon for the passage to Panama, where he would disembark.

While in Lisbon, *Regina* also acquired two new crew members. Neil's agent, Tom, had talked two good-looking TWA airline stewardesses he met on his flight to Lisbon into coming to see *Regina Maris*. After seeing it, the two decided to join the crew. Tim Nossiter recalled the following about this addition to the crew. "I shared the cabin with my newfound love, Sue Frazar from Lake San Marcos. Sue and another girl were both hostesses with TWA, flew to Europe for a backpacking holiday, and happened to sit next to Tom on the flight. They were both very attractive ladies and he of the silver tongue talked them into joining the ship as crew when we were in Lisbon. They never went back to TWA. Sue left the ship with me in Las Palmas but sadly, it didn't last long and she flew back home from Spain to her boyfriend in the States. Sue was a lovely and beautiful person." [9]

With all passengers, crew, and supplies on board, *Regina Maris* finally set sail March 22, 1971, for Cadiz. Captain Nelson, in an article in *News-Pilot,* said his "greatest thrill on the *Regina Maris* was sailing on a broad reach for 350 miles between Cadiz and Casablanca, Morocco." [7] It was a fast and thrilling trip for this 28-year-old captaining his first sailing vessel.

While the ship was in Casablanca, a passenger and several crew members traveled 130 miles to Marrakesh to buy a brick of hashish. Doug Eldon, a crew member who joined the ship in Lisbon, recalled, "The lore was that the man who sold it to them then ratted on them to Interpol, getting paid handsomely for the sale and handsomely again for being an informant. Interpol came on board in Casablanca but couldn't find the hashish despite a pretty thorough search." [6]

Charlie Clements, who had joined the crew in Barbados, recalled in a 2010 email to the author, "In every port we visited, the ship was searched. The young Brit, [Ian Dawson], who assisted Cookie, [John Bird] told me they stored it in the cap on the top of the mainmast. In port, if the ship was moving an inch caused by the wake of a passing motorboat, the top of the mainmast would move about six or eight feet. Customs inspectors seldom went higher than the second crow's nest, because of the heights and motion." [8]

Fred Leeflang remembered, "I was in the cabin of a guy called Don. He showed me a stash of marihuana spread out on a newspaper. He told me proudly, 'That's what a kilo looks like.' Another guy, from Beverly Hills, I forgot his name but he was on board with a girlfriend, told me the reason why he took this trip. He said, 'First we visit Morocco, and get Camel Shit, then we will be in Jamaica, and get some Jamaica Red, and when we reach the west coast of the Americas, we'll find Panama Red, Acapulco Gold, and don't forget what we will find in El Salvador.' " [4]

Tim Nossiter recalled, "I wasn't aware they bought a brick of hash in Marrakesh but they didn't have to go that far as I was offered a brick just walking up the street from the ship. You had to be careful though as we were warned undercover police were selling it to catch people. The bastards never told me where the stash was. I could have had a very happy cruise. I did know there were drugs aboard though and actually I may have had the odd smoke but can't remember." [9]

The next port of call was Las Palmas in the Canary Islands, 540 sea miles to the west. In Las Palmas, one of the two lockable 40-gallon oak casks was filled with Madeira wine. The second was reserved for rum. Doug Eldon recalled having a clear plastic tube connected to the cask of rum and leading through the bulkhead into his bunk. [6]

Tim Nossiter stated, "Doug may have had a tube from the rum barrel but it was actually me who started it as I ended up in that only cabin on deck, with the rum barrel straight outside the porthole. It was very funny as we would all line up for our tot of rum from the captain (and a terrific captain Paul was). He would undo the padlock on the tap and dispense it out, whereas all you had to do to get a drink was give the wooden plug on the top a bit of a hit to remove it and you could enjoy as much as you wanted. At nighttime the old tube would be poked out the porthole and disappear into the barrel." [9]

Tim Pickthall, from South Africa, and Tim Nossiter, from Australia, left the ship in Las Palmas for home. They had been members of the crew during the Australian bicentennial voyage under the Wilson brothers in 1969-'70. [4]

After three days of sightseeing and a final provisioning, the ship was off again across the Atlantic to the West Indies. There were many warm relaxing days and rum-blurred tropical nights. A 15-day, uneventful voyage brought them to Bridgetown, Barbados, as their first landfall.

Two days later, they set sail for Port Antonio, Jamaica, by way of Martinique, Antigua, the Virgin Islands, and San Juan, Puerto Rico. Fred Leeflang has a memory that, on approaching Antigua, "skipper Paul Nelson decided to show off to all the yachtsmen who were there and we sailed almost fully rigged into that little bay. The yacht harbor is a little bay with a high pirate feeling. At the last moment, we turned into the wind and dropped the sails and the anchor. Indeed we gave a nice show and all the people on the shore were impressed." [4]

Fred went on to state, "The original route plan was to leave Puerto Rico and sail to Haiti, but when we arrived in the bay near Port au Prince, we saw artillery shelling the hills behind the city. So we sailed on to Jamaica." [4]

Before landing in Port Antonio, the pilot brought out a doctor, who administered penicillin, as some members of the crew had contracted gonorrhea, according to Doug Eldon. [6] In Port Antonio the rum cask was refilled with dark Jamaican rum.

The next stop was Cristobal, Panama, and after going through the canal, the ship sailed up the coast to Punta Arenas, Costa Rica, and on to El Salvador. In Acajutla, El Salvador, the main port, Charlie Clements recalled "We stopped to get water, I believe. The port authority motored out to where we had anchored awaiting his clearance before anyone could go on shore. A sailor or two, I don't think they were passengers, was swinging from the deck off a line from one of the yard arms into the water … the problem was the lack of a bathing suit. The Port Captain arrived with several escorts armed with automatic rifles … they looked pretty menacing. He told the Captain there was no way they were going to allow a ship full of 'heepies' on shore. Meeting ended. We weighed anchor and left. I think El Salvador was in one of those periods where they cut people's hair at the border, if they looked too much like a hippie. Little would I know that I would return to that police state in the midst of its civil war about 10 years later … with a beard no less! I recall, too, that we tried to make port in Cuba, but they would not grant us permission … maybe El Salvador and Cuba were reading the Interpol reports about our ship being full of dope?" [8]

The ship continued sailing on up the coast of Central America, stopping in out-of-the-way places. They made port at Bahia La Tortuga, Mexico, and on up the coast of Mexico, stopping at, Zihuatenejo, Acapulco, Puerto Vallarta, Mazatlan and Cabo San Lucas. In Puerto Vallarta, Captain Nelson misjudged the channel due to some missing buoys and ran the ship aground on a muddy sand bar in front of some of the big beach hotels. The ship and crew could not extricate themselves so a tug was called and easily pulled them off with no damage except to their dignity. [3 and 6] Henk Ahrens remembered, "Some of the passengers, Big Jim Ryan, Bobby Freeman, Tony Avanzino, and Steve Bovan, came back from a trip ashore bragging about working as extras in a movie and seeing Elizabeth Taylor and Richard Burton. Steve Bovan was a pretty well-known 'Funny Car' driver in California. He died a few years later in a crash." [3]

Charlie remembered, "that 'Cookie' [John Bird] and Ian had cooked the rest of the hashish, maybe a half pound, into a huge pan of brownies. Cookie and Ian went around the ship offering them to anyone who would eat one, but not telling everyone what was in them. Most of the crew knew. Within half an hour most began to feel funny and Cookie 'fessed up. I was on the wheel at that time and my recollection is that it came on like gangbusters. I stayed high for 24 to 36 hours. I had never had a marijuana or hashish high like that, nor have I since. Those on board will remember that it was a motley crew, with long hair and beards, multiple piercings, the least innocuous of which were ear rings, and Henk with a sheepskin vest even in the hottest weather and a shitting, squawking parrot [actually a great green macaw] clinging to his shoulder. So every port we pulled into they could tell the crew were all dopers even if Interpol hadn't relayed the report of the double dealing hashish-Walla." [10]

Henk Ahrens's memory of the Ensenada, Mexico, port of call adds to the marijuana smuggling episode. He reported, "We ended the voyage in Ensenada where the passengers were leaving reluctantly. They had assumed that they were going to sail to L.A., but there were problems with shipping regulations, as it was explained to us. Neil Davis arrived after we had been in Ensenada for a week to prepare for our grand entrance into Los Angeles Harbor. During that week we had a visit from the Federales that were looking for dope. I remember jumping on the dock in the morning to go get some 'shore food' and seeing four Federales coming down the dock with machine guns and a dog. When I tried to get back on board they would not let me. Needless to say they did not find any drugs. Some of our 'hip' passengers had purchased a few 'keys' in North Africa that they had hidden in the septic tanks that were accessible in the passageway below decks by a hatch in the floor. They were hoping to retrieve it when they met up with the ship again when it visited Los Angeles. The Federales were not happy and harassed us for a few days. They blamed my parrot Yopi for the debacle, because he bit the drug-sniffing dog in the nose and supposedly ruined him for work." [3]

Fred's following comment completes the smuggling episode: "When we docked in Wilmington, California, at the yacht harbor, we met some of our former passengers. One of them came for his stash of marihuana that was rolled in the topsail. He stashed it there the night before we entered a port and when we left a port he took it out. In Ensenada, he couldn't take it with him over the border so he left it rolled in the topsail until Wilmington." [4]

On June 11 1971, *Regina Maris*, "under full sail and bearing down like an anachronism from the last century, sailed past buzzing helicopters and power boats through Angel's Gate into Los Angeles Harbor," reported John Hart in *News-Pilot*. [11]

One headline on her arrival in the Long Beach area was "Her Sails Inhale the Wind." [9] *Regina* docked at Newmarks Yacht Center, berth 204, in Wilmington, and for the next seven days the ship was made ready for a new group of passengers.

A recent email from Captain Paul Nelson corrected some of the dates and port of calls in this chapter based on his log book entries. (12) A letter from Paul to his family concerning the relationship he had with the owners appears in Appendix E.

CHAPTER 11
SCHEVENINGEN HARBOR, NETHERLANDS, TO LONG BEACH, CALIFORNIA, 1970 - 1971

1. Greg Cook, interview with the author September 3, 1993, at the *Regina Maris* reunion, Greenport, New York.
2. Captain John Aage Wilson, *Under Steam and Sail, Reminiscences of a Sea Captain* (Sussex, England: The Book Guild, 1990).
3. Henk Ahrens, emails to the author, February 3 and 6, 2011.
4. Fred Leeflang, emails to the author, February 11 and March 22, 2011.
5. Ward Murphy, interview by the author, Shelter Island, New York, July 20, 1994.
6. Doug Eldon, telephone interview by the author, January 16, 2011.
7. Jim Norris, "Square Rigger Becomes Part of Sailors' Life," *San Pedro News-Pilot* (California), June 19, 1971.
8. Charlie Clements, email to the author, December 31, 2010.
9. Tim Nossiter, email to the author, May 23, 2011. (At the time of the email, Tim was skipper of the *R.V.Penghana*, Marine Discovery Centre, Jetty Road, Woodbridge, Tasmania.)
10. Charlie Clements, email to the author, January 2, 2011.
11. John Hart, "Sailing Ghost Arrives," *San Pedro News-Pilot*, June 12, 1971.
12. Paul Nelson, email to the author, May 10, 2017.

CHAPTER 12

LONG BEACH, CALIFORNIA TO PAPEETE, TAHITI
June – August 1971

Author's note: Because I was so closely involved in the events detailed here, I will use the first person in this chapter.

The next two months of *Regina Maris's* life were inextricably tied to my own. I am begging the reader's indulgence for what will follow. That ship changed my life. As the ship's historian, this is the period in *Regina's* history where my objectivity can become lost. I can only speak for myself through my photos, a personal diary I kept while on board, and memories that have been altered by time, age, and, hopefully, wisdom.

My story starts with a woman and a broken heart. The woman in question and I had been dating for two years. I was 23 and ready to get married. I asked the all-important question, so confidant in her answer that I had already booked passage on a cruise ship to Greece for our honeymoon. (I may have mentioned the honeymoon trip to her as an incentive for a positive response.)

Her rejection of my proposal produced a desire for escape, as well as a chance to follow the dream of sailing on a tall ship. That dream had started when I was a small boy watching and wondering about the four-masted schooner *Forester* stuck in the mud flats in Martinez, California. I visited that old ship many times, gathering information about her as I grew older.

I had been introduced to sailing by my uncle, who had a Melody class-one design cat boat that we sailed around the San Francisco Bay area. I had also spent a week the previous year sailing on the 101-foot, two-masted gaff-rigged schooner *Adventurous* around Puget Sound. She had been launched in 1913, and my experience on that old ship now moved me to seek out *Regina*, for hanging on a wall outside my office in Linfield College's admissions department was a poster picturing a beautiful wooden tall ship and advertising an itinerary of island hopping from California to Papeete, Tahiti. The summer break was rapidly approaching and in less time than friends and family could imagine, I was off to Wilmington, California, to meet a new woman, named *Regina*.

Upon my arrival in Wilmington on June 14, 1971, two days before sailing, I was put to work filling water tanks, stowing supplies for the cook, and cleaning staterooms. (Although I was a paying passenger, I was eager to take part in running the ship.) From Henk Ahrens, still with the ship after the sail from The Netherlands and Lisbon, I started learning the function of the many lines that controlled the sails. Henk still had his prize possession, Yopi, the great green macaw. Yopi had the run of the ship and spoke Dutch, mostly swear words I was told, and the only English he knew were the two words, "Hello, Dolly."

I met all the other passengers and crew, including Joyce Kerin, part-owner of the ship with her brother, Neil Davis; Joyce's daughter Stefanie; and Neil's sixteen-year-old son, George Davis. I also met Paul Nelson, the captain, and was put to work stowing food in lockers with John Bird, the cook, who was described this way in the local San Pedro paper: "He has hair like a whirling dervish and eyes that burn with the knowledge of a glittering past." [1] They were an interesting bunch. I always felt a psychologist would have had a field day on *Regina*, for she attracted the most amazingly strange collection of humanity, myself included.

After we were all on board and our belongings stowed, we had to sign ships' articles, which included a proviso that we would not engage in excessive drinking. This caused a great deal of discussion. There had been so much "drunken debauchery" on the previous trip that the owners felt restraint was needed. Nevertheless, I remember that as we cleared port the bar was open, and with 55 gallons of dark Jamaica rum and the same amount of Madeira wine on board, quantity would not be a problem.

As we were preparing to leave, I recall Deek Miles, the cruise director, telling us that because of the Jones Act, the ship, registered in Malta, was not allowed to board passengers in U.S. waters. Therefore, he told us, we were going to "slip out" of port to avoid the Coast Guard. In fact, however, we snuck out saluted by fireboats, helicopters, and yachts, and, seemingly, every resident of Long Beach and Wilmington waving goodbye. We even stopped traffic on the Vincent Thomas Bridge (Interstate 710).

We were to be 22 days at sea until we reached the island of Nuka Hiva in the Marquesas. Life was grand — what more could you want? A great ship, interesting people, calm tropical seas, and an escape from all things on land. Notice that food was not on the above list. Former owner John Wilson had left a great deal of canned reindeer meat on board. We had reindeer meat as stew, sandwiches, meatloaf, and any other way the cook could dream up. It caused a great deal of Donner and Blitzen guilt. Many of the discussions we had centered on food. A large Mahi Mahi was caught and we could all taste it as it was hauled aboard. The Shellbacks (sailors who had previously crossed the equator) on board warned that if we kept it, King Neptune would be offended and we lowly pollywogs (sailors who have not crossed the equator) would pay dearly for our transgression. Needless to say we tossed the fish back.

We made excellent time as we headed to Tahiti. When we could, we put up the studding sails. Setting them took some time, but with a steady breeze they could be up for days. With the trade winds' steady push, these sails would gather more wind and increase the speed of the vessel. With two acres of canvas set, *Regina* would move right along.

The midday meal was served on deck. Sandwiches with juice or Kool-Aid were the mainstay. *Photo by author.*

When we reached the Equator on July 1, 1971, King Neptune came on board and we pollywogs were inducted into the "mysteries of the deep." Each lowly pollywog was inspected by the Royal Doctor, second mate Paul Maskell, for defects, and, depending on your crimes, different levels of torture were meted out. The Royal Barber, first mate Roger Callan, would remove a lock of hair from some but shear other pollywogs nearly bald. The more you fought, the more torture you received. John Bird, the cook, was the Royal Baby and his stomach was smeared with bilge grease that required a kiss from each inductee. The last rite was to drink a cup of seawater mixed with wine vinegar, state your crimes, and ask forgiveness on bended knee from able bodied seaman Doug Eldon, Neptune Rex himself. The gauntlet would be repeated if you did not accomplish this last act. The drink was so foul that I could not speak and I was in danger of repeating the ordeal. Fortunately for me, a pollywog behind me started to cause some trouble and the Royal policemen were called away. Neptune looked me in the eye and said, "Lend a hand, you're now a Shellback."

Now a Shellback, I went back in the line and helped induct the remaining pollywogs. Mostly good fun, but some used the free-for-all to get even with others for personal reasons. When you confine forty people in a small space for a long time, conflicts are bound to arise.

The next day the ship's company was called and informed that Charlie Clements, one of the crew, had become ill with what Roger Callan and Captain Nelson had determined to be hepatitis. We all felt very vulnerable and alone out in the ocean, 1,500 miles from land. We did manage to raise a fishing boat, 700 miles away, by radio, and asked them for advice. The result was that we quarantined Charlie on top of the wheelhouse. The ship's company was told to avoid contact with him and we all hoped for the best. A group of young women waited on him hand and foot, not caring if he had infectious hepatitis or not (the diagnosis was not certain.)

Charlie, a distinguished graduate of the Air Force Academy, had been a C-130 pilot in Vietnam but had gradually begun to feel what he was being asked to do there was immoral. The day before the U.S. invaded Cambodia, he refused to fly further missions and was subsequently placed in a psychiatric ward. After six months, he was discharged with a 10-percent mental disability and had come almost straight to Los Angeles.

In Marina del Rey, he had met Neil Davis, who told him that if he wanted to pay his own way to Barbados he could join *Regina's* crew as an ordinary seaman, even though he had no sailing experience. Neil told Charlie he would be a welcome addition to the crew, who were too often "drunk or stoned." Charlie had been offered $1 and a shot of rum a day and, of course, room and board. [2]

As for me, besides standing watch and handling sails, I worked sanding, varnishing, and cleaning and served on galley duty. I also spent several four-hour stints in the engine room with Danny Spears, the chief engineer. It was a hellhole of noise, heat, and oil stink.

The rum ration ritual Captain Nelson had started on the initial voyage to Los Angeles continued. At four o'clock, the crew and passengers who had worked that day would receive their rum ration. The captain still kept the key to the cask, and he now had a special bronze cup, with a line-drawing of *Regina Maris* on its surface, that held nearly two shots. The crew would gather around up in the bow and each in turn partake of this 18th-century mariner's sacrament. It was very important to down the entire contents of the cup without a gasp or splutter. It is a wonderful tradition to end a day of hard work in the hot sun. The rum soothed aching muscles and helped develop shipboard camaraderie.

Landfall. After 20 days at sea, old salt and passenger alike would long for the dark smudge on the horizon. The clouds would form over the islands and act as a beacon for the helmsman. *Photo by author.*

We arrived at our first landfall, the island of Nuka Hiva, in the Marquesas, on July 7. There was some concern about whether we would be allowed to land with a hepatitis patient on board. There was no physician in Nuka Hiva, only a clinic with the equivalent of a physician's assistant. Charlie would have to stay on the island until he was well enough to travel again, and no one knew how long that might be. The Merck Manual, which had been the source of most of what we knew about hepatitis, mentioned that a return to physical activity too soon could lead to a dangerous relapse. We all thought Charlie Clements was the luckiest guy alive to be able to stay on the island, but no one begrudged him the luck because of all he had been through before.

Charlie's temporary home, Nuka Hiva, was first discovered in 1791 by the American fur trader Joseph Ingraham on the vessel *Hope*. At that time the population was estimated to be about 80,000. By 1926, only 2,000 people were left on the island, due to contagious disease spread by Europeans, and when *Regina* arrived, the population was still only 2,660. For a first port of call after 22 days at sea, it was a wonderful place. There were cold beer, friendly faces, and lots of places to explore.

One night the local traditional dance team was practicing for Bastille Day celebrations to be held in Papeete later in the month. The team was excellent, their rhythms and movements mesmerizing. It was in Taiohae Bay that Herman Melville, as a boy of 16, jumped ship. I had read his book *Typee*, and I told others on board about his adventures with the cannibalistic natives in the next valley, where he had been captured and fattened up as the main course.

Inspired by this story, eight crew members and passengers set out following Melville's path up and over the 2,000-foot mountains and into the next valley. The captain agreed to sail around to Controller Bay and the village of Taipivai to pick us up on the next day. It was a long but incredibly beautiful hike. We were told that the last act of cannibalism in this valley had been in 1912, when three Catholic priests had been consumed. Greg Stover, a passenger, who was on the hike, remembers finding a giant stone wall that was dry stacked with the joints perfectly cut so that there was no space between the stones, an engineering feat seemingly beyond the technology of the existing inhabitants. Such evidence of technological achievement was one factor that inspired the Norwegian adventurer and ethnographer Thor Heyerdah to build his raft *Kon-tiki* and sail it to the Marquesas from South America.

Some friendly children showed us a large temple or "tohua." It had 11 original, still-standing Tikis, wooden or stone carvings found in most Polynesian cultures and perhaps representing deified ancestors. In the past, warring villages would capture one another's warriors in battle and then sacrifice them on stone platforms guarded by Tikis. When the European colonists arrived, all the first people's religious sites were destroyed, or the heads and phalluses were removed from the Tikis. Those actions successfully put an end to the ritual cannibalism and changed the culture, paving the way for Catholicism's success. There is now a small Catholic chapel in the center of the village.

Spending the night among these first people was interesting. They were all so friendly and giving, sharing what they had with us for a simple meal together. The ship arrived the next day. All the crew had enjoyed the visit with these unique people.

We sailed on to Hiva Oa. Greg Stover remembers that "the very night we dropped anchor at Hiva Oa I contracted the worst case of stomach poisoning in my life. Was very dehydrated, ate nothing and was 'pissin' out of both ends' (Willie Preston's remark) and confined to my bunk except for trips to the head for the entire time we were on the island. I did get to see the French infirmary one rainy night, which made all the difference. I was seaworthy by the time we weighed anchor. There was some debate as to the cause (bad water/food at Nuka Hiva) but at least half of the roster was afflicted after we left the island." [3]

While poor Greg was sick, I was able to enjoy all that Hiva Oa had to offer. I visited Paul Gauguin's grave in a lonely cemetery overlooking the little bay. The whole local community was celebrating a wedding we were able to attend. The Catholic ceremony was filled with a cappella voices singing in Marquesian, beautiful to hear, beyond words to describe. After the church ceremony there was a procession down to the reception area and all along the way was more singing as the whole community lined the road. Winding their way through the crowd beside the bride and groom as they walked was a group of old women chanting. We learned later that the women were giving an oral recitation of the couple's lineage. Afterwards was a wonderful community feast. On our last day on the island, the Chinese owners of the local grocery store provided a sumptuous lunch for some of us from the ship, presumably because we were such good customers.

After that, *Regina* headed on south to the coral atolls of the Tuamotus and the village of Rangiroa. From the ship, the village looked to be just some metal-roofed, palm-thatch walled huts on a pile of sand. But it had great coral to dive on and crystal clear water. When it came time to leave, we found that *Regina's* anchor had become tangled around a monster coral head clearly visible in the nearly 100 feet of water. There was talk of Howard Swehla, a passenger with scuba equipment, going down to fix it, but by skillfully maneuvering the ship around in a circle we were able to untangle the anchor chain and haul it back aboard.

The ship then sailed on to the Society Islands, stopping at Bora Bora, where we anchored the ship so its stern was at a short dock in nearly 100 feet of beautiful clear water. To do this, the two large, 1,000-pound anchors in the bow were set to starboard and port as the ship slowly backed up to the dock. Another smaller anchor was rowed in the dinghy far off the stern on the port side, and on the starboard side aft we were tied to a large palm tree. Greg Stover recalls that "on the last day on Bora Bora, the *Regina* sideswiped a small unattended sailboat as we were leaving the harbor. Their hull was scratched and a few of the railing rods that support the decorative railing lines were broken." [3]

There were heavy, 15-foot seas as we went out through the pass between the coral reefs that ringed the island and into the ocean. We nearly holed our hull with the starboard anchor as we attempted to get it up to the cathead and secured. Greg remembered, "Paul Maskel climbed down on the flukes to secure the starboard davit cable to the anchor crown. Several times he and the anchor were submerged in green foamy water, followed shortly by a nerve-rattling thud against the hull." [3]

We made port in Raiatea on Bastille Day. The town was filled with people, and we were docked at the foot of main street in the middle of a carnival of activities. I had read that there was the best example of a Tahitian temple, or Mare, just down the coast so I organized a group of passengers to rent motorbikes to go see it. Dorothy and Alexis Yerxa, from Sacramento, and Pat Quiter from Hollywood, and I, set out on an adventure. It was a long way through beautiful off-the-beaten-path country to get there. The temple was a grand site, but we had to get back to the ship before it sailed. We pushed those motorbikes' engines to their limit and possibly terrorized the locals as the four of us raced for the ship down the dusty roads.

On Huahine, our next island, we had a wild, drunken pig roast on the beach. When it was time to go back to the ship in the wee hours there were more people than the launch could handle. Two inches of freeboard and a load of drunks was a disaster in the making. The launch made it all the way out to the ship anchored in the harbor, but it sank at the side of the ship when a drunken occupant lunged for the ladder. The outboard motor had to be disassembled in order for it to dry out and new electronics installed.

Our next stop was the island of Moorea, where we anchored in Cook's Bay along with a French Navy cruiser that had just returned from the islands of Moruroa and Fangataufa in the Southern Tuamoto Archipelago. The French were preparing those islands for an atmospheric nuclear bomb blast. Two hundred nukes were set off at the two island test sites between 1966 and 1996. There were many French sailors on the Moorea enjoying some rest and relaxation. Some of our crew visited their ship and some sailors came to visit *Regina Maris*. *Regina's* company, singly and in groups, toured the island with its wonderful sites and had a party at the Club Med one evening.

Next we sailed to Papeete, Tahiti, where we tied up at the wharf across the boulevard from the yellow-painted Quinn's Bar, visited the year before by *Regina's* crew under Captain John Wilson. By long-standing tradition, visiting sailors carve their names or messages in the wood of the bar or booths, and we left a few of our own.

We toured the island and did some more scuba diving on the reefs. Many dance groups, from all of French Polynesia, were still giving demonstrations of their art, which we all enjoyed. Some of us went to a fancy French restaurant for a contrast in cultures.

For the majority of passengers, the time in paradise was up. It was time to go back to the States and our other lives. Seven well-salted, rowdy *Regina Maris* veterans were on the Pan Am flight from Papeete to L.A. We did have a good time, possibly at the expense of the other passengers and attendants. I have since become friends with one of those attendants and apologized profusely for our actions.

Regina Maris returned to California with another group of passengers, reversing her path through the islands and on to Hawaii, leaving Papeete August 3 and arriving at Pier Eight in Honolulu on the first of September. Carol Leonard, a 29-year-old teacher from San Francisco, and a passenger on the cruise from Papeete, was asked in an interview for the Honolulu Star Bulletin about her shipmates. She said "We are a very mixed bag, the oldest is 68 and he climbs the rigging, and then there's Harold and Bertha, they're retired. Most of us are young." The reporter added, "and just a shade on the woolly side." [4]

Yes, wild and woolly.

CHAPTER 12
LONG BEACH, CALIFORNIA TO PAPEETE TAHITI

1. Dick Emery, "Her Sails Inhale the Wind," *Independent Press-Telegram* (Long Beach California), June 12, 1971.
2. Charlie Clements, email to the author, January 2, 2011.
3. Greg Stover, emails to the author, January 2 and April 26, 2011.
4. Pierre Bowman, " 'Mixed Bag' of Passengers: 24 Tourists Sail Pacific on Barkentine," *Honolulu Star Bulletin*, September 2, 1971.

CHAPTER 13
ONE QUEEN VS TWO TYPHOONS
1971 – 1973

When Joyce Kerin, one of *Regina Maris's* owners, arrived back home in September 1971 after the trip to Polynesia and back, she decided she wanted out of the business. Fellow partner Greg Cook remembered her telling him and another partner, David Wiseman, that her brother, Neil Davis, had been embezzling funds from the corporation. Greg said Joyce told him Neil had inflated the purchase price of the ship and kept the difference and that he had used the corporation's checkbook as his own. [1]

According to Dolores Davis, Neil's widow, however, the allegations against him were untrue and Joyce's claim was groundless, a ploy to gain control of her parent's estate and cut Neil out of his inheritance. [2] But the damage had been done to Neil's reputation. Greg, David, and Joyce voted him out of the corporation. Greg then bought out Joyce and David, gaining 100% ownership in Trade Wind Cruises. [1]

During the winter of 1971-72, the ship made four round trips from Ensenada, Mexico, to Acapulco. The three-week, one-way trip cost passengers $1,500 and the vessel was always completely booked, carrying 50 passengers each trip.

Van Fowler, a crew member during these trips, recalled in a letter to the author, "On the last trip of the season, upon our return to Ensenada, the Federales were tipped off that a load of marijuana was on board the ship. The ship was searched and nothing found, but during her yearly overhaul in dry dock during the next week, all the sanitary waste lines were found to be plugged with a green organic material." [3]

After the last coast-of-Mexico trip, the first mate, Roger Callan, left the ship having served five years with the Wilson brothers and one year with Trade Wind Cruises. Captain Paul Nelson left as well, after one year of service. A new captain was needed. The Mexican government did not care if the captain of a vessel had a proper license, so Greg Cook asked second mate Paul Maskell to fill that position. Although Paul had extensive sailing experience, he had never applied for his captain's license. The insurance company, Lloyd's of London, accepted Paul's credentials and experience and approved his appointment as acting captain. Shortly after his stint as *Regina's* captain, Paul did apply for and receive a master's certificate for any ship in any sea. [4]

The crew was put to work on the ship while it was in dry dock, but they were disgruntled with their pay of $40 to $50 a month plus food and berth, and they demanded higher wages. A mutiny of sorts took place with the crew refusing to work on the maintenance and repairs. Greg Cook fired them all except the newly promoted captain, Paul Maskell; the newly promoted first mate, Doug Elden, who had been a crew member since Lisbon; and the newly promoted second mate, Ari Pronk, with the ship since the Netherlands. Then Greg hired 12 new crew members. [1] The ship was due to be recaulked in dry-dock before the upcoming sailing season, but that was not done because of the time lost dealing with the wage dispute and hiring new crew." [3, 5]

On May 1, 1972, *Regina Maris* set out with 50 passengers, plus crew, for an uneventful and enjoyable trip to French Polynesia.

Evan Logan, who had joined the crew in April along with other hands Miguel Evans and Cathy Rollins, described the voyage as follows: "We had a fine 21-day passage from Ensenada to Nuku Hiva, in the Marquesas Islands, then visiting Rangiroa, in the Tuamotos, then on to Bora Bora, Raiatea, Huahini, Moorea, and Tahiti." [5]

When the ship arrived in Tahiti, Doug Elden disembarked and returned to the States. Ari became first mate and Miguel Evans became second mate. For the return trip, Evan recalled, "We retraced our route to the Marquesas, motored east along the equatorial counter current, headed north to Cabo San Lucas, and then proceeded northward following the Baja California coast to Ensenada. We were lucky that we did not encounter the usual storms found in the counter current." [6]

The additional motoring required extra fuel, which was carried on deck in 20 55-gallon steel drums. The ship arrived back in Ensenada July 25.

Hoping for a quick turnaround, the crew immediately began cleaning the ship and restocking supplies and fuel. They needed to be prepared for a new group of passengers ready to set off on their adventures to paradise on July 31.

Evan Logan recalled, "We departed Ensenada with 58 people on board. Greg had oversold the crew-trainee and passengers' tickets. There were mesh hammocks in the passageways, along with people's gear and extra people sleeping on deck." [6]

Eight days later and 1,500 miles into the voyage, the ship encountered typhoon Celeste. *(See Appendix F for a NOAA account of the storm.)* For three days the ship battled 30-foot seas and winds in excess of 55 miles per hour... First mate Ari Pronk remembered, "Three sails were blown out by the howling winds. First to go was the lower topsail. Then the staysail was put up, but it blew out also. Next, an inner jib sail was put up. It blew out also. Finally, the storm sail was put up and it held." [5]

Ari, at the helm, ran the ship before the wind in order to out sail the heaviest part of the storm by sailing with the wind on the starboard quarter. During this time, Captain Maskell and chief engineer Bill Wilburn were busy in the engine room trying to find out what the problem was with the 8-71 Detroit diesel main engine — it was refusing to start.

It was determined that this was due to a broken camshaft. The second engine, a 2-71 Detroit diesel utility engine, normally used as a generator for electricity when sailing, also failed. Additionally, the "Lister," a small generator used just to keep freezers and minimal electricity going during "quiet" sailing, when the other engines were off, overheated and could be used only sparingly. [5]

The tremendous twisting of the ship during the storm caused the caulking between the planks on the hull — caulking that had not been redone when the ship was in dry dock — to loosen and *Regina* began taking on water — a substantial amount thanks to the heavy seas. It was later estimated that she was taking on about 2,000 gallons per hour.

Because the ship was on its starboard quarter, it was rolling heavily, and the rolling caused the water to come over the sides and remain on the deck amidships. A wall of water would travel down her decks, filling the space between the rails like a swimming pool.

This added weight pushed against the ship's buoyancy and slowed her recovery from each wave. As the scuppers removed the deck water, the bow would rise into another wave. With water everywhere and the continued rolling, people had to time walking from the wheelhouse to the galley in order to remain relatively dry. To prevent people from being washed overboard, ropes were tied as safety lines from forward to aft on both port and starboard sides, which people held onto as they walked across deck. [7]

Regina's two bilge pumps, used to pump water out of the ship, were also not working. The primary bilge pump was powered by the 8-71 Detroit diesel main engine, now out of commission.

Despite these problems, the ship maintained headway with her sails and could continue on. Passenger April Beach, who eventually married second mate Ari Pronk, remembered in an interview with the author, "Crew members took turns trying to operate a manual bilge pump on the foredeck. This pump was not large and was operated much like a farmer's well pump after being primed. In spite of the continued hand pumping, it would only spit out a mouthful of water at a time. A bucket brigade would be needed. So the crew and passengers had to form a line leading from the bowels of the ship, up the steps of the hatch at amidships, across the deck to the railing. They would pass buckets of water upwards along the brigade line to be emptied over the side of the ship. Then, the empty buckets would be passed back down the same line to be refilled. The brigade, still in good humor, and working well as a team, decided that passing bottles of wine up and down the line to drink would be a good idea. This kept up the 'spirits' and energy levels since nobody was able to eat much for about 36 hours. The cook worked tirelessly to make sandwiches for everyone, but the energy expended to keep the ship afloat far surpassed the caloric intake." [7]

Deirdrie "Shark" Lindsey, the assistant cook, recalled in an email to the author, "I became cook for the trip to Tahiti when we were hit by typhoon Celeste. That was the best experience I have had at sea! Yahoo!! I remember 3 days of 120-knot, gusting winds, black as night, and the seas were total chaos, no pattern at all, bailing with buckets and cooking whatever I could hold on to! I made five passages on *Regina*. I bought supplies and made the menus. What an incredible experience. Paul Maskell was the best! Just for the record I cooked some great meals on that little diesel stove. On the Mexican coastal trips I cooked Thanksgiving and Christmas dinner, 2 turkeys, with mashed potatoes, gravy, and all the trimmings. I made 120 pancakes for breakfast -- that was two apiece for a hungry crew; seconds were offered! My hammock was strung between the bowsprit and the net, what a glorious spot. I was also the witch doctor at the equator crossings." [8]

The radio operator had limited experience with the ship's equipment, and attempted in vain during the storm to contact the Coast Guard or another ship. Robert Eisberg, a passenger and professor of physics at the University of California at Santa Barbara, wrote a detailed report to the Marine Supervisor of the F.C.C. concerning the use of the radio. The report is at times technical, dealing with frequencies, crystals and kilohertz, but it conveys the true emergency of the situation and how hampered their attempts were to successfully make radio contact and receive assistance. (*His account of the experience is reproduced in Appendix G*).

April remembered, "We were able to get one radio communication out for an S.O.S. after many attempts to do so. We reached 'Ocean Station November,' over 1,200 miles away in Hawaii, as the radio waves were transported beyond normal limits due to a 'freak' in the atmosphere. (Freak radio waves are a true phenomenon. This was recently documented when they determined that Amelia Earhart had indeed been able to radio from the Howland Island area all the way to Florida when she was lost.) When we made radio contact with the station, and gave them our coordinates, everyone on board cheered. I [later] named my daughter November partly for this reason."

Edward Bartlett, captain of a WC135B Storm Mission plane tracking the typhoon from McAllen Air Force Base, sighted *Regina Maris* as he completed a flight through the eye of the storm on August 10. In his short radio contact with the ship, he appraised her plight and radioed Hickam Air Force Base in Hawaii, asking them to send pumps. Captain Bartlett dropped marker dye so a Coast Guard plane could spot the ship, waggled his wings, and headed for home. [9]

Alone again in the storm-tossed seas, the bailing brigade, though tired, was renewed with the conviction that they had been spotted and continued bailing as they waited for imminent rescue. Just before dark, a plane was heard and all were relieved at the sight of it. Five high-speed gasoline pumps were dropped by parachute, along with the fuel to run them and a radio. The crew had to lower a lifeboat and row in the rolling seas over to the equipment, a daunting task given the conditions and the weariness of the crew. [7]

Over the radio Captain Maskell learned that the Coast Guard Cutter *Mellon* was on its way from Hawaii to their location 1,200 miles away, and that there was a massive search on for two other ships that were feared lost. Six hundred miles northwest of *Regina,* the Indian freighter *Vishva Tirth* learning of *Regina's* problems, altered her course toward the stricken barkentine. This relieved the *Mellon* from having to assume towing duty.

Evan Logan recounted in a 2010 email to the author, "The whole complement was manning the two deck pumps and several bucket brigades round the clock for 36 hours. I thought it was the greatest thing ever. I couldn't understand why Captain Paul always looked so worried. We had two days of calm after the Coast Guard dropped us motorized bilge pumps and *Vishva Tirth* took us in tow."

Thirty-two *Regina* passengers were transferred to *Vishva Tirth* upon her arrival. The only injuries were a broken nose on one passenger and a possible broken rib on another. Both were treated by the *Vishva Tirth's* on-board physician. [9]

For the tow, *Regina's* anchors were detached from their chains and the sixty fathoms of chain was attached to a tow cable. The chain's weight acted like a shock absorber against the surge of the two ships and the sea.

But *Regina* was not yet out of trouble. Evan's account continued: "Two days later [after the arrival of *Vishva Tirth* and the start of the tow], we met Typhoon Diane. Diane blew 85 knots with 50-foot seas for five days. *(See Appendix F for a NOAH account of the storm)* The second day of the blow, Capt. Paul came into the galley where five or so of the crew were sitting talking. In the group were Tom Maguire, Nick Calvert, John Campbell, Howard Breen and a couple more I can't remember.

"Paul said, 'There is an Irish pennant [a loose line, strand, or rope end left hanging untidily] on the royal yard. If that sail gets loose it could take the yard with it. Can someone go aloft and secure it?'

"We all looked at each other with an unspoken, 'Oh shit!'

"Then, like a fool, I volunteered. Maguire followed me out of the galley and said, 'Hey, if you don't make it, can I have your *Ashley Book of Knots*'? We both laughed." [6]

Regina's owner Greg Cook was surfing in California when he learned of *Regina's* plight. Knowing that this disaster and the cost of the towing the ship to port, if that should be needed, would bankrupt Trade Wind Cruises, he radioed Captain Maskell aboard *Regina* and told him to abandon ship. The captain consulted the crew, and they refused to go along with this order. They saw no reason at that point to leave the ship they had worked so hard to keep afloat. [5 and 7]

Greg then suggested that the ship be towed to Panama so that "the passengers would at least get a trip out of it." [1] Paul Maskell felt that the ship could make it on to Papeete on her own, but it was unknown if the necessary engine repairs could be done in Tahiti.

However, the discussion was actually moot: The decision was up to the captain of *Vishva Tirth*, which had been on her way from Japan to Panama when the captain heard *Regina's* distress call. *Vishva Tirth's* captain had decided to tow the ship to San Pedro, California, for he did not want to face the Panamanian legal system and the red tape that would ensue. Greg had been required by the Indian Government, which owned *Vishva Tirth*, to post a $70,000.00 security bond to cover the cost of the towing. [1]

After the storm dissipated, *Vishva Tirth* had to stop to change the engine oil. Paul Maskell warned *Vishva Tirth's* captain of potential damage if the loss of forward motion caused the two ships to collide, but the warning went unheeded. The weight of the chain, seeking the bottom, pulled the two ships together. Some of *Regina's* crew took gaff hooks and tried to fend off *Vishva*, but this last-minute attempt failed to prevent damage.

Evan Logan remembered, "We were all on the fore deck including Capt. Paul.

The jib boom was scraping against the side of *V.T.'s* hull. One of their Indian crew picked up an aluminum ladder and tried to fend off the jib boom. The ladder was wrenched from his hands and fell into the sea. Then as *Regina* rolled closer and closer the starboard yardarm of the course yard struck a cabin top and broke upward, almost in slow motion. (None of us had the presence of mind to slack the yard lifts and sheets. If we had there would have been little or no damage.)" [6]

Regina's bowsprit hit *Vishva*'s port side aft. The force of the blow drove the bowsprit back and pulled out the six 1-inch diameter bolts embedded in three inches of solid oak. The head stay broke free from the bowsprit. *Regina* bounced back and hit *Vishva* again, breaking off the tips of the two lower yardarms. People feared that the whole foremast was going to come down without the support of the stay, but a temporary head stay was fashioned from the top of the mast to the end of the bowsprit and in not too much time, the towing operation was under way again. [4]

Evan Logan recalled something positive that came out of their experience with Hurricane Diane: "That was where I got the idea to build the 'Logan's Locker.' When we were in the hurricane many of the galley's tinned food stores were stowed in the bilge under the fo'c'sle. When the bilge was filled with water the labels came off the tins and kept clogging the deck pumps. When we were safely back in San Pedro, Paul asked me to build the box on the fore deck to stow the food stores. After that was finished Nick Calvert said he had been in submarines when he was in the navy, and they had a place called Hogan's Alley. Then he said we should name the box Logan's Locker. For some reason the name stuck. I think the box was demolished during one of her subsequent sinkings around Long Island." [6]

On August 22, *Regina* and *Vishva Tirth* limped into San Pedro Harbor after seven days of towing. Their route had taken them through the 70-mile-per-hour winds and massive seas of Typhoon Diana. It had been another uncomfortable and frightening experience for *Regina*'s crew and passengers, but there had been no additional damage or injuries after those mentioned above.

The Coast Guard cutter *Point Camden* assisted *Regina* into her berth, to the welcome of family, friends, and hundreds of curious onlookers. [7] Many passengers were interviewed by the media. April Beach summed up her experience, "The hurricane was the best carnival ride I've ever taken." [10] She was also quoted as saying, "The girls helped with the bucket brigade when we ran into Celeste. We all wore lifejackets and were just too tired to think of anything but to get the water out of the bilges." [10]

But other passengers were not so happy. A group of them sued Greg and Trade Wind Cruises for $1.2 million. That suit was eventually settled for a total of $35,000, but most of the passengers, including some who had sued, rebooked on the next trip.

The insurance had covered the $10,000 towing bill and the damages to the yardarms and bowsprit. The main and auxiliary engines were rebuilt at the Rodriguez shipyard in Ensenada. [1] By November 1, the ship had been fully repaired. Because of the notoriety of her most recent voyage, Trade Wind Cruises was overwhelmed with applicants wanting to go to the South Pacific. Greg booked the ship for two more round trips with passengers eager to take a voyage to Tahiti.

A new captain was hired to replace Paul Maskell, as he had not yet applied for his captain's license. Paul was offered the job of first mate, a downgrade, but he declined to sail on *Regina Maris* under those conditions. Additionally, first mate Ari Pronk was offered the job of second mate. He also declined this posting. Neither man, who had both worked so hard to save the ship, ever sailed on her again. [7]

Evan Logan, who was still a crew member, recalled those next trips as follows. "The next voyage to French Polynesia was uneventful, similar to the first I took. When we got to Tahiti, Miguel jumped ship with the cook, (my ex-girlfriend, Deirdrie) and I became second mate." [6]

While the ship was in Papeete, on her last turnaround in Tahiti in the fall of 1973, Jeff Berry, captain of *Brig Unicorn* had an experience with *Regina Maris*. "I was working there (in Tahiti) then and the situation aboard was that [*Regina's* crew] were ready to mutiny unless they got a new master, and more money," he said. "I remember being approached and given the chance of a lifetime to be her master. Well, I went aboard her and looked around. Most of the spares were used up, so she had been living on her bodily fat since the Australian Bi-Centennial celebrations. I looked in her bilges and found the limbers [holes cut on the underside of the floor-timbers on each side of the keel to allow bilge water to drain aft to the pumps] were all choked with rubbish. I refused the honor, considering the next master was commanding a ship living on borrowed time." [11]

In Berry's unpublished book, *Square-Rigged Skipper,* he makes a further comment on *Regina Maris* and the importance of following sailing routes. He says, "To illustrate the fact that sailing ships must follow sailing routes across oceans, I well remember the Maltese-flagged barquentine *Regina Maris*. In 1972, she routinely sailed between Acapulco, Mexico, and Papeete, Tahiti, then directly back with stops in the Marquesas Islands. The Trade Wind blew her from Mexico fair and true to Polynesia. That was no problem. However, the return trip was made at her top speed, motoring along the same route that she sailed out from Mexico. That put the eye of the wind directly on *Regina Maris'* bow. Most properly the ship should have sailed north past the Hawaiian Islands till she fell in with the strong westerlies, then she should have closed the Mexican coast from that direction. However, that would have taken more time and her owners wanted to maximize their investments by recruiting as many passengers as possible, classified as 'contributing crew.' I recall touring *Regina Maris* in Tahiti. She didn't have enough fuel capacity to make the long passage under power east to the New World, so she was forced to deck load fuel drums. The main deck was completely filled with 55-U.S. gallon drums, 44-Imperial gallon drums, or 200-litre fuel drums, depending upon where they originated. These containers were covered by plywood, which formed a raised deck. This system worked, but it was not too popular with the contributing crew, who had paid a lot of money to make their individual personal adventures come true. They thought they would be sailing away in a tall sailing ship on a voyage between Mexico and the islands of the South Seas. Not aboard a cramped, noisy, smelly motor ship that happened to have sails. The scheme could have worked, had that ship followed the proper routes, but her landlubberly owner, with little knowledge of the sea, wanted to maximize his profit. As a result, *Regina Maris* motored between Polynesia and Mexico for several more voyages." [12]

On the return passage to North America in the fall of 1973, Evan Logan remembered, "the planned route by way of the equatorial counter current was met with fresh trade winds and 20-foot head seas. As *Regina* pitched off the back of a wave we were nearly in free fall until reaching the bottom of the trough with 2-gees gravity. The forward heads were regurgitating sewage onto the fo'c'sle deck. That was as close as I have ever been to being seasick. We had to turn and run for Hawaii to buy more diesel fuel. Several weeks later when we got back to San Pedro we learned Greg had put the boat up for sale and found a buyer, a Captain Willoughby, from the U.K. In the intervening two months we did a coastal cruise down to Acapulco and back to Ensenada, Mexico, on May 29, 1973." [6]

Greg had decided to sell the ship since he had done very well with his investment, grossing nearly $700,000 for the first year, and about the same the next. He had plans to buy a McDonald's franchise. [1]

John Staply, a yacht broker, had found a buyer, Brictec Finance Ltd. of Plymouth, England, and the deal was signed and sealed. Brictec made a $250,000 deposit for the ship, but then Staply absconded with the money and fled to Liberia. He was caught and put in jail but the money was never recovered. The ship exchanged hands without Greg's ever receiving a payment.

Former *Regina Maris* owner John Aage Wilson sued Greg for the remaining $120,000 that was owed on the note to him. Greg had hoped that Wilson would not come all the way to California from Norway for the litigation, but he did. Greg had to sell his 10 rental houses and his used car company to pay off the debt. He eventually did acquire his first McDonald's franchise and by 1993 had expanded his holdings to 15 franchises. [1]

The post-*Regina* fate of two other important crew members is worth noting. **Roger Callan** played a significant role in the ship's history, sailing with the Wilson brothers for five years and Trade Wind Cruises for one, serving as cook, second mate, and first mate. For a year after leaving *Regina Maris* in September 1971, Roger traveled around the U.S., during which time he met his future wife, Angelika. Returning to the U.K. he re-entered the hotel industry, working as a chef in several hotels, and in 1974 moved to Germany to serve as chef in several top restaurants. In 1977 he returned to England, where he studied automotive engineering and became a motor vehicle engineer in 1981. Returning to Germany, he became a service manager for General Motors and in

1989, a service manager for Winnebago Europe. Staying in the motor home industry, he moved into management positions after obtaining business management training and worked for Teschner Motorhome, of Brehna, Germany, until retirement. He is now fully retired and living in Germany and Naples, Florida.

Paul Maskell, who sailed on *Regina* with the Wilson brothers as crew and second mate and then became captain under Greg Cook, wrote a letter to the author on September 6, 1993, after visiting the ship in Greenport, New York. He said, "Just stepping back down onto the deck of the *Regina Maris* again after so many years was of course the most nostalgic of events. Each one of us feels a personal relationship with *Regina*. Going to Greenport for me was like coming back to visit an old girlfriend. Seeing the ship brings back so many intimate memories. My personal association with *Regina* was a love affair that changed the whole course of my life, and for which I will be forever grateful."

In a phone conversation with the author on January 17, 2011, Paul said that for awhile he ran the office of Windjammer Cruises in Trinidad, then retired and moved back to Miami. Later, Windjammer CEO Danny, only son of the family who owned the company, died and Paul was persuaded to come out of retirement and run the company. He then sailed the company flagship *Yankee Trader* three times around the world.

CHAPTER 13
ONE QUEEN VS. TWO TYPHOONS

1. Greg Cook, interview with the author, September 3, 1993, at the *Regina Maris* reunion, Greenport, New York.
2. Dolores Davis, wife of the late Neil Davis, telephone interview with author, with her daughter Diana assisting, July 18, 2012.
3. Van Fowler, letter to the author, dated July 24, 1992.
4. Paul Maskell, interview with the author, September 3, 1993, at the *Regina Maris* reunion, Greenport, New York.
5. Adriaan Pronk, interview with the author, September 3, 1993, at the *Regina Maris* reunion, Greenport, New York. Also email to the author, February 13, 2011.
6. Evan Logan, email to the author, December 31, 2010.
7. April Pronk, email to the author, February 13, 2011.
8. Deirdre "Shark" Lindsey, email to the author, February 6, 2011.
9. "Hurricane Survivors," *San Pedro News Pilot* (California), August 22, 1972.
10. "Battered barkentine limps into L.A. port*,*" *Press-Telegram* (Long Beach, California), August 22, 1972.
11. Jeff Berry, email to Carol Simons, February 11, 2011, compiling a history of

Regina Maris.
12. Jeff Berry, *Square-Rigged Skipper*, January 2009, Part II, Chapter 4. This is an unpublished book. Jeff was captain of *Brig Unicorn* and also sailed on the *Golden Hinde* across the Pacific in 1979.

CHAPTER 14
NEW Owners and PASSAGES
September 1973 – April 1974

In 1973, Captain R. Michael Willoughby, Bill Shand-Kydd, and Peter Olley were looking for a vessel to operate as a mini-cruise ship in the Seychelles Islands, in the Indian Ocean, where Bill was building an upscale hotel. To pursue their plans for the ship and the resort, the three men formed Brictec Finance Ltd. of Plymouth, England. The yacht broker John Staply of a Chichester yacht brokerage firm contacted the three partners with details about *Regina Maris,* which was well known in maritime circles through media coverage of her rounding Cape Horn and circumnavigating the globe. In addition, the two full-length movies of her voyages had been distributed throughout Europe.

Captain Willoughby, Mike to his friends, flew to Hilo, Hawaii, to inspect *Regina,* which was returning from Tahiti and on her way to Ensenada, Mexico. In a letter to the author of November 18, 1996, he wrote, "I arrived on this beautiful volcanic island to await the ship, and after two days, she anchored in the small harbor and I went on board to inspect her. I found much wrong with her but nothing that could not be put right by a good crew and time." [1]

He felt she was too small to carry the barkentine rig and was better suited to be a brig. He stated in the same letter, "The Wilson rig was a botch up by a yard that must have designed it from a book but with little understanding of why things were done."

On Mike's return to the UK, the partners discussed using *Regina* as a short-voyage cruise vessel and agreed that she would be suitable for such an enterprise. They decided to make an offer on the vessel, contingent on a survey by Lloyd's of London to be conducted after the ship arrived in Ensenada May 29.

By June 1973, the survey having been completed, and positive, Mike and his Brictec partners put down a $250,000 deposit on the vessel. On October 13, 1973, after the delays described in Chapter 13, the new firm Brictec at last took ownership of *Regina Maris* in Ensenada.

Once again *Regina Maris* was in the very capable hands of a knowledgeable sea captain. Born July 29, 1912, Reginald Michael Willoughby was 12 years old when he first went to sea, as a cadet on the Blue Star Line, which had pioneered the use of refrigeration in ships. By 1931, at the age of 19, Mike was fifth mate with the Blue Star Line and later went on to became second mate on the coaster *Britannic.* During the rebuilding of the brig *Henrietta,* he learned to rig the square rigger and later served as a deckhand on her. He also worked as a deckhand on the Thames barge *Success,* then skippered the ketch *Windward* from the UK to Trinidad. After that, he signed on as fourth mate on the passenger liner *Incosi,* and, just before World War II, served as second mate on the Tanker *Cerinthus.*

Joining the Royal Navy at the outset of the war, he served on submarines, working his way up to lieutenant commander and then to the position of senior officer of the Seventh Submarine Flotilla in Campbeltown, Scotland. He had also been in La Coruna, Spain, in 1942 in the submarine HMS *Sealion,* waiting for enemy cargo ships trying to reach Germany from northern Spanish ports. After the war, he continued serving in the Royal Navy as senior submarine officer for the South East Asia Command, then retired from the Royal Navy in 1947.

Between 1947 and 1952 he held, as he states, "various interesting but non-marine jobs," but during this time he also owned and skippered a 75-foot ketch, *Pas de Loup.* In 1958, he started a charter business in the West Indies with that vessel along with a Monrovia-registered, 160-foot, 500-ton schooner, *Te Vega,* and a 65-foot ketch, *Georgiana.* Until 1960, he was master of *Te Vega,* making transatlantic voyages that gave him experience in the charter business.

From 1960 until 1968, Mike was the certified engineer for Shalimar Shipbuilding in Calcutta, which built barges, tugs, and a 2000-ton cargo/passenger vessel for the Nicobar Islands. For the Indian Army, he designed and built a 17,000-foot "rope way" (an aerial passenger tram with gondola cars) descending 6,200 feet from Darjeeling to Singla on the Rammon River. And he served as chairman of the Indian Shipbuilding Association, chairman of the Government of India Advisory Council on Shipping, and consultant to the Indian government for the new deepwater seaports of Paradeep and Cochin.

In 1968, Mike returned to the UK to become master of the Sail Training Association's three-masted topsail schooner, *Sir Winston Churchill.* With STA, he made 15 cruises, training a total of 630 boys and girls. The ship and its students took part in the 1968 and 1969 Tall Ships races from Gothenburg, Sweden, to the Orkney Islands, off Scotland's north coast, and on to Kristiansand, Norway, and in the 1970 race from Plymouth, England, to Santa Cruz de Tenerife, in the Canary Islands.

On September 19, 1973, even before *Regina's* sale was final, Mike had hired John Fisher as chief mate and John Blowers as bo'sun to stand by the vessel and look after Brictec's interests. The men were put to work, along with Mike's wife Patch Willoughby to correct some of the faults in the rigging and prepare *Regina* for sea. They removed the moon- and skysail yards from the foremast, then shortened the fore topgallant mast. Mike felt that the lack of the "pocket handkerchief sized sails made little difference to her sailing capabilities and improved her appearance considerably." [1]

Another improvement was the addition of a 25-person life raft to the four 12-person rafts already on board. And the crew corrected the problem with the "fore lower mast cap's being too low and the lower topsail crane's position being fitted to the topmast and not to the cap." [2] See diagram below.

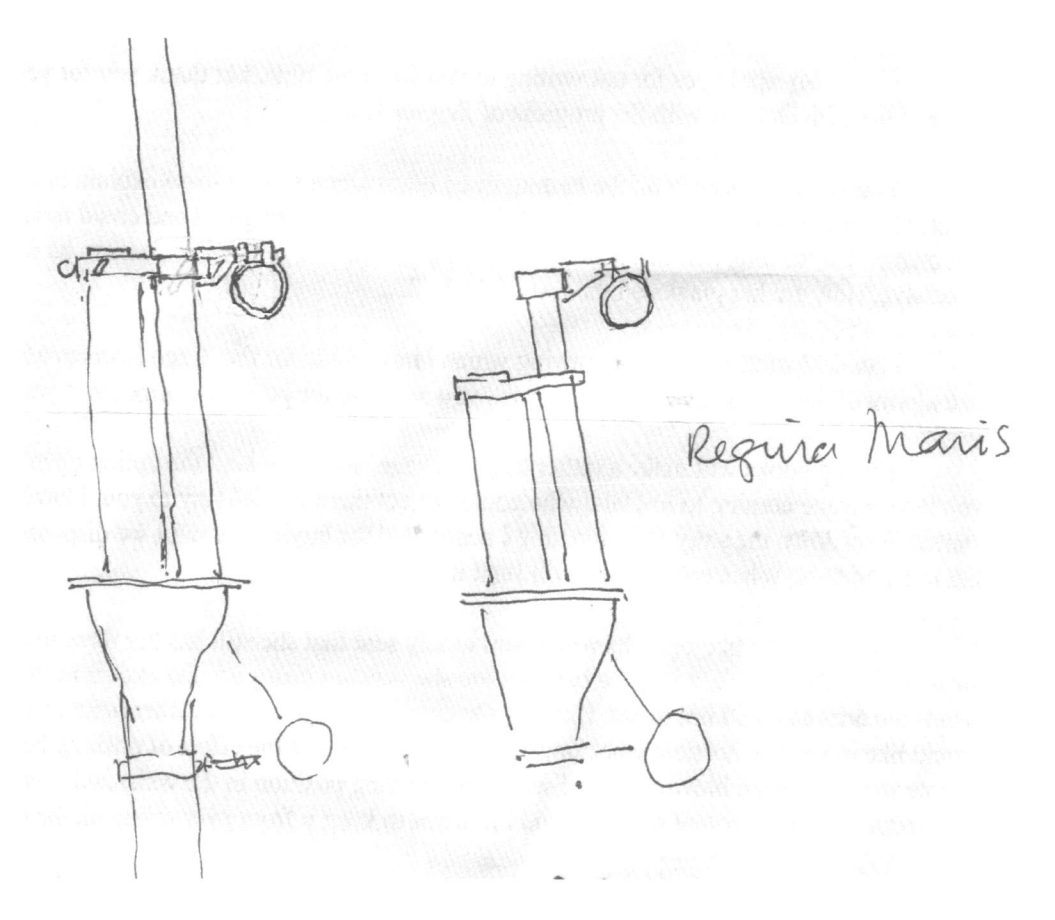

On the left, the corrected fore lower mast cap and the lower topsail crane fitted to the topmast. On the right, the original configuration. This drawing was done by Mike Willoughby on the back of his November 1, 1996, letter to the author. Also see the comment by sailmaker Jeremy Brown in endnote 3.

Patch was given the job of wiring up all the shackle pins. Starting with the foremast and ending with the mizzen sheets, that meant a total of 221 shackle pins. Mike noted, "This was a very hard job for a young woman who had never been on a ship before." [1]

Early in the sale negotiations, Mike had contracted the travel agency Thomas Cook Ltd. to advertise a voyage on *Regina Maris* from Ensenada to the UK via the Galapagos Islands and Cape Horn and to fill 12 berths for the journey. The agency was instructed to accept only physically fit persons between the ages of 20 and 40, since all who signed on would be required to take active part in working the ship, including standing watches, working aloft in any weather, and helping out in the galley.

About a month after *Regina*'s purchase was finalized, a bus arrived at the ship carrying 11 passenger/crewmembers. Six were from the UK, three of them well over 40. Three were Australians, all in their late 50s. Completing the group was a German couple in their late 70s who had suffered three years in a Nazi prison camp during the war and had limited physical abilities.

When he saw this group, Mike's first thought was to "send the over-forty's back to the coach and Thomas Cook." He relented but regretted his decision for the entire trip. The passengers were allotted cabins, and the mate had the task of making sailors out of the group. The younger ones quickly became crew members and went to work. The others tried but were unable to work aloft and as Mike said, "wandered around the ship looking lost and miserable." [1]

Regina Maris left Ensenada October 20, 1973, bound for the Galapagos — the Cook agency had advertised the voyage as "going around the Horn with a stop in the Galapagos Islands." However, the agency had been negotiating with the Ecuadorian government for permission to visit the islands, and as the political winds changed, the government had vacillated between allowing visitors and banning them completely. Mike had hoped that the Cook agency would be successful by the time the ship arrived there, and he sailed without having secured a visitation permit.

During the passage south, the weather was very calm and the engine had to be used for long periods, using up a great deal of fuel. This excessive use caused a small fire in the after peak, as hot gasses from the engine had leaked from a cracked exhaust pipe. No serious damage was done. In addition, a strong vibration in the propeller shaft reduced the ship's speed. Both problems, though seemingly minor, slowed the voyage and figured in later lawsuits.

Tom Maguire, who had signed on with the new owners in Ensenada, had worked on the major refit at the shipyard. In a 2014 email to the author, he stated, "After we left, and started to use the engine, the vibration would start and just get worse. The consensus was that when the shipyard workers 'aligned' the shaft to the engine ... they didn't! Willoughby and others assumed they just pried the shaft to the engine." [4] Also see this endnote for more information on the vibration issue.

Tom Maguire (left) with Captain Mike Willoughby. *Photo by David Marks*.

While the ship was motor- sailing south, the scanty news radio broadcasts were full of the impending oil embargo by Middle East countries. Patch Willoughby recalled in a 2014 email to the author, "Our Simrad radio wasn't up to the job of keeping us informed," leaving much unknown. [5]

Mike had a hard decision to make — keep to the original course plan and head for the Galapagos or abandon that advertised destination entirely. Since at that time the islands had no commercial fuelling facilities, motor-sailing directly to the Galapagos would require the ship to return to the mainland for fuel after leaving the islands and before venturing south to Cape Horn. Oil supply restrictions along the South American coast could also present a problem. In an email to the author, Patch remembered it was the "overthrow, and subsequent death of [President Salvador] Allende in Chile [September 11, 1973] that prevented us from pushing on to Santiago." [5]

The fuel situation became the final factor in Mike's decision to alter course and head for Panama, where the volume of international shipping would hopefully insure an adequate fuel supply. *Regina Maris* dropped anchor in the crowded Panama anchorage on November 21, 1973. They had covered 3,542-miles at an average speed of 4.62 knots.

While *Regina's* crew awaited word on the oil embargo, the media was also filled with news of the Watergate fiasco. This kept the passengers occupied as the days dragged on, and, according to the log books for this time; they also accomplished a great deal of work, from mending sails to realigning the engine with the propeller shaft. Every day but Sunday was filled with work.

Negotiations with the Ecuadorian government about visiting the Galapagos Islands went on and on and eventually broke down completely. The visit was canceled.

As the oil embargo spread to more countries every day, rounding the Horn also became out of the question.

The voyage was falling apart. The disgruntled passengers were demanding their money back and the ship seemed to be stuck in Panama Bay. When arrangements were at last made to transit the canal, all but four passengers left the ship and contacted their lawyers to file huge lawsuits against Cook Travel and Brictec Finance Ltd.

Regina was moved into Balboa Harbor to buoy #3 on November 25. On November 28, the Royal Yacht *Britannia,* bound for the Galapagos with Princess Ann and her husband, Captain Phillips, on board for their honeymoon, took on a full load of fuel oil from the Royal Fleet Auxiliary tanker. This added to Mike's frustration in dealing with the authorities. After much daily negotiating, the RFA agreed that the small quantity of fuel *Regina Maris* needed would not materially affect the world oil shortage. On December 10 the ship was moved to the fuel dock and took on a full load of diesel oil and fresh water. On Dec. 11 at 8:15 a.m. the canal pilot boarded, and the ship motored through the canal and anchored in Colon at 8:00 p.m.

Patch remembered the canal passage well: "The Canal Pilot who joined us for the Panama canal passage was called Mr. Christian and the look on his face when it was time to get going was classic. He had changed out of his uniform into Bermuda shorts, flowery shirt and plastic mac to enjoy his day 'yachting.' The poor chap didn't know where to start, and Mike was not a man to interfere with a Pilot. Of course, he took over when requested. We had to have manual handlers at the locks because the stern bitts had been ripped out during her pervious transit of the canal, so it was quite a day." [5]

The next morning they set off for Antigua, British West Indies, in a force 5 wind. This was the first time since leaving Ensenada that the ship was really sailing. Mike said in a letter to the author, "The wind was on our port bow and we were taking spray on board and occasionally putting our lee scuppers under water. Some of the crew were having the time of their lives and others were suffering from seasickness." [1]

The ship averaged 7 knots for the first 24 hours of the trip. On December 16, the main bilge pump failed so the course was changed for Kingston, Jamaica. On the night of December 18, a sudden gale came up to force 7, and the ship hove to till morning light. They entered Kingston Harbor under full sail with force 4 winds and anchored by noon on the next day. Their average speed for the 853-mile passage from Colon to Kingston had been 5.6 knots.

The ship stayed at Port Royal in Kingston Harbor until the pump was repaired, then set sail for Antigua December 24. With light easterly winds, they made very slow progress, and by December 30, they sighted Bahia de Naba, Dominican Republic. On January 1, 1974, the cook and the two engineers refused to work any longer, so Mike headed the ship back to Port Royal, Jamaica. Patch Willoughby took over the engine room and one of the crew tried his hand at cooking.

With the wind at their stern, they made 7 knots for the return passage to Port Royal and anchored January 5. On the 9th the ship was moved to the dockyard and secured. Due to the lack of funds and the resulting problems with crew members and creditors, the ship was put up for sale. Mike's two partners gave up any interest in the ship as lawsuits loomed. He made an appeal to Cook Travel to take over their interest, but that failed. After some negotiations, however, Mike's own bank was eventually willing to finance the ship's return to the UK.

From January 10 until March 19, the ship remained at the dockyard, getting many stopgap repairs to her stem and haws pipes. All her deck planks were recalked and several seams in her hull were repaired, stopping a worrisome leak.

There were many crew changes during this time, with some new members signing on and others signing off. They went through three cooks and three engineers, and tension was high among the crew. The crew members who had refused to work on the previous voyage "continued to sit, looking morose" [1] and doing nothing until Mike obtained money to pay them off. According to Patch, "Mike managed to keep everyone fed by getting a job with the boatyard to design a concrete fishing boat." [5] When the bankers finally came through with the money to pay the dockyard, the ship was made ready to make sail for Plymouth, England.

With 19 crew members, including Mike and Patch, *Regina Maris* set sail on March 19, with fresh food stores and full water and fuel tanks. In Mike's words, "It was a wonderful relief being out at sea, away from the nerve-racking business of having enough money to feed people and pay the bills." [1]

By midnight they had all sail set and were making 6 knots passing Morant Point, on the east end of Jamaica. For the next 10 days, with a steady breeze, they tacked ship every four hours at the change of watches, sailing between 345 and 110 degrees. According to the log book, at midnight on March 31, they passed the 1,500-mile point, averaging 5.23 knots. The wind force was 8 and they were making 6.5 to 7 knots under reduced sail, with water shipping forward, in lightning and squalls.

Another log entry stated, "April 1st, Rough sea, heavy westerly swell, taking water on deck. Wind force 5/6 under full sail. Thunder and lightning at mid-night so took in the royal and topgallant and main and mizzen topsails but rain came without much increase in wind never more than 8. By dawn under full sail again."

This slightly water-damaged photo was taken by *Mike Willoughby* during the Atlantic crossing of March-April 1974.

By April 8, the ship had passed the 2,500-mile point, averaging 5.16 knots. They set the starboard stuns'ls on April 12 and the port stuns'ls on the 13th, passing the 3,000-mile mark at that time. The log entry for April 21 states, "Passed 4,000-miles. Running short of vegetables and certain other food stuffs. Diet very limited by contents of the freezers and store room."

They sighted Lizard Head, the southernmost point in England, at noon April 26 at a distance of 10 miles and spent the next two days tacking on and off the land against force 5 easterly winds, making little progress. They did not have enough fuel to get into Plymouth under power against the head sea and wind, so they toughed it out for two more days. Eventually, on April 28, they arrived in Plymouth and passed through the locks and into Millbay with a line ashore at the North Quay. The voyage was complete, totaling 4,811 miles at an average speed of 5.13 knots in 40 days.

Mike arranged with the Sail Training Association for *Regina* to take part in the 1974 Tall Ships race from La Coruna, Spain, to St. Malo, France. He had not been in this La Coruna since 1960, when he had taken *Te Vega* there after losing his bowsprit in a force 11 gale in the Bay of Biscay.

It took the months of May and June to get the ship ready to sail again. At the Denton Shipyard on the Thames, the poopdeck was re-calked and a new Deca Navigator Mark 21 radar system was installed, as well as a new VHF radio telephone. The 2-71 generator was overhauled and the windlass hydraulic system was serviced. The ship was re-surveyed by Lloyd's, and the suggested additional repairs were made. A new flax foresail and flying jib were delivered.

As the 16 sail training students, age 14 and above, arrived on July 11, they were put to work cleaning everything on the ship from stem to stern. The sail training program started on July 12, with the captain's and two mates' talk with the cadets, followed by training in basic sail handling. The water tanks were filled and 4,000 gallons of fuel were taken on, as well as provisions for the voyage. Two separate log books were kept for this voyage, one by the paid ship's crew and one by the trainees. There are decided differences between the two, with personal comments, unique handwriting styles, and creative spelling by the trainees.

All plain sail was set on July 14. The wind force was 7 to 8 knots, providing a real challenge for the trainees on their first day out. In the channel, seas were heavy and visibility poor. When the mizzen peak parted, it was taken down, along with the mizzen sail. Mike felt that the ship sailed better with no sail set on the mizzen mast.

In fact, after the long voyage from Panama across the Atlantic, Mike felt more strongly than ever that *Regina Maris* should be a brig. In an unpublished memoir sent to the author in 1996, he stated, "I am fairly certain that the Norwegian yard rigged her as a barquentine without any reference to the vital CE/CP characteristics they were building into her. She is not a good sailing vessel as a barquentine as the CE is always too far aft if any sail is set on the mizzen and in strong winds the main sheets need to be slackened off far too much in order to get the CE forward. As a brig the mainmast can be positioned to produce a good balance under full sail in all wind strengths. As a brig with a longer bowsprit she will go like the proverbial clappers, and come into her own as a sailing ship." [1] For more information on CE/CP characteristics, see endnote 6.

In the same memoir, Mike also said he felt that the wheelhouse should be removed, as it had the effect of pushing her head around up into the wind when it was blowing hard. He felt that most of the conversion could be made with the existing timber. He just needed the money and the time — but he never could amass sufficient funds. He made an additional comment in his letter of November 18, 1996, that is interesting: "The Norwegian riggers had no say in the hull lines, which are as near perfect as on any ship I have ever been to sea on. I never saw green sea on board however hard it was blowing."

On July 16, as they neared Royal Sovereign Light Vessel, two female trainees asked to be put ashore. Like many of the trainees, they were suffering from sea sickness, but they were told it was quite impossible for them to be put ashore. The next day, with the ship near Les Casquets, France, the same two girls again pleaded to be set ashore. The captain gave them the same answer. The wind force lessened and the next five days at sea saw a practice fire drill and lots of setting and furling of the square sails to practice for the upcoming race.

In heavy rain squalls on July 22, the girls' watch shortened sail to slow down the ship's approach to La Coruna. Two girls then went out on the royal yard to put the gaskets, and four girls went out on the topgallant yard. The whole process took them nearly an hour in horrible weather but they did it. When the job had been completed, Mike looked into the mess room to tell them they had done a good job and found that the two girls who had been on the royal were the very same two who had wanted to be put ashore. In his 1998 letter, he recalls, "When they eventually left the ship the same two gave me thanks for everything they had learned on board, and special thanks for the self-esteem they had acquired from working aloft." [1]

John Blowers, who had served as bo'sun on *Regina* since Mexico, recalled in an email to the author that during the Tall Ships race, "one watch was made up of all young women in their 20s and they had the six-berth cabin and often moaned that they had no privacy. The day after we reached La Coruna, the *Malcolm Miller* came into port and the women all wanted to look at the beautiful modern ship. After being showed around the ship and seeing the trainees' quarters with 36 bunks and hammocks they couldn't wait to return to *Regina* and their beautiful cabin." [7]

The ship anchored in La Coruna harbor on July 23. Shore leave was granted by watch, and everyone had a fine time in the three days there. On the morning of July 26, a water barge topped off the tanks, and the race started at noon. They weighed anchor and set off for St. Malo under full sail. A BBC film team that was to cover the voyage had been delayed and had to hire a boat to chase after and join them as they were leaving the harbor.

On the evening of July 27, they sighted and passed two right whales. *Regina's* crew momentarily lost their focus on the race, and the school ship *Royalist* drew ahead and disappeared into the darkness.

On August 3, *Regina Maris* finished the race and tied up alongside the St. Malo dock. The rise and fall of the tide there is 45 feet and the dock is equipped to handle that change, but late arrivals had to raft up to *Regina's* starboard. The 115-foot school ship/mega-yacht *Astral* tied up first, then the Bermudan ketch *Halcyon,* 95 feet with bowsprit, tied up to *Astral*. On August 6, *Eendracht,* a 117-foot steel schooner, finished the race and tied up to *Halcyon's* starboard. This made a four-ship raft and meant that anyone wishing to go ashore or come back aboard had to cross the other ships. This kept the trainees on *Regina Maris* busy checking every one coming and going and made for a noisy and fun time, with the cadets meeting many other trainees from different countries.

When it came time to leave St. Malo on August 8, the wind was out of the north, which made sailing difficult, and the channel crossing required a long series of tacks. *Regina Maris* arrived in Portsmouth after most of the celebrations on the other English ships were over. *Regina*'s crew and trainees had their own party, and all trainees went off to their homes by August 10, 1974.

On August 15, 1974, *Regina* sailed to the Campers and Nicholsons yard in Southampton, where Mike had arranged to have the generator on the main engine and the 2-71 auxiliary generator repaired and to see if the consistent leak from the stem could be found. The ship was tied up to the shipyard's dock in the River Itchen at Shamrock Quay, William Street, Northam, Southampton. The crew was put to work cleaning and drying all the sails, and the next day the sails and all their gear were sent ashore for storage. The ship was cleaned and all unused provisions were removed. The crew signed off and the log book for August 16 says "ship out of commission."

At this time, two notable crew members who had served on *Regina* from Ensenada until the end of the Tall Ships race left the ship for other pursuits.

John Blowers, the bo'sun, was one of Mike's stalwarts, having served with him on *Winston Churchill*. He went on to have an extensive career serving on many tall ships. He helped restore the former Baltic trader *Aquila Marina* and sailed her from Portsmouth by way of Gibraltar to the Balearic Islands off Spain and on to Villefrance sur Mer, near Nice. In a Southampton shipyard, he lent his shipyard and sailmaking skills to the bark *Marques;* the museum ship *Kathleen and Mary,* a three tops'l schooner; and the former Baltic traders *I.P. Thorsoe* and *Lindo*. In a London shipyard, he worked on the polar research ship *Discovery*. He then received an offer to become the sailmaker aboard *Sea Cloud* and became bo'sun for her first season in the Caribbean and then when she went back to Germany for a refit. On leaving *Sea Cloud* in 1985, he joined the crew of *Atlantis* for the summer season in the Mediterranean and the winter Caribbean season, then returned to Germany, where he now lives. [7]

John Fisher, who had served as *Regina's* chief mate, also went on to a distinguished maritime career. He sailed on the brigantine *Phoenix* during a transatlantic charter and in 1987 took command of the Jubilee Sailing Trust's bark *Lord Nelson* for 12 years. *Lord Nelson* is a training ship built with the mission of providing disadvantaged people a chance to go to sea and gain nautical skills. Since then John has commanded the other JST bark, *Tenacious,* making her maiden voyage in 2000, and all others until his retirement from JST in 2005. Along the way, he found time to sail as mate on various other sailing vessels, and, in semi-retirement, as relief master on the mainmast barkentine *Pelican of London* before retiring fully in 2010. [8]

With a skeleton crew aboard to watch the ship and do basic maintenance, *Regina* remained at the Campers and Nicholsons yard for a year and a day while legal issues were settled, the necessary work was finally done, and new adventures began to take shape.

CHAPTER 14
NEW OWNERS AND PASSAGES

During Mike's command and ownership, seven logbooks were kept on *Regina*. They are full of the day-to-day workings of the ship — sail settings, compass headings, noon sites, endless work and repair details — and Mike's comments on the crew, both favorable and deplorable. Mike sent the logs to the author and asked that they be used in telling *Regina*'s story. They have been used extensively.

1.   Michael Willoughby, *Regina Maris, Four and a Half Years in the Life of an Old Sailing Vessel*. Unpublished memoir mailed to the author November 18, 1996.
2.   Michael Willoughby, letter to the author, dated November 1, 1996.
3.   Jeremy Brown, letter to the author dated October 27, 2014. Sailmaker Jeremy Brown, who signed on with Mike and *Regina Maris* in Southampton, England, in June 1975, made the following comment related to this chapter: "The sketch of the lower topsail crane in this chapter is puzzling. I think it was raised from the lower mast cap iron in 1974 the yard was swung from the lower mast cap, but supported by a band above, rather than a leg from below. This was why the upper topsail yard didn't lower as close as it should, needing a downhaul as well as sheets and clew lines to keep control of the yards at all times. We did mess around with changing this lash-up at various times, but ran into other complications. The topgallant had been deepened in Southampton, but this made the upper topsail a tough fit, you really had to sheet it home hard, but still the halyard, which was wire, took a beating braced up. I seem to recall the topsail halyard sheave was also below the futtock band. This caused chaffing on the topgallant foot, a problem I only got sorted when we got to Bermuda in '76 by cutting an excessive roach into it. None of these awkwardnesses are apparent in Willoughby's rather tidy profile drawing."
"Most of the sails were still from the Wilson era when I joined in '75, getting old by then — her rig had many awkwardness that were tough on the gear — but [the rig was] extremely well made. The ill-fit of sails on the foremast indicated to me that there had been several changes and repairs to spars, since a sailmaker who made sails that good would have made sure they fit originally."

4.   Tom Maguire, email to the author, October 21, 2014. This email was very helpful in substantiating the seriousness of the engine/prop vibration. Before receiving the email, the author had only heard that the vibration issue had been downplayed by some in the tall ships world along with lawyers for the disgruntled passengers, who claimed, "Mike never intended to go around the Horn; the vibration and oil embargo were just excuses not to go." These disgruntled passengers directed many lawsuits at Mike and Thomas Cook Ltd. travel agency, suits that followed Mike and the ship for years. Now it appears that the vibration was a real problem.

5.   Patch Willoughby, email to the author, October 23, 2014, which provided key information on the radio reception issue.

6.   George Zinger, email to the author, January 17, 2015. George, a naval architect from Shelter Island, New York, wrote, "CE/CP Characteristics refers to the relative positions of the Center of Effort (CE) and the Center of Pressure (CP), also known as the Center of Lateral Resistance (CLR). The CE is the fore and aft location of the center of area of the sail plan and the CP is the fore and aft center of the underwater profile of the hull and its appendages. If the CE is considerably aft of the CP the vessel would tend to turn into the wind like a weather vane. The center of area of the above-water portion of the hull and superstructure can also effect the effective location of the CE."

7.   John Blowers, email to the author, December 11, 2014.

8.   Jenni Atkinson, writing about the Mariners International 2011 annual dinner, held October 29, 2011, at which Captain John Fisher was guest speaker. Article published on the website, www.marinersinternational.org.

CHAPTER 15
SOUTHAMPTON TO THE BLACK SEA
1974 – 1976

While in Southampton on a cold winter morning in early 1975, the famous Polish film director Andrzej Wajda walked down the jetty and, upon seeing *Regina Maris*, said, "Fantastic, fantastic, exactly what I want!"

Mike Willoughby reported this incident in a 1978 article in *Sea Breezes*. [1] Wajda was looking for a square rigger to use in a movie of Joseph Conrad's story "The Shadow Line," which he was making with Thames Television. At that time, *Regina* was the only British-registered square-rigged sailing vessel available for charter, and, at Wajda's request, Thames Television contacted Mike. After seven months of negotiations with Thames and the Polish National Film Corporation, an agreement was at last signed to charter *Regina* for a period of seven weeks, beginning after her arrival in Varna, Bulgaria.

Patch Willoughby remembered that "the original plan with Thames TV/Film Polski was for filming to be done in the Baltic — it had to be a 'soft currency' area — but the discussions took so long, (this was the height of the cold war) we missed the weather and had to trek to the Black Sea." [2]

Apart from the drawn-out negotiating process, the only other action on *Regina* during this time was a fight between two men aboard visiting Tom Maguire, who had been serving as third mate and sailmaker since joining the ship in Ensenada. One participant, Tom said in a 2014 email to the author, had the other pinned against the wall. "…with his hand, he searches the table and finds a table knife and gouges it into the other's eye. Well, not as bad as it sounds. The knife got the skin around the eye. Anyway, he goes to the hospital, it gets reported to the police."[3]

The fight, Mike reported in his *Sea Breezes* article, "resulted in the culprit and myself appearing in Southampton Magistrates Court. The verdict was a severe warning not to repeat the use of a knife in any future arguments; the case was then dismissed."[1]

Another court issue arose with a ruling on July 4, 1975. The ship's creditors had sued Mike and, according to The Times of London, "the Admiralty Court yesterday granted an order that the tall ship, Regina Maris, be appraised and sold by the Admiralty marshal to pay a debt." [4] After stalling until he received a partial payment from the film companies, Mike was able to pay the creditors, and the sale of the ship was canceled.

After the bill was paid, a complete survey was conducted by Lloyd's, and the Campers and Nicholsons yard started the work in late July. A great deal of planking was removed due to rot and replaced, then re-covered with the copper sheathing. Timbers in the stem were replaced as well.

During the refit, David Marks, a new deckhand, recalled in a 2014 email to the author: "Tom [Maguire] was such a natural leader and very knowledgeable about all aspects of RM. I can still remember Tom walking through the cabins in the morning during the refit, waking us up with an egg in his hand telling us to set a good eggxample and get up and be eggcited about the day." [5]

During the refit at the Campers and Nicholsons yard in Southampton, *Photo by David Marks*

    With the work completed and a new crew aboard, the ship was made ready for sea and left the shipyard's #23 berth at 6 p.m. August 18, 1975. By 8:40 all plain sail were set and she was at sea once again, bound for Varna, Bulgaria, on the Black Sea, and a new adventure in movie-making.

    On August 20, a fire was discovered in the aft peak, caused by the auxiliary engine. The log stated, "The heat from the exhaust started the paneling in the Saloon smoldering, smoke but no flame, dealt with buckets of sea water." Their course was altered to Falmouth to make repairs. Patch recalled, "When we left Camper and Nicholsons in Southampton en route to the Black Sea the ship started to stink of fuel and we discovered that the fuel tank tops had not been secured. Diesel was sloshing everywhere. There wasn't time to do much about it in Falmouth where we had to wait for the Camper and Nicholsons representative to inspect the ship, as it was their fault." [2]

    The repair was completed on August 23 and they again set out to sea. However, they found that the work had not been done satisfactorily, and the ship returned to the anchorage for further repairs. *Regina's* engineer signed off and left the ship soon after anchoring. Finding a replacement became a problem — prospective applicants would take a look down into the engine room and leave. Finally a new engineer was found and on August 31 the ship was once again at sea.

Their troubles, however, were still not over. Once they were underway it became apparent that the work done to fix the leak had not been successful. The pumps had to be manned, and many log entries include measurements of bilge levels. After quite a few days spent trying to pinpoint the leak, the crew discovered it was coming from the port cable/chain locker. Once that area was calked and the leak was down to a trickle, they found another leak on the starboard side of the stem. Pumping manually 15 minutes every watch kept the levels in the bilge even. On September 3, the crew brought all the anchor chain from the starboard locker up and flaked it out on deck. Calking was packed into the leaking areas. The chain was re-stowed and the leak was slowed.

The ship called at Gibraltar on September 7 to take on water and fuel oil. According to the log book, while the ship was in the harbor, the bilges were dry, but a diver was hired to look for a leak in the stem area, below the waterline. In order to raise the bow out of the water, all the chain from both anchors was put on the bottom of the bay. Open seams were found and calked, and no sound of water entering the hull could be heard. With a dry bilge, they set sail for Varna on September 10.

While the ship was still in Gibraltar, Patch recalled, "the Royal Navy lent us a Navigator as 2nd mate to replace David Reynolds, who we had to send home with a tooth abscess. This Navy chap, Cameron Femie, had been in command of a minesweeper — but couldn't take a noon sight, much to Mike's horror. To have a serving British Naval officer on board, on a trip to Varna, home of the Russian Navy's Black Sea fleet was a brave move, but we got away with it. And the officer learned how to take his noon sight."[2]

Regina proceeded under power for four days, as there was little wind and the temperature hovered around 80 degrees. A great deal of ship traffic changed course to inspect *Regina Maris,* and many photos were taken by their crews and tourists. It was very calm and hot, so swimming was in order. Captain Mike sent seaman David Marks up to the topgallant yard arm to watch for sharks. Mike spotted him looking at the sky and paying little attention to the sea surrounding the swimmers, so, in his best captain's voice, he shouted, "Marks!"

The panic of the swimmers "was quite something to behold, in about five seconds they were all scrambling up the shipside and on board, lying breathless on the deck feeling they had escaped sudden death. It is surprising how the name *Marks* can resemble *sharks* to swimmers," Mike commented in a 1996 letter to the author. [6]

On September 15, when they were south of Sardinia, the wind came up and the heavy weather (force 7 to 9 winds) opened a leak in the forefoot. The ship made for Cagliari, Sardinia, for repairs. The main generator was also giving them problems. Mike remembers that while in the Cagliari harbor, there was a "southeast wind and with it came red desert dust which produced wonderful sky effects as the sun went down."[1]

Mike contacted Thames TV, who informed him that filming had to begin soon. Weather reports, however, forecast head winds in the Mediterranean, which would make for a long sail, and therefore, *Regina* would be towed by tug to Varna. The ship sailed on September 20 and met the tug east of Sicily on the 22nd. It was a Greek vessel, *Pirana II*, built in 1930, with a vertical stem. "We did not feel out of place being towed by that splendid little vessel," Patch recalled. [2] *Regina Maris* was towed for 897 miles through the Aegean Sea, the Sea of Marmara, and the Bosphorus to Varna, Bulgaria.

The log book had little to say about the towing, but in a 1996 letter to the author, Mike recounted an event that occurred as they approached the bridge across the Bosphorus at Istanbul. The crew asked to go aloft to enjoy the view from 130 feet above the deck. About twenty of them climbed up to the fore royal yard. "As we got nearer, first one came down the mast, and then another and finally the rest scuttled down as though the devil was after them. The clearance under the bridge is 230 feet and as we neared the bridge they thought I had made a mistake of 100 feet and we were going to lose our masts, and they had no intention of coming down with them. This is a very disconcerting optical illusion that can be most alarming when going under a bridge with a clearance of only a few feet."[6]

Once they arrived in Varna September 29 and tied up at the dock, an armed guard was assigned so no one could board or leave the ship. After the first day they had to anchor in the exposed bay rather than at the protected dock area, and they experienced no end of trouble with Bulgarian immigration and customs officials and police. The crew had surrendered all their passports and the ship's documents upon their arrival, but it was four days before they were given entry clearance. In this police state, the use of a radio telephone was strictly controlled, and try as they might, they could not talk with the movie people on the dock except by sign language.

When they finally received clearance to enter, they sailed up the coast to Baljik, using charts that showed many prohibited areas, including two large underwater mine fields. Mike states, "I doubted that they were real and hoped they were marked on the chart to keep us within sight of the Coastguardsmen ashore, and to keep hostile vessels operating well off shore, but the wind being north it meant my sailing on short tacks or encroaching on the minefield areas, which I am afraid I was forced to do once or twice."[6]

Patch recalled that they learned "the mine field we were sent to was a real one. We discovered this when the Pilot vessel refused to come alongside, saying that as a wooden vessel we were OK. They hadn't thought about our copper sheath." [2] *Regina* has often been referred to as a lucky ship. Once again her luck held.

Once in Baljik, the crew finally met the Thames and Polish film production personnel, including the actors, makeup, wardrobe, film crew and prop men. Representing Thames TV were Jolyon Wymhurst, director; Udi Eichler, assistant director; Mike Darlow, producer; and David Naden, film editor. The Polish National Film

Corporation crew included Andrzej Wajda, chief director; Wijtola Sobolinski, camera director; Bolym Wieslaw, chairman of the Polish National Film Corporation; and the actors Bernard Archard as Captain Elis, Marek Kondrat as Joseph Conrad, Stanislaw Tym as Jacobs, Graham Lines as Burns, Tom Wilkinson as Ransom, and John Bennett. [7]

The *Regina* crew's first task was to remove anything that was twentieth century from the ship or disguise it in some way. Deck lights, electrical cables, radar scanner, aerials, hydraulic pump — all had to disappear for the camera's eye. They used extra sails and studding sail yards as camouflage. Some equipment, such as the extra oil and grease drums and the 25-man life raft, had to be stored ashore for the duration of the filming. The ship's name on the stern and on the lifeboats and life rings all had to be changed.

Filming started October 4, with most done at the dock or with *Regina* sailing in the bay. The ship was filmed going out to sea, returning, setting sail, furling sail, and anchoring, all, Patch remembered, with "interminable cups of coffee, tea, hot soup, lighting cables, cameras, actors, costumes, seasickness, and above all, the calm driving force of Andrzej Wajda making a film. 'Camera, action…cut.' " [2]

The movie set in Bulgaria where a dock in the small port of Baljik, was transformed to resemble Bangkok. *Polish National Film Corporation photo.*

The weather was stormy, with blowing rain that was perfect for the film, although if the intensity of the storm was too great, there would be no filming. There were night sequences for which a large generator had to be hidden on deck to support the extra power demands of the lights and cameras. There was also a set built at the dock depicting Bangkok, where Joseph Conrad joined his ship, and for the ending of the movie, the set was modified to become Singapore. Baljik's modern concrete pier, passenger ship terminal, and cargo complex were transformed into outdoor markets and shops with sampans at the dock. Truckloads of earth, straw, trees, and flowers covered the concrete. Hundreds of Vietnamese refugees became Siamese merchants, boatmen, and coolies selling vegetables and fruit or guiding their flocks and driving carts. [1]

On days without filming, when it was stormy or major set changes were being made, unnecessary crew would spend time in the only bar in Baljik, having their pockets drained. Mike wrote, "Once a week the local Commissars met in a large room below a balcony where I and a few of the crew drank beer. They sat around a long table consuming vast quantities of beer and sandwiches while dealing with the problems of running the town. We watched the proceedings with great interest as occasionally the discussions became acrimonious, but to our disappointment they never came to blows." [1]

During the filming of Joseph Conrad's story *The Shadow Line*. Photo by David Marks.

Near the end of the month, a large ocean-going tug came into the harbor. Mike was told that the film crew was going take the tug and film *Regina Maris* sailing to Varna. On the day of the filming, the wind was northerly at force 7, ideal for scenes showing the ship, wild wind, and heavy seas. The tug waited for *Regina* to set her sails, but Mike waited for the tug to head out to sea because he knew that with all sail set the ship would leave the tug in her wake. This was explained to the tug captain, who insisted that Mike set sail immediately. He did, and *Regina Maris* took off at 12 knots. The scene called for no one on deck except for the actor playing the helmsman, dressed in period garb. Mike and the rest of the crew were hiding below decks. After half an hour, Mike looked and saw that the tug was two miles astern and pounding badly. Relieving the actor helmsman, he put the helm over, and the tug caught up. Another attempt was made, with the tug struggling to keep up and some very seasick cameramen trying to film the ship. The wind increased to force 9 by the time they reached Varna and docking was difficult, but by midnight they were secured. [3]

Mike recalled, "The English and Polish actors, the film crew and our crew all became great friends and our mess room took on a very special atmosphere, with schools of chess, ludo, Mastermind, Monopoly, and cards. The film artists were drawing the players and [there was] one delightful Pole playing a guitar and singing plaintive Russian and Polish folk songs." [1]

Socially the language problem was nonexistent, Mike felt. It was, however, a real problem during the filming and with the officials. He recounted one instance when the ship had a generator failure, and repairing it took a Bulgarian electrician, a Russian who spoke Bulgarian, a Polish man who spoke Russian, and a Polish lady who spoke French to Mike's wife Patch, who spoke French and relayed the translated information to *Regina's* British engineer. Despite the complicated technical translations, the generator was fixed.

After a wonderful farewell party when the filming finished on October 30, *Regina's* crew made the ship ready for sea, reversing the camouflage treatment and retrieving the stored items, filling all tanks with fuel and water, and stocking up on stores. Getting clearance to leave became a problem when the immigration officer could not find the ship's papers or the crew's passports. The authorities mustered all the crew on deck and conducted a complete search of the ship for contraband or stowaways. The Bulgarian official who had taken the missing documents was on vacation and had to be traced down to determine where he had placed them. The whole process took hours, and not until the authorities used an axe to break into the desk where the documents had been secured were the papers finally retrieved. Ten minutes after they got the documents back, *Regina* was off, heading for the Bosphorus. After three days of sailing, they dropped anchor outside the harbor of Piraeus, Greece.

On November 7, 1975, the ship was moved and moored stern-to in the yacht basin of Zeas Marina, with the gangplank over the stern rail for easy access. For the next two months, the crew worked every day on the ship, repairing and cleaning, sanding and varnishing. The sails were cleaned, dried, and stowed away. The plan was to use the ship as a charter scuba expedition vessel, but by the New Year those plans had fallen through.

Mike paid off the crew, some of whom, like Tom Maguire, had been on board since Mike had taken over the ship in Mexico. Tom had also been on *Regina* during the hurricane trip in the Pacific in May of 1972 Don Ward, a seaman who had joined the ship in Jamaica, was also a long-timer. Sailmaker Jeremy Brown had joined *Regina* in early July 1975, when she was in Southampton, and would stay on until June 1977, when the ship was under new ownership in Boston. David Marks had joined in May 1972 and would stay until March 1976. Of course, Mike's wife Patch was with him for the entire adventure, which came to an end on March 15, 1976, when Mike sold the ship to George Nichols, a prominent Boston medical researcher and sailor. As Mike said in his *Sea Breezes* article, "The responsibility for the ship was fatiguing."

Her price was 85,000 pounds sterling. Mike and Patch bought a van for 100 pounds and drove it across Europe to England, having a wonderful time, according to Mike in a 1997 email to the author. He sold the van for 150 pounds on arriving home in England. [8]

In a 2013 email to the author, Jeremy Brown summed up his experience sailing on *Regina*. He also answered a question about Mike's decision to cancel the Horn rounding and go to Panama instead: "The Willoughby era was, even more than others, painfully underfunded. So I have no doubt that getting her back to the UK before [the oil embargo] and things really fell apart would have been a driver in Willoughby's mind." [9]

Jeremy continued, "The Black Sea trip was much the same, with the added complication of the two film/TV companies, each with somewhat different agenda, and no doubt all sorts of misunderstandings about who paid for what. Willoughby seemed to have a number of backers who drifted in and out of the picture — I don't think he had much resources of his own — and the ship was still being haunted by various claims and liens, going back to the hurricane incident. I was not privy to the sales negotiations, although it was quite clear before, during, and after that Willoughby and Nichols did not get along and had quite conflicting styles." [9]

He went on to state, "Willoughby was a submariner, quite 'old school Navy.' Nichols brought his New England patrician airs, and the assumptions that Europeans find so arrogant in some Americans that just because of who they are, they can do whatever they set their hearts to. In my humble opinion neither was a natural sailing ship man."

Comparing the two captains, Jeremy wrote, "Willoughby managed by strength of will, he was happy to sail when conditions permitted, but just as happy to motor, or, as happened on our muddled progress to the Black Sea, accept a tow. By contrast I think Nichols had a very strong image of the sailing captain he thought he was, and did a good job of acting it out. But in my time with him [Nichols], it was Tom Maguire who provided the core leadership and kept things going."[9]

In a side note about the ship, Jeremy stated, "The beginning of the end for *Regina* occurred; I am convinced, when she was hauled in Gloucester in '76. Whilst up on the ways with just bilge chocks, the surveyor had all the rigging slacked off to inspect/replace lower ends. She was never the same after that." [9]

Nevertheless, *Regina* had more years of sailing ahead of her, and the many crew members who had gotten her to this point themselves went on to new adventures.

Mike Willoughby, after selling *Regina Maris*, had an extensive career that included the following activities and more. He surveyed and designed rigs of various vessels for the Maritime Trust and other organizations, including the sailing vessel, *Kathleen and May,* a complete rebuild. He designed the rigs for the bark *Gannet,* the full-rigged ship *Warrior*, and the topsail schooners *Pascel Flores, Result,* and *Captain Scott*, as well as *Astrid,* a brig, and the schooner *Dodi*.

He became a rig consultant to both the Russian and the Japanese navies for their sail training ships. The owners of the full-rigged ship *Christian Radich* hired him as a consultant for the ship's rig design. His design was used for a Norwegian galeas that is now a museum ship. (A galeas, in Norway, is a heavy, cargo-carrying ketch.) Michael designed a five-masted full-rigger *Windrose* for the Australian Wool Corporation, which was never built, and a 2500-ton, 210-foot tall skysail bark for the Renaissance Trust, which was completed in 1997.

Also in 1997, Michael wrote and published the book, *Square Rig Seamanship, for Masters, Mates and Crew*. He was also the new construction surveyor for three Burness-Corlett 600-ton vessels built in Norway and Italy in 1998. In that year he was also hired to engineer and design the rig for *Stavros S Niarchos* and *Prince William,* which were completed in 2000.

Late in Mike's life, painting marine scenes, mostly ships, became his passion, and he achieved great success, with his works shown and purchased for substantial amounts by maritime museums. At age 85, he took on the project of restoring a centuries-old barn into a new home.

Michael Willoughby's obituary follows, as it appeared in the "Crossing the Bar" section of *The Cape Horner Journal,* the newsletter of the Amicale Internationale des Capitaines au Long Cours Cap Horniers (AICH). It was written by journal editor Chris Roche.

"Mike has died aged 96 years on the 29th November 2008; Mike was a Naval Architect of some stature with a love of sailing ships. When he proposed a design for a new sail and rig plan for *Windrose,* a sail liner project, he could only get funding for the design of a vessel along traditional lines as in what we already know works. The project fell by the wayside. I was with Tiger Timbs and *Eye of the Wind* when refitting in dry-dock at Tommy Nielsen's yard Gloucester. One evening the centre of the town was closed off to let low loaders through. These were carrying the masts and yards for *Stavros S Niarchos*. We watched as they were craned over the walls and into the sheds for finishing by Tommy. The wire rigging had all been specified to be 'wormed parceled and served' in the old way of the Cape Horner's. Mike was the managing Architect for that job. Mike had been in poor health these last few years I had a letter from his wife Claire saying that they had eighteen wonderful years together, he had legs lungs and memory problems but still smoked and they could have plenty of laughs together. It was Mike's wish to be buried at sea, and that has been arranged. Mike came to the presentation at which the Cape Horner's gave a Cape Horn Medal to the *Kruzenshtern,* the Russian 4 mast barque at Southampton. I remember him hating the angular shape of the enclosed bridge, it looked so 'motor ship and ugly,' he said." [10]

Jeremy Brown continued his interest in sailmaking aboard *Our Syanen*, now *Pacific Swan*. He married Jill, who had also served on *Regina,* leaving the ship in 1977, and then fished in Alaska. She and Jeremy joined the crew of the tall ship *Sea Cloud* in 1980-81 and again in 1984-85*,* Jill as OS, AB, and sailmaker, Jeremy as sailmaker, bo'sun and sometime third mate. Jeremy went north to fish in 1982. In 1985, he and Jill bought their first troller ("It is a method of hook and line fishing that baffles the more pedestrian," he says) and fished together until 1992. Jill then stayed ashore, first with an oil-spill response company, then getting qualified as an acupuncturist and herbalist. Fishing has taken Jeremy from the Bering Sea to the Southern Ocean, although he now stays on the West Coast and Gulf of Alaska. [9]

Deckhand **David Marks**, after the filming of the movie in Bulgaria, returned home to Jersey, Channel Islands, and worked on the local hydrofoil ferry service between the Channel Islands and St. Malo, France. He then emigrated to Australia in 1979, where he now works in the geotechnical engineering field, and is married, with four children, two grandchildren, and a dog named Cadbury. David visited the United States in 2013 for the *Regina Maris* reunion. [5]

Tom Maguire, the sailmaker and sometimes third mate who had been with *Regina* since Ensenada, stayed on after her sale to George Nichols and sailed under him to Boston. He continued a life at sea by signing on in San Diego with the three-masted schooner *California,* which in his words, "someone stuck yards on and called it a barquentine." [3]

His next ship was the three-masted Baltic Trader *Sophia,* where, as he says, "I got the Captain's' job on that 'hippy dippy ship,'" which had just finished a round-the-world trip. Evan Logan was also on board at the time. Tom also sailed on *America* with Captain John Guthrie. After that voyage, John offered him the bo'sun's job on his yacht. Tom flew to the Seychelles and joined *Dwyn Win,* a gorgeous two-master. "But after a while," Tom states, "that too wasn't what I was looking for so I wrote off to the Germans in Kiel, who had just bought *Sea Cloud.* I got their address from a mate I met on the dock in Martinique." [3]

Tom joined the *Sea Cloud* crew as second mate and stayed for eight years. After four years, he received a new license and sailed as chief mate. Luckily for Tom, on the license the inspector had written, "also 2nd mate, steam and motor vessels upon oceans."

So when his girlfriend became his wife and he needed to make real money, he got into the U.S. Merchant Marine. He started on bulkers as second mate, got a chief mate's license and sailed as chief mate until August of 2005, then went to a brand new ship, the *Alliance New York*, a car carrier. The ship's name later changed to, *Prestige New York*, and has now gone back to the Norwegian flag and her original name, *Hoegh New York*. Tom is now officially retired and, "for some strange reason, I don't miss any of it." [3]

In 1976, *Regina Maris,* with George Nichols, a serious sailor and researcher, in command, set off for yet another incarnation, this time as a research vessel traveling the world to explore the complexities and beauties of cetaceans and their environments.

CHAPTER 15
SOUTHAMPTON TO THE BLACK SEA

1. Michael Willoughby, "*Regina Maris* in the Black Sea," *Sea Breezes*, January 1978.
2. Patch Willoughby, email to the author, October 23, 2014.
3. Tom Maguire, email to the author, October 21, 2014.
4. The Times of London, Court Rulings, July 4, 1975, pp. 4-8.
5. David Marks, email to the author, October 22, 2014. David also provided ideas and memories at the 2013 *Regina Maris*.
6. Michael Willoughby, letter to the author, dated December 28, 1996.
7. Thames TV, Freemantle Archive sales, 1 Stephen St. London, UK Ref# 1163.
8. Michael Willoughby, letter to the author dated April 18, 1997.
9. Jeremy Brown, email to the author, October 20, 2014. Jeremy also provided ideas and memories at the 2013 *Regina Maris* reunion.
10. Chris Roche, journal editor, "Crossing the Bar" section, *The Cape Horner Journal*, the newsletter of the Amicale Internationale des Capitaines au Long Cours Cap Horniers (AICH). November 2008.

CHAPTER 16
THE ORES YEARS BEGIN
1976

November 1974, George Nichols was in Southampton, England, searching for a ship to serve as an oceanographic research vessel. He and Peter Seamans had gone to the Campers and Nicholsons yard to inspect the schooner *America*. In *Whalewatcher,* the journal of the American Cetacean Society, which dedicated its entire summer 1988 edition to *Regina Maris,* George recalled his first encounter with the ship, in the yard for repairs between the STA race and the Black Sea movie adventure. He wrote, "It was not really until we were walking under *Regina's* bowsprit back to the car that I realized that this was the barkentine whose picture had appeared in so many brokers' ads. Curious about whatever inspired anyone to own such a ship; I asked if we could visit. Stepping aboard was to step back in time. On deck everything was massive workboat, from the windless to the spars towering up into the darkness. Below we walked into Victorian elegance gone to damp, mold and decay. The engine room was a jumble of rusty, partly torn-down machinery. The whole impression was 'disaster' and neglect. How was I to know that I would sail her for eight years?" [1]

While George was making his first visit to the ship, Mike Willoughby was busy negotiating the film contract and dodging creditors. George continued his search for a suitable research platform; it took him many other ships and ten months to realize that *Regina Maris* was, as he said in the same article, "nearer to the working vessel we were looking for, for our whale research and teaching, than anything else I had seen. High bulwarks, plenty of bunks and lots of room on deck to handle the oceanographic gear we planned to use were appealing enough to warrant a low offer, provided she passed a survey and was indeed put back into working order." [1]

George said later in the same article, "Her rig, her age, and her rather lurid past all frightened us, but she was all that was available that fitted our needs and that we could afford." [1]

Regina had been put up for sale in Piraeus, Greece, and it was there that George and Mike agreed on a price of $170,000 and completed the purchase on March 15, 1976. Then George; his wife, Ann, and a volunteer crew sailed *Regina* from Piraeus across the Mediterranean to the Canary Islands. George stated in the *Whalewatcher* interview, "Before that none of us had ever sailed a square-rigger ..." [1] This statement seems hard to believe since George became a renowned tall-ship master. His sailing experience had started long before and his family's sailing heritage preceded the *Regina Maris* purchase.

George Nichols Jr. was born in Manhattan, New York, in 1923 to Jane Norton Morgan, daughter of John Pierpont Morgan Jr., and George Nichols. Both the Morgan and Nichols families had a multigenerational history of yachting and yacht racing. George Sr., along with his father-in-law, J.P. Morgan Jr., Cornelius Vanderbilt, Arthur Curtiss James, George T. Bowdoin, Henry Walters, and Gerard Lambert — a group known as the Morgan Syndicate — built the J-Class yacht *Weetamoe* for the America's

Cup in 1930. George Nichols Sr. was the skipper and sailed her in the defender trials of 1930 and 1934.

George Jr.'s father taught him to sail on Long Island Sound at the family's summer home on Long Island's north shore. After graduating from Harvard University, young George attended medical school at Columbia University and completed a year of post-graduate work at Harvard Medical School in Boston. During the war he did research on Navy divers and became fascinated by cetaceans' breath-holding abilities, according to a 1993 profile in *Whalewatcher* by Sherryl Taylor. [2] After the war, he obtained a teaching position in biochemistry at Harvard Medical School, and later he became dean of academic affairs and eventually secretary of the Faculty of Medicine. He practiced at the Peter Bent Brigham, New England Deaconess, and Cambridge hospitals; served as chief of medicine at Cambridge City Hospital; and was director of the Cancer Research Institute in Boston. He published many cancer research papers concerning bone marrow extracts and diagnosis. Sherryl Taylor's profile noted that "George became disillusioned by the 'politics of academia' and made a remarkable decision: He left medicine and set out on the path that led him to Gloucester Harbor and *Regina Maris*." [2] George wanted to combine his research skills, love of sailing and fascination with cetaceans into an educational program. This desire eventually led him to Corwith Cramer.

In 1969, Corwith Cramer, with his friend Edward "Sandy" MacArthur, had developed the Sailing Education Association (SEA.) A partnership was formed, though MacArthur supplied most of the money. "As the official name implied, the organization's concept was to operate a deep-sea sail training ship that would serve an association of educational institutions that could not individually afford a deep-sea vessel …. We didn't want to teach people how to sail," said Cramer. "What we wanted to do was to take them to sea so they would learn to love the sea." [3]

The two partners bought the schooner *Westward,* and George Nichols joined the organization's board of directors. Within a year, Cramer and MacArthur disagreed about how SEA should be organized, so MacArthur withdrew his funding. George Nichols assumed the organization's debt for the *Westward* purchase.

On New Year's Day 1972, fifteen high school and ten college students arrived in San Diego to get on *Westward* for SEA's first voyage. Describing this inaugural excursion, Lucy Helfrich, author of SEA's official history, stated, "The President of the Board, Dr. George Nichols, [and] the publisher of *SAIL* Magazine, Bernard Goldhirsch, also sailed during a portion of the first trip. All 24 bunks were filled. Their voyage was a fascinating one. *Westward* and her students sailed from San Diego, down the coast of Mexico, offshore, stopping at some of the remote islands off the Mexican coast, to the Galapagos and the Cocos Islands and then through the Panama Canal, ending in San Juan, Puerto Rico. The last leg was a hard trek, 1,000 miles straight upwind into the Trades. The students disembarked after nine weeks, having had the adventure of a lifetime."[3]

Near the end of 1974, according to Lucy Helfrich, "Cory Cramer and George Nichols, who headed the board, came to an irreconcilable difference in the philosophy behind SEA. Nichols wanted the educational program to focus on research; Cramer insisted that SEA's program be a broad, multidisciplinary study of the oceans, with a research component. This dispute became heated to the point where neither Nichols nor Cramer would concede to a compromise. The board settled the issue by siding with Cramer's philosophy, and Nichols promptly resigned from the chairmanship and withdrew his funding of the note on *Westward*." [3] SEA continued on without George's funding, with the help of another board member. Today the organization has two ships and is known as SEA Semester.

By this time George and his wife, Ann, had purchased the schooner *Rambler* and set off to explore the world. According to Sherryl Taylor's 1993 column, George felt, "he missed involvement with people — he guesses he's not quite nomadic enough for exploring as a permanent lifestyle. He returned to Boston and established Ocean Research Education Society or, ORES, a non-profit, educational membership society." [2]

In an interview with Harvey Oxenhorn, included in *Tuning the Rig,* his book about *Regina*, George stated, "Whereas SEA stressed oceanography and introductory education, ORES planned to concentrate on new research." [4]

At this time, the early 1970s, interest was growing worldwide in marine mammals, particularly whales. Their diminishing numbers and increased quotas allowed by the International Whaling Commission (IWC) prompted environmental groups to become active in the preservation of many species. Good science on the lifecycles and habits of whales was lacking, and ORES would attempt to rectify that situation. Harvey Oxenhorn wrote, "By going to where the animals were, the new program could stress original research over more structured education, and by spending most of her time at sea, an oceangoing ship would serve as a platform, 'a crossroads,' where all kinds of people doing all sorts of research could contribute and explore." [4]

Asked to rank his goals for ORES, George said "he would place first-class research and good education together, as 1A and 1B." The Outward Bound-type aspects of the experience would rank "a distant second." [4] George Nichol's scientific goal for the organization was more than realized. Over the years, ORES scientists and student scientists published hundreds of research documents, which can be found by searching in Google Scholar for "R/V Regina Maris whale research."

George Nichols Greenland 1981 by Scott Cordes MD

    The plan for this new organization was to sail their newly purchased oceanographic research vessel *r/v Regina Maris* in the Tall Ships Race of 1976, which came to be known as Operation Sail, or Op Sail. The race started in Plymouth, England, on May 2. But for the *Regina* crew, the first leg was across the Mediterranean to Gibraltar. There they were joined by Exy and Irving Johnson, owners of the brigantine *Yankee,* who had been signed on to fill out the transatlantic crew with additional experienced hands. (The Johnson's voyages and adventures have been documented by the National Geographic Society.)

    Regina Maris and her new owners joined the race for the second leg, from the Canary Islands to Bermuda, on May 23. By June 10, all ships had arrived in Bermuda. The race's last leg, to Newport, Rhode Island, started June 20. The ships began to arrive on June 25, and an inshore regatta with awards given under the auspices of the American Sail Training Association and the Sail Training Association of Great Britain was held June 28 through 30. By July 1, all the ships had left Newport for their designated starting points for the ship parade. Those with masts higher than 125 feet proceeded outside Long Island into the Atlantic to the anchorage off Sandy Hook, N.J. *Regina* was among them. Ships with shorter masts sailed through the "Race" into Long Island Sound and on to the anchorage in Gravesend Bay, Brooklyn.

    Operation Sail 1976 took five years to plan and had more tall ships than the previous event, in 1964. Even the then Soviet Union sent the *Kruzenshtern* as a gesture of international celebration. The parade of ships was to be the centerpiece for the New York area Bicentennial celebration, which included the traditional International Naval Review bringing together an armada of modern war ships.

On the Fourth of July, the two fleets of tall ships met up at the Verrazano-Narrows Bridge and paraded up the Hudson. They were escorted by 60 naval warships from 30 countries and over 200 other historic sailing craft. The river was filled with spectator watercraft as well. The parade passed Liberty Island, Governors Island, and Ellis Island. President Gerald Ford reviewed the parade of sailing ships from the deck of the *USS Forrestal*, which gave a twenty-one-gun salute.

The ships sailed under The George Washington Bridge, turned around and headed south at the entrance of the Harlem River and the Spuyten Duyvil Bridge. The Tall Ships then sailed to their assigned berths along the waterfront at piers 84, 86, 88, 92, and 97. On July 6 there was a ticker tape parade from Battery Park to City Hall and a mayor's reception for the 6000 sail training cadets from 30 countries.

Later in the week, *Regina Maris* sailed for Boston Harbor, where the parade of ships was to take place on July 10, with *USS Constitution* leading the fleet of 65 ships. *Regina's* course took her through the Cape Cod Canal connecting Cape Cod Bay in the north to Buzzards Bay in the south. While going through the crowd-lined canal, she was preceded by tug boats and the Coast Guard streaming water from their fire hoses. [6]

After her return to Boston, *Regina's* first voyage as a research vessel was north to Newfoundland and Labrador. Hal Whitehead, now with the biology department of Dalhousie University, Halifax, Nova Scotia, recalled his experiences on this journey, in a 2011 email to the author: "I first went aboard *Regina Maris* in 1976 off the coast of Newfoundland as a beginning whale researcher. I loved her from the start. Over the next 5 years I did a fair amount of research from her, surveying whale populations off Newfoundland, Labrador and in the Caribbean. My colleagues on the research projects from *Regina* and my own little sailing boats between 1978-1981, which led to my PhD (at Cambridge University) on humpback whales in the western North Atlantic, were largely people that I met on *Regina Maris*. They became my closest friends. Some of them still are. That was the experience on *Regina*. But above all I was taken with the old boat herself, climbing her rigging, fighting with her sails on the yardarm, feeling her move with the ocean. I gained huge confidence in dealing with the ocean, as well as dealing with people, from my times on *Regina*. Great times, and, for me, very important times." [7]

This sentiment has been echoed again and again by those who have sailed and studied on *Regina*.

This history cannot possibly chronicle all the events that must have taken place during *Regina's* 42 voyages as the ORES research vessel. With the journal's permission, excerpts from the 1988 "*Regina Maris* issue" of *Whalewatcher* have been used in the following four chapters to tell the ship's story through the words of scientists, crew, and students who sailed on those 42 voyages of discovery. Every effort was made to contact the contributors for a retrospective comment and/or an update about their activities since their *Regina Maris* experience. Some **recollections not** in the original *Whalewatcher* issue have also been included.

Below is a list of *Regina Maris's* voyages **as an ORES research vessel,** as reported in the *Whalewatcher* **issue.** [1]

1976
- Piraeus to Boston via Gibraltar, Tenerife, Bermuda, and New York.
- Boston to Newfoundland and Labrador and return.

1977
- Boston to Silver Bank, Dominican Republic, and return via San Juan, Puerto Rico, and Bequia.
- Boston to Newfoundland and Labrador and return.

1978
- Boston to Silver Bank to Miami.
- Miami to Punta Arenas, Costa Rica, via the Panama Canal, the Galapagos, and Cocos Island
- Punta Arenas to Mazatlan, Mexico.
- Mazatlan to La Paz via the Sea of Cortez as far north as Puerto Citos.

1979
- La Paz to Bahia Magdalena and return.
- La Paz to Socorro in Revillagigedo Islands and return with a visit to Puerto Vallarta.
- La Paz to San Pedro, California.
- San Pedro to Juneau, Alaska.
- Juneau to Seattle via Glacier Bay and the islands.
- Seattle to San Pedro via San Francisco.
- San Pedro to Puerto Plata, Dominican Republic, via Cocos Island, Panama, and Haiti.

1980
- A winter on Silver Bank and return to Boston via eastern Bahamas.
- Summer in Massachusetts Bay.
- Boston to the Gulf of Paria and Barbados.

1981
- Barbados to Silver Bank for the winter season with return to Boston via eastern Bahamas.
- Boston to West Greenland and return.
- Boston to Puerto Plata via eastern Bahamas.

1982
- Silver Bank for the winter with return to Boston via Washington D.C.
- Boston to West Greenland and return.

- Boston to Puerto Plata via eastern Bahamas.

1983
- Silver Bank for the winter with return to Gloucester via Nassau and Bermuda.
- Gloucester to West Greenland and return.
- Gloucester to Puerto Plata via eastern Bahamas.

1984
- Silver Bank for the winter with return via Charleston and New York.
- Massachusetts Bay and Georges Bank until retirement in Gloucester.

CHAPTER 16
THE ORES YEARS BEGIN

1. *Whalewatcher*, Summer 1988, which issue was devoted entirely to *Regina Maris*.
2. Sherryl Taylor, ACS Personal Profiles, *Whalewatcher*, Fall 1993.
3. Lucy Coan Helfrich, "A History of the Sea Education Association, its Campus, and its Founder, Corey Cramer." This article was abridged by John P. Mordes M.D. for the Hopkins Grammar School, Class of 1965, website and is used here with the permission of SEA, Inc.
4. Harvey Oxenhorn, *Tuning the Rig*. (New York, NY: Harper Perennial, 1990.)
5. Francis E. "Van" Fowler, letter to the author dated July 24, 1992.
6. Hal Whitehead, email to the author, October 7, 2011.

CHAPTER 17
R/V REGINA MARIS HEADS TO THE CARIBBEAN
January 1977

Early in 1977, *Regina Maris* made the first of many trips to the Caribbean as an ORES research vessel. Aboard was Dr. Kenneth C. Balcomb III, who had joined the ORES staff under Dr. Nichols to teach oceanography, marine mammal science, navigation, and seamanship aboard *Regina*. George and Ken set out to photo-identify humpback whales in the North Atlantic Ocean and calculate their population size after decimation by early 20th century whaling, a quest they collaborated on for many years.

Ken was eminently qualified for his new role aboard *Regina*. Born in New Mexico and raised there and in California, he graduated in 1960 from American River College, Sacramento, and was majoring in philosophy at the University of California, Berkeley, when a fish- and wildlife-management course rekindled his lifelong passion for animals. He transferred to UC Davis and graduated in 1963 with a bachelor's degree in zoology.

In 1967, he joined the U.S. Navy and trained as an aviator and oceanographic specialist. In 1972, he enrolled as a PhD student of Dr. Ken Norris at UC Santa Cruz, working with whales and also sailing on the schooner and sail-training ship *Westward*, captained by George Nichols.

When he was not sailing on *Regina*, Ken returned to the West Coast, and in 1976, he launched his long-term study of resident southern killer whales, or Orcas, in the Pacific Northwest, using photographic techniques developed by Dr. Mike Bigg of Canada's Department of Fish and Oceans. Today Ken lives on San Juan Island, Washington, where he continues his premiere study of Orcas in collaboration with government colleagues Dr. John Ford and Graeme Ellis at DFO Nanaimo, and Dr. Brad Hanson at the National Marine Fisheries Service, (NMFS), Seattle.

The rest of this chapter is Ken's journal account of ORES' first — hair-raising — trip from Boston to the Caribbean, from the Summer 1988 "*Regina Maris* issue" of *Whalewatch*.

4 January 1977

After an extensive refit and innumerable delays, *r/v Regina Maris* pulled away from Lewis Wharf and motored out of Boston Harbor at 1500 today. A small crowd of well-wishers and a TV cameraman gathered ashore in a light snowfall as the crew, students, and carpenters huddled on deck in silent goodbye. I think nobody thought it possible that we would ever set out to sea, especially to the North Atlantic in the dead of winter. We hadn't planned to be so late, but numerous unavoidable delays since mid-November had destroyed our schedule and created disbelief that this old wooden ship would ever be anything but a dockside curiosity, complete with a cast of colorful characters. Dr. George Nichols, our captain, knew that we would leave – his constant effort had made the whole program possible, and his charge through every delay was sooner or later going to get us going. I also knew that we would leave, and that the final moments would pass quickly, so with each delay I got more and more prepared to depart.

As if by grand design, when we finally did cast off, we had just about everything we will need in the science program, from lathes to radio tags to hydrophones and motor-driven cameras. We also had a floating cetological library that is first rate. The laboratory, which we will construct underway, will be superb. It is above decks, spacious, and divided into two parts — wet and dry — which will house the dining gear/photolab and the electronics shop/library, respectively. In short, we have everything, including fine people, necessary for the near impossible task ahead: to photo-document and follow a significant number of humpback whales from the "wintering grounds" of the tropical western North Atlantic to the "summering grounds" in higher latitudes. If we are successful, we can then have greater confidence about estimates of population, stock integrity, and migration routes than what we now have and we can make meaningful recommendations to national and international organizations for conserving these magnificent creatures.

By sunset at 1635, we were off Thieves' Ledge heading for the Cape Cod Canal. The seas were quite calm, as if to bid us fair passage.

5 January 1977

Sunrise was 0730, by which time we were through Cape Cod Canal and Buzzards Bay and out into the North Atlantic to about 41° N x 71° W. The weather was still remarkably fine so we ran with the light breezes and the main engine due south toward the Gulf Stream and warmer climates. The water temperature all day was 7° to 8° C and the air was 2° C.

Sometime around noon the main engine threw out an oil seal and quit running. Our speed dropped from about six knots to one as we barely wafted along in the diminishing wind. The only working bilge pump runs off the main engine, so we had a little problem there.

At 1645, a loose school of over 50 *Delphinus delphis* came toward us from the south and played around us for awhile. It looked funny to see them wheel around in front of the bow as if to catch our pressure wave, and then almost halt as they found there was none to ride.

Sunset occurred as the dolphins arrived and we were approximately at 41°14'N x 71°0"W. It appears that we will not be able to get the main engine running at sea. I guess that means we are going into port — the question is, where? In the old days they sailed these ships everywhere, and I'm sure George can do it, too. I just wish we had more going for us right now.

6 January 1977

Sunrise found us drifting at 40°09'N x 71°43' W, or thereabouts. The Coast Guard has not yet found us, but they are looking. When they find us it is said we will be towed to Long Island. The seas are miraculously small for this time of year — only about 2 feet. If it were rough we'd really be uncomfortable, so we can count this as a blessing, really.

Shortly before noon we were found. But by then our main engine was running again — Rich Mula, Jim Goebel, and I had collected the hot leaking oil in a coffee can under the engine and dumped it back in through the oil filter at intervals frequent enough to keep us going. Since we didn't need a tow but our condition was still awkward, the Coast Guard escorted us as we motored toward Newport, Rhode Island.

We arrived in the middle of the night and anchored off the Newport Shipyard. The weather had treated us beautifully all day and evening, allowing us to reach port in relative comfort and in good time. Our thanks are due the U.S. Coast Guard for standing by until we were safely inshore.

7 January 1977

By morning it was snowing a sticky wet snow that blanketed everything. The anchor was weighed right after breakfast and we motored over to the shipyard pier. Immediately upon arrival the shipyard crew took out all the defective motor to be repaired, and they started working on repairs to the main engine leak.

By evening a veritable blizzard raged outside, and those of us who had done did their drinking in the afternoon huddled below decks in the cold dampness of the ship and listened to it blow. Even though we were tied to the dock, the ship rocked and tossed as if we were in a gale far at sea. In the early evening, the ship's anemometer pegged consistently at 50 knots, and later we learned that a record 94 knot gust was recorded ashore.

8-11 January 1977

In Newport Shipyard. Blizzard conditions.

12 January 1977

The engines were started at 1030 after all repairs had been completed and all last minute shore details taken care of. Small craft warnings along the coast call for freezing spray today, with 15 to 25 knots of wind. It should be miserable out there — we shall soon see.

At 1110 we cast off from the dock of the Newport Shipyard, and by noon we were clear of the harbor with stays'ls up and the iron spinnaker purring away. At last, we're off to Puerto Rico and sunny climes.

Outside, all afternoon and night, we were "Seasick Maru" as we clashed with the seas and laboriously made our way South. The decks and rigging were frozen over, requiring that we frequently break off the ice with sledge hammers and mallets and cast it overboard, lest we become top-heavy and capsize. We expected that, as did the sailors of yesteryear who ventured out onto the North Atlantic in winter.

During the night the seas built to mountainous size; as the ship tossed and rolled in furious gyrations, everyone's clothing was pitched upon the deck and saturated with fuel oil and bilge water that sloshed up the side of the ship, over the ceiling and across the deck. The stench below was almost unbearable, but the real aggravation was having all our warm clothing and foul weather gear saturated with the stuff so that the stench was always with us.

13 January 1977

It snowed in the afternoon, but by midnight we had apparently entered the Gulf Stream — the water temperature rose dramatically to 20° C from the 3-5° C it had been. Apparently, one can go out on deck in shirtsleeves, but I haven't done it yet. It is now 0100 on the 14th and I'm preparing to finish cleaning the cabin deck to see if I can rid us of these fumes.

14 January 1977

We were definitely in the Gulf Stream — I could comfortably stay aloft for two hours (0830-1030) this morning in spite of a stiff westerly breeze. I searched the port forward quarter to a distance of three or four miles with binoculars and naked eye, and saw no whales or marine mammals. There were about a dozen ringed gulls with us through the morning, one with crude oil all over the belly. I'm hoping to see sperm whales soon, as we approach the Charleston Ground of Yankee whaling days.

Our noon position was 35°47'N x 70°54'W. By nightfall we were really into lousy weather. The seas piled up to 20 feet and more, and it blew a bloody gale out of the Southeast. The ship pounded and tossed into it all night as the wind came slowly around to Southwest, building very confused seas. As usual, the bilge water cascaded across the deck and throughout the ship bearing its foul smell. The decks topside were dangerously awash, and many things broke loose, including a bucket of pine tar in the main deck hatch. It dissolved the calking and oozed through the deck and dripped onto the port table and bunks in the new saloon. Gawd, it was incredibly messy stuff! It also covered the main deck and, no doubt, whatever was in the main hatch with it — three inflatable boats, outboard motors, etc. The stench makes it nearly intolerable to stay below deck, and the slippery dangerous awash conditions make it awkward to survive above — one could easily be washed overboard in the heavy seas that rolled across the decks.

15 January 1977

It was still rough at breakfast, so I just had a few pieces of orange and hit the bunk for awhile. The saloon was a scene of misery — dripping seawater and pine tar from the overhead; bilge water and fuel oil sloshing across the floors; sad, wet, seasick faces sitting around a bowl of oatmeal from which the spoon could barely be removed, it was so pasty. The main bilge pump won't work and the bilge is full, so folks rotated pumping the hand pump on deck. I got into it for awhile — it was fresh air on deck, and the activity was good as well as useful.

Our noon position was 34°56'N x 69°15'W, about 400 miles on our way and 1000 to go. We're past the storm that we went through last night, but we've got another one coming up tonight. This is crazy!

In the evening we saw another ship plodding southeast. We did not feel like we were all alone then, but I still wish we were already in Puerto Rico.

16 January 1977

The storm raged all night, causing a few moments of terror, but abated by morning and it was time to assess the situation and put things in order. Our noon position was 32°29'N x 68°29'W, 813 miles from Puerto Rico. We are all looking forward to getting there.

In the late afternoon we scrubbed the decks to remove pine tar, fuel oil, lube oil, etc. that had accumulated. Jerry Brown, the bo'sun, and the watch section cleaned the main hatch and restowed it. It was a mess getting the pine tar off all the gear, but paint thinner did the trick. Fortunately, the seas were not too rough and the weather was clear but partly cloudy for our chores. Spirits were up considerably by the end of the day when cleanup was finished. When we changed filters we shut down the main engine, so George had the sails hoisted. It was very mellow to sail along at sunset with the feeling of being cleaned. We can take another storm now, but I hope it is a little one. One is due tonight — they must spawn out here.

At the evening meal we learned a few more details about the storm we went through night before last. George says it was a no-kidding Force 12 hurricane wind, and it rocked us a fully 45 degrees over port and starboard in its fury. At one point the spray from the bow went as high as the fore-top-mast (80 feet). A container ship reportedly broke apart somewhere to the west of us.

17 January 1977

It was rocking and rolling enough to make sleep difficult all night. As usual, fuel oil and bilge water sloshed across the decks and the stench was suffocating. Most of the day was lumpy, too. We've passed through the region of three gales a week into the region of two gales per week — Big Deal It is still rough all the time.

Dinner was very good — roast pork, mashed potatoes, apple sauce, etc. For dessert we had cherry pie, *sans* crust. It seems that Adolph, our cook, accidentally dropped the crust dough on the deck and then stepped on it before he could pick it up. The rest of the dinner also fell on the deck, but apparently it was more concealable than a grimy footprint in the pie crust. Anyway, dinner turned out well the best meal of the expedition thus far.

18 January 1977

It stayed rough most of the night with occasional squalls, and then it calmed down with morning. I spent the day in the engine room with Rich Mula and Jim Goebel, trying to get things running.

Our noon position was 28°13'N x 67°09'W, which by my calculations puts us 819.11 miles out of Newport, Rhode Island and, more important, 600.62 miles from Cape San Juan, Puerto Rico, which bears 170.5°T. We could make it by Saturday noon, or sooner if the engines keep running.

Morale was running high in the evening, perhaps because of the good weather and one beer per person allowed by Captain George.

19 January 1977

The seas are building again today under a steady NW blow. The engines are still running, though, so we should be able to pump bilges and keep headway even if it does get terrible again. It sure is monotonously lousy out here.

It calmed briefly in the morning, but only long enough for the winds to swing around to the southwest and blow like hell. The seas were very confused and building. Our noon position was 27°17'N x 66°00'W, or about 537.49 NM from Puerto Rico. That may be as close as we ever get, because we went backward from noon on. We aren't in a storm, we are in a whole string of them, and they are howlers. Most people got out on deck to enjoy the first couple of them — seas crashing over the bow and rails, and spray enough to shower everybody at once. Pass the 'Joy' around, we'll all get clean (and salty!). I took one shower, then helped Rich shut down the main engine to check the oil and reset the valve cover gasket. Then I took another shower in the spray and ran around snapping pictures with my Nikonos. The afternoon storms were getting more ominous as the day progressed. The winds were 50-60 knots between storms, and 80 or more knots in them — and the seas were getting huge! It was getting fearful again. George took the helm for awhile at supper, lest we be buried under a mountain of water. The lee rail was buried continuously, and it took expertise to simply keep us from broaching or plowing under.

This stuff went on into the night, going from bad to worse. Water cascaded into the ship through every unplugged hole and down the ladders. As I sat at my desk, three 3-inch waves of water rushed across my feet with every roll. It was quite frequently terrifying as we were set literally on our beam; but always *Regina Maris* righted and plowed ahead in stride. Oh, sometimes she would reel recklessly during a particularly complex combination of motions, but always she felt strong. Still, I could not sleep for fear that at any time we would broach and swamp, leaving the ship a watery tomb from which escape must be immediate, if at all.

20 January 1977

It is now 0230 as I write these notes, and we are still afloat! I thought things had calmed down a bit in the last half hour, but just a bit ago we went through some hellacious motions that suggest the helm was lost temporarily. Even now I'll bet we're rocking a full 45 degrees from upright, and hundreds of gallons of water are crashing down the ladder well. The rails must be alternately inundated. My feet got sloshed again by another wave that poured through the ceiling. Stuff is clattering to the deck in the galley. Come on big horse! Get us to Puerto Rico…if we make it, I promise to never go any place like this again. One storm a month is as much as I will stand for.

We survived the night, and saw the seas diminish to an acceptable state by noon. To everyone's surprise, we'd even made some progress — to 26°05'N x 65°46'W. The seas last night were 30+ feet, with an occasional 50-footer — let's hope that we don't get into any bigger ones ever. The ship always felt sound (but wild), and I've implicit faith in George's seamanship, but I don't trust this damned ocean! One of these troughs could be bottomless, so far as we're concerned.

The afternoon was lumpy, but clear and pleasant sailing with a following NW wind. We're keeping the main engine running because it also runs the bilge pump, and we need that. Dinner was the best food that we had in thirty hours, and very little of it rocked upon the deck, or went uneaten. Adolph complained that everybody showed up to eat, with a disproportionate number at second sitting — but everyone got fed.

21 January 1977

At last! A full day of reasonably good weather. Our noon position was 23°39'N x 65°56'W, only 319.60 NM, 176.4°T to San Juan. No more storms are reported to loom before us, so we should make it by Sunday night.

22 January 1977

Our noon position was 21°10'N x 64°40'W, about 177.7 NM on 197.1°T to San Juan, by my calculations.

23 January 1977

At 1500 we motored into the harbor as crowds gathered on the headlands and promontories of the fort to watch us. Ann saw a whale just before we entered the harbor. No dolphins came to escort us. At 1530 we tied off at the Coast Guard station and almost everybody went ashore for a little while. A bunch of us gathered at the "club" and had a few beers. Tours were given of the ship to interested Coast Guardsmen, and at 1830 we all had a party aboard ship. By then it was raining ferociously, obviating the need for a freshwater washdown.

We all had a good night's sleep, tied safely to the dock. Tomorrow, work routine starts at 0800. ...

After his journal recounting of that first hard voyage, Ken also noted in the *Whalewatcher*" issue, "Thus began *r/v Regina Maris* expeditions to the Caribbean Islands and shallow banks, which were the historically known wintering grounds of the Western North Atlantic humpback whale population. Conditions improved considerably for students and crew and the ship, once the sun soaked in and the whales were found. The later were found in most abundance on Silver Bank, north of the Dominican Republic. Accordingly this bank was the primary winter research area each year for *Regina Maris* expeditions until her retirement in 1984."

CHAPTER 18
VOYAGES 1978 THROUGH 1980

From 1978 to 1980, *Regina* continued her research mission in the Caribbean; expanded it to Mexico, the West Coast, and Alaska; and appeared in a public television series. This chapter looks at those years, primarily from the recollections of several *Regina* crew members, as published in the summer 1988 "*Regina Maris* issue" of *Whalewatcher,* along with some recent updates. (Portions of some contributions have been condensed or summarized.)

The Royal Yard
Hal Whitehead

Dr. Whitehead is based at the biology department of Dalhousie University, Halifax, Nova Scotia but spends a great deal of time at sea conducting cetacean research from the 40-foot cruising vessel *Balaena*. His graduate students research a variety of cetacean topics, and his own work focuses primarily on the behavior, social structure, and population biology and conservation of sperm whales, as well more general questions of social structure in mammals and cultural evolution. He wrote the following in *Whalewatcher.*

Regina had many special places, and in each there was a different way to see the ocean she sailed. Down in the net below the jibboom the dolphins broke the surface to blow an arms-length beneath, keeping station. The top of the mainmast, *Regina's* highest point, was the best place to measure icebergs. If one of those Labrador icebergs reached above the horizon, it was over 30 m tall. But, for me, the most special was the royal yard. The royal was the highest squaresail on the foremast, and the royal yard was the horizontal timber from which it hung.

The attractions of the royal yard included its height above the sea and remoteness from the rest of the crew down on deck. The royal, the smallest squaresail, was the easiest and most satisfying sail to furl alone. The royal yard was also a fine place for watching whales. Throughout the winters of 1978 and 1980 two of us would sit on the royal yard as *Regina* sailed transects across Silver and Navidad Banks, the breeding grounds of the humpback whale in the West Indies. Sitting on the yard, one each side, our backs against the foremast, we scanned for humpbacks. We saw breaches in the distance and tiny calves nestling by their mothers' sides, we saw the dark green coral heads of Silver Bank, and the spatial patterns of the whales scattered over this strange remote patch of ocean but, back-to-back, we did not see each other.

As we censused the whales we often talked. Our positions on the royal yard dispensed with the ambiguities of eye contact, and there was nothing else to do but watch and count the whales. Some of those I censused with on the royal yard have been friends ever since.

The royal yard gave a unique view of the whales. It swayed slowly far enough above the ocean to allow a view of overall pattern. It was there that I pondered the hypothesis that a humpback breaching in one area might provoke another to breach a few thousand meters away.

At times when we were not censusing, the royal yard gave a distance from the research. As George Nichols maneuvered *Regina* for Ken Balcomb to take fluke photographs I would climb to the royal, and watch the whales as a human, not a scientist. Far above, I would try to find a perspective on the research, the extraordinary animals we were studying, the wide ocean and, of course, the great old wooden boat on which we lived. [1]

Glacier Bay, Alaska. *Photo by Jeff Gilbert.*

Regina Maris in Southeast Alaska
Peter J. Bryant

Dr. Bryant is Professor of Biological Sciences, University of California, Irvine, carrying out research in developmental biology, genetics, and stem cell biology. He also finds time for his "real love," the study of biodiversity and ecology. For many years he has been documenting the local diversity of plants and animals as well as intertidal life, and he has also studies wild populations of whales, including conducting population assessment and photo-identification work on the gray whales of Laguna Guerrero Negro from 1976 to 1982, with the sponsorship of the American Cetacean Society and the National Marine Fisheries Service. From 1977 to 1980, he was the founding president of the Orange County Chapter, ACS. From 1981-1982 he served as vice-president and in 1982 as president of the ACS. He has also worked on determining the age of subfossil remains of the Atlantic gray whale, the most recent of which were discovered on a beach in his home town, Torquay, England.

Peter served as guest scientist on board *Regina Maris* during the summers of 1979 and 1981 and wrote in *Whalewatcher* of his experiences on Expedition #16 in 1979. Their main objective was to study and document "bubble-net" feeding of humpbacks — a phenomenon originally discovered in 1929 — in Glacier Bay, Frederick Sound, and other areas of Southeast Alaska. He wrote the following in *Whalewatcher*.

> We planned a very elaborate series of observations, measurements, and acoustical studies on bubble netting but we saw so few bubble nets (only about six altogether) that this project was simply not possible. We concentrated instead on studies of the behavior of the whales, and of their geographic distribution in relation to the availability of krill.

The year had seen a "dramatic decline" in the population of humpbacks in Glacier Bay, he wrote, noting that the ship was in the bay for two days and confirmed that only three whales were present. The expedition moved on to Frederick Sound, where whales were more abundant, with an estimated 80 whales in and around the sound, about the same as had been observed in previous years. Peter wrote:

> Frederick Sound was a wonderful place to observe other kinds of whale behavior, especially breaching. One animal breached 50 times in a row as it sped across the Sound! We formed the opinion that this kind of multiple breach was simply a way for the whale to take deep breaths while swimming at top speed. Dolphins do this — why not whales? We got to know some of the whales individually by both markings and behavior patterns — including some that became curious about the ship and swam

around under the jibboom, one that would lie on its back slapping the surface alternately with one flipper and then the other after every dive, and one that trumpeted like an elephant with each blow! We also had plenty of opportunities in Frederick Sound and other parts of Southeast Alaska to watch other marine mammals including killer whales, Dall's porpoise, harbor porpoise, harbor seals, and Steller's sea lions. Birds sighted included marbled murrelets, northern phalaropes, bald eagles, and surf scoters. The tidepools were full of surprises, including sea cucumbers, giant barnacles, sunflower starfish, and huge hermit crabs. Some of the wildlife, including humpback salmon and Dungeness crab, provided delicious feasts for the crew and students!

Regina was a beautiful, majestic vessel, and looked very much at home in the timeless, unspoiled scenery of Southeast Alaska. We often went ashore in small boats. ... Looking back at *Regina* in the distance, in bright sun and still air on a glassy sea, we imagined ourselves in a different century. The early explorers of the region included La Perouse, James Cook, George Vancouver, and John Muir, and we got some idea of how they must have felt as we explored completely uninhabited islands and coves. As we climbed the mountains separating the fiords, *Regina*, far below us and looking like a toy boat in a bathtub, was the only sign of human presence.

Regina was not only an ideal floating whalewatching platform with observation posts at all levels between sea level and about 90 feet; she was also a well-equipped oceanographic vessel. One of the most interesting ways of studying ocean life is to examine the many different kinds of organisms that come to the surface in a plankton tow. We were especially interested in the depth distribution of different potential food organisms, so we used a technique called the vertical plankton tow, in which two large "bongo" nets are lowered to a certain depth and then hauled upward through a specific depth range. A water sampling tube is attached to the nets and can be closed by sending a weight down the line when the nets are at the desired depth. With [research assistant] Karen Miller and Toni Boettger [Bryant's future wife] supervising, students participated in plankton tows and in the identification and counting of the krill and other organisms that come up in the nets. ...

Our krill samples contained the expected species *Euphausia pacifica*, *Thysanoessa spinifera*, and occasional specimens of *Thysanoessa longipes*. We were able to keep samples alive in tanks on board the ship, so that we could make observations of their behavior ... [The organisms in the tank] were quite a challenge for the photographers among us, as

Regina's gentle motion caused the water in the tanks to slosh back and forth and the animals to rapidly jump in and out of focus. There are some things best done ashore!

When the scientific work of Expedition #16 was finished, *Regina* headed to Seattle. Peter recalled in *Whalewatcher*:

> The trip down the coast from Alaska to Seattle was quite hair-raising at times. My bunk happened to be just under the shelf where a collection of strange remains and artifacts, including some heavy mammal skulls, were being stowed. This was perfectly safe on the port tack but not on the starboard tack! At about 0500h I was rudely awakened by a shillelagh and several other heavy items falling on my head as we came about suddenly in order to avoid some shallows that were causing steep seas. Upon poking my head out through a hatch to see what was going on, I realized that we were in a force 10 gale with a scandalized mainsail, making only 2 knots with the engine roaring at full ahead! Although *Regina* rode storms amazingly smoothly, the lurches can still make moving around the ship quite an adventure. Under these conditions the usual meal schedule is modified slightly — a large can of soup is tied to the mast in the galley, you try to scoop some out as you slide past while trying to keep your balance, then you try to drink some of it and keep it down long enough to do some good. ...
>
> To me, any piece on *Regina* is incomplete without at least a few words about George Nichols. George runs a tight ship, consequently a safe one, but he also makes everyone welcome and takes a personal interest in every one of the students. One of the wonderful things about trips aboard *Regina* were the lasting friendships that were formed, and George is responsible for creating the atmosphere where that could happen. George was kind enough to invite me on two trips as guest scientist, at a time when I was (as now!) very much an unknown quantity as far as marine mammal science is concerned. He gave us all an opportunity to see what we could do, and we made some very useful contributions to humpback whale biology. We learned a tremendous amount, mainly from George, about ships and the sea, about whales, but most of all about how to work hard, sometimes under the worst of conditions, and to stay happy while doing it! I would also like to thank Roger Payne for getting me involved in this project, for his inspiration, and for many useful discussions. [2]

A Love for Her
Toni Bryant

Toni Bryant, then Toni Boettger, sailed on the same 1979 Alaska expedition Dr. Peter Bryant discusses above, and later they married. She shared memories of that trip in a phone conversation with the author on December 21, 2011.

Toni signed on as crew because of her interest in whales, and she thoroughly enjoyed climbing the rigging and working aloft — buckling in the safety harness made her feel safe. They saw many whales, icebergs, eagles and bears as they cruised the coast.

On the trip back south, on the outside of Vancouver Island, they ran into a very bad gale. All but four crew members were sick and unable to keep on their feet. George, Peter Bryant, a fellow named Patrick and Toni crewed the ship for two days as the storm pushed the ship toward the coast. They couldn't steer and drifted under bare poles. The cook made a pot of stew, tied it to a post in the galley and went to his bunk.

Toni still felt safe and protected by *Regina*, as if the ship were a "being," and she developed a deep love for the ship that brought her safely back to shore. Years later George Nichols confided to her his assessment of the peril they had been in during the gale: "I thought we had bought the farm." [3]

A Rough Passage
James Perran Ross

Dr. Ross is currently associate scientist in the department of wildlife ecology and conservation, University of Florida, Gainesville, where he advises the Florida Fish and Wildlife Conservation Commission on stakeholder management and Florida conservation issues, including gopher tortoise and manatee conservation, threatened species listing, and conservation policy and planning.

Perran's career has focused on international conservation biology, specializing in the application of sustainable use to conservation and management of sea turtles and crocodilians in developing countries. He has been a consultant and advisor to World Wildlife Fund International, CITES, IUCN, US AID, ICBP and the US Fish and Wildlife Service.

His many other positions include serving as a visiting lecturer at University of Massachusetts and Williams College and as executive officer of the Crocodile Specialist Group and a member of the IUCN/SSC Marine Turtle Specialist Group and Reintroduction Specialist Group. Perran wrote the following in the *Whalewatcher* issue devoted to *Regina*.

> The basic plan seemed sound enough. Pick the gap between late hurricanes and early fall gales, wait for a passing front and ride the northeaster across to Bermuda. Our skipper, Bill Mabie, a Camden, Maine, native and former mate in *Regina*, felt that we could make up time

lost in a lengthy yard period in Gloucester, and our crew and complement of students were all eager to go. Easily said, but the land seems to put out sticky strands to delay a sailing ship and I never knew one yet that could keep a schedule, least of all *Regina*.

But at last we were ready to go — out to sea with a last glimpse of Gay Head light fading in the fog as the promised Northeast front picked up.

Things went well at first. The three days delay had allowed the student crew to settle to their tasks, their watch mates, and the ship's routine. Sails were set, sheets hauled home and *Regina* rollicked forward with bone in her teeth, Bermuda-bound in the evening of the 8th of November, 1980, running with a Northeast gale.

How to tell of that crossing? It was fast — I grant you that; Gay Head light to Saint David's light in four and a half days. Four and a half days of hell.

The wind blew 30, 40, up to 50 knots and on up from there. By the morning of the second day we had *Regina* trimmed down to a storm trysail on the mizzen boom and a staysail forward and she still made 6 or 7 knots. The great, gray, spuming seas rose up astern like mad whales, *Regina's* stern rising, rising, rising, then the sudden rush and surge as she plunged her jibboom into the sea and ran like a surfboard down the face of each wave as it passed. That is where you had to watch her on the helm as she would try to broach across the foaming mountains of water. It was two hands at the wheel, lashed in, for half hour tricks and beaten black and blue by the spinning wheel spokes at the weary end of each watch.

The wind howled and the sea roared and the sleet and spray blew horizontal and stinging into your eyes and *Regina* rolled and creaked and of course she leaked. *Regina* always leaked, usually just a little. But the workings of those eighty-year-old timbers and fastenings opened up seams and dribbles and squirts, and the water came in everywhere. Nowhere very much but everything was wet. The water sloshed around the bilge and ran up in foul gushes into your bunk. The water ran down the walls and conduits and into the electrical junction boxes starting smoky little fires. The water dripped down your neck and dripped into your food and decks and soles were a slimy mush of bilge and spilled food.

Four hours on, eight hours off, at least in theory. But when half the students are sick and terrified and things break loose and blow out, then it's all hands. Never mind that you just got off to sleep, huddled in your damp blankets, or that you must take your turn again in just two hours. Up and out. Blown out sails to cut away and replace, blocked pumps to clear, smoldering junction boxes to disconnect.

The worst was doing a trick on the wheel. *Regina* had a very direct cable steering drive and so when the waves surged up and hit the rudder the wheel would kick and buck and it took two people to hold it. When it got away from you it would spin and pummel you with the spokes as you tried to regain control and the ship would swerve across the seas and take a great roll and the water would crash across the deck three feet deep. That's where I nearly ended a promising career.

We took over the watch at midnight of the third night, tired, sore, and afraid of that wheel and its bruising spokes. There were small signs of progress — the water sloshing across the deck was warm and filled with phosphorescence indicating our passage beyond the Gulf Stream. We had become used to 50-knot winds and fifteen foot seas, and battled numbly from watch to watch counting our blessings in a cup of lukewarm soup or a last pair of dry socks.

I took the wheel with another, and fearful of the spinning spokes decided not to clip my safety harness to be free to dodge the bruises. As so often happens it takes a new helmsman a minute or two to find the balance point with the wheel, usually the cause of a transient wiggle in the wake; this time and with these seas a momentary exposure to death's door. My vivid recollection is that realizing we were slightly off course I looked to windward to see an immense wave cresting over the bulwarks broadside on. I had time to realize there was green water breaking high up the ratlines even as *Regina* rolled away from the huge sea and then I was swept off the wheel. It is a somber moment when you realize that you are afloat, in a storm, in winter, in the mid-Atlantic and that your companions will not be able even to turn the ship, let alone come back and look for you. If you go overboard out there you are dead. It was quiet and the water was surprisingly warm and I was beginning to make calculations about kicking off my sea boots when my flailing arm clunked into something hard and painful. The sound came back on and I realized that I was within the confines of the bulwarks, inside the boat. Afloat and within a foot of being carried over and out but — this time at least — safe.

Regina has never, to our knowledge, had a death on board or lost a crew member to the sea. This is remarkable in view of her long history and the very real hazards of large sailing ships. While she was uncomfortable in a heavy sea, she was also an excellent sea boat with the gull-like ability to float over rather than through the waves that ship designers hope for but cannot ensure. She carried many hundreds of us safely to our destinations through everything the ocean could throw at us. I logged 20 voyages and thousands of miles on *Regina* between 1980 and 1984 and I don't regret a minute of it. [4]

In a letter to the author dated November 9, 1992, Perran wrote, "My position on board was officially 'supercargo' — professor and research biologist, but a lifetime interest in ships and sailing made me a useful extra hand and I daresay I could steer, splice and lay aloft and furl, with any of them (as well as maintain my credibility with my students). My usual bunk was aft by the starboard main chains and she has many times, in heavy weather, shaken me awake with a frightening crack of stressed rigging and a spray of dirty bilge water coming over the ceiling. But there was always a basic trust that the vessel was well built, and if not dry, at least sound.

"I have lots of stories, like every other *Regina* hand. Once we sailed the ship with just four hands and setting every sail (except stunsails) to show it could be done; fine tuning her sails in the lee of Cape Cod with a strong southwesterly and coxing an honest nine knots out of her; sailing her backwards to the dock, without the engine, during the Boston tall ships (a remarkable act of seamanship by Captain Nichols that went totally unremarked by the crowd and organizers); being arrested by the Barbados coast patrol (erroneously); and ports of call — obscure (Acklins Island, Mira por Vos Key, Horseshoe reef, and Aves.) The voyages to Greenland were well documented by my good friend Harvey Oxenhorn's *Tuning the Rig,* which I can attest is a most accurate presentation of many of the characters, who I knew well, including George Nichols, and the 'flavor' of *Regina* voyages at that time."[5]

A Totally Unsuitable Crew Member
Carol Lew Simons

Carol Lew Simons is an editor and writer living in Southold, New York, and editor of this book. A student on Regina in 1980, she wrote this recollection of an experience not quite like those of other contributors.

A tiny ad in a 1979 *New Yorker* promised six weeks in the Caribbean crewing an old square-rigger and studying humpback whales. I was fascinated by whales, and this trip sounded like just the ticket.

I called ORES and explained that I was not a sailor, not young (38), not athletic, and quite acrophobic. The ORES staffer assured me I'd be fine and wouldn't have to climb the rigging. I signed up, eager to leave my Manhattan apartment for the open sea.

ORES sent detailed information about required gear and the delights of whale study, but not so much about getting to the ship: Fly to Santo Domingo and take a taxi to Puerta Plata.

In the Santo Domingo airport, in April 1980, I met up with two other *Regina*-bound women. No obvious taxis presented themselves, and none of us had any Spanish, but we managed to find a wild-looking man willing to drive us to Puerto Plata, in a beat-up car with the passenger doors wired shut.

We made it to Puerto Plata and easily found some *Regina* crew and George Nichols, who escorted us to the ship. She looked huge, and boarding required walking up a very narrow gangplank, which I did with neither grace nor bravery. The ship was creaky and old, strange and forbidding, permeated with a strange odor I came to recognize — and love — as compounded largely of diesel, wood rot, salt water, canvas, motor oil, tar, and sweat.

We were told to pick one of the bunks ranged around the main salon and advised that most leaked and their occupants usually slept in black plastic garbage bags. Somehow, however, I managed to find a relatively dry berth. At once we received an appallingly detailed briefing on crewing the ship, most of which was completely over my head. Panic set in and stayed around for awhile.

On this first night, George Nichols was reserved and pleasant but not especially interested in the five new crew staring at him. The rest of the crew was even less concerned. The cook was ill and everybody else looked grubby, surly, tired, and formidable. When I mentioned not climbing the rigging, the information was not well received.

A different problem became evident during our first briefing: The whales had taken off on their northward migration a day or two earlier. Instead of following them, the ship had a grant to search for the extinct Caribbean monk seal, which some enterprising fisherman had reported seeing. For two weeks we sailed from one remote Bahamian island to the next seeking this wild goose and seeing no cetaceans except a few dolphins and the carcass of a toothed whale.

We had lectures on whales and on sailing square riggers, but in the first week, we newcomers grumbled among ourselves about the inhospitable crew and the lack of whales. Looking back, I see we were like spoiled tourists who had expected a deluxe cruise and had accidentally stumbled onto a real sailing ship with a real crew who had been at sea for six months, just wanted to get home, and expected us to pull our full weight as crew. Period.

Learning the ropes (literally) proved totally baffling to me, and in six weeks, I never did get everything straight. Usually I misunderstood the orders that flew at us, but I believe that only once in the entire voyage did I come close to accidentally killing another crew member, the bo'sun — remarkable given my intractable ineptitude.

On the positive side, I loved sleeping on the ship, soothed by her rocking, creaks, and groans. I loved being at sea, especially out of sight of land, and standing watch, especially from four-to-eight a.m., as it grew light. I quickly gained great respect for the first mate and head of my watch, Tad Pennoyer, George Nichol's nephew, a very competent and invariably kind and helpful young man, and the other crew as well. I discovered I didn't get seasick and loved rough weather (but reading other entries in this book, I realize we did not see much really terrible weather).

My good inner ear and eyesight meant I could take the wheel in stormy weather, when others were seasick or couldn't see through rain-spattered glasses. I had trouble handling the wheel (I'm barely five feet tall) and knew nothing about being a helmsman, but I tried. And because I wouldn't climb the rigging, I got to coil the anchor chain — a hot, dirty task I was glad to do to show that I was willing to work hard and get dirty. These were small jobs, but at least I could try to do something.

One day about two weeks into the trip, I was sitting on a little Bahamian island beach, looking across at *Regina* riding at anchor, seeming to float above the blue-green water like an apparition from long ago. Suddenly it hit me how amazing this adventure was. My constant, low-level anxiety evaporated in that instant and I was suddenly very happy. The other newcomers must have had similar experiences because we all stopped griping and began appreciating this unique experience.

We never did see humpbacks, but it didn't matter anymore — being on the ship was enough. We stopped for several days in Bermuda, painting the ship, forming friendships, and drinking too much beer in Bermuda bars. Between Bermuda and Gloucester, we were in pea soup fog for several days. Because our radar was broken and we were basically invisible, we had to be quiet and listen for other ships. Watch duty included cranking a little manual fog horn. It was cold and wet and scary, but that did not dampen my enthusiasm.

The day the weather cleared, somewhere between New York and Gloucester, as if to compensate for the lack of humpbacks, a blue whale swam close to the ship — an awesome sight, for it was just about as long as *Regina.* By the time we got to Gloucester, we new students were very sad to take our leave.

After I returned to New York, I couldn't get my land legs, and in a way I never really did. In 1987, I bought a house in Greenport, an old sea- and whaling port at the far eastern end of Long Island, and left the city for good. And one day in 1991, I opened the local newspaper to an astounding headline: "*Regina Maris* coming to Greenport." When the ship was towed into the harbor, I went aboard. She was terribly broken and battered, but one whiff of her and I was back standing watch on the open sea. Over the years, I spent much time working with many fine people trying to save the ship. It was a quixotic project, but I'm glad we tried. *(The Greenport restoration project is covered in Chapters 22 to 24.)*

Regina's greatest gifts to me were the experience of sailing and the introduction to the special world of people who love sailing wooden boats. In fact, I ended up marrying one such person. His sailing experience is long and deep, mine short and shallow, but we had certain places and people in common — he had even known George Nichols in Puerta Plata. Without *Regina*, my husband and I might never have had a first conversation. [6]

Regina on Public TV

In the early spring of 1979, a film crew from the Public Broadcasting Service visited *Regina Maris*. The 13-part TV series "Cosmos, A Personal Voyage," based on the book by Carl Sagan, Ann Druyan, and Steven Soter, needed film footage of the tall ship and the ongoing whale research.

Regina is featured in episode 11, "The Persistence of Memory," with shots of the ship from water level looking upward to the rigging and Carl Sagan talking about whale communication and songs. He demonstrates the use of an oscilloscope in studying whale song frequencies, and he is seen walking the deck, with crew behind him working the lines and tending to the ship's operations to ensure she runs quietly so that whale songs can be studied.

In episode 13, "Who Speaks for the Earth," *Regina* reenacts the first contact between the French explorer Jean-François de Galaup La Paruze and the Tlingit native people of the Gulf of Alaska. The crew is shown working on the ship at sunset. Canoe-level shots show the tribal chief approaching the ship and then realizing that it was the work of men and not the Black Raven God he had feared it was.

PBS released the series in 1980.

CHAPTER 18
VOYAGES 1978 THROUGH 1980

1. Dr. Hal Whitehead, *Whalewatcher*, Summer 1988.
2. Dr. Peter Bryant, *Whalewatcher,* Summer 1988.
3. Toni Bryant, telephone interview with the author, December 21, 2011.
4. Dr. James Perran Ross, *Whalewatcher*, Summer 1988.
5. Dr. James Perran Ross, letter to the author dated November 9, 1992.
6. Carol Lew Simons, email to author, April 14, 2013.

CHAPTER 19

VOYAGES 1981 THROUGH 1983

The years 1981 through 1983 saw *Regina* add Arctic adventures to her usual work in the Caribbean, with three trips to West Greenland. Several crew members here supply their recollections of these and other challenging but rewarding passages. Except where noted, these were first published in the *Whalewatcher "Regina* issue"; portions of some contributions have been condensed or summarized.

Greenland Voyages
Judith S. Perkins

Judy Perkins served as an instructor for ORES and a scientist aboard *Regina Maris*. She is now a research associate with Long Term Research Institute, Lincoln, Massachusetts. Her *Whalewatcher* contribution included several excerpts from her journal kept on *Regina's* 1982 trip north. These journal entries are dated and italicized here.

July 10, 1982

Sailing along the sea with only the horizon in view changes one's perception of time and space. One is so accustomed to landmarks. Even the fixes seem to advance along the chart like dice rolls on a board game. In transition from land to sea-shelf. Trying to decipher our position by reading the seascape. Glad to be using my senses again, feel them sharpen, become acute. We caught myctophid fish in the plankton net, so probably we are south of Halifax near the colony of Leech's petrels. Murres and puffins will come as we approach Newfoundland, the potheads in the Davis Strait, then the dark phase fulmars and ice off Greenland.

I remember sailing to Newfoundland in the 1970's and thinking it was so far north, so remote. Now it had become a stop on a journey more than 800 miles nearer the pole. The Davis Strait is one nasty body of water, 1800 fathoms deep, abyssal, with gales brewing and blasting every few days. Somewhere off Cap Farvel, the southern tip of Greenland, the sky changes, the atmosphere thins and becomes crystal clear, the weather patterns change; you enter the Arctic. I always wanted to photograph the Greenland sky, its clouds. There are strange, ghoulish tones layered in a gray collage, always changing, never cumulous, more wispy, lenticular, long washes filtering polar light. Often the sky and sea cannot be separated.

Vast, powerful, magnificent, awesome, and *cold* are Greenland words. Even they are inadequate. Greenland is an island of extremes: sheer size (840,000 square miles) covered with ice-cap (780,000 square miles); glaciers [including] the Humboldt-Jacobshavn ... which calves icebergs every five minutes; vast, deep fjords (Scoresby Sund, King Oscar, Franz Joseph, Sondre Stromfjord); frozen land and sea; carpets of wildflowers; fields of cotton grass; tall, jagged mountains; smooth, rounded glacial valleys; constant daylight.

The Commission for Scientific Research in Greenland and the Danish Foreign Ministry granted us permission to conduct our three-year research project: to assess the size and distribution of the West Greenland humpback whale stock and to study the local marine environment. The International Whaling Commission, in particular, wanted to know if the annual harvest of 10 humpbacks was appropriate for this stock. As important to us was to teach and make available our techniques for estimating population sizes to the Greenland Hunter and Trapper's Association, which included the whalers. In addition, catch statistics needed to be managed more efficiently and by the Greenlanders because the system of reporting these data directly to Copenhagen meant no one in Greenland knew when and if the quota had been filled. In this educational mission, we were successful only up to a point because, in my opinion, Greenlanders as a culture are not accustomed to keeping records of any kind. Also, we were "foreigners," and whether we made sense or not, we were suggesting how they should manage their resources.

After three summers of tracking along the banks off West Greenland, whose names all of us could rattle off like the alphabet — Store Hellefiske (great halibut), Lille Hellefiske, Sukkertop, Tovqussaq, Fyllas, Fiskenaes, Danas, Frederikshaab— we had estimated the humpback stock to contain about 270 whales and confirmed that the largest aggregations occurred primarily around Fyllas Bank, directly off Godthaab, and secondarily off Frederikshaab about 120 miles south.

We found Sukkertop Dyb (trench), separating Fyllas and Tovqussaq Banks, to be an ecological "hot spot" between 62°-70°N: plankton tows consistently yielded large volumes of copepods (and freezing cold hands); humpbacks, finbacks, and sperm whales were most abundant there. Temperature profiles showed a pronounced downswelling that brought warmer (1.5°-3°C) surface water to depths of at least 50 fathoms. Another fertile area was about 60-70 miles southwest of Frederikshaab, along the continental slope where the cold West Greenland Current and the Irminger Current converge. In 1981 and 1983, the copepod concentration there was immense … and in 1981 we encountered pack ice, where there is often great productivity along [the] edges.

July 15, 1981

1105. A white line glows on the horizon — the isblink. This is the pack ice, not in floes but sharp, jagged, melted remains of hummocks. The white is highly visible and reflects light, creating a bright band in the atmosphere just above the horizon. It is a spectacular if not eerie sight, awesome in its cold, hard, angular appearance. The most appropriate welcome to the Arctic. The water temperature dropped to 1.5°C from the earlier 5°C and a freezing wind hit us. About the same time four bottlenose whales spouted off the bow and swam toward the ice. Nearer the ice edge, a large bull sperm whale lay at the surface bobbing up and down like a log. When we got closer, it rolled forward and lifted its gigantic flukes and sounded.

In Greenland it was hard to make plans because the weather made them for you. The summer of 1982 could be called "gales, whales, and tails" in that order. In addition to ORES research, two Danes were aboard conducting a minke whale survey between gales, a most frustrating situation.

July 30, 1982
Gale all day long, topping 50 knots. We've been hove-to for more than 36 hours on Store Hellefiske Bank drifting 2-3k northward. Since 1400 yesterday, the barometer has dropped from 29.74" to 29.35" and is still going down. Last night, I jostled around in my bunk, ship creaking loudly, and went topside at 0345 to make sure things were secure in the lab. We motored away as a flotilla of bergs began descending on us. It was dark and raining, hard to see, so it was a bit hairy.
The seas built up to about 20' with Waikiki crests, mean and big. The roaring seas and howling winds belied the relative comfort down below. Regina is rocking us like a cradle on these cold north seas.

Greenland presented another face a few days later

August 3, 1982
We left Godhavn yesterday at 1930 heading directly for station 3 (on the minke whale survey) again. It was sunny and clear, a lovely day. Ahead, the white fog turned out to camouflage pack ice! In it were some huge icebergs. From a distance, it looked like a white-washed Manhattan. I climbed to the maintop and saw dense pack ice, a wondrous and frightening sight. Only two days ago we were hove-to right here in a gale.

We learned it was better to find a secure anchorage than sit out the gales because they drained so much of our energy. Our haven from gales on

Regina Maris next to Evighdesfjord Glacier on the West cost of Greenland in 1983. *Photo by Kraig R. Hankins.*

Fyllas Bank was a snug cove, Haabets ∅ Havn (Hope Island) at the entrance of Godthaabfjord, where we saw a wolverine and jigged a wolfish whose stomach contained macaroni and cheese, fresh scrapings from dinner!

Were it not for bad weather, we might not have witnessed the … splendor of Greenland in summer. To me, the coast near Sukkertoppen and Hamborgerland is without rival. … The icebergs were also fantastic. They were spellbinding. One of my favorite memories is of an evening in 1981 when we drifted at the mouth of Jacobshavnfjord with young icebergs surrounding us, beginning their long journey across Disko Bay en route to destinations off Newfoundland. Being a Saturday night, we were allowed to have one beer at dinner, reward for the earlier "field day" clean-up. After eating, people brought instruments on deck-concertinas, guitars, violin, recorders, and pennywhistles-and started a concert, complete with dancing, popcorn, and an audience of icebergs.

Regina was an equal match for Greenland's grandeur. She enhanced the scenery. Perhaps what Greenland is to wilderness and elemental beauty, *Regina* is to sailing vessels and the manifestation of human craft. She looked as if she belonged there, among the icebergs, deep in the fjords.

Regina also generated a certain Greenlandic spirit. It became a tradition to celebrate crossing the Arctic Circle by producing an "Arctic Revue." The idea was to dress as incongruously as possible for a parade on deck.

July 21, 1981
Yesterday the "Arctic Revue" was held at 1500. It was a good show, bravely carried out by many bathing beauties and skimpily clad gents in temperatures of 4°C. Baggywrinkle worn as a grass skirt, bathing suits with sou'westers and safety harnesses, and bare legs stuck into Newfie sneakers were the rage. Photos were taken all around and water began to be splashed about. Horrified yells came from Harvey (Oxenhorn), who was clipped onto the main stays'l sheet and unable to escape his cold baptism. "Very refreshing," they all said later, dressed once again in woolens, hats, and boots.

Then there was the official opening of the Greenland golfing season when Al Stearns, accompanied by caddy Root Lieberman in tuxedo, teed off from a bergy bit in Fiskenaesset Harbor. As the ice drifted closer to land, Greenlanders took pictures of Al swinging his club. Another year, John Calogero skied down the glacier in Evighedsfjord, and Richie Perkins windsurfed among growlers at the foot of the glacier.

In the fjords we found exquisite wildflowers — campions, saxifrages, harebells, azaleas, fireweed, 3-5 inch willow and birch trees branching horizontally along the ground, meadows of yellow poppies and cotton grass, which the Inuit used to insulate their boots and to make wicks for their seal oil lamps. There were moraines of all kinds, glaciers with meltwater streams flowing underneath, and views that appeared deceptively close when they were 10 or 20 miles away. Between bog and bug, we saw an occasional fox, hare, peregrine, nesting jaeger, and caribou, an occasional Inuit fishing camp, and ruins of old Norse settlements.

In the towns we explored and indulged in local offerings. The sight of unfamiliar things and bizarre contrasts from the mix of indigenous and European cultures remain in my mind most vividly. There were walrus skulls airing on top of tool sheds and whale entrees on hotel dinner menus. You could buy steak tartar and frozen raspberries from Denmark in the supermarket or muktuk, blubber, intestines, seal meat, loons, kittiwakes, and other country food at the open market in Godthaab. Four story apartment complexes had slabs of fish and other meat hanging from the windows. Seal skins stretched on frames adorned the balconies along with racks of caribou antlers and various furs. In larger towns, not only were there taxis, but they were Mercedes, Volvos, and Audis!

We would grow weary from the excesses of town life and like true nomads were ready to go back to sea. *Regina* was a welcoming home; there was always a pot of hot coffee on the stove, good food, wool mittens and socks lining the radiator to dry in the main cabin, someone writing in a journal, people napping in bunks (red curtains closed) or reading (red curtains open), the unmistakably delicious smell of pine tar in the focs'le, the familiar rock and roll of the ship, the quiet of the paneled, red cushioned aft saloon and its "home sweet home" lantern hanging above the table, and a thousand other things that were part of *Regina*.

We worked hard those Greenland summers and found ourselves rewarded in many ways. It was a tremendous privilege just to be there and to sail where so few people have been before. I remember an afternoon on our way home, when *Regina* seemed to blend so beautifully with the life and rhythm of the sea, and I thought how all of us on board had adapted to this motion and now moved so naturally in tune with it.

September 3, 1982.
We're racing along at 6-7k under sail with SE winds, passing the Newfoundland coast about 70 miles offshore of the Funk Islands and Cape Freels. The seas are choppy but the ride is smooth. I'm sitting on the windward side beside Doo's bait locker and the pilot house, watching hundreds of shearwaters and some fulmars and kittiwakes soar gracefully, bank and arc skyward then dip low again. The quarter deck rail rises and dips in rhythm with the birds, a perfect duet.

Regina seemed to change everyone who lived and worked aboard her, to stretch them in positive and compelling ways. Kim Smith once said to me, "*Regina* has good karma." She drew people to her and held them in her grip. As one of those victims, I will always treasure my voyages on *Regina* with deep gratitude. Thank you *Regina*, thank you, George. [1]

Big Fish Story
Gregg Swanzey

After voyaging to the Arctic aboard *Regina Maris* in 1981, Gregg Swanzey went on to captain such venerable vessels as the sloop *Clearwater* on the Hudson River, the schooners *When and If* and *Te Vega* for Landmark School's Watermark Program, the schooner *Bowdoin* for Outward Bound and then served many years as captain and executive director for the schooner *Ernestina,* the official vessel of the Commonwealth of Massachusetts. His most remarkable achievement might be sailing trans-Atlantic three times as captain aboard *Te Vega* with his wife and two daughters aboard.

Today, Gregg has gone ashore for a bit to work for two land trusts in New York — Mohonk Preserve, near New Paltz, and the Kingston Land Trust. He lives in the Rondout section of Kingston with a view of the tidal Hudson River, knowing he can always jump on a boat and go anywhere on the globe.

On July 29, 1981 we sailed into Itividley Fjord, Greenland, just a couple of days after leaving Disko Bay on our trip south. We anchored in a shallow arm of the fjord within easy reach of glaciers, mushrooms, mussel beds and a freshwater lake full of Arctic char. There was an Inuit family set up for the summer to dry the char which they caught in weirs in the stream before it ran into the fjord.

Captain George Nichols and I, in anticipation of the possibility of capturing and eating some Arctic char, both brought our fly fishing rods and an assortment of flies. We took off for the lake as soon as the anchor was down. George proceeded to hook three char, much to my frustration since I couldn't get anything to come near my hook. He was rightly proud of his catch.

I decided to try my hand at saltwater fishing the next day. Patrick Wadden, Brenda Ashly, Harvey Oxenhorn, and I went out with cod jigs and reels of monofilament in the jolly boat to the nearest drop off of the bottom — I had checked it out on the depth finder as we came in. We got our gear ready and drifted over the spot as we jigged.

We did pretty well, caught lots of medium-sized cod and pollack and finally decided on one last drift. The lines went out and soon mine hooked the bottom — or so it seemed — but a steady pull got results. This was the biggest fish I had ever hooked! He ran a couple of times and I took a couple of turns around the thole pins to tire him. We gasped at the huge shape which appeared below the boat!

He broke the surface. In the excitement I nearly went overboard to grab him by the operculum and the cod jig. Harvey grabbed me by the belt as Patrick picked up an oar to whack him. The boat tipped to the gun'l as we rolled and that fish slid in. We lashed him tail and head.

A 54-inch, 100-pound halibut was hauled on board *Regina* with the boat falls. That fish fed the boat for three meals!

George and I each had gotten the fish story we'd come to Greenland for. [2]

A Life-Changing Ship
Earl Henderson

Earl Henderson is believed to be living in Annapolis, Maryland.

My experience on *Regina Maris* literally changed my life. I had never been on a boat before I joined her in 1981 and have been working as a professional sailor and captain ever since. In those years my fondest memories of sailing, from two weeks of daylight to green flashes to beautiful night sails (still my favorite time to sail) to many, many whales and dolphins to golfing off the stern, are of times on *Regina*. To date the most awesome experience of my life and my most often told story is free diving with a 40' (or so) humpback on Silver Bank and being eye-to-eye for what seemed at the time as an eternity within a distance of 20' of the eye (almost touching the flipper's tip). Until then I had thought that the "sense" that others had told me of when in close proximity to these phenomenal creatures was hogwash. I have never felt threatened or seen what I thought was threatening behavior from these animals. They are amazingly forgiving of our terribly inhumane acts toward them.

Even after 11 months of personal experiences and new places, the most incredible occurrence aboard *Regina* was the repetition of exciting, active, quality people whom I will never forget and for whom I will never cease giving thanks for helping my (sometimes slow) maturation. All of my experiences, without exception, were positive and all of those people, without exception, made definite, sincere, positive, and mostly major contributions to my development. When I find myself in the position of instructing, the major point I try to convey to my students is what I was taught on *Regina Maris* — and that is to never stop learning, and to try to be constantly aware of learning something at all moments in time. [3]

A Step Back in Time
Nicola Wadsworth Bloedel
Nicola Wadsworth Bloedel – student, deckhand and cook on *Regina Maris* – is now a portrait photographer in Seattle, Washington.

Stepping aboard *Regina Maris* was like stepping back in time. Sailing aboard her provided a glimpse of yesteryear, when tall ships were popular vessels. No wonder so many of us read the ship's copy of Sterling Hayden's *Voyage, a Novel of 1896* with such relish. Of course, we had a much easier time than the crew aboard Neptune's Car! Thank goodness there weren't any Otto Lassiters aboard the *Regina M*aris! Instead we were a group of people enjoying our time at sea, enjoying life from decks of a three-masted barkentine, out on the North Atlantic.

Regina Maris was my home for a period of 12 months spread over two years. I arrived as a student, returned as a deckhand, and came back another time as ship's cook.

I first boarded *Regina* as she was tied at the New England Aquarium's dock in Boston, in October 1982. I was a student on the Expedition 42 trip (Boston to Puerto Rico via Bermuda and the U.S. Virgin Islands). There was so much to learn that first time — the names and positions of the rigging, the navigation, the stars, general seamanship (like tying a good knot!), getting used to the watch schedule, and naval time. Not to mention learning how to pump the heads properly! Then there was "boat talk," like saying "down below" instead of "downstairs." Any difficult chore on board was called a "character building experience" — fixing a plugged up head; shaking the anchor chain back into its locker; standing watch in wet clothing. My student trip was one of the last trips done with all the classes held on board, so we had to deal with watch schedules and class schedules, sometimes together, while underway.

As a deckhand (January to May 1983) I enjoyed teaching students about seamanship aboard our proud vessel. I was in great shape with all the yard climbing and sail maneuvering that we did. Of course, as a deckhand my arms got terrific workouts keeping up with the sanding, rust-busting, painting, and varnishing. We seemed to start at the top of the worklist, work our way down it over the weeks, and at the end of the list we'd have to start back up at the top again. The sea doesn't allow any brightwork to last for very long.

We had the best cook on board while I was a student and deckhand: Danny Bareiss was his name and it was his first time cooking on board a boat. It was no small feat preparing our meals in *Regina's* galley, dealing with a temperamental diesel stove/oven. I know, because for five months (January to May 1984) I was *Regina's* cook. It takes a lot of energy to prepare three meals per day (sometimes two sittings per meal), seven days a week for the 35 people on board.

The day usually started off at 0530h with kneading dough for six loaves of bread. Breakfast was always a big meal to get everyone going, although if you snoozed through it you lost out on having it. No sooner had the dishwashers and the galley slave finished up than it was time to start on lunch. I usually could get a mid-afternoon break which meant a nap in the jolly boat (I couldn't be seen from the deck, at least) or whale watching. I was lucky enough to have an assistant, Julie Hoffman, which made things considerably easier. Working together, we would be able to crawl off to our cabin by 2100h. Planning the menu and stocking up the boat was always a treat. We had to make sure that there was enough of everything because if we ran out of something, there wasn't a grocery store out on Silver Bank. Our buying trips in Puerto Plata (Dominican Republic) quickly improved my fluency in the Spanish language.

When I was the cook I did miss being a deckhand. There was nothing better than climbing the yards to furl sails. I was surprised to read in the early pages of my journal that I dreaded the thought of going up in the rigging at night. That quickly changed! As a deckhand I always volunteered to go aloft to overhaul the buntlines, which meant hanging onto the yards "by your eyelashes!"

My fondest memories of life aboard *Regina Maris* include:
- Watching for the green flash as the sun set while anchored out on Silver Bank. One time, just as we saw the green flash, a humpback whale breached near the horizon, appearing to leap over the setting sun. And, if that wasn't enough, a second and a third whale breached right after that, a little closer each time;
- Climbing aloft to furl the Royal under a clear, starry night in a warm breeze;
- Riding through the street of Puerto Plata on a donkey cart while buying supplies for the ship;
- Trying to chop out the next night's dinner (frozen chicken bodies) in the pantry freezer with a crowbar because the freezer's crushed ice melted when the ship's power was off for awhile and when the power went back on the ice froze in one solid block. This happened more than once and required my climbing into the freezer locker, wearing a pair of shorts, a T-

shirt, and my gumboots, wielding a crowbar to get the meat out. This method resulted sometimes in little hack marks on the meat served — a source of amusement for everyone at the table;
- Riding out the gale off of Cape Hatteras during our sail north to Newport, Rhode Island, in April 1983. For three days we were violently tossing and rolling around. We had the hand pumps going on the deck; we lost our windsock and anemometer up on the masts; we lost a plank up near the rail and a door in the bulwarks; the engine door tore off; and the lower topsail (squaresail) tore to shreds. You name it, it went crazy, and we SURVIVED!;
- Last but not least, seeing my first whale ever — a humpback sighted NW of Navidad Bank on January 11, 1983, at 0914h. It breached not two miles broad off the starboard bow and I was, to say the least, impressed. [4]

Close Encounters of the Cetacean Kind
Ken Balcomb

In addition to Ken's account of Regina's first voyage to the Caribbean (Chapter 17), the 1988 *Whalewatcher* issue included the following journal entry from 1982.

10 January 1982, Silver Bank

We started out this beautiful cloudless day by putting the deflatable boat over the side to try getting some tail photos using that precarious platform. Immediately the 25hp outboard started running rough, so we replaced it with the 15hp outboard and headed north about three miles to try to get photos of a lobtailing solo. The 15hp, of course, started running rough once we were well away from the ship, and it quit entirely when we got near the whale. We could see the ship, so there was really no danger. Besides, the engine had quit under duress, and there was every reason to believe that it would run again. It eventually did, and we limped back to r/v *Regina Maris* just in time for lunch. Oh well, it is only half a day gone by.

The afternoon ... more than made up for the false start of the morning. We first went after a trio of whales, one of which stayed near the surface and acted agitated at the other two. All three fluked frequently, so it was a good bet to follow them. The agitated whale had a small bite out of the hind margin just to the left of the notch, and [the whale] was of approximately equal size (to the other two). Its flukes were mostly white with two short black scratches on the starboard side. One of its companions had dark flukes with a grayish splotch on the starboard side. As we followed these whales we saw two rowdy groups of LOTS of other blows within three miles. One of the rowdy groups came conveniently close to us so we turned toward them.

As it turned out we didn't have to go very far. They came over and ran a couple of circles around us so we stopped. Then they played "Ring Around *Regina*" for awhile, charging around and around us like a frolicking school of dolphins. I counted eleven whales on the surface at once, and I suspect a twelfth was tagging along underneath. I don't know how long they did that, but it was at least a half a dozen revolutions. Then I jumped into the water and joined them. They swam around and around me, at first excitedly as they had been, and then slower and more inquisitively. I hung upside down over them and made noises in the water. Visibility was not good, so they had to get within a whale length for me to see them very well. Several times the whole procession did so…underneath and alongside me.

Some of the whales left, but six of them kept on circling, so one by one most of the people on *Regina* who wanted to swim with whales got their chance. At one point all of the whales swam directly at us, and one faced me and gave a trumpeting scream before abruptly diving fifteen feet in front of me. I dove with it, but of course could not keep up as it plunged toward the bottom. I don't remember if I took any pictures as we faced off — I was pretty excited. The trumpeting scream must have been very directional because Jennifer, who was about thirty feet to my left, did not hear it.

Well, we all went swimming with them until the ship had to leave to find an anchorage for the night. As we left, the whales charged along behind us like dolphins again. When we anchored about four miles further south, they charged around and around us again. When the anchor was securely set and the light was fading I went back into the water to see if I could swim under them and identify their sex. They would not let me get under them, but they all faced me at one point, and as I dove down they excitedly dove and turned away. At that point I was able to see that one at least was a male. By then it was getting kinda spooky and shadowy, and George started talking about shark-feeding time, so I got out. The whales moved off a bit anyway. I don't think they liked me as much as I liked them. All of this stuff really happened today, but what does it mean?

In the evening, Denise (Herzing) and I did the dishes in the sweat hot galley, and afterwards I climbed out to the tip of the bowsprit to cool off and watch the clouds pull a blanket across the moon. To the north the sky brightened in flashes of lightning from the thickest clouds. A storm is approaching, but for now it is calm with gentle waves to rock us to sleep. From my perch in the furl of the flying jib the world looks altogether well. [5]

Greenland 1983
Mari Smultea

Mari Smultea is with Moss Landing Marine Laboratories in Moss Landing, California. This is her contribution to the *Whalewatcher "Regina* issue."

The ORES Greenland 1983 expedition aboard r/v *Regina Maris* to evaluate whether the West Greenland feeding stock of humpbacks could withstand continued aboriginal whaling was a journey of firsts. First of all, only hard-core whale fanatics or cold-loving masochists would choose to endure their "summer" in sub-zero temperatures. Yet a diversity of people was attracted to this atypical expedition.

The ever-faithful mascot of our motley crew was a plastic pink flamingo on a stick. Feeling and acting as if we were trailblazing pioneers, we planted flamingos at the heads of glaciers, at the foot of a fjord, at the base of an ice-carved mountain — desolate and pristine places where it seemed no one else had reason to come before us. We claimed these territories under the auspices of *Regina Maris* in the name of the Pink Flamingo.

It was also a journey of personal firsts: Third mate Richie Perkins' windsurfing expedition in front of the womb of a massive ice-blue glacier, weaving his sails through the iceberg maze; new icebergs being calved before our eyes, the kittiwakes swarming over waters upturned by the explosive splashes. Al Stearns, the cook, and John Calogero sleeping with their skis crammed into their tiny bunks to be the first to ski a remote snow-capped fjord island. Then, after ice-climbing our way up treacherous glacial fissures, the entire crew tee'd off at the crest, shooting our golf balls wildly toward the sea-valley far below us, *Regina* a mere dot testifying to our climbing feat, our ever-faithful flamingos watching over our freezing martinis. Crazy Eric Hutchins "dipping" into a 2° C iceberg pool, a frozen smile of defiance and victory pasted to his blue face. Then perusing the backstreet markets of the capital of Gotthab among the toothless grins of the native Eskimos while they gnawed on muktuk and other nameless, shapeless delicacies.

For me the entire experience was a first: furling sails at 70 feet, crossing open ocean in a storm, being mesmerized by voraciously feeding humpbacks. But my lasting first was the incredibly vitalizing and addicting energy created by the people of ORES, absorbed through my pores to the depths of my soul. My experience with ORES was the most influential and rewarding experience of my life, both personally and professionally. It still inspires me as I continue with the adventures of whale science. [6]

There for the Ship
Bert Rogers

Bert Rogers is now executive director of Tall Ships America (formerly the American Sail Training Association) in Newport, Rhode Island. The organization's mission is to encourage character-building through sail training, promote sail training to the North American public and support education under sail. Bert recalled his experience on *Regina* in an email to the author in 2011.

I joined the ship in September of 1981 in Boston to further my learning in tall ships. I had recently left the very traditionally run Brigantine *Romance* under Captain Arthur Kimberly, who had a lot of deep sea experience. Traditional sailing and seamanship were my passion. As bos'n, I was focused on the working of the ship. My efforts and skill aloft were recognized by George Nichols and I was promoted to third mate. I worked hard teaching the other crewmembers marlinspike seamanship.

In the year I served on the ship, I sailed under Captain Herb Smith and Captain Lawrence "Tex" Kilduff. I was eventually given a field promotion to chief mate, which I felt I was not ready for, as *Regina* was only my second ship and I did not have much inshore, near-costal experience. I initially declined but finally accepted the position under some pressure and with many reassurances from the captain.

I had to adjust to the ways of a research vessel. The science being conducted on board was secondary to my personal mission, and it was a while before I understood what the research was all about, so focused was I on the ship. But when they anchored over Silver Bank in the seemingly open sea, I had the realization that they were on a "Marine Safari," and the relationship between the ship and the science became clear to me. Being introduced to the rich biosphere of the sea was an uplifting and life-changing event for me, and I learned that helping the scientists achieve their research goals was very satisfying.

In the spring of 1982, the ship was sailing from Puerto Rico to Washington, D.C., as George Nichols, who was promoting the Sailing School Vessels Act, wanted *Regina* to be present for congressmen to tour and get to understand the workings of a school ship. This act was being considered in Congress at the time. The act was important for all school ships that used paying students as crewmembers.

Captain Tex gave me the task of readying the ship for a "Bristol" inspection upon arrival at the Gangplank Marina in D.C. As chief mate, I used this opportunity to express my passion for tall ships and seamanship, and I made the crew and students work long, hard hours attempting to make *Regina Maris* into a showpiece. They were successful in their efforts but my driving force was not very carefully calibrated, to say the least, and caused a rift in the fragile fabric of shipboard relationships.

The ship then returned to Gloucester for yard work in preparation for a voyage to Greenland. It was there that George spoke with me about his concern for maintaining good shipboard relationships and said he felt I needed more time at a lower rank to improve my skills. He then offered me the second mate position, which I declined. I then moved on to other ships, including *Alexandria* (née *Lindo*), *Sea Cloud*, *Spirit of Massachusetts,* and others, constantly honing my seamanship skills. [7]

CHAPTER 19
VOYAGES 1981 THROUGH 1983

1. Judith S. Perkins, *Whalewatcher*, Summer 1988.
2. Gregg Swanzey, *Whalewatcher*, Summer 1988.
3. Earl Henderson, *Whalewatcher*, Summer 1988.
4. Nicola Wadsworth Bloedel, *Whalewatcher*, Summer 1988.
5. Ken Balcomb, *Whalewatcher*, Summer 1988.
6. Mari Smultea, *Whalewatcher*, Summer 1988.
7. Bert Rogers, email to the author, October 13, 2011.

CHAPTER 20

REGINA'S LAST ORES YEARS
1983 – 1986

This chapter covers *Regina's* final years as a sailing research vessel, including more recollections from the *Whalewatcher "Regina* issue," some partially condensed or summarized.

Photo-identification
Ken Balcomb

In Chapter 19, Ken Balcomb described the first — unsuccessful — attempt to use auxiliary craft for photo identification of whales, (which was then followed by a fine encounter with humpbacks). Auxiliary boats, however, did prove successful for photo-identification, and the *Whalewatcher* issue includes an entry from Ken's journal describing a day spent in that activity with Steve Katona, David Mattila, Richard Sears, Greg Stone, and Phil Clapham.

20 February 1984

The weather remained beautiful today, even though the breeze picked up to about 15 knots. We got underway with *Regina* at 0959 after launching the deflatables, and I got on the bowsprit. Immediately we found an active trio of adults — I believe two males and a female. One male, the outside animal, was pushed away by the other male every time it tried to get close to the female. The female blew much less frequently than the other two and seemed very relaxed about everything.

At 1119 we had two cows with their calves approach one another and then veer off at about 50 feet apart. One of the calves was tiny and gray and its fin was laying clear over on the portside. I estimate it was *very* recently born. The other calf was more blackish gray, though it too was small and the fin was slightly bent — 10 days old! (I estimate). Interestingly enough, the only escort we observed arrived with the gray calf mum and left with the black calf mum.

After lunch we found a reasonably friendly pair of whales, so Sal and I jumped in and the pair swam around us for at least three minutes in super clear water. One thing was very apparent — same as yesterday — the male was always the closer animal to me and it would get between me and the females when I swam toward [them]. We swam around with these whales until 1409.

After leaving those two, we went for a cow/calf/escort that were lobtailing. The cow had a notchfin, but I didn't get a very good photo of it.

Steve and David saw her too, and thought she might be the one we saw yesterday, but that one didn't have a calf. We worked around with these for awhile until 1434 and then we headed closer to the reef to anchor.

We anchored at 1558 and had a swim call. I came below to write my notes. When Steve and David came in, Steve raved about swimming with a pair that was probably the same pair that Sal and I swam with. Steve also noted that the male would not let him get near the female — was even aggressive about it. David touched his flipper, however, and it immediately drew it back. Later Richard Sears also went in with this pair, but in that encounter one of the whales went straight to the bottom and singing commenced. Then the other whale swam to the bottom and both swam away. Little bits and pieces of behavioral observations may someday add up to a story. [1]

A Dream Made Real
Phil Clapham

Phil Clapham, who started out on *Regina* as a student, is with the Cetacean Research Program, Center for Coastal Studies, Provincetown, Massachusetts. Serving on *Regina* satisfied an urge he had had from early childhood to sail on a tall ship. The following is from his longer *Whalewatcher* contribution.

By the time ... I [sailed] aboard *Regina*, in the spring of 1983, I was already familiar with her near legendary status as a research vessel. I had seen her from afar... and the sight briefly rekindled the embers of [an] old dream. I had always had a soft spot for Baltic traders... there was a steadfast quality about them ... that quietly commanded respect. I looked forward to the trip — a week's excursion to the Great South Channel southeast of Cape Cod — with much excitement and not a little trepidation....

When I first stepped aboard *Regina* in Newport, Rhode Island, I can honestly and unequivocally say that it was love at first sight. I was immediately infected with that widespread and thankfully incurable condition that Perran Ross once termed "*Regina* fever." The cruise itself was not what could be termed a great success: Great South Channel in May is known for fog, gales, and cold, and we had all three. Much of the trip was spent in vainly trying to escape either damp, cold conditions, or the cheery sight of a variety of people losing a variety of meals at a variety of unpredictable intervals. But despite the less-than-auspicious circumstances, I was extremely content, happy just to be there and to find that, cold and vomit notwithstanding, the experience was as romantic and as moving as I had imagined it might be. The trip home, made in a gale, was particularly memorable: *Regina* heeling to port as we ran through the night, her deck ablaze with phosphorescence every time a wave washed across it.

My second trip aboard *Regina*, in early 1984, remains in my mind as one of the most stimulating experiences of my life. David Mattila and I were conducting a cooperative study, with ORES and the College of the Atlantic, on Silver Bank, studying the population composition and habitat use of the humpback whales that winter there. A more magical setting could hardly be imagined: sixty miles out to sea in a magnificent reef system, companioned by nothing more — and nothing less — than seas and sky and some two thousand whales. And there were memories to match: during daylight one could find oneself sitting forty feet out on the bowsprit, or high up in the rigging, watching *Regina's* bow cutting through water of purest aquamarine. Nights were no less enchanted: lying on the foredeck, in darkness utterly uncompromised by any artificial light, gazing in wonder as the slow sway of the masts swept across the blazing star fields above. It was a wonderful time, and for much of the cruise I felt as if I was alive and awake in a dream of my own making — which, in a very real sense, I was.

The generosity of George Nichols in allowing so many people to experience *Regina* was, I believe, a gift whose value cannot be overestimated. Without her and the work of the many people — scientists, students, and crew — who were fortunate enough to find themselves sharing a small part of her long life, we would know a great deal less about whales than we currently do. And, as important as this, was the gift that *Regina* herself was able to give — for magic is hard to come by in these modern times of ours, and *Regina* was magic in the making. [2]

Photo shows the fluke of a humpback as it sounded off the side of the ship. Notice Master George Nichols leaning on the starboard railing. Photo by John Quackenbush.

A Student's Life

Kathy Kelly

The *Whalewatcher* issue included several journal entries from Kathy Kelly that provide a vivid picture of a student's daily life of aboard *Regina*. Kathy now lives in Katonah, New York.

The First Day
On our way to Gloucester from Boston. We've plunged right into the thick of it all, and though the jungle of anonymous lines seemed overwhelming last night during our brief orientation watch, after handling some of them it immediately becomes less frightening and more friendly. This morning the watch mate took us together on our watch to familiarize us with some knots, then we checked our safety harnesses in preparation for our first ascent into the rigging.

While the onlookers from the party-boats and pier provided us audience, we swung over to the shrouds and fearlessly clambered up… up the ratlines, over the little platform, and on further to the upper topsail. No problems. Until you look down, and that first jolt suddenly makes your knees just a trifle rubbery. It seems precarious with just that little foot line between you and the next spar, and for a few tense seconds while you get yourself under control, you wonder if you'll succeed for two months.

Watch Schedules

We were divided up into "watches," with a watch mate and deckhand for each group. Ours is the fore watch (the other two being the main and the mizzen). While on deck during a watch we were responsible for standing lookout, doing the logs (engine and environmental), taking a turn at the helm, watching for whales, etc., being available for sail handling, etc. The watch period ran four hours, with one hour at each assigned "station" until late afternoon, when there were two "dog" watches, each two hours long. This broke up the rotation so that the same group would not always be standing watch during the same time slots. A really long day would be one when you started out at midnight, standing watch till 4 a.m. You'd then be back on deck at noon till 4 p.m., then *again* from 8 p.m. until midnight. One particularly pessimistic entry, no doubt written during a "long" watch day, read: "Isn't it astounding that we paid so much money to stand out in 4-degree weather, with the rain battering our faces, the cold water seeping through cracks in our warm clothing and making our mittens sodden, winds lashing out and throwing showers of frigid seawater over us? Isn't it astounding?? My scarf and mittens still haven't dried out from this morning at 4:00, when the six of us, dripping and exhausted, ponderously lowered ourselves back into the cozy womb of the main salon." (Of course, the one advantage to the long watch day was that once I was done you got to enjoy a full night of uninterrupted sleep — no small luxury!)

Climbing Aloft

This morning, after being relieved at the helm, we handled some sails, and then Joan, Clay, and I went aloft to overhaul. This maneuver involves climbing into the rigging in order to feed out some slack on the bunt and bunt-leach lines. I managed to scramble right up and out into the first three yards, but on up to the t'gallant I ran into a small problem. A little "deck" projects out over the ratlines, but the distance from the last rung of the ratline to the next foothold was too far for my short legs, and in my bumbling effort to pull myself up, I slipped, and for one or two heart-stopping seconds was hanging, unclipped, by one arm and one leg. Despite the overly vivid images coming to mind of my crumpled body sprawled all over the deck below, I caught my breath and moved up, but was considerably shaken. On the way back down, I found a nice solid point to clip my safety harness into before letting myself out and over that ledge again. God, sometimes I wonder what in the world I was doing way up there, anyway.

Food

Another peculiarity of shipboard life is ocean-going jello. Al has made jello a couple of times now, but it never gets quite the way it ought to. Usually it freezes and separates, so you get liquidy blobs mixed in with large flakes of ice. Actually, it doesn't taste bad at all. Last night we had strawberry jello with apricots and pears in it, and whipped topping. After people had had their spoons in it digging around a couple of times it got pretty funky looking, so someone dubbed it "Red Tide."

"Starboard List" brownies — everything on board tends to exhibit special little oceanic quirks; jello, cakes, brownies, anything that has to sit awhile while cooking usually comes out slanted in the pan, one side shallow and the other side deep, depending on the list of the ship.

Sounds

This old lady makes more of a racket than anything I ever heard. The creaks and cracks and thumps and bangs and knocks are enough to wake the dead. It's a measure of how tired we all get that we can even sleep through such a din. Every now and then you wake up in the dark of your bunk, and it sounds like all Hell breaking loose around you — wood creaking, pots and pans bashing around in the galley — you wonder if *Regina* has collided with the world's biggest iceberg, and you start remembering where you stowed your survival suit. Of course, there's never anything amiss, and George's words come back to reassure you before you doze off again: It's a ship that doesn't creak in weather that you ought to worry about.

Laughter

One of the nicest things about this trip is the laughter. There's so much of it, it happens so often — not a meal goes by without some instance of hilarity, not a day passes that you don't break up laughing at something. Of course, there are certain people who tend to instigate it, but there's no lack of wit among the rest, and often one remark is enough to catalyze an entire chain of jokes and one-liners. It's probably a good thing, especially with so many people living together in such close quarters for such a long period of time [3]

Evan Logan Recalls *Regina* in 1983-1984

Evan Logan served on *Regina* during the early '70s in various crew positions and then spent seven years on the top'sl schooner *Sofia*, five of them doing a circumnavigation. He returned to crew on *Regina* from 1982 to 1984, then captained the schooner *Rambler* for a year, also for ORES. Today he is based in New Zealand, from which he sails *Alvei*, a three-masted main topsail schooner that provides sail training and delivers medical aid to remote island communities. In a 2011email to the author, he provided the following recollection of his *Regina* experience.

In September, 1982 I rejoined *Regina* in Boston, Massachusetts, as first mate. A fellow named Larry "Tex" Kilduff skippered the first expedition south. We stopped off for a visit at Bermuda, then sailed on to St. Thomas to clear in. Then we sailed over to a bay on the east end of St. Johns, where the students did their coral reef ecology studies. The first expedition finished mid-December. We dropped off the students and scientists at St. Thomas so they could fly back to the States, and the crew took *Regina* to San Juan for the Christmas holidays and to wait for the next group of students. Larry, aka "Tex," went back to the States. Seems he and George had had a differing of opinion and Tex got fired.

In early January 1983, the crew and I took *Regina* to Puerto Plata, Dominican Republic, to meet the next group of students and scientists and begin humpback whale surveys on Silver Bank. George flew to meet us in Puerto Plata. He seemed quite happy with the state of things, and I got promoted from first mate to captain.

For the rest of that season we did humpback whale surveys on Silver Bank working out of Puerto Plata. For one survey we were out for a whole six weeks on Silver bank. Fortunately for us, an 800-ton tramp freighter named *Polyxeny* ran up on the north end of Silver Bank. Except for the perimeter, Silver Bank is poorly charted, and the freighter was an excellent radar target, allowing us to make an accurate chart of the area. Ken Balcomb was leader of the Silver Bank humpback research and the main photographer.

We returned to Boston by way of the Bahamas, riding the Gulf Stream north along the coast. Stopped in at Charleston, South Carolina, and put out to sea again to ride out the last storm of the spring season. (See photo below)

That summer of 1983 we spent doing Minke whale surveys in the Davis Straits and along the west coast of Greenland. George skippered

Regina for that expedition; it was my first experience sailing in ice, and I sailed as mate.

From the fall of 1983 through the winter of 1984, *Regina* again did humpback surveys on Silver Bank. The last expedition of that season started in Puerto Plata, we did two weeks on the bank, then sailed through the Bahamas and cleared at Nassau for the passage north to Charleston and back to the new ORES office at Gloucester. [4]

R/V Regina Maris in the last spring 1983 storm, 150 miles East of Cape Hatteras. Waves stove in the engine room door and smashed up the steering box. *Photo by Evan Logan*

Regina on TV: "The Voyage of the Mimi"

While continuing work as a research vessel, *Regina* added to her TV and film résumé by appearing in "The Voyage of the Mimi." This 13-part TV series, produced by Bank Street College of Education, New York, and released by PBS in 1984, was also an interactive video/computer program that provided hands-on laboratory experiences related to the science featured in each TV episode, such as using fluke pattern matching to study whale populations; reading nautical charts; triangulating with radio beacons; and testing water for pH, salinity, and temperature.

In the series, the actress Judy Pratt, a Gallaudet University student who had spent a summer as a student on *Regina,* plays Sally Ruth Cochran, a graduate research student. Episode 6, "Home Movies," shows Sally doing whale research on *Regina*. Filmed off

Silver Bank, the episode shows many research activities on the ship and includes good footage of George Nichols up aloft watching for reefs and calling down instructions to the crew on the wheel. Scenes show film being developed in the darkroom and Judy Pratt and Ken Balcomb matching fluke photographs. The main salon is shown, as well as all the bunks and the galley, with a Thanksgiving meal being prepared. Other footage covers the making and usage of baggywrinkle, and the film also shows census runs, with the crew observing and Ken recording data. In footage of Judy and Ken snorkeling, they see many calves and grown whales, some of which are singing. Judy, who is deaf, feels it on her body. And another sequence shows using the hydrophone and observing the vibrations on the oscilloscope with voice print recording comparisons. The *Regina* segment closes with the crew hauling the anchor and getting ready to set sail.

The End of an Era

In 1984, ORES retired *Regina* and used the three-masted staysail schooner *Rambler* for all offshore activities. In a letter to the author in1992, when *Regina* restoration attempts were underway in Greenport, New York, Ken Balcomb provided one explanation for the ship's retirement: "The real reason she is not still sailing around doing her thing is that she was incredibly expensive to maintain. I remember in the 12 years I was the chief scientist seeing quarter millions after half millions of dollars spent on her, and she was always leaky and stopping just short of threatening to sink. She was held together with love, patience, immense amounts of work, and more than a little grace from the heavens." [5]

Indeed, during the 12 years of ORES ownership, keeping *Regina* well maintained consumed a large part of the organization's budget. Ann Nichols remembers very expensive yard bills and stated in an email to the author, "The ship was hauled out in the fall of 1976, when planking had to be replaced and the copper bottom removed. The mechanicals always needed attention." [6]

And Richard Perkins, responsible for much of the ship's maintenance, recalled in an email to the author, "Generally there were two haul-outs a year, usually for four weeks around May and June, and then another in the fall before heading south, although for the fall year period she may have stayed in the water. She was hauled out in Gloucester, Massachusetts, during the years I was aboard, over on Rocky Neck. There was major yard work on her in 1982 with additional planks replaced in 1983 and 1984." [7]

Evan Ginsberg, who sailed on *Regina* and *Rambler* in the fall of 1984, remembers, "*Regina* lost her insurance slip from Lloyds in the fall of 1984 as did most of the fleet of tall ships then serving as school ships after the 117-foot *Bark Marques* went down in a gale off North Carolina losing 19 of her 28 crew members. She was hit by a sudden squall and a large wave, knocking her down on the starboard side, the main hatch was breached and water flooded into the interior of the ship. Built in 1917, *Marques* did not have watertight compartments. All ships without sealable water tight compartments supposedly lost their insurance as a result of the *Marques* tragedy. When the insurance was lost, ORES bought *Rambler*, a 120-foot three masted, high aspect Staysail Schooner, with a 13-foot deep fin keel, in Tenerife, Canary Islands. *Rambler,* formerly *Idus De Marzo* had been built for an Antarctic expedition several years before. The new ORES research vessel made the Atlantic crossing to pick up students waiting at the Virgin Island Ecological Research Station at Little Lamesure Bay in the North end of St. John , USVI. These students/crew, were the last to sail *Regina* and had left her in the industrial harbor of San Juan, Puerto Rico. After picking up the students and crew, *Rambler* then tracked sperm whales with hydrophones over the trench, east of the VI down to Bequi. Evan Shepard was captain and Hal Whitehead was chief scientist."[8]

After *Regina's* retirement from ORES, Evan Logan recalled in his 2011 email, "*Regina* sat on the inside of the dock at the ORES office in Gloucester until June of 1986." [4] ORES continued offering six-week courses in whale studies until 1987, when the organization disbanded. She was listed for sale by several brokers, who were waiting for new adventurers and dreamers.

On Tuesday, March 14, 1989, The Gloucester Daily Times carried an article with this headline: "Dr. George Nichols, ORES founder, dies."

The front-page article, by a staff reporter, was more than an obituary — it provided insight into a man with a mission and many dreams. Excerpts from that article follow.

"Dr. George Nichols, whose love of the sea led him to sail around the world and to found the Ocean Research and Education Society (ORES), died unexpectedly Sunday (March 12th) of a heart attack while skiing on Mount Attitash in Bartlett, N.H. Nichols, a Manchester resident, was the husband of Ann (Ratcliffe) Nichols. He was 66. Nichols was known locally as the founder and director of ORES, an accredited college program that took students around the world, which moved to Harbor Loop in Gloucester from Boston in 1983. ORES taught more than 1,000 college students and hundreds of schoolchildren about the ocean and what lives in it. ORES scientists compiled research on marine mammals and their habitats. ...

"Twenty years prior to George's death, a local author and historian, Joe Garland, met him and said of George, 'He was an extraordinary guy. He was a leader in this country at seeing the sea as being part [of] maturation and education for young people.' Garland goes on to say that Nichols was, 'a great friend of Gloucester, full of vigor and passion, an individual whose energy, imagination, and inspiration will be very sorely missed by anyone who knew him.' ...

"Most recently, Nichols was leading an effort by Gloucester Marine Railways workers to buy the company from its owners. Nichols, who volunteered many hours of his time to the union, wanted to save the boatyard to help preserve the city's commercial fishing industry. ...

" 'Our union and the men in the yard are real grateful for everything he did for us,' said Rand Wilson, organizer of the local 815 carpenters' union. Wilson said that Dr. Nichols' work for the union was all voluntary. 'He had complete confidence and trust of the men in the yard,' Wilson said. 'He had no trouble at all grasping the problems and frustrations of the working individual's life.' ...

"Nichols sailed his three-masted staysail schooner *Rambler* from Europe across the Atlantic to Puerto Rico in 1984. He had returned in July from a two-year sea voyage around the world with his wife and two of their children. ...

"Nichols was survived by his wife, Ann; two sons, George III and Pierce; two daughters, Susan and Domenica; and five grandchildren." [9]

A memorial service for Dr. George Nichols was held March 21, 1989, at the First Unitarian Church on Middle Street, Gloucester. Over the years, ORES scientists and student scientists have published hundreds of research documents, which can be found by searching in Google Scholar for "R/V Regina Maris whale research." George Nichol's primary goal for the organization has been far more than merely realized.

CHAPTER 20
REGINA'S LAST ORES YEARS

1. Ken Balcomb, *Whalewatcher*, Summer 1988.
2. Phil Clapham, *Whalewatcher*, Summer 1988.
3. Kathy Kelly, *Whalewatcher,* Summer 1988.
4. Evan Logan, email to the author, January 7, 2011.
5. Ken Balcomb, letter to the author dated February 21, 1992.
6. Ann Nichols, email to the author, December 31, 2010.
7. Richard Perkins, email to the author, September 26, 2011.
8. Evan Ginsberg, Facebook posting on Friends and Crew of the Regina Maris site, May 10, 2017.
9. "Dr. George Nichols, ORES founder, dies," The Gloucester Daily Times, March 14, 1989.

CHAPTER 21
IN MARINA BAY, MASSACHUSETTS
1986 – 1991

In June 1986, ORES sold *Regina Maris* to brothers and partners Peter and William O'Connell, of the O'Connell Management Co. Inc. of Quincy, Massachusetts, for about $500,000.00, as reported in article in *The Patriot Ledger*. [1] The brothers' company was the principal developer of the 400-acre, $96 million Marina Bay residential-commercial project in the Squantum section of Quincy, on the south shore of Boston Harbor.

In April, the O'Connells had sent their director of development, Walter J. Hannon Sr., the former mayor of Quincy, on a quest to find a historic vessel for use in their development. Walter had called a former Army friend, Newport ship restorer Paul Dunn. Paul knew of *Regina's* availability and suggested Walter take a look at her. "As soon as you saw the ship," Walter said, "you immediately fell in love with it." [1]

James L. Frye, then the manager of Marina Bay Boston Harbor Marina Corporation, remembered the following in a 2011 email to the author: "I was involved in negotiating her purchase in as much as I was there playing the junior role to Walter Hannon Sr., who was actually representing the O'Connell brothers in the negotiation and purchase. We met at ORES with Captain John Wigglesworth, and it seemed clear to me at the time that John had accepted his task to sell the ship most reluctantly and, although pleased to have a buyer, he was a bit chagrined in agreeing to the purchase price and sale. I do remember that there was considerable room between the asking price and the selling price, but Captain Wigglesworth was hard pressed to turn away the check that Walter Hannon laid on his desk. We purchased the ship for cash right on the spot, no survey, no reservations (even I, as a relative neophyte, had suggested a survey be performed before the purchase, but it was not done) the only condition being that the ship would be delivered to Marina Bay by Captain Wigglesworth." [2]

Captain John W. Wigglesworth had served as a relief captain on *Regina*, sailing her in the Pacific, the Caribbean, and off the Labarador coast on ORES research voyages. After George Nichols died, John took on more of a leadership role in ORES, which was financially strapped. Selling *Regina Maris* became necessary. At that time, he was quoted as saying, "I feel sad. I'd like to see it keep sailing, but at the same time the cost of doing it is prohibitive. So I think this is the best life for the ship." [1]

The O'Connell brothers planned to turn *Regina Maris* into a seasonal floating dockside restaurant, with a glass covered deck and canopy. It was to be like the tugboat *John Wannamaker,* which had been docked at Marina Bay and converted to a restaurant, The Edmund Fitzgerald. For many years that restaurant had enjoyed great success, and the belief at the time, according to Jim Frye, was that "a sailing ship would be an even bigger draw and a more dramatic experience." [2] The O'Connells had budgeted $500,000 for the conversion. They hoped to have the restaurant open in May 1987 and planned to use the Barrett family restaurant chain to operate it. They had visions of having a turn-around ceremony each year for preservation purposes, but not to coincide with the *Old Ironsides* traditional event, according to Anthony Yudis in a July 1986 *Boston Globe* article. [3]

Regina was delivered from Gloucester to the commuter boat launch in Marina Bay, under the power of her well-worn 8-71 diesel, by Captain John Wigglesworth. [1] John and a crew of 10 took the new owners and 35 of their friends and employees on *Regina's* last sail, a voyage of 21 nautical miles. As there was nothing but an uncooperative headwind, however, the only actual sailing was the dropping of the lower topsail inside Boston Harbor, achieving an additional half-knot of speed. The O'Connell company helicopter escorted the ship, filming the event.

"Tall ships and waterfront communities go hand in hand," said Peter O'Connell, who stood on the ship's bowsprit as she pulled into Marina Bay before 200 onlookers. "And we deserve one, the way I look at it.... To have it here in Quincy, the City of Presidents, reinforces our connection to the sea." [1]

Regina arriving at Marina Bay in Squantum (Quincy) MA in 1986.
Photo by Joan Vaughn.

Jim Frye took on the day-to-day responsibility for *Regina*. In an adjacent warehouse, he stored all the sails and other equipment not needed for a restaurant. One of the first things done to *Regina,* he recalled, was "removing the bulkhead walls that made up the quarters below and opening up the space for restaurant seating. We quickly discovered this to be delicate and difficult work, preserving her structural integrity whilst trying to create the necessary space."[2]

Consultants were hired to design a lighting plan for the ship and its masts. Thirty thousand decorative lights and cables were placed on the ship, creating sails made of lights. "The idea was to get her lit up so folks would be excited and intrigued during the build-out of the housing complex and be eager for their dining experience when she was ready," Jim Frye recalled. "The lighting project was expansive and she was magnificent when illuminated, looking as if she were floating just above the water at night." [2] The lights could be seen from Interstate 93 and all over the South Boston Harbor area.

"There was a great deal of time spent in planning and designing the restaurant space," Jim noted. "It became clear pretty quickly that there wasn't going to be space enough for a kitchen and the necessary number of seats below decks. The cooking for The Edmund Fitzgerald was done landside adjacent to the ship and brought aboard by waiters. We couldn't use the same kitchen because *Regina Maris* drew more water than was available where The Edmund Fitzgerald had been. As a matter of fact she was sitting in the only part of the marina that could accommodate her, and we drove the clusters of dolphin piles specifically to moor her there."[2]

Once the lights were installed, the restaurant renovation got underway, but plans stalled due to the complexities mentioned above. The O'Connells decided to insure the vessel, and that required that *Regina* be surveyed. In the fall of 1987, Jim Frye arranged to have the ship towed to Cashman Marine Company at the Boston Graving Dock, the former Bethlehem Shipyard, in East Boston. It was agreed that the most cost-effective way to haul her would be to wait for and take advantage of any opening in the yard's schedule rather than set a specific date for the survey. Fall turned to winter.

At 3 a.m. January 15, 1988, it was -6° F with a wind chill of -50° F. *Regina* was tied to the dock at Cashman Marine, locked solid in ice. The bilge pump failed. When the weight of the water was too much for the ice to hold her up, down she went in 33 feet of water while still secured to the dock. The night watchman told Jim Frye, "One minute she was there and then I heard a loud cracking sound and all I could see were the tops of her masts." [4] *Regina Maris* lay on the bottom, and she stayed there for two and a half months.

During that time, the plan for re-floating her was developed. Many ideas for how to raise her were proposed, complicated by fears of other winter storms and ice doing damage to her rigging. Salvage experts were concerned with the age of the vessel and whether a hull weakness existed. Underwater photos revealed she had rolled on her side and settled into six feet of mud and muck.

The plan that developed required that she first be rolled upright with airbags attached to her lower side and then inflated. Next divers would plug all the openings in the hull, the four companionways, and the hold's entrance. The divers also would have to remove mud under the ship in order to thread three 2-inch diameter cables around her that would be attached to steel "H" beam spreaders high over the deck. The three cables would then be attached to three cranes, two on the dock and one on a floating barge amidships. The slings at the bow, amidships, and stern could then lift her and the tons of water inside. [4] As she was being raised and the deck reached the surface, a trash pump with the capacity of 50,000 gallons a minute would be used to empty the hull. [5]

    Jim Frye feared "the boat's aging wooden planks might be damaged by the cables slung under the hull. When they were lifting before she broke the surface, we were concerned that it be a uniform lift from all three cranes." [6]

    During the actual lift, the cranes smoked and groaned, making it necessary to stop lifting and reposition them so that the strongest was at the bow, where the ship had the most mass. Once the deck was exposed and the pump turned on, it took only half an hour to have her floating again. [7] She was raised on April 1, 1988, Good Friday, and by 2:27 p.m. she was floating and tied to the dock, her decks covered with bushels of mussels and mud. The only apparent damage was that the top ten feet of the mizzen mast had been broken off when the lifting sling became tangled in the mast's rigging.

    When asked about her condition, Jim Frye said, "But she will be looking as good as new soon. We are going to move her two piers away at high tide tonight and place her in dry dock. We'll hose the crud off her and then check for damage and make necessary repairs in the coming weeks. We'll repair the masts esthetically, but not so she could get under sail again."[5]

    Once she was hauled out, she was searched for large leaks, but none was found. It was determined that the bilge pump had malfunctioned due to the extremely cold weather. A survey was then done by Gilford "Tiffy" Full, of Marblehead, Massachusetts. The survey revealed that *Regina* needed a great deal of real restoration to be insurable and worthy certification. "As a matter of fact," Jim Frye wrote in his 2001 email to the author, "as I recall the surveyor was reluctant to make much comment on the record preferring not to prejudice those that might evaluate her condition for insurability. [2]

    After the haul-out and all the bad news about her, *Regina* was towed back to Marina Bay and the restaurant plans were "effectively scrapped," Jim said in his 2011 email, "The tops of the masts had been broken off," he continued, "and of course the remnants of spending months on the bottom of Boston Harbor didn't enhance the appearance of the ship. To the best of my recollection the ship was never actually insured. The ship was re-lighted but to a much lesser degree and she was to sit with no plan beyond being an attraction of sorts for the marina. It was a sad time for those of us that respected her history and as I said I still feel like we had disrespected her in some way especially as the outcome did nothing to enhance her history or her future. Unfortunately her time at Marina Bay was only folly. " [2]

Former owner and captain John Aage Wilson had made inquiries in 1986 into re-purchasing the ship and restoring her to glory, but when he heard about the sinking in Boston Harbor, he commented, "That was probably the ship's destiny and it would be impossible to save her." [8]

In October 1989, Thomas Cox replaced Jim Frye as manager of the Marina Bay complex and *Regina Maris*. It was up to Tom to protect the ship from further harm and find a way to use her so as not to incur any additional expense for O'Connell Management. He started looking for a buyer.

CHAPTER 21
IN MARINA BAY, MASSACHUSETTS
1986 – 1991

1. Eric Sorensen, "Motoring Home, Tall Ship Ends Era," *The Patriot Ledger* (Quincy, Massachusetts), July 1986.
2. James L. Frye, email to the author, April 20, 2011.
3. Anthony Yudis, "Tall Ship to Become a Restaurant," *Boston Globe*, July 1986.
4. James L. Frye, phone call with the author, September 2, 1992.
5. Andrew L. Andrews, "Crew Raises 80-Year-Old Ship from Harbor with Little Damage," *Boston Globe*, April 2, 1988.
6. Alan Levin, "From the Depths of Despair," *Boston Globe*, April 2, 1988.
7. Della Klemovich, "Cranes Lift *Regina Maris* from Muddy Sea Bottom," *The Patriot Ledger*, April 2, 1988.
8. "*Regina Maris*: The Sail Ship with Eternal Life," *Faederlandvenneil* (Norway), March 13, 1993. Translated by Peter Wilson.

CHAPTER 22
TO GREENPORT, NEW YORK
February – September 1991

A tree farmer in Connecticut named Hijo Knuttel had been following the saga of *Regina Maris* in the news while she was in Boston, having seen her at Marina Bay in the spring of 1990. According to a 1991 *Suffolk Times* article, he had said to his friends at that time, "Gee that's incredible. ... After that, I never really slept the same — I always thought about her." [1]

Many months later, on the coldest day of 1990, Hijo sneaked on board the ship at Marina Bay. He recalled, "She was a mess and taking on water but a lovely ship with beautiful lines." [2] The dream of saving the 82-year-old ship was developing in Hijo's mind. But with a young family and responsibility for the family business, he was in no position to bring the dream to fruition. He contacted Robert Val Rosenbaum, a former classmate from his days at Landing Boat School in Kennebunkport, Maine. A yacht designer with offices in Riverside, Connecticut, Bob Rosenbaum shared Hijo's dream of restoring a historic ship.

Later, when the ship was in Greenport, Bob was asked by a *Newsday* reporter how he found *Regina Maris*. He said, "I don't know if I found her or she found me. Everyone turns into a kid when they see a ship like this" [3]

After visiting the ship, the two men decided that Bob should buy her and together they would work on her. During the early months of 1991, Bob started negotiations with Tom Cox, now managing Marina Bay and responsible for *Regina*. They came to an agreement and on March 20, 1991, signed a contract for Bob to purchase the ship for the sum of "ONE DOLLAR AND NO CENTS ($1.00)". The contract required Bob to insure the vessel against loss, sinking, and liability, to protect the sellers from responsibility. Marina Bay gave Bob until June 17 to vacate the free dock space the company was providing, after which a $300-a-day fee would be charged. The contract also required that Bob apply for a seasonal marina dockage license from the local authorities and that a constant watch be maintained on board *Regina* while she was docked at Marina Bay

"Before I knew it, he had purchased it," Hijo recalled. "I helped Bob fix her up by supplying paint, a generator, pumps, T-shirts to sell, and my time and labor."[1] The two men realized that restoring *Regina* was a task beyond their personal means. But they felt that if they could find a community that would sponsor the project and supply volunteers and funding, restoration could be accomplished and the ship could possibly serve as a sail training vessel. [2]

Before all that could happen, though, Bob had his work cut out for him. Meeting all the requirements of the contract was one thing; finding a community to support the restoration of the ship was another. His research lead him to the city of New Bedford, Massachusetts, which had some interest in the vessel, but negations broke down. As he continued searching, Bob fondly remembered the eastern end of Long Island, New York, where he had summered in the 1960s, and especially the small Village of Greenport, which he had first visited when he was 12.

Greenport, on the North Fork of Long Island's East End, boasts a beautiful waterfront and one of only two large, deepwater ports on eastern Long Island (The other is in nearby Sag Harbor.) In the early 1990s, a growing population of well-to-do second-home owners was moving into the village and the surrounding areas. Vineyards and other agribusinesses were bringing more and more visitors to communities just west of the village, and Greenport itself was in the process of revitalization. Government officials and other community leaders had developed a vision for the future, and central to that vision was the village's becoming a tourist destination, primarily by capitalizing on its waterfront and strong maritime history.

Greenport had been home port to 111 whaling ships between 1795 and 1891. From the mid-to late 1800s, village shipyards had built and launched 120 wooden sailing ships, and fishing and shellfishing had long been mainstays of the village economy. During World War II, Greenport Yacht and Shipbuilding, owned by Steve Clarke, a village trustee in 1991, had built 59 minesweepers, tugs, and rescue boats of up to 278 tons, and it had a 400-ton railway. The village also had two other yacht-building and restoration yards, with talented restoration workers.

The village had obtained grants for several waterfront enhancement projects and had already accomplished one major one, the rebuilding of the historic lighthouse known as Bug Light, east of the village. The East End Seaport and Marine Foundation (EESMF), founded in 1990, had undertaken the lighthouse restoration, and the project had been spearheaded and orchestrated by Merlon Wiggin, an engineer by trade and an EESMF founder. The lighthouse structure had been prefabricated at Steve Clarke's shipyard, and it had been floated out to the foundation on a barge and lifted into place in just one day by local marine contractor John Costello, also a village trustee. The grant-writing, subsequent fundraising, and fabrication were all done by local volunteers, and Bug Light gave leaders confidence that the small village could accomplish great things.

Other plans in the works included turning the train station into a museum and home for EESMF; converting a burned out restaurant and derelict marina complex into a waterfront park; and re-establishing the marina docking space. Merlon and his wife, Isabel, were instrumental in the grant-writing and fundraising for all these projects.

In addition to Merlon and Isabel Wiggins, Steve Clarke, and John Costello, other players in community development projects included Bill and Jan Claudio and their brother- in- law Jerry Tuttle. Together they owned two dockside restaurants and provided dockage for restaurant patrons and marine services to transient boaters. They owned one dock at the foot of Main Street large enough for a ship that could be an attraction.

Bob Rosenbaum had once worked part-time as a bartender at Claudio's Restaurant. He recalled in a 1991 *Newsday* article "having long talks with the owner, William

Claudio, about the village's whaling history and its tall sailing ships. ... His dream was to see a big ship tied up at the dock by his restaurant."[3]

When Bob had purchased *Regina Maris* in March, he had called Claudio's Restaurant and spoken with a Bill Claudio. It took Bob a while to understand that he was speaking with the son of the man he had worked for years ago. After the confusion was sorted out, "Bill Claudio asked me if I wanted to tend bar ... I told him, 'I have a tall ship.'" [3]

This piqued Bill's interest and he discussed the ship with other town leaders. In early June 1991, the village government, under Mayor Bill Pell, business owners, and the EESMF contacted Bob Rosenbaum and started negotiating an agreement to make Greenport *Regina Maris's* new home.

At the time, Steve Clarke said in an article in *The Traveler Watchman* that early indications suggested that the ship was too heavy for his marine railway. His facility could handle vessels under 400 tons, and an estimate being bantered about in the community was that *Regina* weighed in at 500 tons. "If we don't get it, it's not because we just turned it down without a real hard look," Steve said. "We want it, but we have to protect ourselves. There are so many things that look right about it, but you have to look at everything."[4]

Merlon, with the verbal support of the marine foundation and other community members, sent a draft agreement to Bob Rosenbaum on June 12. Bob's free dockage at Marina Bay was up on the 17th, and he had to move fast. His major challenge was the cost of moving the ship to Greenport, estimated at $9,000. According to the agreement, EESMF was to cover that cost, although other issues were involved that needed further negotiation, including final approval by the foundation's board of directors. So Bob did not sign the document, but he did contact a towing company to move the ship. *Regina Maris* arrived in Greenport June 19, 1991, and was tied up at the Claudio family dock at the foot of Main Street.

Many community members were thrilled to see the tall ship docked in their quaint historic village. It was picture perfect. The media, loving the story, swarmed over the ship, and tourists came to see it and spend money in the village. Local pride swelled and optimism was in the air.

A volunteer group was organized to start the restoration, which later became Save the *Regina Maris* Ltd. (STRM). Over 70 skilled and unskilled workers from all over Long Island came to help with the restoration. Donations of labor, equipment, and money started coming in.

Along with this flood of good will, the steady work of negotiating among all the parties continued. Some EESMF board members, village officials, and community members, did not fully support the ship's becoming their responsibility. Some saw her as a potential liability that could take energy, focus, and funds from other community projects. Nevertheless, all parties finally signed an agreement on July 11 that eased most fears and concerns and also included some interesting points. Prefacing the document was a discussion of the U.S. Coast Guard definition of a "permanently moored vessel," which is viewed as "substantially a land structure." A Coast Guard inspection would be required to certify that *Regina* would indeed be "substantially a land structure." This classification would allow the ship to be moved to a shipyard for hauling or to a temporary hurricane mooring.

In the agreement, EESMF was to pay for the towing from Boston to Greenport. (This fee was payable upon *Regina's* arrival, but the towing company subsequently agreed to accept installment payments.) The foundation also agreed to raise funds for *Regina's* restoration as a permanently moored vessel and dockside attraction. Free dockside electrical service would be provided, and the foundation agreed to make all the appropriate applications to all governmental regulatory entities — village, town, county, state, and federal. The agreement's point #6 played an especially important role in *Regina's* future:

"EESMF will arrange for the installation of mooring pile clusters so as to provide a safe mooring of the vessel at Claudio's Main Street Dock. The placement of the storm mooring would be a joint effort between the Foundation and the Owner with the initial plan to have a tall ship mooring installed by the Navy similar to the ones that the Navy accomplished in Newport."

Also according to the agreement, Bob Rosenbaum's responsibilities, in addition to having the ship towed to Greenport, included having the ship hauled out for inspection "depending on the convenience of the owner, shipyard and funding availability." And Bob had to actively pursue the restoration, with the immediate goal of having the ship available for on-deck tourist visits. Getting *Regina* into this condition would obviously require a great deal of work, and the agreement allowed just one year to accomplish the task.

The agreement also spelled out many specific tasks to be done, including repairing the hull below the waterline; sanding and caulking the decks; inspecting and insuring the safety of the rigging, which task included replacing the two missing top masts; and general repair and painting topside for cosmetic reasons. Bob had to provide liability insurance for all visitors and have the ship available for 10 individual weekend days for EESMF on-deck functions, at no cost. One final provision was to "enter into an agreement with the Claudio Family Corporation to include appropriate provisions for the control of the vessel if it is abandoned, or no restoration is done for one year, or loss of insurance."

Bob had already started the processes of getting *Regina* accepted on the state and national registers of historic places and of forming a not-for-profit organization, but the paperwork for both tasks needed constant follow-up and prodding. With the signing of the agreement, those tasks were to be shared by EESMF, and they fell primarily into the capable hands of Isabel and Merlon Wiggin. Bob now felt he wasn't alone in trying to save the ship, for much of the community was behind the project. Crowds constantly wanted to visit, and so many volunteers were around all the time that Bob didn't have much privacy. The burden of sole responsibility for the ship had been lifted.

By August much had been accomplished. The free electric service provided by the village and phone service had been installed. Volunteers had cleaned, painted and repaired enough to make the ship safe and presentable for tourists to be on the deck. The tons of debris and rusted mechanicals destroyed in the Boston sinking were beginning to be brought up from inside the hull for disposal — *Regina* had to lose some weight so she could be hauled out at the yard. Steve Clarke was starting to build a new set of rails that would be heavy enough to handle the hopefully trimmer vessel at his shipyard. There were hopes for a spring haul-out in order to scrape and inspect the hull, replace rotten planking and then repaint. Permits to install additional dolphins (pilings) to help hold the ship at the dock in high winds and seas had been applied for, and the funds to do that work had been raised. Merlon had submitted a request to the Navy, through Representative George Hochbruecker (D Coram), to install in Pipes Cove, somewhat west of Greenport Harbor, a storm mooring large enough to hold *Regina,* or any military vessel, that would allow the ship to swing with the wind in storms. The village planned to use the ship as a centerpiece for their September Maritime Festival, which would feature a wooden boat regatta and local marine tradesmen demonstrating their skills. A complete restoration was years away, but having the ship seaworthy and sailing again was a dream many in the community shared with Bob Rosenbaum. In a *Newsday* article of August 11, 1991, he is quoted as saying that by 2008, on the ship's 100th birthday, "We'll sail her around the world."[3]

In the second week of August, the U.S. Weather service was observing ominous weather changes in the Caribbean. By August 15, a tropical storm was brewing, and it was traveling up the coast. On the evening of August 17, it became Hurricane Bob. By Sunday, August 18, with sustained winds of 100 miles an hour, it began accelerating north-northeastward. It was predicted to hit the East End of Long Island on the evening of Monday, August 19.]

What to do with *Regina Maris*? The plans for such an occasion that had been laid out in the agreement between Bob Rosenbaum and EESMF were just that — plans. Nothing had yet been done to keep the ship safe. Bob met with Merlon and other community members on August 17 to develop a plan of action. Emergency, "fly-by-the-seat-of-your-pants" options were discussed. *Regina* could be towed out to open water and anchored — but she had no power to run the pumps required to keep her afloat. It was not known if her anchors were functional. And where was this place she could be anchored so that the expected winds would not drive her up on some beach? The permits had just arrived for the installation of large storm dolphins in her present slip. But there was no time now to install them. [5] She could be left where she was and tied up between Preston's marine supply stores dock and Claudio's dock, but with an expected storm surge of 8 to 12 feet, the ship could end up stuck between the buildings in the middle of Main Street. The third option was to move her to the heavily built railroad dock, a short distance from her present birth, and tie her off between the very large dolphins there. But if she broke loose there or capsized, it would shut down the vital ferry service to Shelter Island. The last — unthinkable — option was to scuttle her at the dock.

The end result of the meeting was the decision to charter a tug and tow the ship to the railroad dock. Merlon, in an August 30 *Newsday* article, said that "the first time he could get together a tugboat and smaller towboats was first thing Monday morning and there were fishing boats at the dock presently and they had to be shuffled around to make room for the *Regina*." [6]

The harbormaster, Ed Swensen, on Sunday had cleared a space for *Regina* at the railroad dock. The tug was expected to arrive at 11:00 a.m. Monday, August 19. Everyone in the community was scrambling to get their boats, houses, and families ready for the storm. Bob knew of the proposed plans, and he knew the tug was coming. He just had to wait.

On Monday morning, a frantic call came from the tug skipper saying he had overslept and one of his tow boats had mechanical problems. Hurricane Bob had sped up overnight, and it was clear that time had run out for any plan to be accomplished. Bob, two musician friends who were staying on the ship, and some volunteers tied up the ship as best as they could. They removed all the personal effects and abandoned ship. Bob called the fire department and had them begin to pump water into the hull to scuttle her lest she end up in the middle of Main Street, but, Bob recalled, "the department lacked sufficient pumping capacity to finish the job before the storm hit." [6] (It would have taken 1.7 million gallons of water to fill the hull.)

A deliberately-scuttled Regina Maris weathers Hurricane Bob Monday morning at Claudio's dock in Greenport New York. Photo by Judy Ahrens from her book "The North Fork" which features photographs from her years at The Suffolk Times.

Hurricane Bob hit Greenport around noon Monday, August 19, with sustained winds of 75 mph; after the eye passed over, gusts up to 90 mph were recorded. The ship was still partially buoyant and bounced off the bottom with every wave surge, damaging the hull. But sometime during the storm she lost all buoyancy and settled into the bottom mud, where she would stay for 13 days.

After the storm cleared, Bob took stock of the situation. There was little damage above the waterline. However, he recalled, "The electrical system we put in is destroyed. The cabin houses, which had been completely refurbished, are now completely destroyed. We had six months of straight restoration to the boat. Although the ship is insured, I think we're set back a year or a year-and-a-half from where we started. Cashwise, just for materials, we had somewhere between $30,000 and $50,000 into the vessel and the labor of the 45 volunteers who had been working on the vessel here for a month."[6]

Tuesday, the fire department tried to pump the ship out, but after three hours, pumping had not substantially lowered the water level in the hull. Also on Tuesday morning, ORES alum and editor of this book Carol Lew Simons, then living in Greenport, headed out to Claudio's dock, "to find Bob Rosenbaum and Merlon Wiggin near the dock in the rain yelling at each other," she recounted in an email to the author. "I saw Merlon seem to grab at and push Bob — but he may very well have just been making a point by jabbing his finger in the air and accidentally connected with Bob's chest. Bob was furious, yelling, 'He hit me, you saw it!' to everyone around. It looked like a serious fight was imminent, but it didn't happen.

"I talked with Bob right after that incident. He was furious with the entire town, which he felt had not supported the project as it should have. He was staying at the Townsend Manor Inn, which itself was pretty wet, and I invited him to stay at my (dry) house for a few days.

"Bob believed that Merlon, and perhaps Bill Claudio, I don't recall, had deliberately delayed getting help for the ship until it was too late. He thought Merlon wanted *Regna* to be scuttled, perhaps to grace Greenport harbor like the hulks of boats in Wiscasset, Maine. Bob recalled, as did I, that Merlon had often mentioned that those old wrecks were the most photographed attraction in Maine. Bob thought maybe Merlon hoped *Regina* could serve a similar purpose in Greenport.

"But the animosity, perhaps paranoia, was definitely two-sided. Merlon and Bill were sure Bob had planned to scuttle the ship. I believe they thought he wanted the insurance money and was a major crook and con artist. That opinion was reinforced later in the *Regina* saga they felt, when Bob took all the artifacts, including the wheel and the binnacle, from the boat. Merlon and Bill thought these things belonged to the town or the organization that had formed around *Regina*. Neither party seemed bothered by the fact that they actually belonged to *Regina*.

"And while fingers were being pointed all around, *Regina* just got wetter and more rotten and farther away from the dignified retirement she deserved."[7]

On Saturday, August 24, dock builder John Costello, with large capacity dock-building pumps, and fire departments from Greenport and nearby East Marion and Orient, tried once again to pump out *Regina*, but they were unsuccessful. Shortly after that, volunteer divers Mat Sisnni from Stony Brook, Paul Casciotta from East Hampton, and Doug Murphy from Greenport attempted to assess the extent of the damage. Doug, as reported in *The Suffolk Times,* said, "They could find no signs of major damage to the hull, she's probably sitting on top of something we can't see."[8]

The same article quoted Bob Rosenbaum as saying, "The divers had been able to inspect 60 percent of the hull, but access to the rest of the ship was blocked by the bay bottom. We think she has sprung a plank or is holed, but we just don't know."[8]

Regina was on the bottom once again and now the center of a controversy and a blame game. Bob claimed that EESMF and Merlon had failed to respond to the impending storm emergency. EESMF felt that Bob had been too hasty in his decision to scuttle the ship, since help had been on the way, even if the tug had been late and the storm early. Community members not involved with the decision-making loudly vocalized their hindsight opinion that *Regina* could have survived at the dock since the storm surge had not coincided with the high tide as had been predicted. Blame and counter-blame flew, tempers flared, and threats were made. The once-united community was becoming divided. Examples of the diatribe reported in the local press follow:

August 29, 1991, The Suffolk Times *quoting Bob Rosenbaum:*

"We knew the storm was coming three days ahead of time, but Merlon Wiggin didn't show up until just before the storm arrived. I personally blame Merlon Wiggin for not towing the ship to safety. I will not talk to him, nor will he set foot on this ship. And as long as he's in the picture, the *Regina Maris* will not be part of the Maritime Festival [planned for September]. An invitation to Mr. Wiggin to sit on the *Regina Maris* board of directors also will be withdrawn." [8]

August 30, 1991, Newsday*:*

Mr. Wiggin expressed regret this week that "elaborate" plans to assist the *Regina Maris* made in advance of the storm fell through on the morning of August 19 due to a variety of circumstances, including the hurricane's unfashionably early arrival. "I understand why Bob is disappointed, but by the time help arrived Monday morning it was too late. He had already decided to sink the boat. I hope that any differences with Mr. Rosenbaum can be worked out, and that the *Regina Maris* will remain in Greenport. I will insist that a written agreement reached between Mr. Rosenbaum and the EESMF be honored." [6] [Merlon was concerned about the planned Maritime Festival.]

September 5, 1991, The Suffolk Times

"If [Mr. Rosenbaum] was so serious about this, he would have had a plan before the hurricane," said Village Trustee [Steve] Clarke. Steve went on to say, "I say this because he didn't call me until it was too big of a job to complete before the storm. Even then I didn't know what he wanted. Nobody did. He blames Merlon for waiting until the last minute, but I think it's the other way around."[9]

September 5, 1991, The Suffolk Times

Merlon stated, "The EESMF's attorney notified Mr. Rosenbaum that it expects a full refund of the $10,500 spent bringing the boat to Greenport if he is not around to fulfill his end of the contract." Merlon also sent a letter to all of the foundation members that stated, "It recently came to our attention that Mr. Rosenbaum may not have set up the standard 'not-for-profit' foundation type accountability for donations. Until we receive conformation from the IRS, we feel, in consideration of you, the members and supporters of our foundation, we should not be promoting financial support to the *Regina Maris* Foundation."[9]

A meeting was called on Wednesday, August 28, that included Mayor Bill Pell, village trustees Steve Clarke and John Costello, and Merlon Wiggin. The group came up with a plan to raise the ship, if Bob would let them, since communications by this time were very strained. From the meeting, Bill Pell called Bob and told him of the plan, and scheduled a 10 o'clock meeting for the next day to discuss it. Bob told him that he had called Russell H. Tripp, owner of Bay State Towing Company, to come down, pump out the ship, and tow her to D. N. Kelly and Sons shipyard in Fair Haven, Massachusetts, for repairs and continued restoration. Bob also said, "If I can come to an arrangement with the village, I will bring the ship back to Greenport." [6]

Bay State Towing divers arrived the same day as the meeting to do an underwater survey and plan what equipment they would need for the refloating operation. The divers reported spotting what they termed as a "1/4 inch split in the hull" during their survey and preparation work.

On Saturday, August 31, Bay State Towing pumped out *Regina* in 25 minutes, and by 3:20 p.m. she was being towed to Fairhaven by *Russell Jr.*, a former U.S. Coast Guard tug. Russell Tripp, in a 2011 telephone conversation with the author, remembered that while towing the ship, the sea's rocking opened more seams, and her water level kept rising until they turned on another 6" pump. [10]

Kevin McLaughlin of D.N. Kelly said in the September 5 *Suffolk Times* article, "The tug with the *Regina* in tow arrived safely at the shipyard on Sunday and [the ship] is now floating waiting to be hauled out." [9]

The dock at the end of Greenport's Main Street where *Regina* had been tied up was empty. The three masts that were taller than the church spires were suddenly gone. The thousands of people who came to stare at and learn about the ship were there no more. The tourist magnet was gone. Greenport had lost its tall ship. Her loss was keenly felt.

CHAPTER 22
TO GREENPORT, NEW YORK

1. Margaret O'Neil, "Home Again: Regina Maris Back in Village for Good," *The Suffolk Times* (Mattituck, New York), October 24, 1991.
2. William Dobriner, "The Nine Lives of *Regina Maris,*" an unpublished article by William Dobriner. He gave a draft copy to the author in 1993.
3. Mitchell Freedman, "History Is Standing Tall In Greenport," *Newsday* (Long Island City, New York), August 11, 1991.
4. Tim Kelly, "Agreement, Maybe on Tall Ship Offer — Barkentine Owner Mulls over Marine Foundation's Conditions," *Traveler-Watchman* (Southold, New York), June 17, 1991.
5. Robert Val Rosenbaum, *Wooden Boat* On-Line Forum, January 6, 2011.
6. Bill Bleyer, "Smooth Sailing It Wasn't," *Newsday*, August 30, 1991.
7. Carol Lew Simons, email to author, March 1, 2012.
8. Troy Gustavson, "*Regina Maris* Still Sunk and Sabers Are Rattling," *The Suffolk Times*, August 29, 1991.

9. Margaret O'Neill, "*Regina Maris* Arises and Departs," *The Suffolk Times*, September 5, 1991.
10. Russell H. Tripp, telephone conversation with the author, June1, 2011.

CHAPTER 23

FAIRHAVEN, MASSACHUSETTS
September 1 – October 22, 1991

The shipyard in Fairhaven was no haven for *Regina Maris*, nor for Bob Rosenbaum. Shortly after the ship arrived on September 1, Kevin McLaughlin, manager of D.N. Kelly and Sons shipyard, inspected *Regina* and decided not to haul her without an additional bond from AIG, the ships insurer in case she broke up during the hauling out process. He felt an 83-year-old wooden vessel that had been sunk twice would pose a risk and present special problems. Kevin was especially concerned that her "bottom was not sound enough." [1]

After days of discussions and negotiations, however, AIG refused to post the additional bond at that time, and the ship was not hauled. The insurance company did agree to pay Bay State Towing owner Russell Tripp to watch the ship and maintain the pumps until she could be hauled out. He and his crew worked down below in *Regina,* patching and caulking all the leaks they could find so that, he said, "a single 4-inch diameter pump would keep her bilge level low while only idling." [2]

Bob Rosenbaum was in a very difficult position. Again he was on his own, without a town's support, the owner of a derelict ship with no way to fix her. He was at the end of his rope, overextended in every way. He was threatened with a law suit by the Village of Greenport for breach of contract and by a tug company and two shipyards for lack of payment. He decided to scuttle the ship. To do this he had to make an application to the Massachusetts Environmental Protection Agency, which did give him permission initially. But the media picked up on the story and a public outcry arose. Ship lovers from all over New England did not want to see *Regina* go to the bottom and be lost forever.

Because Bob had requested permission to scuttle the ship outside the 12-mile limit, the federal EPA got involved. Partly because of the public outcry, the agency came to believe the ship might have historic significance, overturned the state's scuttle permit, and referred the case to the National Park Service. The park service has to certify anything that seeks listing on the National Register of Historic Places, for which Bob Rosenbaum had applied. In researching *Regina,* the federal EPA also sought the advice of the Massachusetts Historic Commission. Eventually the commission said it did not believe the ship qualified for the National Register of Historic Places because she had been in the country for fewer than 50 years. [1]

All this took time, and the ship could not stay at Kelley's shipyard because they would not haul her. On October 8, Bob arranged for Russell Tripp to tow her, with his tug, *Russell Jr.*, the 40 miles to Newport, Rhode Island, where she would be docked. The media storm was feverish, and the harbormaster there refused to allow tug and ship to enter the Newport harbor because he feared *Regina* would be abandoned. Russell was forced to tow her back to Fairhaven and dock her at Lindberg Marine, rafted up to another vessel while still also tied to *Russell Jr.,* on October 9. [3]

Meanwhile back in Greenport, Merlon Wiggin was frantically reaching out to Peter Stanford, president of the National Maritime Historical Society (NMHS), who had many connections in the maritime industry and had been successful in saving many historic ships. Together they contacted Captain H.D. Robinson of the Coast Guard — captain of the Port of Providence and an acquaintance of Merlon's. They convinced Captain Robinson to place a non- removal order (#0491) on *Regina* so she could not be moved from Fairhaven, because it was feared the ship would be scuttled. This order threatened Russell and Bob with a $25,000 fine from the Coast Guard if they tried to carry out their scuttling plan. Since Russell, as he told the author, had been quoted in the media as saying, "the *Regina* should have her masts chopped down and be sunk with a bucket dredge," [2] the public focus was on him, and the media made him the villain. "There were lots of threats against me and my tug," he said. As the days went by, he incurred more expense and endured more ire from a public that was calling for the ship to be saved. [4]

Back in Greenport — behind the scenes and under the media radar for the most part — the East End Seaport Museum Foundation (EESMM) and Merlon Wiggin were pulling every string they could to get the ship back. They held many discussions with Hijo Knuttel, who had become the conduit to Bob Rosenbaum since all other communication with him had broken down. Merlon and Peter were hoping to buy time for a new organization to be formed that might save *Regina Maris* from what they felt was an untimely end. AIG and their underwriters were planning to seize or arrest the ship to gain control of the situation, but that process would take 60 to 90 days.

Eventually the National Park Service issued a statement saying in part that *Regina Maris* had no significance for American history and could be scuttled. [1] The federal EPA was then allowed to issue Bob Rosenbaum a permit to sink the ship out beyond the 12-mile limit. Though he had his permit, he still wanted to gain as much financially as possible from this nightmare of an investment. He went to Lindberg Marine and said he wanted to do some work on the ship. They told him to leave and that he could not work on the ship without insurance to do so. Bob provided proof of insurance and proceeded to remove from the ship all the portholes, hatches, cabin doors, and belaying pins; the ship's wheel; and anything else of value he could before he and Russell took her out to be sunk.

At this point, the Coast Guard, having received word from Merlon Wiggin that a new organization was taking over the restoration, [2] set out to stop Bob, whom Russell Tripp remembers seeing, chainsaw in hand, getting ready to cut off the figurehead and take down the masts. The young Coast Guardsman assigned to watch over *Regina* acted just in time, and he deserves a great deal of credit for confronting Bob and preventing his removal of more artifacts.

Considerable luck was also involved. According to Phil Colararusso of the federal EPA, "The only thing that kept the boat from being scuttled turned out to be the time it would take to cut down its 92-foot masts, which could be a menace to navigation." [5]

Moreover, the new restoration organization was only in the process of forming. Since there had been no sale at that point, Bob was actually within his rights to do as he pleased with the ship. Merlon and Peter Stanford had used their close ties with the Coast Guard to step in where they legally had no jurisdiction to keep the ship from being scuttled. Bob was furious, and rightfully so. He was being persecuted by the press and the Coast Guard, with only Russell Trip working to help him. Bob would not talk to Merlon because the two had become mortal enemies. Peter Stanford was working with Merlon, so Bob felt that Peter, too, was not to be trusted. Hijo Knuttel was talking to Bob but, their relationship was strained.

Author's note: Because I was so closely involved in the events detailed in the rest of this book, I will use the first person from here on.

After the Coast Guard stopped Bob's scuttling plans, *Regina's* fate was still unclear. On Long Island, there ensued a very intense week of bargaining, marked by a great deal of subterfuge, over the basic issues of which community would have the ship — Greenport or Sag Harbor — and what the new restoration organization would look like. I will attempt to sort through the history of this confusing period as objectively as possible, since I was a player in it, along with my wife, Penny, and ORES alum and this book's contributing editor, Carol Lew Simons.

Penny kept notes on the conversations we had with everyone involved in the change of ownership and the development of the restoration organization. Hijo, who, with Bob's lawyers, was working out details of buying the ship, had a friendly relationship with Penny, Carol, and me, and we all shared a passion for restoring the ship to sailing condition. Merlon was a powerful force in the village and was, to his credit, capable of accomplishing incredible things. But we had varying degrees of trust in him because his methods were often uncompromising and overbearing.

In a phone call to Penny and me on October 17, Hijo said that he was going to buy the ship. He needed money for the tug to bring her back to Greenport, and we assured him we would find the funds. (That was accomplished, with Carol's help, through Everett Holland and other members of the Greenport business community.) Hijo said he had an agreement with Bill Claudio for 30 days of dockage in Greenport.

Further complicating matters, Hijo also told us he had discovered that Bob had offered *Regina* to Greenport's neighboring deepwater port, the Village of Sag Harbor. Hijo had learned that Andrew Boracci, publisher of *Eastender Magazine,* had been instrumental in persuading Sag Harbor to enter into a contract with Bob to host the ship for preservation. Hijo did not know how far along these negotiations were, and he needed that information in case his Greenport plans fell through. He asked us to contact Andy and try to find out.

On the morning of Friday, October 18, Hijo called Penny with further details of his negotiations with Bob and Greenport. Bob had kept adding provisions but lawyers for both parties had approved a basic agreement. One provision stipulated that the vessel could never be sold to Merlon; another gave Bob the right to review any decisions about the ship's future. Hijo was uncomfortable with these provisions, but he was getting help with the negotiating from Peter Stanford and Merlon.

That afternoon, Penny contacted Andy, who said he had just spoken with Bob. Andy said Bob had settled with his insurance carrier and was able to pay all his bills, thus ending the law suits. Bob had said he had insured the ship for $500,000 and the insurance company had settled his $50,000 claim for the hurricane sinking and damage.

Andy also told Penny that the proposed arrangement with Sag Harbor had been negotiated among Bob, the mayor, and the director of the Sag Harbor Whaling Museum. The Sag Harbor group had set up an escrow account of $5,000 to cover expected costs and had an additional guarantee of $50,000 from Pat Malloy, a local businessman. They were setting up a committee to oversee the restoration but, as part of the deal, were still attempting to retrieve all the artifacts Bob had removed from the ship. Sag Harbor's plan was to push the ship into a sand berth to save on pumping. The village had no shipyard in which to do the restoration but people were looking into possible sites. Sag Harbor did have ample dock space for *Regina* once she was restored. The mayor's main concerns were liability, the environmental impact of the sand berth, and the complications of working with state DEC. Nevertheless, the Village of Sag Harbor was planning a grand entrance for *Regina* into the harbor.

Later in the day, we gave all this information to Hijo, and he, Penny, and I discussed the pros and cons of each community. In the end, Greenport won out because it had a shipyard to carry out the restoration, and the ship's pre-existing connection with the community was very strong. Greenport also had the maritime museum next to a proposed site for a possible sand berth. Hijo had also received many promises of unlimited help from Peter Stanford and others in the ship restoration community. Hijo realized that Merlon was going to be a formidable force to reckon with.

At this point, the chronology is hard to pin down, for many players were working simultaneously. Hijo was working with Peter Stanford and Merlon Wiggin to form a new organization, while he was also negotiating with Bob Rosenbaum. Bob was still looking for a better deal from Sag Harbor. And Peter and Merlon were pulling every possible string with the EPA and the Coast Guard to stop Bob from scuttling the ship. But time was running out for Hijo and the ship, as the EPA had actually given the green light for scuttling and Bob and Russell were ready to act.

In the last hour, Save the *Regina Maris* Ltd. (STRM), a Delaware corporation, was formed, with three directors: Hijo, as president; his friend Vince Mow, of

EnviroSource Technologies, Inc., in Merion Station, Pennsylvania; and Bill Taylor, of Sterling Yacht Sales, in Mystic, Connecticut, whom Hijo did not know but whom had been suggested by Peter Stanford. An advisory committee was also formed, comprising Merlon Wiggin, as executive director of the East End Seaport and Marine Foundation; Peter Stanford, who lived in Hudson, New York; and four people whom Peter had recommended and whom Hijo did not know: Tom Cox, of Marina Bay in Quincy, Massachusetts; Ann Nichols, wife of the late George Nichols of Ocean Research and Education Society; Robby Robinson, of Tabor Academy in Marion, Massachusetts; and John Wigglesworth, of Sea Education Association, Woods Hole, Massachusetts, the one-time relief captain of *Regina* who had been involved in her sale to Marina Bay. [6]

At some point in this period, Hijo actually purchased *Regina* from Bob Rosenbaum for $1.00, to keep her safe until the new organization's paperwork could be finalized. At last, on Friday, October 18, 1991, while the organization was still in the process of filing for non-profit status, the ship's ownership was officially transferred to STRM Ltd. Peter Stanford commented, "It was very close, we came very close to losing this very important piece of maritime history." [7]

Bill Taylor, one of the original directors of STRM, wrote in a 2012 email to me, "I was invited into the triumvirate that acquired the vessel at the request of Peter Stanford, who was passionate about NOT letting tall ships get scuttled. He feared this would be her fate since no one wanted her. He prevailed on me to do what I could and I said yes because we had some friends in common. I was the money-partner for Hijo and Vince and their dream of saving the ship. They wanted this badly and begged me to help. We did a lot of work together when the vessel was 'on the ropes' after Hurricane Bob to actually save the ship from being lost altogether. I owned Sterling Yachts at the time, which was based in Mystic. We specialized in the restoration of antique and historic vessels. *Regina Maris* was proposed to me by Vince & Hijo to be a project for my company to restore."[8]

Two details of the purchase agreement are of note. An option in the contract to purchase the equipment/artifacts that Bob had removed stated, "For an additional sum of $200 the seller will grant STRM Ltd. the right of first refusal on the sale of any or all of the items for 60 days at prices to be determined at that time." Bob had removed most of the interesting artifacts and STRM wanted them back, so the organization was willing to agree to this clause in hopes of raising the funds in the time allotted. Bob had estimated the value of the removed items at $10,000 and he was hoping STRM would find the money to pay for them. [1]

The second important provision of the purchase agreement made STRM responsible for any liens against *Regina Maris*. Two had been filed, one by the Lindberg shipyard, where she had been tied up in Fairhaven, and the other by Russell Tripp for 10 days of dockage and towing. The two liens amounted to $12,000. [9]

With the purchase details finalized, the next major step was to get *Regina* back to Greenport, which required getting the non-removal order #0491 lifted. The application to the Coast Guard to lift the order states, "Present plans call for the removal of the vessel to 'Claudio's Pier' in Greenport where temporary hull repairs will be attempted as we await the outcome of a permit application to dredge a nearby backwater to form a platform where she can either be beached and repairs carried out at low tide, or permanently moored and possibly backfilled to provide a permanent historical exhibit."

In a 2011 phone interview, Russell Tripp told me he had been paid around $100,000 for his month and a half of looking after the ship for the insurance company. He owed Lindberg Marine dock fees, and he had to pay his crew and cover his fuel costs. "I broke even and am still friendly with all parties involved. Sometimes that is as good as it gets." [2]

Russell was retained to deliver the vessel to Greenport after Captain Robinson of the Coast Guard lifted the non-removal order. Richard Scholes, manager of Lindberg Marine, still has a belaying pin Bob Rosenbaum gave him when the ship was at his yard. He remembers having a good working relationship with Bob, and in the end all the yard bills were paid with the insurance payoff. [10]

Although STRM now officially owned *Regina* and financial and regulatory issues in Massachusetts appeared to have been settled, *Regina's* fate was still far from certain.

When Hijo first purchased the ship, he visited her in Fairhaven. "When I walked on her ... I felt she was raped," he said in a 1991 *Suffolk Times* article. "Rosenbaum, he pulled the wool over my eyes. He was never going to share her with people. This boat is too much for one person. It's for generations. It links the past with the present and becomes more valuable the older it gets."[4]

Despite his good feelings about the ship herself, Hijo had been made very uncomfortable during the negotiation process by Merlon's often high-handed approach. Penny and I reported to Hijo on Sunday, October 20, that Bill Claudio was talking about an article Andy Boracci had published about the ship's going to Sag Harbor. We noted that this information was circulating in Greenport, causing anxiety. The pro-ship people were saying, "Get *Regina Maris* here at any cost." The con-ship people were saying, "Let Sag Harbor have her."

In a phone call with Hijo on October 21, we reported that in a closed-door meeting of the Greenport Village Board, Merlon had said he represented Hijo. None of us, including Hijo, knew what had transpired. The rumor was that the Village Board had decided to sink *Regina* at the railroad dock as soon as the ship arrived, before they had a permit from the DEC to do so. Another rumor was that in the meeting the Village Board had agreed to change the terms of the relationship between EESMF and the village, and there were also rumors of a shake-up in the EESMF board. Hijo said he felt like "the spider had set its web, and he was the fly," and he said to Penny and me that he was thinking of taking *Regina* to his riverfront home in the town of Windsor on the Connecticut River.

While all this was going on, *Regina Maris* was beginning her second voyage to Greenport. *Russell Jr.*, with *Regina Maris* in tow, left Fairhaven for Greenport at 9:30 a.m. Tuesday, October 22, 1991. "By that evening off the coast of Rhode Island, she was braving 12 foot seas with knee-deep water on the deck," said Hijo, aboard for the trip. [9]

At the same time, *HMS Rose* was docked in Greenport, leaving the next day for Bridgeport, Connecticut, on a nine-month tour carrying an original copy of the Bill of Rights to 24 cities. Many people in Greenport thought when she arrived that she was *Regina Maris* returned from the deep. On the next day, when *Rose* continued her journey, she passed *Regina* being towed by Russell's tug. Hijo Knuttel said, "The *Rose* sailed right up to *Regina* in Gardiners Bay around 5 p.m., fired its six guns, and sounded its horns while its crew members gave the barkentine a salute." [9]

Upon her arrival just after dark, *Regina* swarmed with people attempting to organize shore power and bilge pumps to keep her afloat, since Russell Trip wanted to removed his diesel pumps, untie *Regina*, and be rid of his 54-day burden. I went below to the engine room and placed the largest volume trash pump deep in her bilge next to the original mechanical pump, which I had helped rebuild with Danny Spears 20 years earlier crossing the Pacific. My first sensation being on board again with my face in her bilge was the smell of her: She still had that "*Regina* scent" — a mixture of salt, fuel oil, wet oak and human odors. That brought back many memories.

Back in Greenport again, with new owners and a new lease on life. *Photo by Penny Kerr.*

The morning after the ship's return to Greenport, a steady stream of visitors stopped by her berth at Claudio's dock to stare at her disheveled appearance. Stripped of all her finer details, she took on the appearance of a "ghostly pirate ship" as some of the younger observers exclaimed. Amy Swensen, 4, told her father, Greenport harbormaster Ed Swensen, "Hook is back!"[5] Bill Claudio enjoyed smiling at people as they visited the ship. "She's back," he said to one man, "I bet you never thought you'd see it."[5]

On October 24, *The Traveler Watchman* reported details of the October 21 Village Board meeting that gave members of the fledgling STRM hope that the village would play a larger role in the preservation of the ship. The article reported, "The board started the environmental review process for dredging out an area next to the railroad dock. If the state and federal agencies grant the necessary approvals, as officials expect, the boat will be placed with its port side against the bulkhead, its bowsprit facing the pier (and the harbor). The dredged materials would then be placed around the hull, in a fashion used to maintain the whaling ship *Charles W. Morgan* at Mystic Seaport. The ship could then be floated at any time."[4]

After the October 21 Village Board meeting, some village officials expressed positive sentiments supportive of STRM. Steve Clarke, village trustee and shipyard owner, said, "I can't believe that we're seeing it back. But this is what happens when people care about something." [4]

Trustee John Costello commented, "The new owners have assumed all financial responsibility, and will post a bond to cover the cost of removing the ship when the hull becomes unsafe in 15 or 20 years. This is the direction we should have taken when the vessel was here before."[4]

So under the auspices of STRM Ltd., an organization whose board of directors and advisory committee together included only one local person (Merlon) and one person (Vince) whom Hijo, president of the board of directors, really trusted, *Regina Maris* resumed her life as a dockside tourist attraction.

Everyone involved knew her success in that role would be greatly enhanced if the artifacts Bob Rosenbaum had removed were returned. However, the fledgling STRM could not raise the funds necessary to purchase the lot within the time specified in the purchase agreement. Bob Rosenbaum waited the required 60 days and then started disposing of the artifacts in December 1991.

Some of the ship's parts and pieces showed up in New England chandlery and maritime antique shops. Bob loaded up the remainder of the artifacts and drove to California. In early July 1992, he attempted to sell the ship's wheel to Ed Zelinsky, a director of the National Maritime Historical Society who had sailed on *Regina*. In a personal letter to me in 1992, Francis "Van" Fowler — a San Francisco real estate mogul who had crewed on *Regina* and had donated generously to STRM — wrote, "Ed reports that Bob had the wheel tied to the back of his pick-up truck and was driving it around to various people trying to sell it for $2,500. Bob called Ed [Zelinsky] later in the month to tell him that he sold the wheel and that he was discouraged trying to make a living selling used cars and was having a problem with his girlfriend so he was going back to restore ships on the East Coast." [11]

I have made countless phone and email attempts over the past 10 years to encourage Bob to provide comments on his experience with the ship. He has been given multiple opportunities to tell his side of the story, with full editorial review. In each case, Bob promised he would send information or a written statement, but he never followed through. He would offer face-to-face meetings and then be unavailable.

Many in the community and media often cast Bob as a villain, and he may have been one. But he was also victimized by powerful forces beyond his control. He evidently did continue on in the maritime field, for he describes himself in a profile in Wooden Boat's On-Line Forum of January 6, 2011, as "a Professional boat designer, surveyor, project manager, and captain. He holds a USCG 500-ton Master of power and sail with over 30 years experience. Previous owner of many wooden historic vessels including a 3-masted barkentine, coastal ferry, staysail schooner and misc. power yachts. I worked as a senior designer for Sparkman & Stephens in the early 80s and again in the early 90s as well as Holland Marine Design." [12]

CHAPTER 23
FAIRHAVEN, MASSACHUSETTS
September 1 to October 22, 1991

1. "Regina Maris Saved from the Deep," *New England Coastal News*, October 15, 1991.
2. Russell Tripp, telephone interview with the author, June 1, 2011.
3. Jeff Lindberg, telephone interview with the author, June 2, 2011. Jeff, now owner of Lindberg Marine, shared notes from the diary of his father, who had been the owner but was unwell at the time of the telephone call.
4. Tim Kelly, "*Regina Maris* Returns Under New Management," *The Traveler Watchman* (Southold, New York), October 24. 1991.
5. Mitchell Freedman, "Tall Ship Weathers Several Storms; Hurricane and Legal Wrangling Can't Keep Barkentine Down," *Newsday* (Long Island City, New York), October 24, 1991.
6. Peter Stanford, personal letter to Merlon Wiggin, which came into the author's possession after Merlon's death. Information about the makeup of the board was also in the local news at the time.
7. Ebba Hierta, "First sunk and then homeless, *Regina Maris* wins fight for life," *Soundings Magazine* (Essex, Connecticut) January 1992.
8. Bill Taylor, email to the author, April 30, 2012.

9. Margaret O'Neil, "Home Again: Regina Maris Back in Village for Good," *The Suffolk Times* (Mattituck, New York), October 24, 1991.
10. Richard Scholes, telephone interview with the author, June 1, 2011.
11. Francis E. "Van" Fowler, letter to the author, July 24, 1992.
12. Robert Val Rosenbaum, *Wooden Boat,* On-Line Forum, January 6, 2011.

CHAPTER 24

GREENPORT, NEW YORK
October 24, 1991 – August 25, 1998

Regina Maris's bowsprit and figurehead were facing up Main Street. Her masts could be seen from all over town. Nearly 100 Greenporters, proud of their seaside community, signed up to help restore the ship, some willing to provide labor of any type, others offering specific skills and services.

Much had to be done to repair damage from the Hurricane Bob sinking. A new electrical panel had to be installed, along with wiring to the pumps and lights. To receive Coast Guard certification as an "approved moored attraction," the ship had to be made safe for on-deck visitors. Divers were working below the waterline, patching and caulking. Many of the original volunteers jumped back into jobs they had been doing nearly two months earlier. A phone system was installed because the ship needed her own line and answering machine to handle all the incoming offers of donations. And there were letterheads, brochures, and donation cards to design and print.

Hijo Knuttel was spending weekdays at his Connecticut nursery business and weekends on the ship, sometimes bringing along his wife and three children. It was a busy time for him, overseeing all the work and setting up the new organization. Merlon and Isabel Wiggin were a great asset to the fledgling organization and helped Hijo a great deal with the complexities of dredging applications and obtaining non-profit status. During the first meeting of STRM Ltd., held October 28, 1991, many tasks were delegated to eager volunteers.

The divers reported that they had already caulked all the leaks but one and that the bilge pump was now working intermittently. John Costello of Costello Marine reported that the dolphins that were supposed to have been installed before Hurricane Bob would be going in as soon as the following week. Their installation would make the ship more secure during storms and high tides. Also at this meeting, plans were made for a fundraiser and information session for the public.

On Wednesday, October 30, at 4:00 p.m. a weather emergency was declared over the Civil Defense network. The "perfect storm" was going to hit the area with huge high tides, the first at 2 in the morning of October 31. These high tides could push *Regina* up and into Claudio's Restaurant or Preston's store, leaving both building and ship unsalvageable wrecks.

John Costello and the harbor master had a plan to move the ship to a more protected berth, between two larger docks on the lee side of Claudio's dock. As the Hamptons' publication *Dan's Papers* reported on November 15, "The call went out through the village to come and help, and hundreds of volunteers answered." [1] They swarmed the dock and pulled the ship, stern first, 300 feet southward to the end of the100-foot wide pier, around the gas dock at the southern end of the dock, and then 300 feet northward into the more protected slip, securing her with her bow facing out and into the oncoming seas.

This maneuver would be repeated many times over the coming years, usually at the last minute and under inclement conditions, and moving *Regina* became something of a community event whenever a suitable tug was not available, which was most of the time. As the years went on, however, fewer and fewer people showed up to help. After all, the volunteers had their own homes and businesses to tend to in major storms.

For the perfect storm of 1991, however, many people answered the call and worked together, united in their desire to save *Regina*. "I was so happy," Isabelle Wiggin said, "it made me want to cry. She wanted to live. She had come back. Now she was home." [1]

Regina Maris weathered the storm. And in the process, as Dan Rattiner, founder and editor-in-chief of *Dan's Papers*, wrote, "I cannot think of a single thing that has so united any town on the eastern end of Long Island as *Regina Maris* has this time united the people of Greenport."[1]

After the storm, the ship was moved back to her original position at the foot of Main Street, with the help of a small tug and many willing hands. On Saturday, November 1, a volunteer work session was organized at which Mike Kortchmar was introduced. Chosen by Merlon to head the restoration effort, Mike had a boatyard in East Marion, just east of Greenport, and considerable experience restoring wooden boats. At the work session, a large dumpster was filled with debris from the Hurricane Bob sinking.

The Saturday work session, attended by large numbers of volunteers, became a constant for the next seven years. In addition, a select crew of senior citizens started showing up Tuesday mornings and continued to do so for *Regina's* entire time in Greenport. The Tuesday crew had the skills and the time needed to maintain the ship and keep her afloat. Mike Kortchmar made John Woodhouse the unofficial chief of the Tuesday workers, who also included Robert and Barbara Cameron, Charlie Digney, Charles and Mabel Ley, Bob Maus, Don and Jeri Prince, Ted and Karen Schroeder, and Rich and Robin Suess. The wives helped organize the work crews for the Saturday sessions, ran the ship's store, and planned fundraisers. Jeri Woodhouse, John's wife, was especially active in fundraising and also served on the STRM board at one point. Without the efforts of all these volunteers, *Regina* would not have survived for as long as she did.

As restoration work proceeded, with many volunteers envisioning *Regina's* sailing again, another plan was also being floated. For *Regina* to obtain approval as a moored attraction, the Coast Guard required the ship to be placed in a permanent berth. At a November 7 Greenport Village Board meeting, Merlon Wiggin presented a proposal to dredge 600 cubic yards of sand from the southwest side of the bulkhead next to the old railroad station, which was soon to be the new Maritime Museum. The ship would then float there at storm high tides among eight pilings. Merlon presented this proposal as a representative of STRM, but the STRM board had never actually agreed on this as a solution. In fact the proposed plan was a concession to those STRM members who wanted to keep the option open for *Regina's* sailing again and not just bury her in sand. [2] After discussing the proposal, the Village Board voted 4 to 1 in favor of it, with one dissenting vote cast by William Allen, who maintained his long-standing argument that the villagers had not had enough say in the proposal. Only one resident voiced a negative sentiment, concerned that traffic congestion in the area would increase were the ship docked in the sand berth at the foot of Third Street. [2]

The first of many fundraisers was held Sunday, November 10, at Claudio's Restaurant. The public was invited to meet the board members, enjoy hors d'oeuvres and drinks, and contribute $25 to the restoration fund. Mike Kortchmar was introduced as head of the physical restoration.

One result of this get together was the recognition and open discussion of the need to mend the relationship between STRM Ltd. and community members whom Bob Rosenbaum owed money. He had opened charge accounts in several local stores and had promised others access to the ship in lieu of payment. (In a closed meeting the following week, the STRM board drafted a letter to the editor of *The Suffolk Times* that thanked all who had helped with the ship and also clarified the organization's plans, including assuming responsibility for all the ship's bills, past and present.) [3]

The November 10 fundraiser was packed and very social in nature, so it was difficult to be heard or to speak. One comment that got much less attention than it should have, given subsequent events, was board member Bill Taylor's attempt to share his concerns about the ship's condition. His words unfortunately fell on deaf ears. Most everyone present was buoyed by the success of having saved the ship from certain destruction and by the dream of her sailing again. Also apparently forgotten in the loud and heady moment was the sand berth proposal.

In a 2012 email to me, Bill Taylor wrote, "I worked closely with Dana Hewson, head of the Preservation Shipyard at Mystic Seaport, researching the history of the vessel and organizing a preliminary survey of the vessel by my friend Paul Coble in Newport. Sterling Yachts hired him to travel to Greenport and perform his assessment. This was done in early November, before the first fundraiser. He wrote out on paper for all to see what I had been saying for weeks – since the day I laid eyes on her. Very few people wanted to accept the reality of her condition and most could not grasp the scope that the restoration entailed." [4]

Those who remained undaunted by the issues Bill Taylor tried to raise included Mike Kortchmar. Mike's plan for the ship, which he outlined at the fundraiser, was to "get *Regina Maris* into sailing condition again, eventually. Depending on how fast the money comes in," he said, "she could become a training ship for apprentices in the lost skills of sailing ship building and rigging, moving along the Long Island coast."

Mike had a pool of around 60 active volunteers to draw upon, depending on the tasks at hand. When asked in 1992 by a *New York Daily News* reporter about the restoration tasks volunteers were involved in, Mike said, "The labor is intensive for the volunteers. For example the anchor chain was rusted together and it took four people a whole day to hammer the rust off and drag it out and up on the dock, where it took another half day to get it ... into a steel bin so it can be hauled away for later use." [5]

The ship had to lose weight so that Steve Clarke's shipyard would be able to haul her out. The weight loss issue was the first of many to be addressed. Mike had acquired the services of a naval architect to calculate the ship's weight, which, according to meeting minutes, he told the board was "329 tons, based on her design lines, and 239 tons displacement and for every 4.5 tons unloaded from the ship the water line changes one inch." [6] This information enabled the volunteer workers to determine *Regina's* weight by watching the water line as they removed articles from the ship.

Many months of work followed the initial board meetings and fundraiser. Meetings were attended, problems solved, and money raised, so that by mid-summer of 1992, the hard-working volunteers had accomplished incredible tasks in the restoration process. A 12,000 pound concrete mooring, along with a 500-pound buoy with several thousand pounds of anchor chain, were placed in Pipe's Cove to serve as a storm mooring in the event of another hurricane. However, the ship still needed an electric hydraulic pump in order to attach to the mooring easily. The two robust, three-piling dolphins were in place at the ship's berth at the foot of Maine Street, to keep her safe in heavy wind and sea. Two generators were installed to keep the pumps running in case she had to be on the storm mooring for an extended period. Extra electric trash bilge pumps were on hand in case of a failure. The cargo hatch was reopened to give access to the hold. All the fuel, water, and waste storage tanks and their attached plumbing had been removed. All mechanicals — including the hot water, oil-fired furnace and all its plumbing; the 8-71 diesel main power engine; and the two auxiliary diesel generators — had been cleared out of the engine room. The diesel engines were possibly in good enough shape to rebuild, so they were taken to the shop of a volunteer who would do the work and charge for parts only. The running rigging aloft had been adjusted so her yards were all squared away. Anything that might pose a hazard falling from aloft had been removed. Eager but poorly informed volunteers removed large sections of the oak ceiling to search for leaks. The removal of these sections caused structural problems discovered later.

The forward cabin had been converted into a ship's store, where visitors could buy T-shirts, parkas, polo shirts, mugs, stationary, and various other items, all with a *Regina Maris* line drawing that had become the STRM Ltd. logo. The exteriors of both cabins were scraped and painted and given new weathertight windows, doors and roofs. The hull above the waterline had been scraped and painted, and below the waterline, the divers had made the seams tight. There appeared to be just a leak or too still to be found and caulked, and in the spring of 1992, the ship received Coast Guard certification as an approved moored attraction, which allowed visitors to tour the ship on deck. [7] The hard-working directors of STRM Ltd. had shepherded the organization through the arduous process of becoming a 501(c)(3) non-profit organization by midsummer, and *Regina* was open for business.

Although the physical work was progressing, political conflicts among the STRM board, personalities in the village government, and the East End Seaport Museum and Marine Foundation (EESMM) board created a constant feeling of unrest surrounding the ship and the restoration effort. In his 2012 email to me, Bill Taylor commented, "I spent quite a bit of time and money over a period of about a year creating quite a bit of marketing material for the organization to raise money. But once the ship was safely back in Greenport it became a political football. It got quite ugly in Greenport. Everyone savaged each other in the name of having greater status within the vessel's restoration community. I wanted no part of it. It had absolutely nothing to do with historic ship preservation and everything to do with self-glorification among a select few townspeople. In the end, by mutual agreement, Vince, Hijo, and I donated the ship and the nonprofit to the people of the Village of Greenport in the fall of 1992. Vince and I wanted out but Hijo seemed to cling to the impossible dream of sailing her with other Tall Ships. " [4]

Once again ownership of the ship and the make-up of the board had changed. Hijo remained as president but vacancies left by Vince and Bill were filled by Geri Woodhouse and Maggie Leahy, both of nearby Orient. The make-up of the board changed fairly often over the next years, at one point including me; my wife, Penny; and editor Carol Lew Simons.

One term in the original agreement Hijo had signed with the Village of Greenport was that the ship was to be available for the village's Maritime Festival. She was to have been the queen of the inaugural one in 1991 but Bob Rosenbaum had been holding her hostage in Fairhaven, Massachusetts. In September 1992, however, *Regina* was the centerpiece of the second annual festival. That event had to be delayed one week due to the high tides and winds of tropical storm Danielle, during which *Regina* had again been moved to the protected berth on the lee side of Claudio's dock, with her bow facing the wind and seas. Once the storm passed, *Regina* was returned to the foot of Main Street and made ready for the festivities. She was bedecked with flags, and from her side hung a 10-foot banner, made by Penny Kerr, with *Regina Maris* embossed in silk to welcome all who came aboard. There was live music and the ship's store was open, and *Regina Maris* was joined in the harbor by Naval and Coast Guard ships. The festival included fishing contests, wine-tasting, maritime skills demonstrations, a wooden boat parade and regatta, whaleboat races, and a flyover from the National Guard air/sea rescue helicopter team from Westhampton. Over 5,000 people attended the two-day event, and the majority visited *Regina*. [8]

In the following year, over 10,000 people attended the festival, and in subsequent years the event grew and the crowds increased. [8] *Regina* had become the magnet the business community had hoped she would be, and she worked for the funds needed for the restoration. Each year she took in around $10,000 from donations for tours and other activities, including those during the Maritime Festival. Unfortunately, her expenses usually kept pace with or surpassed her earnings.

On December 11, 1992, a nor'easter slammed into the coast, necessitating the ship be moved again to her safer docking space. The seawater was over the dock and the winds were fierce, but the watchful crew brought the ship through unscathed. Then during the winter of 1992-93, the ice became locked in under *Regina's* stern, a plank popped, and the ship almost sank. John Costello brought his pumps and personally dove under the ship through the ice, managing to put oakum and calking around the popped plank and place battens over his work and the leaking area. Thanks to him and other volunteers, *Regina* was saved one more time.

In September of 1992, Peter Stanford, president of the National Maritime Historical Society (NMHS), visited the ship, bringing from San Francisco Karl Kortum, chairman emeritus of the NMHS and a stalwart of its American Ship Trust. In 1969 Karl had seen *Regina Maris* in the Canaries, when he was serving as mate on the tug *Eppleton Hall* and *Regina* was awaiting a tow to Norway as a result of a dismasting. Karl subsequently contributed to the ship and got others to do so, and he published articles about her in West Coast journals.

This 1992 visit gave Peter Stanford the opportunity to assess the situation in Greenport first hand, and in July of 1993, he wrote a letter to the STRM board strongly encouraging them to join with EESMF in a written agreement that would basically combine the two organizations. Peter implied that his organization, NMHS, could not provide further assistance or powerful support until the merger was accomplished. Sentiment on the STRM board was that this was a power play by Merlon Wiggin, now head of EESMF, and also an effort for the museum to gain access to the donations the ship had been collecting.

While political issues roiled, the restoration work was encountering serious obstacles. Mike Kortchmar's restoration plan hinged on the ship's being hauled out to repair the planking and redo the caulking. Using Steve Clarke's shipyard, 200 feet from where *Regina* was docked, seemed the most practical solution, but Steve was very concerned about the ship's weight. In a conversation with me on March 17, 2012, he said that his railway had been capable of raising 400 tons, but the largest vessel he had ever lifted was 365 tons. "As a shipyard owner, I learned that what an owner stated as the weight of the vessel often differed from the designed weight, and then there were the additions that other owners had added that increased the total weight even more. I like to think of a bathroom scale supporting the vessel in question, it has its limits." [9]

On July 31, 1993, Steve and I took his workboat out and, through a simple means of measurement, determined *Regina's* weight to be 465 tons. At the time, board members, including myself, accepted his figures and his refusal to haul the ship because she was too heavy for his railway. Further research in writing this book, however, indicates that Steve's measurement method or math may have been flawed. At her historical heaviest configuration, with a seven-yardarm foremast and fully fitted out for an around-the-world cruise, Lloyds' of London had stated her total gross tonnage at 189 tons. Mike Kortchmar's naval architect friend had put her tonnage at 329 tons. Somewhere in between the two figures is the truth.

Steve had been thinking about rebuilding an unused railway from World War II that would have a capacity of 800 tons. However, he estimated that project would take some $300,000, which was more than he felt he could invest, because there was no call for a railway of that capacity at this time. The local ferry companies were purchasing larger boats but they were in the 250- to 300-ton range.

This was very bad news for *Regina Maris* and all the dedicated people who cared for her. The question became whether to wait for Steve Clarke to expand his shipyard in some distant future or to move her to a yard that could handle her weight. But the real issue, as always, was money. In August of 1993, LIPA, the Long Island power company, offered to provide the lifting equipment and operators to remove the masts to reduce her weight so she could be hauled at Steve Clarke's shipyard. This was a generous offer but it never came to fruition because the issue of removing the masts became highly contentious, with different factions of STRM Ltd. and the community all weighing in on the decision. If the masts were removed she would no longer be a tourist magnet for the community. But if she were not hauled out to be repaired and made leak-free, she would sink at the dock. During this difficult time Penny felt that the organization needed a newsletter to help communicate with the volunteers and donors. The *Regina Maris Quarterly* was mailed to the membership and made available in local stores.

Of course, Mother Nature always had a major say in human plans for the ship. During this decision-making period, another hurricane threatened, and on August 30, 1993, the crew moved the ship to the lee side of Claudio's dock. The brunt of the storm missed Greenport, and the ship was moved back to her berth on September 2. Preparations then had to be made for the upcoming Maritime Festival, which this year was going to be doubly special for *Regina*. A reunion of those who had sailed on the ship was planned for September 4. The reunion committee had been working for nearly a year and attempted to contact as many former crew members as possible. Ann Nichols, widow of George Nichols, gave the organization all her contact lists for the thousands of students, sailors, and scientists who had served on the ship during the ORES period. The main event of the reunion was held in conjunction with the annual fundraising cocktail party. About 30 *Regina* alums attended, and many of the "old lost crew" sent letters. Peter Stanford spoke and Penny Kerr débuted a new song, "Regina Maris, Queen of the Sea" that was eventually placed on her album "Conscious Contact" and received worldwide air play. The next day the Kerr's hosted a cookout at their home on Shelter Island for the former sailors and owners.

Despite the good feeling generated by the reunion, things did not go well in the fall of 1993. The battle against rot and leaks was fierce and ongoing. Some people were paying attention to the Paul Coble survey of 1992, which had made clear how difficult a full restoration would be. NMHS continued to exert pressure for STRM to join with EESMF, but people were having trouble agreeing on the financial arrangements necessary for the merger and on how to combine the two organizations' boards. Moreover, village elected officials and the business community was becoming disenchanted with the project, and liability for *Regina* was becoming a bigger issue to the Village Board. Neither the means nor the will to fund a full sailing restoration seemed to exist within the community, and it was becoming more apparent to the majority of STRM Ltd. board members that the dream of having the ship sail again was only that.

With all these factors in play, in December 1993, STRM and EESMF finally agreed to combine their forces and boards. No change of name resulted, but the organizations shared board members and fundraising activities, and in fact EESMF became the parent organization, since it had developed a more effective relationship with the village. The previously proposed idea of *Regina's* resting in a sand berth became the preservation effort's official goal. She would become a permanent fixed dockside attraction either in the new Mitchell Park or next to the EESMF's proposed museum in the restored LIRR train station. At last the wrangling over whether to merge the two organizations was resolved, but the process had caused a loss of community support and strained established friendships among the volunteers.

Nor did the new administrative structure protect *Regina* from further mishaps. On February 3, 1994, during a howling rainstorm — which had not been forecast — she sank, but she was refloated within 24 hours. Lighting and phone systems had been damaged, but the preparedness of the loyal workers had prevented serious destruction. After the Hurricane Bob sinking, they had redone the wiring and had placed all electric pump connections, the circuit breaker box and the two gas-powered generators in protected places on the ship or ashore.

The aftermath of the February 3rd. 1994 storm. Photo by *Penny Kerr*.

A month later the ship caught fire and a bulkhead was burned, the flames doing minimal damage. It was determined that a heat lamp had fallen undetected and ignited combustibles.

Restoration efforts and work on the sand berth continued, if slowly, after this incident, and nothing dramatic happened for some time. In June 1995, the city of New Bedford, Massachusetts, made overtures to buy *Regina Maris*. Many Greenporters were falling out of love with the ship and welcomed the possibility, but there was an upwelling of positive sentiment locally and EESMF and STRM Ltd. rejected the request.

Regina Maris continued to do her part for the community by attracting tall ships from all over the world, and she helped put Greenport on the tourism map of Long Island. [10] The Chamber of Commerce and the village government used the ship's image on posters and advertising for community events. The ship was cited in proposals to attract tall ships, including America's Sail '95, and often captains of the involved vessels had served on *Regina* or knew her from past events. She was mentioned in grant requests for the waterfront park revitalization plan competition and referred to in maritime museum fundraising. "We used it any way we could," Mayor David Kapell said in a 1998 *Newsday* article. "What's wrong with that?" [11]

The tourists poured in. *Regina's* visitor log averaged 3,000 entries a year during most of her stay in Greenport, with worldwide representation. [9] From June 29 to July 1, 1995, America's Sail '95 called in Greenport. Attending were *Simon Bolivar*, a 270-foot bark from Venezuela; *Capitan Miranda*, a198-foot, 3-masted schooner from Uruguay;

Zenobe Gramme, a 94-foot Bermudian ketch from Belgium; *Concordia*, a 154-foot barkentine from Canada; *Tole Mour*, a 160-foot schooner from Honolulu; and *HMS Rose*, a 179-foot full-rigged ship then based in Connecticut. *Regina Maris* was the center of activities, hosting a sea chantey concert and a formal dinner for all visiting captains and officers. Later in July, *Regina*, the ship magnet, brought the return of the Danish tall ship *Georg Stage*. Many of the 60 cadets were housed by local families, and a cocktail party and dinner was held in honor of all the cadets and officers. In August 1996, the 177-foot *Gazella*, the world's only other remaining wooden barkentine, arrived from her home port, Philadelphia, to pay her respects to the "Old Queen," as some had begun to call her, usually with kindly intent. The two ships had sailed together fishing for cod and herring off the Grand Banks during the 1930s. This visit was an opportunity for STRM Ltd. to learn about the *Gazella* organization and understand what STRM was up against in restoring *Regina*. The *Gazella* that arrived in Greenport had been completely rebuilt, with only a portion of her original timber remaining. [10] The restoration had required a vast organization and millions of dollars contributed by citizens of Philadelphia.

Even as *Regina* drew ships and crowds to Greenport, serious leaks persisted and had to be controlled. To accomplish this, during October and late November 1995, dock builder John Costello and other volunteers dove under the ship and installed a rubber "diaper" to cover the entire hull, once the propeller and rudder had been removed to make attachment more leak-proof. The diaper did reduce the sinking concern, but ice and extremely low storm tides damaged the diaper, and it was replaced in late 1996. In 1997, the diaper split and the ship nearly went to the bottom, but again the fast-acting volunteer crew saved the Old Queen, and a new diaper was installed. [12]

In the fall of 1997, Donald Buchholtz, a marine surveyor from Texas, completed a new survey of *Regina*. After four days poking about, climbing, and otherwise investigating the ship, he concluded that restoring her to sailing condition would be cost-prohibitive but that a safety and cosmetic restoration for a permanent fixed dockside attraction would only cost around $65,000. Donald also estimated that her weight was down to 314 tons. This report encouraged those involved, and Merlon was energized to start a new search for funding.

A big boost came from the Greenport Business Improvement District in November 1997, when they voted to float a bond for $65,000, $30,000 of which was earmarked for hauling and patching the leaky *Regina Maris*. "This is the kind of incentive we need," Merlon Wiggin said. "Old wooden boats," he added, "always leak to some extent, but we think it's worth fixing, because Greenport is a historic seaport village, and a tall ship like this is one of the most dramatic maritime symbols you can find."

He also noted that EESMF was working hard to obtain the rest of the money, seeking corporate grants — Beck's Beer and Volvo had been contacted — and the organization was planning two major fundraisers for the next summer. One such event was to be tied in with America's Sail '98, the tall ship race from Savannah, Georgia, to Montauk Point, New York, July 11 to 15. The second was Greenport's annual Maritime Festival in September, which customarily attracted crowds and donations. [13]

The volunteers were working continuously to reduce the ship's tonnage in hopes that Steve Clarke would relent and allow his railway to haul her. Donald Buchholtz's December 1997 report had said the ship's weight was down to 314 tons, [14], within Clarke's shipyard's ability. Hope of an imminent hauling arose. Village Mayor Dave Kapell gave public assurances to STRM and EESMF that there would be space for the ship at the new Mitchell Park municipal dockside center that was under construction and expected to be ready sometime in 1998. Dave said, "We don't want the liability, so once the ship is repaired, we'll accommodate it as soon as possible." [13] What exactly the mayor meant by this remark was unclear. What was clear, however, was that *Regina's* future in Greenport was growing less and less certain.

The volunteers were still working to restore all they could above the waterline. Bob Maus, Ted Schroeder, and Bob Cameron took on the never-ending task of scraping and painting the entire ship. A flurry of letters to the editor of the local paper suggested that the best place for the ship was at the bottom of the Atlantic, indicating that community support continued to wane. One volunteer worker, Don Griffing of Blue Point said, "We're going to work on the ship until someone takes it out from under us." [15]

John Pasquarella of Massapequa, a member of the STRM board and a volunteer worker, said in response to the village's concern about the ship's safety and stability, "The hull has been chemically sealed to reduce leakage and a new plastic liner has been put on the outside of the ship to keep it water-tight." [15]

Nevertheless, by the spring of 1998, STRM and EESMF were out of options for the ship. The village had hopes she could still be the centerpiece of the harbor front, but her hull would have to be sound to be a permanently moored attraction. Steve Clarke's shipyard was capable of doing the necessary repairs, but Steve did not want to risk hauling her on his existing railway, even though she had lost weight over the years, thanks to the tons of equipment and materials the volunteers had removed. And, while Steve had started restoring a World War II slipway that would be able to handle *Regina*, it would not be completed for at least another year. Moreover, the dock space the Claudio family had given for nearly the past seven years was needed for other purposes. And, according to John Costello, Mayor Kapell was determined to get rid of the ship, as he felt it was a liability to the village. [12]

In June 1998, the village hired Gillford Full to assess *Regina Maris.* Gillford had been the surveyor and consultant on the restoration of the *USS Constitution,* docked in Boston Harbor. He spent several hours on *Regina,* and his report to town officials and community members offered little hope: "The ship is rotting away so fast you can almost see it happening. Her stern is being held in place by a cable, her bow and ropes and rigging are rotting and about [to] fall and she is now a liability. At some point she is going to become a danger, if she is not already. There is no doubt that there is a lot of history and charisma involved here but you have to get down to earth and realize that this vessel is a bottomless pit and should be disposed of. No ship is built to last forever, and in this case, the expenditure of funds, estimated at $5 million that it would take to restore her, would be better spent elsewhere. My recommendation is that *Regina* should be scuttled at sea." [16]

This assessment contrasted sharply with the restoration price tag Donald Buchholtz had mentioned in his 1997 survey report. However, Donald and Gillford had worked on several projects together in the past, and when questioned about the discrepancies between the two surveys, Gillford said, "A close examination of Buchholtz's report would show that we are not that far apart. It was unfortunate that in the summary he put a price tag on the project of just $65,000. When you read the report in detail it is far, far, more." [17]

Mayor Kapell said he was convinced that *Regina Maris* was "too far rotten to be saved and should be given a respectable burial at sea." [18]

The Village Board at their next meeting voted to have the ship removed by the end of August. Mayor Kapell's response after this meeting was, "You can't be smitten by romance when it involves public safety. I don't think this will hurt Greenport. For the short term and the long term, we've mitigated a huge liability exposure for the taxpayers and residents of the local communities." [18]

Regina had lost her berth, and she had no place to go.

After the meeting, according to *Dan's Papers*, Merlon Wiggin said, "Without the support of the village officials, I don't see how we can proceed. I feel we have no choice but to finalize the plans for at-sea disposition." [17] But Merlon also said in a *New York Times* article of July 5 that he "had till August 26 when the insurance ran out, to find a new home for the ship." He noted that among those expressing interest in the ship were Errol Weston, a film producer and operator of the former Weston restaurant chain, and Mr. Weston's California business partner, Dolph Rempp, who for the last 35 years had owned and operated the land-bound Dolph Rempp Sailing Ship Restaurant near San Francisco's Fisherman's Wharf. [16] (The restaurant, which had been housed in an old three-masted sailing ship, has since been torn down.)

Unfortunately this possible opportunity evaporated as the August deadline rapidly approached. With all the publicity about *Regina,* offers to help poured in. Merlon reported that he had pledges of $10,000 to $15,000 and a promise by one person he would not identify to contribute $50,000. [20] And John Venditto, supervisor of Oyster Bay, a Long Island community some 72 miles to the west, expressed interest in having *Regina* become part of his village's newly redeveloped western waterfront. Unfortunately the dockage space there was to be completed the following year. [19]

Dan's Papers provided a lead to another possible — and most unexpected — source of support, publishing a firsthand account by an individual who said *Regina Maris* had been the rescue vessel for him and others fleeing the Holocaust. [19] In fact, in October 1943, the Danish underground did organize the evacuation by sea of some 7,200 Jews, and 700 non-Jewish relatives, who were taken to Sweden and other unoccupied countries on rescue ships. That evacuation effort is documented on the website of the World Holocaust Remembrance website. [20] The question of *Regina's* participation in the evacuation effort will be discussed more in Chapter 25.

Two Danish organizations — the Ethical Foundation of Denmark, involved in the preservation of transportation-related artifacts, and a business group, Viborg, Pedersen and Kalleso — learned of *Regina's* plight from the *Dan's Papers* article and contacted Merlon in late August. They offered to invest $4.5 million to restore the ship in Greenport or take her back to Denmark so the work could be done at the Ring-Andersen Shipyard. [18]

This all came too late for Greenport, and *Regina*. Funding was only part of the problem, since the ship had to leave the village by the end of August. The timing was good, however, for another waterfront community, Glen Cove, New York, some 90 nautical miles west of Greenport, whose mayor, Thomas Suozzi, had heard of *Regina Maris's* problems. Glen Cove, with a long history as a seaport, had hosted nine tall ships during America's Sail '98, including the 338-foot *Libertad*. The city was in the process of a $20-million waterfront revitalization, and Mayor Suozzi felt *Regina* was just what was needed to be a star attraction for this project. In a *New York Times* article at the time, he commented, "There are only about 200 tall ships left in the world, less than that are made of wood and the *Regina Maris* is one of two wooden barkentines left. The supply of these tall ships is small, but the demand is great." [22]

Dock space in Glen Cove was available immediately, and, moreover, the Holocaust Memorial and Tolerance Center of Nassau County (HMTCNC) was located in Glen Cove. The consensus in the Glen Cove community and especially the HMTCNC was that *Regina* must be saved.

On August 20 and 21 Mayor Suozzi contacted Merlon Wiggin. They reached an agreement: Glen Cove acquired *Regina* for $1, and August 25 was set as the date for moving the ship. Barbara Johnson, a Nassau County legislator, donated the $3,000 to tow the vessel to Glen Cove harbor from Greenport. She said, "I'm an American Jew, and the historical significance of this ship should not be scuttled at sea. Many of my relatives were exterminated in concentration camps. It is also the 50th anniversary of the creation of the state of Israel. What more fitting tribute to Israel and the memory of so many Jews who perished in the holocaust." [23]

For *Regina's* passage to Glen Cove, the Coast Guard required that the battens holding the rubber diaper around the hull be double-secured and additional on-board pumps be installed. As this work was being done, Steve Clarke's shipyard started a major push in the restoration of their 500-ton railway. Timing is everything.

Regina was supposed to leave Greenport for Glen Cove at 2 a.m. August 25, but because of the tides she was towed out of Greenport Harbor two hours earlier. Many Greenporters felt she would be lucky just to make it through Plum Gut's rough water.

A different experience was reported by Rudolph Shubert, a volunteer from Glen Cove who was on the voyage to that port and had served as dock master during Glen Cove's America's Sail '98 festivities. (Rudolph was also serving at that time as first mate on the schooner *Mary E,* berthed in Greenport.) He reported "The tide was running against us, but she slipped right through. She was built to sail, and sometimes it felt like she was under her own power. You forgot she was being towed." [21]

It is worth noting that three people critical to *Regina's* stay in Greenport and the restoration effort there have since passed away. Peter Stanford, of the National Maritime Historical Society, died in 2016, at the age of 89. Merlon Wiggin passed away in October 2008 at the age of 78 and his wife, Isabelle, at age 78, in February 2012.

CHAPTER 24
GREENPORT, NEW YORK
October 24, 1991, to August 25, 1998

1. Dan Rattiner "Look Who's Here! Four Masted Tall Ship Is Back in Greenport—This Time to Stay," *Dan's Papers* (Southampton, New York), November 15, 1991.

1. "New Home for Regina," *The Suffolk Times* (Mattituck, New York), November 21, 1991.

2. Save the *Regina Maris* Ltd., letter to the editor, "Regina Update," *The Suffolk Times,* November 21, 1991.

3. Bill Taylor, email to the author, April 30, 2012.

4. Gus Dallas, "A hull of a restoration job' Square rigger gets new life," *The New York Daily News,* May 17, 1992.

5. Mike Kortchmar, STRM Ltd. board meeting notes, August 3, 1992.

6. William Dobriner, "The Nine Lives of the *"Regina Maris,"* unpublished work, 1993.

7. Bob Liepa, "Maritime Fest Labeled Best Ever," *The Suffolk Times,* September 30, 1993.

8. Steve Clarke, interview with the author, March 17, 2012.

9. *Seaport Journal*, the quarterly publication of the East End Seaport and Marine Foundation and *Regina Maris*, Vol. 2, Spring 1995.

10. Joe Haberstroh, "Fighting to Keep Ship Afloat," *Newsday* (Long Island City, New York), July 5, 1998.

11. John Costello, interview with the author, March 17, 2012.

12. Debbie Tuma, "History Slowly Sinking," *New York Daily News*, November 17, 1997.

13. Donald Buchholtz, report on *Regina Maris,* published by John J. McMullen Associates, New York, New York, December 11, 1997. Mitchell Freedman, "Old Ship's Days May Be Waning," *Newsday*, 1997.

14. John T. McQuiston, "Prospects for Regina Maris Dim," *The New York Times*, July 5, 1998.

15. Dan Rattiner, "Greenport Mourns," *Dan's Papers*, June 26, 1998.

16. Pat Rogers, "Farewell, *Regina*," *The Suffolk Times*, August 6, 1998.

17. Joe Haberstroh, "Fighting to Keep Ship Afloat," *Newsday,* July 5, 1998.

18. Dan Rattiner, "Off to Denmark," *Dan's Papers*, July 31, 1998

19. Yad Vashem, The World Holocaust Remembrance Center web site, http://www.yadvashem.org/yv/en/righteous/stories/historical_background/denmark.asp.

20. John T. McQuiston, "Ship with Proud History Arrives at Its New Home," *The New York Times Metro Edition*, August 26, 1998. Reprinted in *Sea History Gazette* (Peekskill, New York), September/October 1998.

21. "Johnson Helps to Save Proud Ship," *The Westbury Times* (Westbury, Long Island), September 10, 1998.

CHAPTER 25

GLEN COVE, NEW YORK
1998-2002

Before noon on August 25, 1998, with flags flying, *Regina Maris* arrived in Hempstead Harbor, from which a narrow channel leads to Jude Glen Cove Thaddeus Marina, where the ship was to be docked. But as *Regina* entered the channel, she ran aground on a sand bar and had to wait out two high tides before she could float to her new dock. Once there, however, she was welcomed by Mayor Suozzi, who climbed her rigging and declared her a symbol of his efforts to revitalize the city's waterfront. [1] So begins the last phase of *Regina Maris's* life in her new homeport of Glen Cove.

During the process of obtaining *Regina*, Tom Suozzi had gathered into the steering team for *Regina's* restoration the same people who had helped him bring America's Sail '98 to Glen Cove: Sunny Seitier, Tom Hoffman, Charles Chiclacos, David Nieri, and Joe Weiser, who owned the Jude Thaddeus Marina. In early September, the group formed a new 501(c)(3) organization, Friends of the *Regina Maris* Ltd.; planned a monthly publication, *View from the Crow's Nest*; and developed brochures similar to the ones used in Greenport.

During the first volunteer organizational meeting, November 4, members of the dry-docking and restoration team were named: Roger Compton, of the Webb Institute; Pete Jacobson, of Jacobson Shipyard; David Short, a wooden-ship restorer; Gary Neillands, an experienced sailor and captain; and David Reiger, a master carpenter. They were charged with planning the restoration. [2]

What this team proposed, according to Tom Suozzi, was "loading the *Regina Maris* aboard a container ship and sending her back to the J. Ring-Andersen shipyard in Svendborg, Denmark, where she was built in 1908. She would be refurbished there with the help of financing by the two Danish organizations that [had] made contact with STRM Ltd. during the ship's last days in Greenport … and offered to invest $4.5- million to restore the ship in Denmark. …" [3]

The first of many fundraisers was held November 12 at the Sea Cliff Yacht Club. By this time I was serving as ship's historian, and I showed two movies of *Regina's* voyages. Merlon Wiggin presented the Glen Cove group with a model of *Regina*. On loan from EESMF, the model was displayed in the newly named *Regina Maris* Room at the Steamboat Landing Restaurant in the Jude Thaddeus Marina. (The restaurant's outside dining areas adjoined the north-south bulkhead against which *Regina* was docked.) The "fundraiser was a tremendous success with over 90 people present," steering committee member Sunny Seitier noted. [4]

A group of volunteers from the community took responsibility for the day-to-day care of the ship, which was quite demanding. A pump failure or an approaching storm necessitated an "all-hands-on-deck" mode for the dedicated few. Or as Tom Suozzi remembers, "There were months of midnight calls of, 'She's sinking' and a mad rush to the ship to bail her out." [5]

Sunny Seitier wrote in *The Gold Coast Gazette*, "Again a few words of thanks to the 'old reliable' [crowd] — Wade Curry, Larry Demmler, Herb Schierhorst, and Harry Hunt. Thanks to the 'on-the-spot-when-there's-a-problem' crowd — Mike Salentino, Joe Weiser, Dave Nieri, Ted Hoffman, Scott Emerich, Gretchen Geller, Ted Hoffman, Charles Chiclacos and Brett Flipse. These hard-working people kept her afloat and made steady progress on a hit list of necessary tasks, staying just ahead of the rot in some areas, lagging far behind in others." *Regina* continued to function as a dockside attraction for the community, drawing many visitors.

However, in 1999 a serious setback to the restoration plan arose. In February, Tom Suozzi sent local resident Janet Blatt to Sweden and Denmark to research the ship's reported role in helping the Danish underground rescue Jews fleeing the Holocaust. After Janet returned, she also met with Professor Leo Goldberger of New York University, author of *The Rescue of the Danish Jews: Moral Courage Under Stress*. In a telephone conversation with me in 2001, Janet said she felt, as a result of her research and Professor Goldberger's, that *Regina* had most likely carried Jews to safety. However she also felt that without official documentation from the family of the ship's owners confirming *Regina's* role, the necessary evidence was lacking for recognition by the Yad Vashem museum, Israel's official memorial to Holocaust victims and also the world center for Holocaust research. [6]

Asked to comment on the loss of the Holocoaust connection, Tom Suozzi told the *New York Times* in July 1999, "We'll continue to use her as a dockside attraction. She can stay where she is for some time yet. There is no urgency. In time, she could be secured inside a bulkhead or placed up on dry land with the necessary supports, if, as it turns out, there is no hope of ever making her seaworthy again." [7]

Since the ship had arrived in Glen Cove, he continued, the city had received $30 million in state and federal aid for environmental cleanup projects, and 100,000 square feet of new retail space was under construction in the downtown area. "The ship has become our good luck charm and has become a reminder to all who see her that Glen Cove is a beautiful waterfront community with a Gold Coast and maritime history." [8]

In the fall of 1999, the City of Glen Cove applied to be one of the major stops for the Operation Sail 2000 fleet. *Regina's* presence was used extensively to attract tall-ship captains and their vessels to the event, held in July, which the community called Waterfront Festival 2000. A 400-foot temporary dock was built at the Morgan Memorial Park for some of the 11 ships that visited, which included *Kalmar Nyckel*, a 139-foot full-rigged ship from Wilmington, Delaware; *Californian*, a 95-foot schooner from Long Beach, California; and *Morning Star of Revelation*, a 62-foot gaff-rigged sloop from England. Another ship, *Thomas Jefferson*, a replica of the side-wheel paddle steamers that plied the Gold Coast during the 19th century, gave harbor tours. *John L. Hall*, a 453-foot Navy guided missile frigate, was also in port. City officials estimated that 100,000 people attended. Once again, *Regina* had been used to bolster the image of a community and bring tourists and their cash to local businesses.

"This festival is a vehicle to reintroduce the people of Long Island to our beautiful waterfront," Mayor Suozzi told the *New York Times*. In addition, he noted that a mile of that "beautiful waterfront," once a state and federal Superfund site, was now targeted for redevelopment. [9] That fact would soon prove important for *Regina*.

While *Regina* was working hard to benefit Glen Cove and her volunteers were working hard to keep her afloat, negotiations to transport the ship to Denmark for restoration had been proceeding slowly. Early in 2001, however, the Danish organizations backed out completely. The Glen Cove group was still hoping that a grant from either Becks Beer or Volvo would come through. But the likelihood of the Volvo grant declined when the Glen Cove restoration team's estimated costs for the restoration topped $2.5 million. Efforts were made to encourage the companies to launch a joint effort to provide some financial help or otherwise support the project. Talks went on and on, and *Regina* was rotting at her slip. The steering team continued with several fundraising events during the year. But with the likely loss of funding from the large Jewish population in the greater New York metro area, Glen Cove *Regina* lovers faced the same almost insurmountable financial problems that had plagued Greenport's STRM Ltd.

Tom Suozzi's focus had shifted from all things Glen Cove when he decided to run for the office of Nassau County Executive. The rotting *Regina Maris* became something of an embarrassment to him during the campaign, according to a September 13, 2001, *Suffolk Times* article, [10], but after a contentious primary, he was elected county executive in 2001 and served until 2009.

From her arrival in 1998, *Regina* had been docked at the Jude Thaddeus Marina, owned by steering team member Joe Weiser, who also had an ownership interest in the Steam Boat Landing restaurant adjacent to the marina and right by *Regina*. The ship had brought business to the restaurant and marina, a benefit to all involved. As restoration efforts stalled, however, Joe became concerned about his liability if anything fell from the ship's rigging onto the restaurant's outdoor tables. In the spring of 1999, at his request, the ship was moved farther south along the bulkhead. A year later, after failing pumps and a sinking, Joe felt that if the ship went down and could not be raised quickly, it could block access to slips or damage boats renting dock space, and the marina would lose business. [11]

Therefore, to further alleviate Joe Weiser's concerns, on June 1, 2000, *Regina* was moved stern first northward along the length of the bulkhead and into a narrow channel leading westward to Mosquito Cove. According to communications to me in 2013 from Nick DeSantis, former public works director in Glen Cove, however, once she was fully turned into the channel she started taking on water because the rubber liner had been torn loose and ripped. She was quickly hauled to the bulkhead on the northern side of the cove, where she settled to the bottom. Only her masts and cabin top stuck up above the water. [12] There she sat for a year, in a bed of mud against the bulkhead of a former super fund site.

Regina on June 6, 2000. Photo and copyright by Sam Berliner III. All rights reserved.

Nick also related the next major event in the *Regina* saga. A Captain Gerhardt from the state of Georgia had showed up in Glen Cove and volunteered to raise *Regina* without cost to the town if they provided electricity for the pumps he needed. Tom Suozzi, then still mayor, welcomed Captain Gerhardt's offer because it fit into the plan he'd developed after *Regina* sank — have her lifted up and placed on land in the park on the former superfund site, adjacent to the bulkhead where she now rested. Re-floating was the first phase of that plan, and the city provided electric power for Captain Gerhardt. He had divers plug all the leaks they could find; then, using inflated air bags placed strategically within the hull, he refloated *Regina*. The ship, however, was completely dependent on the pumps for buoyancy. [12]

By the end of July 2001, *Regina* was still floating, with the aid of the constantly running pumps. But there was the continual danger that a pump would fail, a storm would sink her again, or both would happen, so the lifting phase of the plan was scheduled for as soon as the necessary equipment could be assembled.

Dave Nieri of the Glen Cove *Regina* steering team, told me in a 2013 email, when "Tom Suozzi made plans to hoist the ship out, they were not conveyed to all of us who had been involved on a 'steering committee.' Former Mayor Suozzi did a lot of wheeling and dealing behind the scenes and we weren't in the loop." [13]

During the refloating process, an organization called Econaval of Baldwin, New York, raised funds to support the lifting and hired Bay Crane of Hicksville to do the job.[10] Econaval planned to lift the floating ship and build a cradle under it on the reclaimed former superfund site just behind the bulkhead where *Regina* had sunk in 2000. They were then going to completely rebuild the ship.

When I heard she was going to be lifted, I contacted Bay Crane to give them the lifting specifications former owner John Wilson had given me, specifications based on the experience of Hoivold Mekaniske Verksted shipyard in Kristiansand, Norway. According to Hoivold's design data and lifting experience with the ship, and based on her rig in 1969, she had seven yards up the foremast and her center of weight balance was just 6 feet aft of that mast. This made her very bow-heavy, a condition not understood by the uninformed. She also had a 98-foot long steel shoe wrapped around her wooden keel, which meant that steel cables could slip along the shoe's length if the ship were not kept in a level or balanced position. Apparently, Bay Crane, a large, very highly regarded corporation, had no knowledge of these design specifics nor of the steel shoe. I don't know if my information ever reached the involved parties. I made several inquiries before and after the lift but I could not contact the actual lifting foreman. Had they had this information, they would have known to lift her with three cranes, as had been done in Boston in 1988. At that time, three 2-inch diameter cables had been placed around her and each were attached to steel "H" beam spreaders high over the deck. The spreaders prevented the cables from crushing the ship. The three cables had then been attached to three cranes with a combined lifting capacity of over 1,000 tons, two on the dock and one on a floating barge amidships. The slings at the bow, amidships and stern could then lift her and the tons of water remaining inside.

Instead, on September 8, 2001, Bay Crane attempted to lift the ship with one 500-ton crane, but all the water had not been pumped out. *Regina* was much heavier than estimated and maxed out the crane's ability to lift. The cables slipped and cut into the hull and bulwarks, crushing them with loud reports. The stern most cable may also have slipped aft off the steel shoe and cut deeply into the wood of the hogged and weakened stern. This opened up her hull so that no amount of pumping could keep her afloat.

As always, weight had played a crucial role. Before volunteers in Greenport removed 140 tons of unsalvageable equipment and rot, Steve Clarke had estimated, perhaps incorrectly, that *Regina* weighed around 465 tons. At this time in Glen Cove, she might have weighed around 329 tons. This would not include the weight of the water inside the hull when the lift was attempted in Glen Cove. A 500-ton crane was not up to the task.

"It could have been better," Nick DeSantis, the former public works director, said in the September 13, 2001, *Suffolk Times* article. "The Bay Crane crew spent eight hours using a 500-ton crane to try and lift the ship. But they finally concluded that they had to go back to the drawing board to reassess the situation. They'll have to use more straps and better straps. It'll take time to work out a solution" [10]

However, *Regina Maris* was so rotten to begin with and so badly damaged after the one lifting attempt that all hope of moving her in one piece was abandoned. *Regina's* hulk sat against the bulkhead and was eventually disassembled.

Some parts of the ship were restored and found a home in the reclaimed superfund site, slated to become a park with walking trails. On February 5, 2002, her restored masts, bowsprit, and figurehead were put in cement there, in an approximately *Regina*-sized footprint. There, too, her elegantly turned mahogany railing was placed around the stern cabin on replica wood bulwarks and hull. The work was done by the Local 7 Carpenters Union and their Empire State Apprentice Program for journeymen and apprentices At the time of the installation in the park, Nick DiSantis told *Newsday* that he wanted to "hang flags from the ship's spars, people will walk through it, bike right through it, as if it were a park." [14]

When I asked Nick in 2013 what had happened to the parts of the ship not used in the park display, he said, "All the planking, ribs and other timbers and parts were disposed of." In the same conversation Nick said that he felt, "Tom Suozzi did everything he possibly could to keep that ship afloat and viable as a restoration."[12]

Regina Maris, February 7, 2002, during her installation in the land berth at the superfund site park in Glen Cove. *Photo and © 2002 by Sam Berliner III. All rights reserved.*

"It made me a little bit sad looking at it, but you ask yourself at some point, 'Can you save everything?' " Doug Shaw, director of the Long Island Maritime Museum in West Sayville, told *Newsday*. [14]

Many other comments appeared in the media during *Regina Maris's* end days, but the one below, in *Ocean Navigator*, sums up her last gasp.

The resting place for *Regina*'s parts and pieces 2002-2017.
Photo by Morton Fox, courtesy of Panoramio and Google Maps.
All rights reserved.

"After years of falling apart, almost piece by handcrafted piece, the three-masted, wood barquentine, *Regina Maris*, Queen of the Sea, has reached the end of her road. After sinking last year in Glen Cove Creek, N.Y., where she had been for the past three years, an effort was made to raise her with a crane. The hull was so damaged by the steel cables that the great ship was finally dealt her deathblow. That, combined with the devastating economic effect of Sept. 11, virtually dried up any potential support to save the vessel. During her time in Glen Cove, despite the best efforts of volunteers, *Regina* leaked like a sieve; it simply couldn't be kept afloat. It was a sad but inevitable end for this great ship."[15]

In 2013, Tom Suozzi sent me the following statement about Glen Cove's involvement with *Regina*.

"Sometime during the course of 1998, the Village of Greenport had announced that it was going to scuttle the *Regina Maris*. I was Mayor of Glen Cove at the time. That summer we had hosted America's Sail, a tall ships event for the ships throughout the western hemisphere. To say that I, along with the residents of my city, had become bewitched by the romance of historic wooden ships would be a gross understatement. The idea of saving this historic ship and permanently exhibiting it on our planned revitalization waterfront seemed too good to be true. It was. The celebrated history of the ship as a vessel used to rescue Jewish refugees trying to escape the Holocaust was enough of a hook to raise the millions of dollars that would be needed to repair and revitalize this old ship, and insure that she no longer spent as much time under the water as she did floating proudly on top of it. The rescue from Greenport, her dramatic transport down the Long Island Sound, and her joyful welcome to Glen Cove Creek were soon supplanted by days and months of water pumps, salvage efforts, and constant attention and fundraising. Unfortunately, research into her background and history could not substantiate that she had been used for rescues of Holocaust survivors. After many attempts to raise funds, and a lack of continued public interest, we decided to disassemble her and display her masts and figurehead along the Glen Cove Creek as a permanent exhibit." [16]

But of course nothing in a tall ship's life is permanent — for *Regina* not even her "final" resting place. On September 16, 2017, I received the following email message from Diana Davis, whose father, Neil, was part owner of *Regina* from December 1970 to September 1971. "As you probably already know the 3 masts of the RM stood in Glen Cove, N.Y., across from the Brewer Marina, for quite some time. The kids around town were using it as a skate park and injuries of those children prompted the city to take the masts down. They are in a dump some where and I want to see if I can salvage a piece of something as a memento. Since I live in a town adjacent I am going to give it a try." [17] This was shocking news that spurred me on to do further research.

I then emailed Dave Nieri, a former *Regina* volunteer who lives in Glen Cove, for more information. Dave replied, "In January 2017 ground was broken by the developer RXR on a mixed-use community located along the shores of Hempstead Harbor to be called Garvies Point, the same land on which the masts of *Regina* were installed in 2002." [18]

Dave agreed to do additional research and take photos with his friend and fellow *Regina* volunteer Charlie Chiclacos. I then contacted Tom Suozzi, now Congressman Suozzi, for help, and he directed me to the current mayor, Reginald Spinello, whose office subsequently directed me to Manny Grella, foreman of the city's public works department. In a telephone interview, Manny told me that in mid- July the masts had been removed and destroyed. However, the city's public works department had salvaged the figurehead. He also implied that they might preserve the rusty hydraulic capstan, pullies, and other hardware from the masts. The city's plan, he told me, "is to use the pullies to decorate the newly completed ferry building." [19]

After I reported this information on The Friends and Crew of *Regina Maris* Facebook site, it became abuzz with hopes that the figurehead might be preserved in a maritime museum, perhaps with the help of Mayor Spinnello and Deputy Mayor Barbara Peebles.

The *Regina Maris* figurehead in the Glen Cove Department of Public Works storage yard, October 30, 2017. blocks can be seen in the foreground. *Photo by David Nieri*.

On October 11, 2017, I contacted The Long Island Maritime Museum (LIMM) in West Sayville and sent them David Nieri's photos. Museum representatives inspected the artifacts in Glen Cove and agreed to take them as a donation if offered by Glen Cove. On October 13, Terry Blitman, executive director of LIMM, contacted Deputy Mayor Barbara Peebles, who told her that the city had plans for the artifacts and they were not available. Upon hearing this, I in an act of friendly persuasion, sent Barbara exerts of this book and implored her to protect the figurehead from the elements.

The rusty hydraulic capstan as it sat in the City of Glen Cove department of public works yard in early October 2017. *Photo by Vinny Martinez Jr.*

On Novemger 16, after the release of the eBook edition of this book, an email arrived from Barbara saying that Glen Cove would like to donate the ship's artifacts to the Long Island Maritime Museum and could I help make that happen. Barbara also said that the figurehead had been moved to the safety of the new ferry building and was no longer out in the elements. With this wonderful news, I contacted Terry at the LIMM to start the transfer process. The museum plans to have the figurehead mounted on a wall, as it would be on the bow of the ship, with historical information displayed below. For more information about the museum, go to http://www.limaritime.org. For additional information and photos of the ship, visit the ship's Facebook site (https://www.facebook.com/reginamaris1908/), and also the *Regina Maris* Society's Web site (www/reginamsociety.org) The *Regina Maris* Society also has an online newsletter, *The Jolly Boat* that can be viewed at http://eepurl.com/rmcQv.

CHAPTER 25
GLEN COVE, NEW YORK 1998-2002

1. John T. McQuiston, "Ship with Proud History Arrives at Its New Home," *The New York Times Metro Edition*, August 26, 1998. Reprinted in *Sea History Gazette* (Peekskill, New York), September/October 1998.
2. Sunny Seitier, "News Flash from the Regina Maris," View from the Crow's Nest, *The Gold Coast Gazette* (Glen Cove, New York, November 1998.
3. Debbie Tuma, "$4.5M bid is wind in ship's sails," *The New York Daily News*, July 23, 1998.
4. Sunny Seitier, letter to the author, December 16, 1998.
5. Tom Suozzi, telephone interview with the author, July 26, 2012.

6. Janet Blatt, telephone interview with the author, September 15, 2001. Janet had met recently with Professor Leo Goldberger of New York University's psychology department and author of *The Rescue of the Danish Jews: Moral Courage Under Stress*, (New York, New York: New York University Press, 1987.)

7. John T. McQuiston, "Admirers of an Aging Ship Still Short of Restoration Money," *The New York Times Metro Edition*, July 19, 1999.

8. Robert Gearty, "Tracking Trail of Rare Tall Ship," *The New York Daily News*, February 21, 1999.

9. David Winzelberg, "Plenty of Tall Ships without Leaving L.I.," *The New York Times*, July 2, 2000.

10. Julie Lane, "Regina to Rise Again?" *The Suffolk Times* (Mattituck, New York), September 13 2001.

11. Charlie Chiclacos, (a member of the Glen Cove steering team for *Regina Maris* who was at the meeting where Joe Weiser expressed his concerns), email to the author, March 22, 2013 and September 20, 2017.

12. Nick DeSantis, telephone interview with the author, March 26, 2013, and email to the author, March 29, 2013.

13. Dave Nieri, emails to the author, April 2, 2013, and September 19, 2017.

14. Joe Haberstroh, "Ship's History Kept in Parts, *Regina Maris* exhibit edited for cost," *Newsday* (Long Island, New York), February 5, 2002.

15. "Celebrated barquentine *Regina Maris* scrapped," *Ocean Navigator* (Portland, Maine) #122 May/June 2002.

16. Tom Suozzi, email to the author, June 17, 2013.

17. Diana Davis, email to the author, September 17, 2017.

18. Dave Nieri, email to the author, September 17, 2017.

19. Manny Grella (public works foreman, City of Glen Cove, New York), telephone interview with the author, September 18, 2017.

EPILOGUE

Though, thankfully, the figurehead may live on, *Regina Maris* herself is gone, gone the way of all things made by man. With her glory days behind her, the final years were not easy. If her obituary were to be written, it would surely say she lived a charmed life, exceeding her life expectancy, reaching the grand old age of 98, and never losing a human soul entrusted to her care. Launched as a three-masted schooner with two square-sail yards on the foremast, she was modified — some say butchered — into a "textbook" barkentine. Others, had they had their way, would have converted her to a brig. Her grand basic lines have sparked much romantic prose, and she took many who dreamed of a life at sea on their first voyage in a lifetime of adventures. *Regina's* sailing around the world helped spark a resurgence in tall-ship seamanship and restoration. Cities around the world started restoring their old ships and sail training gained new meaning and followers.

To restoration purists, *Regina* was ruined when the seven-yardarm foremast was conjured up. Or did that happen when cement was poured into the hull to increase the ballast? Did she lie down on her death bed when the 98-foot- long steel shoe encasing her keel was installed? The existence of that shoe was unknown to many of the shipyards that refused to haul her and to Bay Crane in Glen Cove on her final lift. Did the death knell sound when she was hauled in Gloucester to inspect the lower ends of the masts with just bilge chocks and her standing rigging slackened off? Or was it when her copper sheathing was removed? What about all the quick fixes, poor quality wood, and shoddy workmanship done improperly to maintain her over the years by financially strapped owners? Some felt she was already living on borrowed time when the deep pockets of the Wilson brothers faded into the past. Few organizations can dedicate half a million dollars or more a year to properly maintain a wooden ship of *Regina's* size. ORES gave her all they had, and in the end it was not enough to keep her working at sea.

What is a proper end for a fine ship like *Regina Maris*? Scuttling at sea, which nearly happened in 1991 in Massachusetts? Rotting away in a sand birth near the East End Seaport Museum in Greenport, which, with a slight change of events, could be her situation even now? Or is it a fitting end to go the way of the two highly photographed schooners rotting in the mud of Wiscasset, Maine? Ships like *Regina Maris* are tools, machines humans have created and used to do work and gain financially. In her case, she also fulfilled dreams, started successful maritime careers, and added to the knowledge of the sea and its denizens.

The sight of a tall ship, sails billowing, is stirring to behold. Many people have started following the ways of ships and the sea because of that vision. Perhaps during the past 15 years *Regina's* masts, reaching high in Glen Cove, stirred some soul into following a tall-ship life at sea. Now, hopefully, her figurehead displayed at the Long Island Maritime Museum, along with proper documentation of the ship's history, can continue to inspire thoughts of Neptune's realm and spur still more dreamers to become, in Steve Katona's words, ensouled with a ship.

Regina Maris Lives On

At this writing, all that remains physically of *Regina Maris* are the carved figurehead and a few forlorn parts at the Long Island Maritime Museum in West Sayville, New York. But *Regina's* spirit persists, thanks, especially, to the work of a few dreamers who won't let her memory die.

In 2008, Evan Ginsberg, who in Chapter 20 recounts some of his experiences on *Regina* in the early '70s and early '80s, started a Facebook Group page, *Friends and Crew of Regina Maris*. To date there are 267 members who frequent the Group, sharing photos and memories of their time aboard the ship. According to Steve Nelson, whose major role in preserving the *Regina* spirit is detailed below, ". . . of those 267, I can only confirm that 47 are *Regina* alums who actually sailed on the ship. The rest must be relatives of crew or just tall ship devotees."

Out of the Facebook page grew another idea that further kept the *Regina* flame alive. In August 2011, Ann Nichols, widow of ORES founder and *Regina* owner Dr. George Nichols, suggested on the Facebook Group page that a reunion be held, centered at the Gloucester Maritime Heritage Center, since Gloucester had been *Regina's* home port in the ORES days. Seeing this Facebook post, Steve Nelson, who served as student, deckhand, and third mate on *Regina* from May 1979 through June 1980, volunteered to find and contact more *Regina* alums for a reunion. "I quickly realized," he recalled in an email to the author in 2017, "that Facebook was not the place to find and gather an older demographic like ours — most alums were not on Facebook."

In July 2012, Steve tried to arrange a small, informal reunion in Gloucester of *Regina* alums. *(See Appendix H for the Rendezvous announcement that was posted to the Facebook group in November 2011)*. This gathering did not materialize but it "did lead to the beginnings of the *Regina Maris* Reunion 2013 Organizing Crew," Steve wrote, "which returned to Ann Nichols' suggestion of gathering at the Gloucester Maritime Heritage Center, where we could meet and even create a museum exhibit of *Regina's* history."

In addition to Steve Nelson, the organizing crew consisted of several former *Regina* hands: Ken Balcomb, Roger Callan, Eric Hutchins, Amanda Madeira, Ann Nichols, and Richie Perkins. The group worked on a multi-day event centered in Gloucester that would include a schooner sail, a museum display about the ship, and time for sharing personal photos and *Regina* artifacts.

Partly to support the reunion project, Steve was inspired create an online newsletter, and the first issue of *The Jolly Boat*. "My goal for *The Jolly Boat* was to each month share photos, articles, videos, and news about all the periods of *Regina's* history, so that all the shipmate subscribers would develop a sense of community across all the years and all the ownerships and would anxiously wait each month (or two) for the next bit of history they never knew before. And I wanted to make them feel privileged to be a part of that history — to make them feel like fellow 'Dreamers Before the Mast.' And through *The Jolly Boat* I wanted to create a sense of credibility for the organizing crew that was planning the reunion, a sense that we had our act together and that it would appear worth travelling from Australia or Norway or Washington or England or Germany or Alaska or Maine or wherever."

Publicized through many media, including *The Jolly Boat,* the Facebook page, *WoodenBoat* magazine, and emails to alums whose addresses the author was able to provide, the 2013 reunion took place September 6 through 8, in Gloucester. Sixty-five crew members, plus their significant others, attended, hailing from Australia, New Zealand, Germany, Norway, England, and across the United States.

Attendees of the Regina Maris Reunion in Gloucester in 2013. *Photo by Alessandro Abate.*

Steve Nelson recalled, "I have to admit that I was just amazed both at the number of attendees and how far they traveled to get to the 2013 Reunion. Why would so many believe that a bunch of shipmates with no formal organization would be able to pull together such a complex event? Believe it enough that they would buy a plane ticket, reserve a hotel, and show up at the appointed time and place, wearing a faded, threadbare T-shirt with the picture of a very specific boat on it? Still amazes me. I've enjoyed the time shared (in person and via email) with every one of them."

So successful was the 2013 reunion that plans for a second, to be held on the West Coast in 2015, were soon under way. Steve Nelson made a scouting trip to the Pacific Northwest in the summer of 2014 to check out meeting facilities and hold initial planning sessions with the West Coast organizing committee, which comprised, in addition to Steve Nelson, Ken Balcomb, Darlene Marmol, Jill Likkel, Emile Amarotico, Lee Bruno, Eric Hutchins, and Perran Ross. *(See photo in Appendix H.)* Held August 20 to 23, 2015, in Port Townsend and Friday Harbor, Washington, the event welcomed 25 crew, along with their significant others. The reunion, which offered communal housing and meals at the Fort Worden conference grounds, featured a whale watching trip to the Center for Whale Research on San Juan Island, hosted by ORES chief scientist Ken Balcomb, and an open-to-the-public roundtable discussion among ORES scientists on *Regina's* many contributions to cetacean research.

Regina Maris Reunion 2015 group photo, taken at the Center for Whale Research, Smuggler's Cove, San Juan Island, Washington, August 23. *Photo by Craig Strang.*

"Both reunions," Steve wrote, "were financially scary because we, of course, had to put down deposits on venues, catering, boat rides, entertainment, and the like, and many of the paid reservations came in at the last few weeks. Note that the organizing crews made a common pledge at the outset of planning that we would cover any financial shortfalls, but in both cases, we came out ahead, with some funds leftover."

In march 2015, six months before the second reunion, The *Regina Maris* Society was founded as a non-profit in Washington state to serve as the representing entity for the reunion, handling the cash and paying the bills. Since completing these administrative tasks, it has expanded its mission to discover, share, and preserve the history of *Regina Maris*.

In 2017, reported *The Jolly Boat,* "the Sail Boston 2017 tall ship event provided the excuse for some of us shipmates to get together for a lobster feed at Eric Hutchins' Dogtown Homestead in Rockport, MA. It was small, casual, and a lot of fun."

At the time of this book's publication, the *Regina Maris* spirit still lives on in Facebook, *The Jolly Boat* newsletter, and The *Regina Maris* Society. And Steve Nelson and the author were creating a collection and associated database consisting of the artifacts, photos, journals, log books, films, drawings, publications, audio recordings, interviews, oral histories, and more that together make up the historical record of the ship. Ultimately the collection and database will be donated to a library or maritime museum so it can be available to historians and researchers long after those of us who sailed *Regina* have crossed the bar.

Regina crew can sign up for *The Jolly Boat* newsletter at http://eepurl.com/rmcQv. The *Regina Maris* Society website can be found at *www/reginamsociety.org*. The *Regina Maris* Society Facebook Page can be found at https://www.facebook.com/reginamaris1908/.

Appendix A

Below is a list of share holders and their share amounts.

O. B. Bengtsson	10/77	J. Lund, Lawyer	9/77
Per Reinhold, sea captain	8/77	Carl Nisson, Odakra	4/77
N. B. Bentz, builder	3/77	Jons Peter Andersson, Capt.	2/77
J. A. Backe, Captain	2/77	Carl Holmstrom	2/77
Charles Hvilsom, Copenhagen	2/77	Petter Jacobsson	2/77
Nils P. Johansson, Halsingborg	2/77	Teodor Lindgren	2/77
Anders Magnusson, Captain	2/77	A. H. Magnusson	2/77
Gottfried Olsson	2/77	N. P. Palsson, Raus plant	2/77
Rudolf Ahlman	1/77	Nils Andersson, Lyngso	1/77
Olof Andersson, Leberget	1/77	Agda Bengtsson	1/77
Carl Bjork	1/77	Janne Hansson	1/77
Per Hansson	1/77	Petter Jonasson	1/77
Anna Maria Jonsson, Halsingborg	1/77	Johs. Kristiansson	1/77
Anders Kropp	1/77	Bengt Larsson	1/77
Kristina Jonsson	1/77	Johan och Reinold Moller	1/77
Joel Olsson	1/77	Nils Olsson	1/77
O. R. Olsson	1/77	Reinhold Olsson	1/77
Sven Olsson	1/77	Janne Peter Reinhold	1/77
A. P. Sundin	1/77	C. Sundin	1/77

Appendix B

Year Visited	Sailing Season	Freight Income	# of Ports
1908	3/22 -- 12/1	10,350.45 kr	11
1909	4/1 -- 12/2	10,307.25 kr	10
1910	4/14 – 11/22	11,495.71 kr	18
1911	3/15 – 12/2	16,848.38 kr	25
1912	3/18 – 12/12	19,296.20 kr	18
1913	2/28 – 12/13	19,338.67 kr	17
1914	3/1 – 9/29	9,249.43 kr	13
1915	4/19 –12/7	14,444.85 kr	15
1916	4/28 – 11/20	35,100.32 kr	16
1917	3/12 – 12/13	33,150.12 kr	14
1918	3/22 – 12/14	33,861.82 kr	16
1919	4/17 – 12/9	49,252.87 kr	14
1920	4/1 – 12/14	40,576.33 kr	

Appendix C

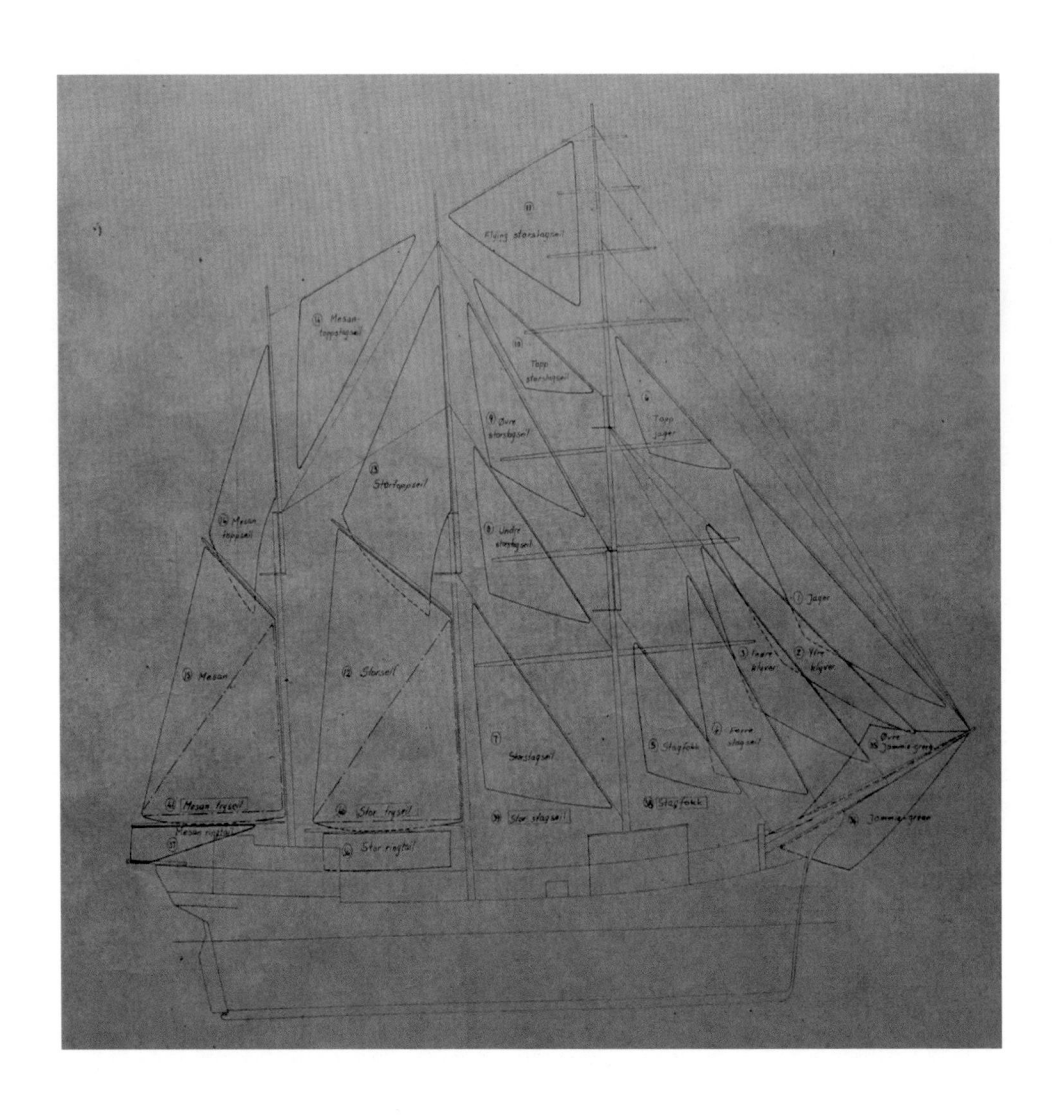

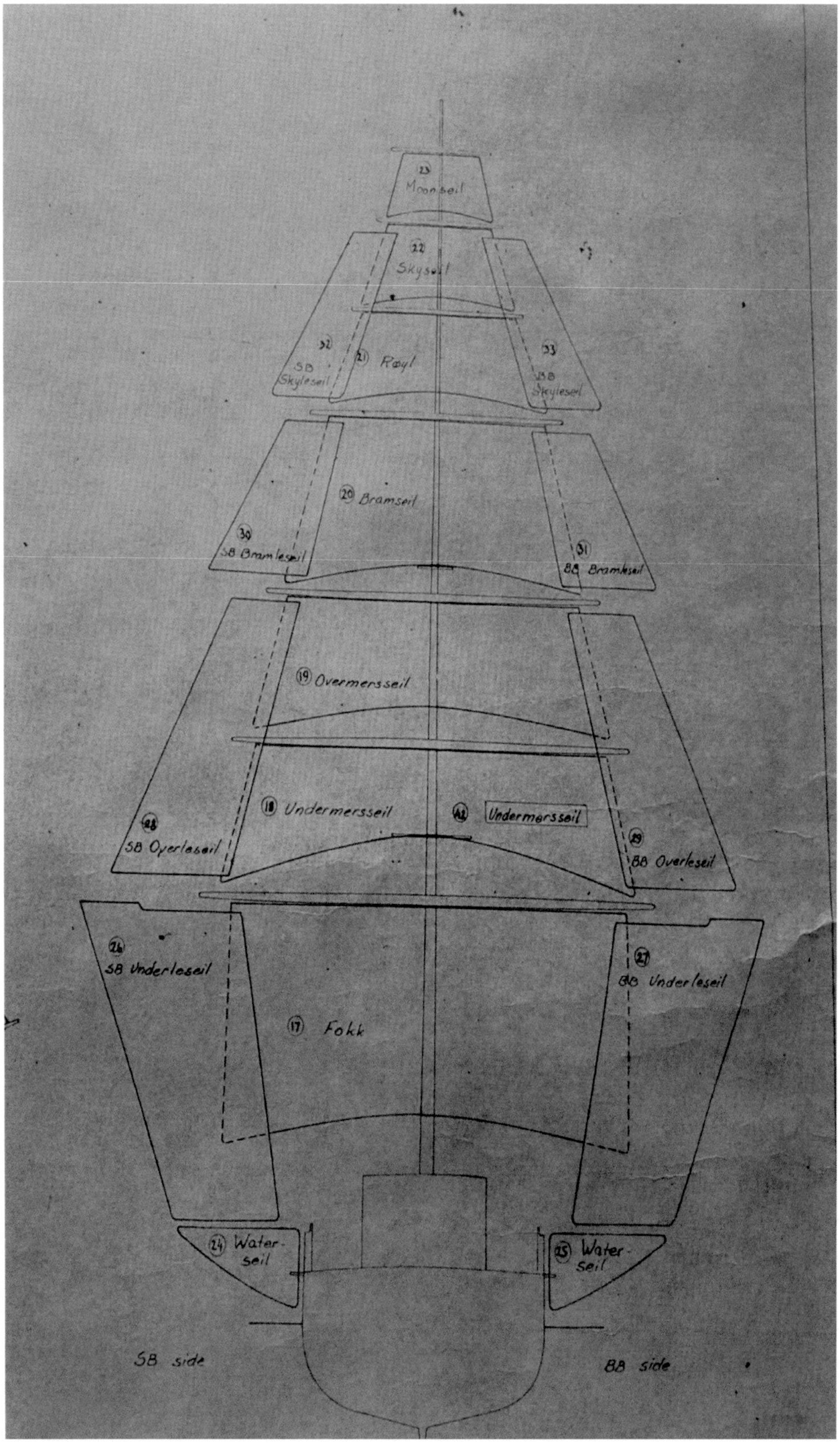

23 Moonseil
22 Skyseil
32 SB Skyleseil
21 Røyl
33 BB Skyleseil
20 Bramseil
30 SB Bramleseil
31 BB Bramleseil
19 Overmersseil
18 Undermersseil
42 Undermersseil
28 SB Overleseil
29 BB Overleseil
26 SB Underleseil
27 BB Underleseil
17 Fokk
24 Water-seil
25 Water-seil
SB side
BB side

Figure 1 Appendix D

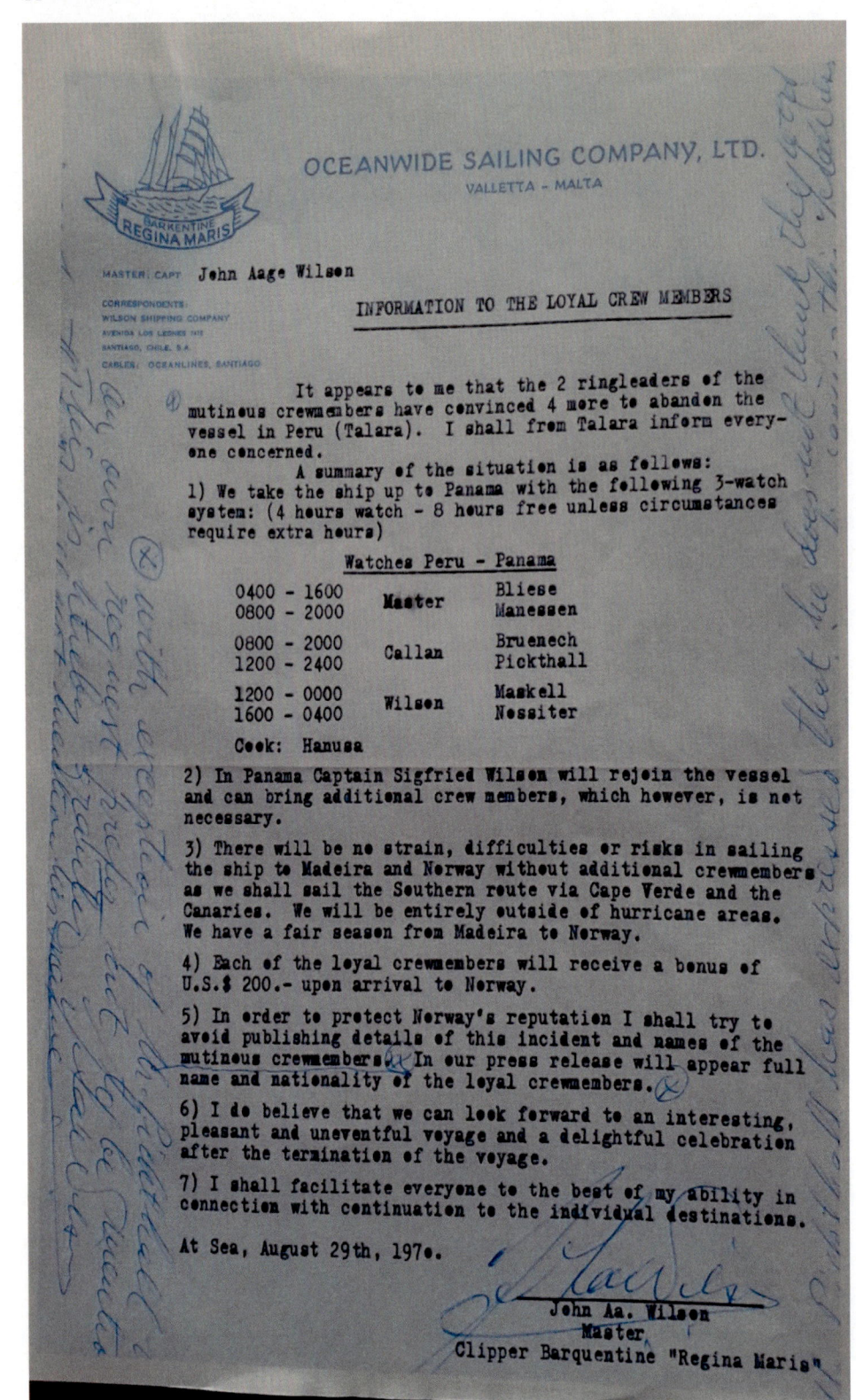

OCEANWIDE SAILING COMPANY, LTD.
VALLETTA - MALTA

MASTER: CAPT. John Aage Wilsen

CORRESPONDENTS:
WILSON SHIPPING COMPANY
AVENIDA LOS LEONES 1972
SANTIAGO, CHILE, S.A.
CABLES: OCEANLINES, SANTIAGO

INFORMATION TO THE LOYAL CREW MEMBERS

It appears to me that the 2 ringleaders of the mutinous crewmembers have convinced 4 more to abandon the vessel in Peru (Talara). I shall from Talara inform everyone concerned.

A summary of the situation is as follows:
1) We take the ship up to Panama with the following 3-watch system: (4 hours watch - 8 hours free unless circumstances require extra hours)

Watches Peru - Panama

0400 - 1600	Master	Bliese
0800 - 2000		Manessen
0800 - 2000	Callan	Bruenech
1200 - 2400		Pickthall
1200 - 0000	Wilsen	Maskell
1600 - 0400		Nessiter

Cook: Hanusa

2) In Panama Captain Sigfried Wilsen will rejoin the vessel and can bring additional crew members, which however, is not necessary.

3) There will be no strain, difficulties or risks in sailing the ship to Madeira and Norway without additional crewmembers as we shall sail the Southern route via Cape Verde and the Canaries. We will be entirely outside of hurricane areas. We have a fair season from Madeira to Norway.

4) Each of the loyal crewmembers will receive a bonus of U.S.$ 200.- upon arrival to Norway.

5) In order to protect Norway's reputation I shall try to avoid publishing details of this incident and names of the mutinous crewmembers. In our press release will appear full name and nationality of the loyal crewmembers.

6) I do believe that we can look forward to an interesting, pleasant and uneventful voyage and a delightful celebration after the termination of the voyage.

7) I shall facilitate everyone to the best of my ability in connection with continuation to the individual destinations.

At Sea, August 29th, 1970.

John Aa. Wilsen
Master
Clipper Barquentine "Regina Maris"

Cont. Page 2   Packets, Tins
                                 or by Volume   Meals

FRUIT:
Applesauce   22   4
Misc. Fruit   55   11
Dried apricots   10 ltr.   3
Raisends   +)   10 ltr.   --
                                                Total 18

OTHERS:
Milk   200   4 per Day
Butter   50 1/2 kg   3/8kg =
Margarine   47 1/8 kg   see above
   dito   24 tins   see above
Sugar   25kg+30packets hard   --
Salt   5 l.+rock salt+powder ---
Tea   enough   --
Coffee   enough   --
Concentrated juice   10 ltr. (1:5)   1 1/2 per day
Jam   enough   --
Milk powder   23 kg   3/8kg per day
Egg powder   20 kg   10
Cake mix.   3 packets   --
Bread (German)   300   3 sl. per day
Baking powder   10   --
Cooking fat + oel   10 ltr.+10kg   --
Ketchup   -88 (None)   --

+) SOUPS:
Bags (1 bag = 10 people)   30   --
Toro Soucewürfel   9   --
Fleischbrühe   2 small glasses   --
                                            guessed Total 15

+) FOOD FOR EVENINGS OR MORNINGS:
Sardines in tomato or oel   450 small   7 per day
Cheese   15 kg   15
Paté   150 small   3 per day
Corned beef   32 small   8
Tinned ham   18   18
Rolled oats (porridge)   24   30
Sago (rice-milk soup)   14   10
Eggs   --   4
Liverpaste   10 (1/2 sticks)   5
Sousage   5   2

BREAKFAST: **Tea AFTERNOON:**
Porridge   44   not   Fish, Meat   60
Sago   small   enough   Veg. greens   46   not enough
Eggs   Portions   Potatoes   30
                                 Rice   30

Evening TEA:
Soup   20   Nudeln   30   48 with potatoes
Meat/Fish   38   Rice   30   or nudeln but
Ham, Cheese, beets, bacon   10   Potatoes   30   only 12 days of
Wurst, Pate, Gürkens, beans with   rice + potatoes
Corned beef, tomatos, radish soup   only with soup.

48 days with meat, rice or nudeln, 10 days w. cheese etc. + soup,
2 days soup!

cont. Page 3

These estimates are based on past experience in <u>tropical</u> conditions!
We do not consider that there is sufficient food on board for 60 days,
especially for men working long hours under cold conditions.

NB: There is only enough for:
a) 44 light breakfast of porridge and sago.
b) No more than <u>50 days</u> of evening tea consisting mainly of potatoes or rice.
c) 48 days of greens
d) 5 slices tinned bread for each man per day.
e) ~~26 kg of carbohydrate~~ 24 kg of sugar - 26 gr/man/day for 60 days

2) SEAWORTHINESS OF THE SHIP:

We consider that it would ~~be~~ not be safe to take the ship round Cape Horn in her present condition. At the moment it takes about 1 hr. and 30 min., after pumping, for the water level in the engine room bilge to reach just above the keel; and 25 min. of pumping to reduce the water level to zero again. Alternatively, the manual pump on deck pumped properly, can keep the water level in the bilges steady.

In view of your promise to take the ship into port if and when the leak gets worse, we would like your guarantee that you will do this as soon as 1) the interval between pumpings becomes less than 1¼ hours, (with the water just above the keel) or 2) the manual pump on deck is no longer able to keep the water level steady.

[signatures]

Signed on 12th August 1970

I expect everyone to do their duty
willingly and seriously — for their own
safety and that of the ship. I shall
certainly continue to do my part.
Strict and immediate obedience to
my orders — and disciplined behaviour is
an important part of the ship's safety.

At Sea   30 - 8 - 1970

Captain,

With regard to your notice addressed, "Information to the Loyal Crew Members", concerning point No. 5 of your summary, we the undersigned do not want our names and nationalities to be divulge to the press of any country.

Also we do not agree with the word, "_mutinous_", that you have used in your notice to describe those members of the crew that wish to disembark at Talara.

Finally we do not wish to be described collectively as "the loyal crew members". We can assure you that apart from any other unforseen difficulties or changes in the voyage, we will do our best to sail the vessel back to Norway. We sincerely hope that the voyage will be a friendly, happy one.

Signed.

TIM PICKTHALL - EXTRACTS FROM DIARY REGINA MARIS
09 August 1970 to 10 September 1970

9/8/70 - left Pitcairn and were told we were going to Cape Horn, not to Chile any more.

10/8/70 - Much talking and complaining about the Captain's decision - main objections were the safety factor, food and advising home. I saw the captain that night who told me we would save 2000 miles and struggling against the Humbolt current and adverse winds and that the journey would take about 5-6 weeks. What we didn't like was the way it had been done and that we weren't notified before Pitcairn so that we could mention it in the letters. The Captain spoke to the crew as a whole. Said he wanted to stress the ship was safe as a house. Most accepted the decision. Water and food will be rationed. So many oranges and bananas on board by the time they are finished they will be growing out of our ears! No bath for 5-6 weeks - what a stink!

11-8-70 - To save fuel the motor was switched off but there was a favourable wind blowing. We had to hand pump the bilge 12 minutes every two hours. Weather was good. Took inventory of food. With daily rations there is just sufficient to last 50 days - 60 at a pinch. But not all of it is right food for cold weather and hard work in storms. As long as the safety factor is there, sufficient food for good health, I accepted the challenge. Had a bath in teepol and salt water - feel much better. Porridge and fruit. Spaghetti & sausage; soup; fruit salad; 5 slices atomic bread (tinned black German bread which we believe was World War II hard rations); tea and fruit.

12-8-70 - Crew meeting when it was decided there would be enough food for 60 days maximum but no longer. This entailed hardly any breakfast or supper but a fairly substantial midday meal consisting mainly of starch. We gave the list to the captain, and the leak was also mentioned. The captain replied that we wouldn't starve and the leak was no cause for concern. Now it remains to see what happens. Just before lunch, Klaus came into our cabin and was approached by Henk over something Henk got carried away and drew his knife. Managed to quieten him down, not a pleasant experience. Getting fed up with all these. Good weather and following wind. Making good speed and if maintained, could be there in 20 days. No breakfast (on dogwatch); fish balls rice and potatoes; bread; cabbage salad; tea and two oranges.

13-8-70 - Temp dropped to 15 degrees C from 21. The barometer was rising 3+- pmb at a time and by 8pm it was 30.49 nearly 50. The highest I have ever known. The lads are very unhappy about the situation. Hope everything turns out alright but I think we are beyond that point. No breakfast (on dogwatch); meatballs, rice and potatoes; 2 oranges; Rice, cabbage, fish, meat and 5 slices bread.

14-8-70 - Barometer still very high 30.44 and temperature 15.5C. The lads are very unhappy and I hope not too much trouble evolves. I am neutral whether we go or not. The captain offered us wine but it has been refused. Porridge; pancakes and orange; fishballs cabbage, potatoes; fish roe, cabbage and rice; German bread and tea.

15-8-70 - Raining (with some hail) and temp dropped to 10.5C as well as the barometer. Today we received beer for the first time since leaving Brisbane. With luck a month today we should be in Montevideo. Pancakes and an orange; meatballs, mixed veg; noodles and orange; noodles, rice, 1 slice atomic bread; tea.

16-8-70 - Weather deteriorated further so we hove to. About force 7-8 with strong an heavy seas. We were rolling like billy-ho and on watch I was sitting in the mess and we had one bad roll and the water came pouring into the galley and mess which was very funny. Captain decided to have the middle and lower staysail set. In the morning we put up the main mast storm sail which stretched us a bit. In the evening we were all called into the mess to be told that we were going to Lima in Peru and no longer to the horn - thereafter Panama, Jacksonville for dry docking, Caribbean and then home to Europe (remains to be seen)! The following notice was put up in the mess:

NOTICE TO CREW OF REGINA MARIS
In consideration of various crew members attitude towards my decisions of necessary changes in our voyage itinerary and refusal of unanimous acceptance of proceeding home by way of Cape Horn, I have consequently had to change the voyage. We are from 1600 hrs on Aug 16, changing course to proceed to Callao, Peru, where the mutinous crewmembers will disembark. Tentative itinerary will be as follows - all dates approximate. etc, etc,

17-8-70 - Weather deteriorated with cold wind force 8-10 and huge seas. We are in a high percentage gale area.

18-8-70 - Storm continues and at peak was said to have reached Force 11. The seas were huge but rain had stopped. Saw a yellow sunrise and full moon at night - all quite eerie. The port pin rail was sometimes right under water and one time I stood on the drums and felt them lift right up - fortunately they are empty. The bob stay chain broke right at the tip of the bowsprit when a sheet bolt sheared right through. Must be a tremendous force exerted by the mast. Spent most of the time below as the spray clears the deckhouse at times. Getting to the mess is a refined art of speed and agility. Barometer went very low then fluctuated up and down then shot up 6 points in an hour, indicating further bad weather and strong winds.

19-8-70 - During the 8-12 watch we saw a rainbow - an amazing sight at night. Captain decided to move out of the storm area - had the port standbys up to set inner and outer job lower and middle staysail. We made a cracking 8 knots but had to be very careful for side glancing seas. The wheel was a battle and had to pay careful attention. Eating can be a trying task.

20-8-70 - Wind dropped but cold and rain squalls with huge seas - averaging about 10ft and the big boys about 15-20ft. Captain decided to run with the sea. Making almost 9 knots so all being well shouldn't be too long before we reach Callao. Who will leave and will they be replaced? One of these days it won't be necessary to wear a sweatshirt under shirt; two jumpers; scarf and towel; plus oilskins; socks and gumboots! Saw a glass fishing bowl (buoy?).

21-8-70 - Weather seems to have improved. Captain said there were about 2,500 miles to go. Only being able to make a slight easterly course but most of the time it is due north.

22-8-70 - Very quiet day. Good breeze SE wind enabled us to make a fair speed. In a few days we will be in the tropics and warm weather again.

23-8-70 - Considerably warmer today with slight wind and calm seas. Had very nice lunch today but no more rum; beer; biscuits or chocolates until Callao. It's been too long at sea with nothing much to do.

24-8-70 - Beautiful day today but I feel sore; bones are stiff and weary. Steering easterly course 60. No wind and temperature going up. Will be able to sleep on deck again soon. Rumours about going to the Horn - am getting sick of the indecisiveness. Rigged up a semi-belly board extending out from the stun sail boom with safety belt. Lowered ourselves down rope ladder and bosons chair to get back. It was terrific fun. Tim N lost his costume which was very funny.

25-8-70 - Beautiful day - water like glass. Deep red sunset - played Chess.

26-8-70 - Rumours still flying about so I asked the Captain what was happening. He put up the following notice: ETA Callao Friday 4 September, then Panama 15 September, then Cristobel 17 September. After that, still undecided. May sail to Europe rather than USA. Will call at Funchal, Madeira on southern route keeping us out of hurricane areas during the season.

27-8-70 - Overcast with cold north wind. Steering easterly course 80. A quiet day.

28-8-70 - Another quiet day. Wind swung to East so changed course to 30 wind just off the bow. Apparently there seems to be something wrong with the motor but not sure. There is also a problem with fuel that we might not have enough. This evening the Norwegians are going to tell the captain that they are leaving in Callao. Interesting to see what happens. The Captain was very surprised. Not much was said. Food has deteriorated because there is nothing good left. Life is full of surprises. Was playing Chess with Klaus when the Captain walked in and said 3 loyal members - Paul was busy typing. A meeting was held with the Captain of the ones who weren't leaving. Weighing up the factors, I have decided to remain - a fairly grim position.

29-8-70 - Everybody was dispirited with what has happened and the Norwegians are swearing blue murder and raving about what they are going to do. We changed tack for a few minutes so as to get some extra fuel on the slant. The fuel position is very dicey and touch and go whether we reach Talara or not, a point which the others will want to drive home. With this food my stomach is really taking a hammering.

30-8-70 - This evening I approached the captain about the written paper he gave me to sign, except I wanted a few alterations, which he readily agreed to.

31-8-70 - Easterly wind this morning. Captain came along and wanted the course set and braced round far as possible. It was touch and go whether it would set. Quite hard holding the wheel. Captain tore Jorgen to pieces because he wasn't on course - he had no reason to say what he did. No sabotage. Another piece of paper going round amongst the remaining 8 about mutinous press release and loyalty. Only remains to be seen what happens.

1-9-70 - Very quiet day, rather overcast with some easterly wind but not as strong as yesterday. The seas are calmer and sailing with the fore and aft up. It's going to be touch and go whether we reach Talara as fuel is getting low. Captain trying to go as far north as possible to get good weather so we can go inland, or get the south east trades. There were no lights today so as to try and save some fuel. Water is being rationed as there is only one tank left. If everything fails and we miss Peru, we could be at sea for much longer as we would have to sail round to the South Pacific islands and try again (this is the method the old sailing ships used).

2-9-70 - Still running with fore and aft up and making about 6-7 knots per watch. Lights are off during the day to try and safe fuel. Fuel position looks a little brighter having sufficient for 7 days which is possible as the further north we go the better the weather should get. Nevertheless it will be touch and go. This afternoon the Captain expressed the urgency of the position to me and said it was a matter of life and death and how important it is that we strike the south American coast, otherwise when the fuel runs out we will drift to the south pacific islands. This would be very well but we haven't sufficient food, water or oil and there is still the pumping to think about.

3-9-70 - Making quite good easterly direction with se wind very consistent.

4-9-70 - Weather still the same, I don't think it ever clears up in this part of the world. Our time of estimated arrival in Talara is Monday night after 6 weeks at sea. The lads are slowly getting themselves organised and packing up and looking forward to their departure. Most of the day was spent getting the ship clean.

5-9-70 - We seem to be in good weather again after constant overcast weather, although the same wind is still blowing. The old man really had us working today - said that pay would be suspended if the work wasn't done. Still a lot of blood and thunder going on. He has offered Joe and Larry a passage to Panama but hasn't said anything to the Norwegians. Jan Erik has decided to stop on.

6-9-70 - Misty day with drizzle, not very warm. The following notice was issued: TO THE THREE CREW MEMBERS - BIE OSTGAARD ZOGBAUM - Who together with Jorgensen and Svendsen have given notice to leave in the first port of all. I have been requested by Zogbaun to take him to Panama, which I refused. I hereby offer one or all of the three abovementioned to bring one or all three to Norway on board the Regina Maris on the following conditions (deviation of home passage approximately 60 days).

1) Payment for food and lodging - Norw.Cr 10 - per day $1.50;
2) One or all shall assist cook - one at the time;
3) The others (other) shall steer 4 hours and take outlook 4 hours per day;
4) Give Master their word of honour that they will strictly adhere to the Master's orders and the ship's discipline similar to the regular crew members.

At sea - September 6th 1970. MASTER

7-9-70 - ETA around noon. Small birds settled on the boat. They were put in a cage near warmth, watered and fed. Saw a fin in the water which turned out to be a porpoise which was joined by many more - Regina Maris patrolling her game reserve! The lads were ready and packed at 11.30 and we sighted south America in the form of oil derricks, fishing boats who harpoon their fish. The land looked like south west Africa - desert and sand. Eventually berthed at 6pm after waiting for another ship to vacate bunkering berth. The captain told the others that a law case would be involved if anything was said in the newspapers. Much to our anger we were leaving soon as bunkering was over which would be about 02.00 hrs. After much bribing with whiskey and cigarettes, it was arranged for the other to go ashore. Managed to get ashore after doing some work and found the others in a restaurant where we had a steak, chips, tomatoes. Out of this world, and beer. We went to find the others to say final goodbyes but couldn't find their hotel.

8-9-70 - Made a successful departure and was woken at 7.30 to set square sails. Not much sleep so the day was spent quietly. Cleaned the cabin - so much space I feel lost. Our first day with 8 passed quite well. Hope this part of the voyage will be a happy and safe one with no blood and thunder. All being well we should be in Panama Saturday/Sunday.

9-9-780 - Crossing the equator today and King Neptune is coming to visit us. I had everything you could think of put all over me - mustard, tomato sauce, egg, flour and then was dunked. Got a certificate commemorating our crossing and was given the name Sir Timothy Slow Motion! Cleaned up, relaxed and had a beer - porpoises joined us again. Very quiet, peaceful evening with calm seas.

10-9-70 - It has warmed up considerably with light sw breeze running with the square sails up, calm seas. Didn't see any dolphins or boats. Threatened to rain but didn't. Keeping very well these days and hope it continues. Tim N moved into the cabin this morning. ETA Balboa daybreak Sunday the magical 13th. End.

Appendix E

A letter from Captain Paul Nelson to his family.

Trade Wind Cruises

2550 VIA TEJON, SUITE 3C

PALOS VERDES ESTATES,
CALIFORNIA

90274 (2 13)378-2605

AUX. BARQUENTINE [11] REGINA MARIS [11],

PAPSTE, TAHITI,

FRENCHPOLYNESIA

MONDAY, 2ND AUGUST, 1971

I think I'll begin from the Panama Canal which gave me my last sight of the Caribbean I like so much. We went through the Canal on the 7th May and as usual it was a hassle. This is a much used American word which means very roughly 'a hell of a lot of work'. This is not to say that the actual transit of the Canal was laborious; in fact it was fairly simple. The worst part was the protracted negotiations with the Canal and Port officials. To reduce the canal fees, water, fuel and port charges. This has been the history of every port we have been to whilst the principal stockholder, Neil Davis, was on board. In every port during that first voyage we had to sit down with the ship chandlers, agents, feed suppliers, launderers and port officials and haggle ever prices. I am all for negotiating prices with suppliers but it was often the case that Davis would try and renegotiate after the goods were received! In several cases bills were not paid at all, and in others they were paid with a lot of bad grace and ugly scenes. As a matter of interest and as far as bills are concerned they have not, to the best of my knowledge, paid their debts in Holland, England or Portugal. This comes to a sum of approximately $25,000.

From the Canal we went to Puntarenas in Costa Rica which was a most unmemorable place. We did not pay our bills here although they were only for about $30. We then sailed to Acajutla in El Salvador which was again a very ordinary port. It was here, however, that one of the most fantastic scenes of the last eight months took places. The story goes back to the Atlantic in the middle of which we stopped the ship so that the passengers could take a swim in the sea. To our surprise four of five of them started swimming in the nude in front of female passengers and two children. Mr. Davis did not like this at all, and from henceforth it was a ship's rule that there was to be no nude bathing. Imagine my surprise when I returned to the ship after a long hot day in Acajutla haggling and hassling over prices to find two of the male passengers in the nude. Walked up to them and told them to put their trousers on, but they refused. I then told them that their pay was stopped (they were being paid $30 a month as working passengers), but they still refused to put their clothes on. I was unsure what action I could take next. So I consulted Mr. Davis. He decided that they should be put off the ship, but of course the passengers refused to leave. Finally Mr. Davis and I went ashore, had a talk with the Captain of the port, and returned with two guards with sub-machine guns. The Passengers had now no choice but to pack their belongings and go ashore to the office of the port Captain. Here we had a long conference and it was decided that they should be allowed to return to ship provided they caused no further trouble. This was mainly at my insistence because by this time I had had a change of heart: it occurred to me that I had not actually warned them that if they did not put on their clothes they would be put off the ship. So ended a distasteful and not untypical incident of that first voyage.

From Acajutla we went to Acapulco which was a far more successful port because Mr. Davis left there.

Acapulco is beautifully situated in a perfect bay, but of course it is very expensive and tourist-oriented. I had very little time there because we now had a chance to paint the outside of the ship. The Mexican authorities were not the most helpful either. In

Acapulco we embarked a couple girl stewardesses, one of whom was Ernest Hemingway's grand-daughter – a very nice girl.

We were in Acapulco about four days and then left for Zihuatanejo – a primitive port a hundred or so miles to the north. From there we set course for Puerto Vallarta, but on the way we pulled into a bay on the coast called Chamela Bay. This was almost uninhabited which made the stop particularly appealing. We also had a barbecue on the beach which completed a perfect day.

I prefer to forget about Puerto Vallarta. Its principal claim to fame is that Richard Burton and Elizabeth Taylor have a summer home there, and of course it is drenched with Americans. We were there for only two days, and on the first I had to get water for the ship. Water has always been a problem because we carry very little aboard and the ship was never designed to carry so many people. The only place that I could get fresh water in the port was at the yatch marina, and the Port Captain invited me to take the ship to the marina so that we could take on water. Little did I know that two buoys were missing from the entrance to the marina, and of course as we were entering the approach channel we went aground? Going aground when you are in command of a ship is like having a crunching accident in a car – it's a terrible felling. Fortunately a tug was on hand to tow us off and we were only aground for less than then minutes. No damage was done, but nevertheless I'd hate to go through something like that again. My main concern was that the tug would claim salvage but a bribe of only $30 helped them forget it. We never took the water.

I hurried away from Puerto Vallarta as quickly as I could and went to Cape San Lucas at the tip of Baja California. This is really beautiful because Lower California is of course all mountainous desert and the landscape is quite haunting. All that is there is a cannery where the tuna boats take their catches, and an expensive hotel for American sports fishermen.

The weather was bad when we left Cape San Lucas and it was a long haul up to Ensenada in Mexico. On the way we stopped as Cedros Island which is a small semi-deserted place but where we could get some fuel. In Ensenada we disembarked the passengers which was an ordeal in itself. All the passengers were unhappy because they were being dumped in a Mexican border town and not Los Angeles as per contract. This was Mr. Davis's idea, the reason being that he disliked the passengers so much he wouldn't offer them the courtesy of taking them to Los Angeles in his ship. The story of the relationship between Mr. Davis and his passengers is a long one, and I haven't enough time to go into it deeply here. Briefly it is the story of false promises in order to get them to come on the voyage at $2,000 per head; innumerable rules and regulations they were expected to follow; poor food and accommodation and unilateral alterations to the written itinerary and schedule. The stories of the enmity between Davis and his passengers would fill a book. It was not all one sided, however. At least a quarter of the passengers were habitual smokers of marijuana which Davis detested; they tended to be very untidy in their habits and as time wore on were careless with the ship's (Davis's) property. This time was all anathema to him. To cut a long story short all the passengers were disembarked in Ensenada except two or three of his favourites. We stayed there about a week and carried out few minor repairs because labour was cheaper than in Los Angeles. Our stay there was enlivened when the ship was put under arrest by the Mexican authorities. One of our erstwhile passengers had informed them that we had drugs aboard, which in the event was true. The ship was surrounded by armed guards, no one was allowed off the ship whilst she was searched, but they never found anything. Finally we set sail for Los Angeles which is only a day's run from Ensenada. There was a good welcome arranged by the Press as you can see from the enclosed photographs. These were taken from helicopters and boats as we entered the harbour. By now I am becoming blasé about the welcome this ship receives in every port she goes to. We are always surrounded by hordes of sightseers and asked the same question over and over again. There always seems to be somebody being shown round the ship. It's irritating after a while because one seldom has any privacy.

We were moored in a yacht marina in Los Angeles and it was a long away from the city center. As usual I had almost no time off because we were preparing the ship for the next voyage to Tahiti and French Polynesia. We were in LA as it is called for exactly a week – from the 11th to the 18th of June. Six out the seven nights were taken up with parties of one sort or another. Three of them were given aboard by the owners for their special guests; one of them was a political party for local dignitary; another was for travel agents and the other at a private home. As you can see it was all pretty hectic, and that is why I had no time to write.

There was an ugly incident before we left LA – or rather two. The last day was mad scramble getting provisions and stores aboard and in the midst of it the Coast Guard were making a formal inspection of the ship prior to our embarking a new load of passengers. One set of stores I was concerned about were the medical stores. Davis had been promising that a doctor friend of his would sort them out and replenish them where required. Of course nothing happened so I presented him with a list of some basic supplies we were short of. He refused to get them. I refused to take the ship to sea without them. He got them! Worse than this was the scene at the fuel deck. We had moved here to fill up all our tanks three or four hours before we were due to sail. Unbeknown to me the owners had just informed one of my seamen (an 18 year old I had hired to in Newhaven) that he could either (a) leave the ship forthwith and be repatriated to England or (b) go on a reduced salary of $30 a month instead of his original $100 a month. I was told all this by all the crew who had convened a special meeting in a cabin and had come to an agreement whereby they would not sail the ship from LA unless the seaman, Bobby, was fully reinstated at his previous salary. The apparent reason for the action taken by the owners was that on the last voyage Bobby had been smoking Marijuana (which is strictly forbidden) and had also slept with one of the female passengers (also forbidden). I was very offended that the owner had neither consulted nor informed me before taking this action, and I also believed that their action was wrong. If a man is to be fired it should be done immediately after the offence was committed and not two or three weeks later; also it was quite incorrect to try doing it only two or three hours before the ship was due to sail for the South Pacific. I immediately had a long session with the owners where I told them that the crew would not sail the ship if bobby was not reinstated; I further told them that I would not take the ship sea unless they agreed to the crew's demands. After a long argument they were persuaded to do as I asked and Bobby stayed on full pay. I took full responsibility for Bobby and my action (Which I think was morally right) and carefully explained to him that drugs were definitely not allowed. The sequel to this story is that a week after leaving LA whilst we were in the middle of the Pacific I caught him, another seaman and female passenger blatantly smoking marijuana on the top of the wheelhouse at night. I had no alternative but to fire both the seaman, stop their work and pay, and told all three of them that they would be put off the ship at the first available opportunity. The other seaman was put off at the first island we called at because he was also suffering from hepatitis; Bobby and his girl friend were put off at the first island which had an airport. I don't know if you have yet seen the catch but it is this: Bobby stayed aboard at my insistence so I felt morally obliged that I should pay for his fare to Los Angeles and they could take care of him from there. They have refused to do even this so I have had to buy him a ticket to New Zealand out of my own money – about $200. There it is …… it makes me wonder if I did the right thing?

This second voyage has been far more successful than the first – the passengers have been more happy and contented although the food has still been poor. We did more sailing than on the last trip because the Trades were much better than in the Atlantic. We had an excellent 'crossing the line' ceremony which the passengers thought great. Davis isn't aboard this trip so people have been far less inhibited. The islands have been very beautiful and up to most people's expectations. As a matter of interest we have been to the following islands: Nuku Hiva and Hiva Oa in the Marquesas; Rangirea in the Tuomotus; Bora Bora, Raiatea, Huahine and Tahiti in the Societies. My favorite is Bora Bora which is particularly beautiful and we were moored stern to a very pleasant hotel. It was here we met a German who owns a night here in Papeete: it opens at 11 o'clock at night and closes at 6 in the morning, and plays classical music for most of the time. This chap, who is extremely generous and very friendly, arranged a great deal of publicity for our arrival here as you can see from enclosed.

Things have been very hectic here as usual. No sooner had the old passengers disembarked than the new ones started arriving without giving us a change to clear up after the others. The mail was very late in arriving. Arrangements were supposed to have been made by the office so that we could refuel here under credit. The credit has only just arrived – a week after our arrival. We are short of crew as men start leaving the ship – they have seen what they want to see and have no confidence in the owners. The food was poor on the outward trip because of the bad buying in Los Angeles; now they have only allowed us $500 to buy fresh provision here – despite my request for $1000. The food is going to be even worse on the homeward trip. I have been trying to telephone Los Angeles for the last two days to clear up some problems, but I can't get through. Now is the time to read the enclosed letter of resignation. As it is written it is not very strongly worded and you will probably be asking "why?". The crux of the matter of the matter is that I have lost all confidence in the owner as fair, reasonable and honest people. They are bad managers as they have antagonized me, my officers and crew. They make very heavy demands of us all without a quid pro quo. The crew are poorly paid (The going rate is now $30 a month), poorly fed, and if the owners had their way over-disciplined. I can't even get their or my linen laundered in three months. We have been living off straight porridge for breakfast, cold meat and cheese for lunch and reindeer meat balls with potatoes and vegetables in the evening. Day after day. As I explain in my letter of resignation they don't trust me with their money to decide what food is fair and reasonable; nor do they trust me to decide what the correct level of discipline is for the men. I know and have been told by many people that the crew respect me and think I am a first class shipmaster and seaman. So do the passengers without exception. I am not soft or lax but always fair and reasonable.

Appendix F

NOAA > NWS > CPHC Home Page > Annual Archives > 1972
The 1972 Central Pacific Tropical Cyclone Season

The Central Pacific Tropical Cyclone Season of 1972

A total of seven tropical cyclones entered or formed in the Central Pacific Hurricane Center's area of responsibility during 1972. In 1972 there were 30 named tropical cyclones of which 22 attained typhoon intensity, in the Western North Pacific. There were only 12 named cyclones in the Eastern North Pacific that year, slightly below the 1966-72 annual average of 15.

The equatorial trough was quite pronounced over the North Pacific during the summer and fall of 1972. Low-level monsoon westerlies (Ramage, 1974) extended from Southeast Asia across equatorial latitudes into the Central North Pacific. Sadler (1972) indicated this anomalous circulation pattern to be associated with large-scale ocean warning and the early beginning of a strong "El Nino". The 1972-73 "El Nino" cycle which began in March of that year (Ramage, 1975) had by fall reached such intensity that it was already equivalent to the great ones of 1891, 1925, 1941, 1957-58 and 1965. Aogust sea surface temperatures at Canton Island were 2.2C above normal, sea surface temperatures off Peru were 5C above normal, and the surface winds at Tarawa Island (1.4N 173.2E) had been prevailing westerly since September 1.

AUGUST 2-22, 1972 (HURRICANE CELESTE)

A tropical disturbance about 450 nautical miles south ?f LaPaz, Mexico on the 2nd moved westward and stalled near 15N 120W on the 4th. It developed gradually into a tropical storm by the 6th near where it had stalled and then moved slowly westward. There were no ship reports nearby when the vessel WGBC about 90 nautical miles south of the center indicated westerly winds of 20 knots and a pressure of 1006.4 mb (29.72"). Ships then remained well clear of the storm, now named CELESTE, until 08/1800Z when the SANTA ISABEL MARU passed 150 nautical miles southeast of the center.

A radio telephone call from the STAR TRACK estimated 80-90 knot winds near 16N 123W at 09/0054Z. During the rapid development to hurricane intensity a 117-foot, three-masted, square-rigged sailing vessel, the REGINA MARIS, with 53 persons aboard, became involved in the storm and was damaged by high winds and rough seas. It began taking on 2,000 gallons of water an hour and issued a distress call. A U.S. Air Force reconnaissance aircraft on a mission to the hurricane was alerted to the distressed vessel. That aircraft found it some distance from its estimated position, guided a rescue aircraft to the ship, and then continued on its mission. The VISHEA TRUTH reached the sailing vessel and took it in tow until the USCGC MELLON took over late on the 13th. Rescue and towing operations were complicated by the after effects of CELESTE and the effects of Hurricane DIANA, which followed 1000 nautical miles and 4 days after CELESTE.

Hurricane CELESTE crossed 140W at 14N about 12/0900Z. For the next 2 days it moved west-southwestward about 10 knots. The storm passed south of the Hawaiian Islands on the 15th. The closest point of approach, at 16/0600Z, was 380 nautical miles south-southwest of South Point on the island of Hawaii. Fifteen foot surf pounded the Puna, Kau, and South Kona coasts of the Big

Island.

By this time CELESTE had gradually turned to a west-northwesterly course and was headed directly for Johnston Island-a small, low-lying atoll, with an area of about one square mile and highest elevation of less than 20 feet above sea level. Extended (72-hour) forecasts provided ample opportunity for precautionary measures to be taken at Johnston. Later, the forecast for CELESTE to pass close to Johnston caused the Air Force to evacuate the entire population of about 500 military and civilian personnel the day before the hurricane struck, as a precaution against the possible escape of stored toxic gases.

On the morning of the 19th northerly hurricane-force winds raked Johnston for several hours as CELESTE's center passed about 25 nautical miles to the northeast. Details on the type, extent and dollar value of damage to the military facilities are not available, although the north and northwest sides of the structures appeared t-o have been sandblasted by blown sand and coral. Intensive preparation for the storm and the center passing north of the island no doubt caused damage to be relatively light. Fears that waves might inundate the atoll did not materialize, partly because of the protection afforded by extensive reefs and large deposits of dredging spoil which lie offshore to the north and northeast of the island.

The Johnston weather station lost about a third of its roof and ceiling tiles, but interiors and equipment were virtually unscathed. Weather instruments that remained in operation throughout the storm recorded the following:

1. A fastest mile of 105 miles an hour (statute) from the northwest at 7:59 a.m. on the 19th- -the greatest in 13 years of record and much above the previous maximum of 49 miles an hour observed in November 1959 and again in March 1964. The gust recorder was inoperative.
2. Gale force winds, from 11:18 p.m. on the 18th to 11:47 a.m. on the 19th.
3. Hurricane-force winds from 3:54 a.m. to 9:18 a.m. on the 19th.
4. A minimum sea-level pressure of 29.04 inches (983.4 mb) at 11:58 a.m. on the 19th. This compares with the previous minimum of 29.58 inches (1001.7 mb).
5. A total rainfall of 6.21 inches was measured in the catch basin of the tipping bucket weighing gage. However, this may be an underestimate, since the funnel of the gage was partially plugged with coral.

Immediately after passing north of Johnston, CELESTE took a sharp turn to a due northward course and began to weaken. Nevertheless, at 21/0600Z the AMERICAN LANCER only about 20 nautical miles north of the center was pounded by 55-knot gales, heavy rain which reduced the visibility to l/2 mile and seas of 10 feet.

CELESTE was downgraded to a tropical storm by 22/1200Z near 21N 172W and rapidly dissipated thereafter due to unidirectional vertical wind shear.

1972: Hurricane Celeste

Date/Time (UTC)	Latitude (N)	Longitude (W)	Pressure (mb)	Wind Speed (kt)	Stage/Notes
08/12/0600	15.0	139.3		85	Hurricane Cat. 2
08/12/1200	14.0	140.2		95	"
08/12/1800	13.7	141.8		85	"
08/13/0000	13.4	142.9		80	Hurricane Cat. 1
08/13/0600	13.0	144.2		80	"
08/13/1200	12.7	145.7		90	Hurricane Cat. 2
08/13/1800	12.6	147.0		90	"
08/14/0000	12.6	148.0	967	95	"
08/14/0600	12.5	149.6		100	Hurricane Cat. 3

08/14/1200	12.5	151.0		100	"
08/14/1800	12.4	151.7		100	"
08/15/0000	12.5	152.6		100	"
08/15/0600	12.5	153.9		100	"
08/15/1200	12.8	154.6		100	"
08/15/1800	12.9	155.8		90	Hurricane Cat. 2
08/16/0000	13.4	156.7		90	"
08/16/0600	13.7	158.0		90	"
08/16/1200	14.0	159.0		85	"
08/16/1800	14.3	159.8		75	Hurricane Cat. 1
08/17/0000	14.5	160.4		70	"
08/17/0600	14.7	161.2		70	"
08/17/1200	15.0	162.0		75	"
08/17/1800	15.0	162.9		80	"
08/18/0000	15.1	163.6	952	85	Hurricane Cat. 2
08/18/0600	15.3	164.5		85	"
08/18/1200	15.4	165.3		90	"
08/18/1800	15.5	166.5		90	"
08/19/0000	15.6	167.0		95	"
08/19/0600	15.7	167.7	943	100	Hurricane Cat. 3
08/19/1200	16.1	168.1		100	"
08/19/1800	16.5	168.5		110	"
08/20/0000	17.2	169.2		110	"
08/20/0600	17.8	169.5		100	"
08/20/1200	18.6	169.7		90	Hurricane Cat. 2
08/20/1800	19.0	170.0		80	Hurricane Cat. 1
08/21/0000	19.5	170.3	981	75	"
08/21/0600	20.6	170.6		65	"
08/21/1200	20.9	171.1		55	Tropical Storm
08/21/1800	21.2	171.6		45	"
08/22/0000	21.5	172.8		40	"
08/22/0600	21.9	173.5		35	"

AUGUST 8-20, 1972 (HURRICANE DIANA)

DIANA began developing in the wake of CELESTE on the 8th. A circulation was first indicated in satellite pictures near 9N 114W at 10/1800Z. Squalls and showers extended out 300 nautical miles from the center. Winds of 20 knots or less were reported 200-500 nautical miles from the center by the SANTA ISABEL MARU, CONON FOREST, and the STEEL ADVOCATE. The CONON FOREST, north of and converging with the storm, altered her course on the night of the 10th. She then sailed parallel to and at nearly the same speed as the storm, which increased to hurricane intensity on the night of the 12th near 13N 124W, remaining in its vicinity until the 18th. The VISHEA TRUTH (VWWT), towing the REGINA MARIS which had been disabled by hurricane CELESTE, was headed northeast ahead of the storm in 30-40 knot winds to rendezvous with the USCGC MELLON near 17N 126W on the night of the 12th. The hurricane center was then about 120 nautical miles to the south. The tow was transferred in strong winds and high seas, and the MELLON, bucking winds of 35-50 knots, headed northeast and east away from the storm. During the night of the 13th an Air France aircraft, on a flight from Los Angeles to Tahiti, encountered part of the storm at 18N 129W and diverted to the east of its normal flight path.

Reconnaissance on the 14th showed no change in either central pressure or maximum wind. On the 15th, Air Force reconnaissance reported DIANA had weakened somewhat. The central surface pressure had risen to 982 mb (29.0011) and maximum surface winds had diminished to 55 knots, causing DIANA to be downgraded to a tropical storm. At this point DIANA also changed course from a northwesterly heading to the west and increased forward speed to 16 knots. The next three reconnaissance observations on the 17th and 18th gave no reports on minimum surface pressure, but all reported maximum surface winds of 45-55 knots with no changes in storm characteristics.

Until 18/1800Z DIANA moved on a steady westerly course at an average speed of 16 knots. At this time the center was 300 nautical miles east of the island of Hawaii and the storm center was forecast to pass very near the southernmost point of the island on the 18th. Early on the 18th, Air Force reconnaissance located the center north of the predicted path and a sharp change in both course and speed of DIANA was in progress. A tropical storm warning advisory was then issued stating the storm would pass north of Hawaii. Reconnaissance on the 19th indicated further slowing and curvature to the north. A reported central pressure of 987 mb (29.15") with maximum sustained surface winds of 50 knots indicated slow weakening.

On the morning of the 20th a reconnaissance aircraft located the center of DIANA 30 nautical miles north of the island of Maui with a minimum surface pressure of 1005 mb (29.68") and, maximum surface winds of 25 knots. DIANA's career was nearly over. DIANA did manage to cause some damage, however. On the morning of the 18th, surf estimated to be 30 feet in height struck Hawaii Island's Puna coast at Kalapana, Kapoho Beach lots and Kapoho Vacationland. At Vacationland, which was most severely hit, the surf swept four homes off their foundations, extensively damaged one of them, flooded another home, washed rocks and debris inland and eroded 200 feet of a private road. Tides at Hilo Harbor rose 4 to 5 feet above normal beginning about 8 a.m. and lasted throughout the day. Although there were no floods, rainfall was heavy over most of the eastern side of the Big Island with pockets of very heavy rainfall. Ten inches fell in a small area northeast of Hilo and 8 inches fell in the Punaluu area southwest of Hilo.

On Maui the only reported storm damage was the erosion of some sand from Hanoa Beach on the eastern shore by surf of short duration estimated up to 20 feet high. One area along the northeast coast received up to 6 inches of rain during DIANA's close approach.

1972: Hurricane Diana

Date/Time (UTC)	Latitude (N)	Longitude (W)	Pressure (mb)	Wind Speed (kt)	Stage/Notes
08/16/1200	18.5	140.4		55	Tropical Storm
08/16/1800	18.3	142.0		55	"
08/17/0000	18.2	143.5		55	"
08/17/0600	18.3	145.1		55	"
08/17/1200	18.4	146.8		55	"
08/17/1800	18.4	148.8		55	"
08/18/0000	18.4	149.9		55	"
08/18/0600	18.5	151.1		55	"
08/18/1200	18.6	151.9		55	"
08/18/1800	18.9	152.7		50	"
08/19/0000	19.3	153.3		50	"
08/19/0600	19.8	153.8	987	45	"
08/19/1200	20.2	154.1		45	"
08/19/1800	20.4	154.3		50	"

08/20/0000	20.5	154.5	982	50	"
08/20/0600	20.7	154.8		50	"
08/20/1200	21.0	155.3		35	"
08/20/1800	21.3	156.1	1005	25	Tropical Depression

APPENDIX G

FROM THE REGINA MARIS BLOG   CREATED BY ALESSANDRO ABATE

POSTED FRIDAY, JULY 17, 2009

Regina Maris in the 1972 Pacific hurricane

My wife Lila, 12-year old daughter Joann, and I sailed on the Regina Maris from Ensenada bound for Tahiti via the Marquesas and Tuamotus. We intended to then fly to Australia where I was to spend a sabbatical leave. The voyage was a "share the work, share the expense" arrangement with Oceanwide Adventure Cruises of Palos Verdes, California. Everyone was assigned a task; mine was to give classes in celestial navigation. For that purpose I brought along a sextant, a nautical almanac, sight reduction tables and a portable multi-band radio to receive the time signals needed for celestial navigation (but I was not the Regina Maris navigator). The multi-band receiver turned out to be useful, as described in the F.C.C. report. But we encountered heavy weather not long after leaving Ensenada and so I never had a chance to teach celestial navigation. In the pounding the Regina Maris was getting from the turbulent seas she began to leak seriously -- very seriously as hurricane Cecile approached. Continuously pumping at full speed strained the two powered bilge pumps. Finally they both failed and we were then keeping the vessel afloat by a large manual pump and bailing. This is where the F.C.C. report begins. The next paragraph provides some information not in the report to be read while reading the report.

I used the International Phonetic Alphabet in my MAYDAY call. For example "Romeo Echo Golf India November Alpha" spells REGINA. Ocean Station November was a Coast Guard vessel located about halfway between San Francisco and Honolulu to collect weather information (this was before weather satellites), provide a place for airplanes in trouble to ditch, and to listen for distress calls from boats.

Single side band is a more sophisticated form of radio transmission normally used at the time by the Air Force jet but not compatible with the older double sideband receiver in the Regina Maris. Because of the hurricane we had not been able to get a "fix" on our position for several days and so knew it to no better than within about 1 degree of latitude and 1 degree of longitude; near the equator that means to within a region of about 60 nautical miles by 60 nautical miles. So the Air Force jet the Coast Guard diverted to look for us said we must make ourselves as visible as possible by spreading marker dye, producing smoke by burning oil soaked rags, raising as much sail as safety allowed, and flashing mirrors in the sunlight. It subsequently told me that what they saw first were the flashing mirrors. The two airplanes that arrived later dropped by parachutes a large number of small gasoline powered pumps and many cans of gasoline. The hurricane had passed by us when the Vishva Tirth arrived, allowing people to transfer to it from the Regina Maris. But some stayed on the Regina Maris to keep the gasoline powered pumps running. Several days after the Vishva Tirth began towing the Regina Maris to San Pedro the hurricane bent back and passed quite near us. The Vishva Tirth crew, who were terrified, said that they are usually able to avoid hurricanes but could not avoid this one because their speed was now limited to the hull speed of the Regina Maris they had in tow. A day later a large Coast Guard cutter arrived and began circling around us. With my multi-band receiver, I heard a message from the cutter to the Vishva Tirth saying they were present to pick up survivors if it or the Regina Maris went down. But it did not prove to be necessary and we all arrived safely in San Pedro 12 days after the tow began.

From San Pedro Lila, Joann and I returned to Santa Barbara, disposed of our filthy clothes, packed clean clothes, flew to Tahiti, spent two weeks there and in Bora Bora, then flew on to Australia. Four years later when applying to Harvard Joann described her experience on the Regina Maris in the essay that was part of the application. Her high school and SAT grades were very good; but the same was certainly true of the many others applying. After enrolling she came across a member of the selection committee who told her that her Regina Maris experience essay was of great interest to the committee and clinched her admittance.

I hope my experience will be interesting to people reading your blog.

Robert Eisberg

Appendix H

Left to right - Darlene (Jackson) Marmol (RMcrew79), Ken Balcomb (RMcrew76-85), Jeremy Brown (RMcrew75-77), Jill Likkel (RMcrew76-77), Steve Nelson (RMcrew79-80)
Photo taken at Sirens Pub in Port Townsend, WA. by Steve Nelson, 8 September 2014.

Regina Maris crew rendezvous

Past Crew, Students, Scientists, Cape Horners

Saturday 7 July 2012

Gloucester, MA

If you are a Regina Shipmate, please drop into the RM Facebook group or email Steve Nelson so we can get you on our mailing list.

- facebook group "Friends and Crew of Regina Maris"
  http://www.facebook.com/groups/53237394912/
- email contact Steve Nelson (crew 79-80)
  nelsbkstg@gmail.com

Tall Ships America
Adventure and Education Under Sail!
29 Touro Street, PO Box 1459
Newport, RI 02840
T: 401-846-1775 F: 401-849-5400
Email: asta@tallshipsamerica.org
www.tallshipsamerica.org

30 August 2013

To all REGINA MARIS Shipmates and Friends:

My deepest regrets, for not joining you in Gloucester for this excellent reunion. I am in Erie PA instead, wrapping up our TALL SHIPS CHALLENGE® Great Lakes 2013 season, which has included more than 20 sailing ships visiting more than 20 ports in the US and Canada, with races in all 5 lakes. It's been a long and successful season, for the ships, the ports, and the visiting public. Just so you know that I am not "missing and presumed lost", but still on watch and on duty in service to the fleet.

I know you'll have a great time seeing old shipmates and retelling old adventures. For what it's worth, I hope you'll all take some comfort in the sure knowledge that the way of the ship continues, in the ships, the programs and in the hearts of the sailors who make up Tall Ships America.

I learned so much in my days in REGINA, as a seaman, as and as a human. I had many unforgettable adventures, and sailed with some great folks. REGINA's legacy is strong and enduring, way beyond just the reunion festivities there in the great port of Gloucester. I witness it every time a sailing ship is outward bound on a deep water passage, with a cargo of eager and slightly scared young student-trainees. It is proven every time they return again, so triumphant in their new skills and competency.

It's good to know that young people still go still to sea, laying down the miles and the adventures end to end until their voyage is done and they're home again, stronger, more alert, and so much smarter about themselves and their place in the world. Maybe only one out of a hundred of these will ever board another ship, but everyone will be a better person, a better citizen, and a better steward for our ocean world.

From my vantage in Erie, I'll raise my glass to REGINA and her people, in deepest respect for the tradition she served and the lives she transformed. Best wishes to you all.

Ever onward,

Capt. Bert Rogers, Executive Director

The mission of Tall Ships America is to encourage character building through sail training, promote sail training to the North American public and support education under sail.

August 30, 2013

WoodenBoat

Dear REGINA MARIS alumni,

When I learned that there was to be a gathering of alumni sailors of the REGINA MARIS, my mind's eye went immediately to an awe-inspiring glimpse of her I caught in the early 1980s as she sailed off of Gloucester. Although I did not then fully understand her past or significance, she was a legend in my world as a pioneering educational vessel—one that would inspire me to pursue a similar educational path and—ultimately—a career around boats and the sea.

When I came to WoodenBoat in the early 1990s and became immersed in a world of historical vessels, REGINA's significance as a vessel quickly unfolded. She was built by the best Danish shipwrights of the best Danish oak, and was a queen among the legendary cargo carriers of the Baltic. She was nearly lost to fire in 1963, but a pair of Norwegians—the brothers Wilson—saw strength in her bones and rebuilt her to the highest standards. Then they sailed her around Cape Horn, cementing a legend and confirming the vessel's ability to undertake a second world cruise in the late 1960s and early 1970s. Subsequent ownership brought her to the charter business in the South Pacific and Caribbean, and then to Greece where, after a role in a film about the life of Joseph Conrad, she was left to die.

But then George Nichols stepped in with his vision for the education program in which you likely first encountered REGINA. He gave the ship purpose and care, and you gave her life. In the decade after he sold her in 1987, her condition declined precipitously.

In 1999, we at WoodenBoat made our own small tilt at her salvation with an article by David Berson. REGINA was then languishing in Greenport, New York, in need of a miracle. Our hope with our article was that a new owner of means and vision would step in and repeat the Herculean feats of the Wilson Brothers and George Nichols, but it wasn't to be. After sinking at her mooring, REGINA was subsequently broken up in 2002.

Now you sailors from all over the United States, Europe, and Australia have converged in Gloucester to celebrate this storied vessel, with your words, memories, and photographs. We at WoodenBoat hereby salute your commitment. For you, collectively, are the living legacy of REGINA MARIS.

Sincerely,

Matthew P. Murphy
Editor

The Magazine for WoodenBoat Owners, Builders and Designers
P.O. Box 78 • 41 WoodenBoat Lane • Brooklin, Maine 04616-0078 207-359-4651 Fax 207-359-8920

INDEX

A

A1-A, 26
Acapulco, 97, 108, 114–15, 263–64
Acklins Island, 163
ACS, 158
Adamstown, 75
Admiralty, 72–73
Admiralty Court, 130
Adolph, 152, 154
Adriaan Pronk, 94, 116
Aegean Sea, 133
Africa, 36
Agda Bengtsson, 246
AICH, 24, 30, 138, 140
aircraft carrier USS Coral Sea, 73
Air Force, 269–70, 272, 275
Alan Levin, 197
Alan Villiers, 29
Alaska, 138–39, 146, 156–57, 159, 166, 243
Albany, 72–73
Albatross, 24, 44, 45,48, 72,81
Alborg, 13, 66
Alessandro Abate, 244
Alexis Yerxa, 106
Alice Wilson, 64
Altamira Cave, 31
Amanda Madeira, 243
Amelia Earhart, 111
American Cetacean Society, 2, 141, 158
American River College, 148
American Sail Training Association, 144
American Ship Trust, 222
America's Cup, 142
America's Sail, 180, 225–26, 228, 231
Amicale Internationale, 27, 138, 140
Anders Kropp, 246
Anders Magnusson, 246
Andrew Boracci, 210, 211
Andrew L. Andrews, 197
Andrzej Wajda, 134
Angelika, 115
Angel's Gate, 98
Anna Maria Jonsson, 246
Annapolis, 175
Ann Druyan, 166
Anne flew home, 39
Anne-Luise, 28
Anne Margrethe, 28, 30
Anne Wilson, 37, 39
Annika Thuvik, 22
Ann Nichols, 189, 191, 212, 223, 243, 141, 143, 154, 190–91
Anthony Yudis, 194, 197
Antigua, 97, 122
April Beach- Pronk, 92, 108,113, 116
Arendal, 21, 24–25, 28, 45, 50, 86–88
Argentina, 37, 39
Ari Pronk, 109, 113
Arne Edvardsson, 22
Arne Ostgaard, 79
Arthur Curtiss James, 141
Ashley Book, 112
Australia, 7, 38, 50–52, 55, 58, 62, 67–69, 71–73, 76, 97, 139, 243–44, 274–75
Azores, 3

B

Bahamas, 46, 146, 188
Bahia Magdalena, 146
Baja California, 109, 264
Balboa, 84
Balboa Harbor, 122
Balearic Islands, 127
Baljik, 133–35
Baltic, 10–11, 17, 21, 130
Baltic Sea, 11, 21
Bangkok, 134
Barbados, 96–97, 103, 146
Barbara Clark, 47
Barbara Johnson, 228
Barbara Kirkbak, 32, 85
Batskarsnas, Sweden 11
Bay Crane, 235–36, 242
Bay State Towing, 206, 208
Becks Beer, 226, 233
Belgium, 17, 225
Bengt Larsson, 246
Bering Sea, 139
Berlin, 28, 33
Bermuda, 128, 144, 146, 161, 165, 176, 187
Bernard Goldhirsch, 142
Bert Rogers, 180–81
Big Jim Ryan, 97
Bill Bleyer, 206
Billdal, Sweden, 22
Bill Mabie, 161
Bill Pell, 206
Bill Shand-Kydd, 117
Bill Taylor, 211–12, 216, 219–20, 229
Biscay, 30, 54, 125
Black Sea, 5, 130–31, 137, 139, 141
Bligh, 74
Blohm, 30
Blue Point, 226
Bobby Freeman, 98
Bob Cameron, 226
Bob Liepa, 229
Bob Maus, 218, 226
Bolym Wieslaw, 133
Bora Bora, 106, 109, 267, 275
Bornholm, 21
Bosphorus, 133, 136
Boston, 36, 75–76, 136, 139, 142–43, 145–46, 148, 176, 180, 185, 187–88, 190, 198, 200, 235
Boston tall ships, 163
Botany Bay, 73
Brad Hanson, 148
Brenda Ashly, 174
Brest, 94
Brett Flipse, 232
Brictec Finance Ltd, 115, 122
Brictec partners, 117, 118
Bridgetown, 97
Brigantine Phoenix, 127
Brigantine Romance, 180
Brigantine Yankee, 144
Brig Henrietta, 117
Brighton, 93
Britain's West Indies, 74
British Isles, 47
Bill Pell, 200
British Merchant Navy, 91
British West Indies, 122
Brittany, 30
Brixham, 30
Brooklyn, 144

Buenos Aires, 38–39
Bug Light, 199
Bulgaria, 130–31, 133–34, 139
Buzzards Bay, 145, 149

C

Cabo San Lucas, 97, 109
Cagliari harbor, 132
Calcutta, 118
California, 4, 91–92, 98–100, 107, 110, 112, 115–16, 146, 148, 157, 179, 215, 232, 262, 274
Callao, 41–42, 45–46, 79, 89, 257–59
Cambridge University, 145
Cameron Femie, 132
Campers and Nicholsons, 127, 130–31, 141
Canada, 225
Canary Islands, 32, 34, 69, 96, 118, 141, 144, 190
Cantabria, 31
Cape Cod, 149, 163, 183
Cape Cod Canal, 145, 149
Cape Freels, 173
Cape Hatteras, 177, 188
Cape Horn, 24, 37, 41–45, 50, 57, 75, 77–78, 80–81, 119, 121, 256–57
Cape Horner Journal, 45, 138, 140
Cape Horn Society, 28–29, 51, 83
Cape Pigeons, 64
Cape San Juan, 153
Cape San Lucas, 264
Cape Town, 69–71
Cape Verde Islands, 33–34, 69
Capitan Miranda, 225
Captain Amasa Delano, 76
Captain Aralt, 25
Captain Bengtsson, 11
Captain Cook, 51–52, 57–58, 71, 74
Captain Edvardsson, 18, 20
Captain Finn Jensen, 18
Captain George, 153
Captain George Nichols, 174
Captain Gerhardt, 234
Captain Gustaf Edvardsson, 16
Captain James Cook, 50, 57, 74
Captain John Aage Wilson, 32, 40, 41, 43, 49, 58, 68, 76–77, 81, 83, 85, 88–90, 99, 196
Captain John A. Wilson, 48, 52
Captain John Fisher, 129
Captain John Guthrie, 139
Captain John Wigglesworth, 193–94
Captain Maskell, 96, 109, 111
Captain Mike, 132
Captain Mike Willoughby, 115, 117, 121
Captain Olof Bengtsson, 10, 14
Captain Paul H. Nelson, 32, 91, 95–97, 99, 103, 108, 262
Captain Robinson, 209, 213
Captain Sigfried Wilson, 28
Captain William Bligh, 88
Caribbean monk seal, 164
Carl Bjork, 246
Carl Holmstrom, 246
Carl Nisson, 246
Carl Sagan, 166
Carol Leonard, 107
Carol Lew Simons, 116, 164, 167, 204, 206, 210
Carthage, 87
Casablanca Morocco, 96
Cashman Marine Company, 195
Cedros Island, 264
CELESTE, 113, 269–70, 270, 272
Center of Lateral Resistance (CLR), 129
Cetacean research, 156, 183, 244
Challenge Cup, 50

Chamela Bay, 264
Channel Islands, 139
Charles Chiclacos, 231–32
Charles Hvilsom, 246
Charles Nordoff, 76
Charleston, 188
Charlie Chiclacos, 241
Charlie Clements, 96–98, 99, 103–4, 107
Charlie Digney, 218
Chichester yacht brokerage, 117
Chief engineer Bill Wilburn, 109
Chile, 24, 28, 36, 44–45, 77, 80–81, 86, 121, 256
Chris Roche, 45, 88, 140
Christovao de Mendonca, 71-72
Christina Theander, 22
Claudio family, 226
Claudio's dock, 200-202, 204, 212, 214, 217, 221, 223
Claudio's Restaurant, 199, 217, 219
Coast Guard, 48, 101, 110–11, 113, 145, 150, 206, 209–13, 218, 221, 228, 265, 274–75
Colon, 122
Columbia University, 142
Congressman Suozzi, 238
Connecticut, 24, 198, 211, 213, 216, 225, 239
Connecticut River, 213
Conscious Contact, 223
Cook Travel, 122–23
Copenhagen, 11, 13, 87, 169, 246
Coruna, 118, 124, 126
Corwith Cramer, 142
Cosmos TV Series, 166
Costa Rica, 97, 146, 263
Covent Garden, 88
Craig Cook, 95
Craig Strang, 245
Crow's Nest, 231, 240
Cuba, 97
Curacao, 82–84
Cutty Sark, 24

D

Dalhousie University, 145, 156
Dana Hewson, 219
Dan Rattiner, 22, 218, 229–30
Danish Jews, 18, 232, 240
Danish newspaper Politiken, 18
Danish school ship Georg Stage, 22
Danish tall ship Georg Stage, 225
Danny Bareiss, 176
Danny Spears, 103
Darlene Marmol, 244, 280
Dauphin Map, 72
David Kapell, 225, 227
David Nieri, 231, 232, 235, 239,241
David Marks, 121, 130–31, 135–36, 140
David Mattila, 182–83
David Moodie, 15
David Naden, 133
David Reiger, 231
David Reynolds, 132
David Short, 231
David Winzelberg, 241
David Wiseman, 108
Davis Strait, 168, 188
Davy Jones, 67
Debbie Tuma, 229, 240
David Marks, 139
Deirdrie "Shark" Lindsey, 110, 114, 116,
Denmark, 8, 11, 13, 18, 22, 28, 45, 66, 86, 172, 228, 231–33
Denton Shipyard, 125

Diana Davis, 238, 241
Dick Emery, 107
Disko Bay, 171
Dismasting, 59, 61, 65, 67, 71, 73, 222
Dolores Davis, 108, 116
Dolph Rempp, 227
Domenica, 191
Dominican Republic, 122, 146, 155, 176, 187
Donald Buchholtz, 225–26, 229
Don Griffing, 226
Don Ward, 136
Doug Eldon, 96–97, 99108–9,
Doug Murphy, 204
Doug Shaw, 237

E

Earl Henderson, 175, 181
Ebba Hierta, 216
Ecuadorian government, 120, 122
East End Seaport Museum and Maritime Foundation199–202, 204–5, 209, 211, 213, 220, 222–23, 226, 229, 231, 239, 242

Egypt, 87
Elbe River, 29
Elizabeth Taylor, 264
El Salvador, 96–97, 263
Emile Amarotico, 244
Endeavour, 71, 74
England, 27–28, 30, 32, 39–40, 49–51, 68–69, 73–74, 76, 85, 89–94, 115, 117–18, 123–24, 137, 243–44
English Channel, 82, 84
Ensenada, 98, 108–9, 113, 115, 117, 119–20, 127, 130, 139, 264–65, 274
EnviroSource Technologies, 211
Eovald Zogbaum, 79
Eric Bjorck, 15
Eric Hutchins' Dogtown, 245
Eric North, 91
Eric Sorensen, 197
Erling Brunborg, 32
Ernest Hemingway, 263
Ernestina, 173
Ernst Fault, 38
Ernst Nilsson, 16
Errol Weston, 227
Essex, 216
Estonia, 13
Evan Ginsberg, 190–91, 243
Evan Logan, 109, 111–14, 116, 187–88, 190–91
Evan Shepard, 190
Everett Holland, 210
Evighdesfjord Glacier, 171, 172
Evivald Zogbaum, 79
Explorers Club in New York, 86

F

Faederlandvenneil, 32, 197
Faervik, 88
Fairhaven, 206, 208–9, 212–13, 216, 221
Falmouth, 131
Fernando Fuenzalida, 28, 30
Fiji Islands, 74
Finland, 13, 17, 28
Fiskenaesset Harbor, 172
Flensborg, 13
Fletcher Christian, 75
Florida, 46, 64, 111, 115, 161
France, 24, 30, 45, 48, 50, 66, 72, 74, 92–94, 124–25, 139
Franz Joseph, 169

Frederick Sound, 158
Frederikshaab, 169
Fred Leeflang, 92–94, 96–97, 99
Fremantle, 7
French Polynesia, 74, 107, 109, 114, 262, 265
Friday Harbor, 244
Funchal, 4, 50, 52, 57, 59, 259
Funk Islands and Cape Freels, 173

G

Galapagos Islands, 119–22, 142, 146
Gary Neillands, 231
Gauguin's work, 74
Gazela Primeiro, 19, 95, 225
George Davis, 101
George Nichols, 136-137 139, 141–43, 148-49 152–53, 157, 160–61, 163–66, 173–74, 179–81, 184, 187–91, 193, 223, 243
George Nichols Jr, 141
Georges Bank, 147
Georgia, 226, 234
Gerard Lambert, 141
Geri Woodhouse, 221
German concentration camp, 23
German occupation, 23
Germans, 18, 36–38, 139, 267
German submarine, 17
Germany, 7, 11, 17–18, 27–29, 36, 38, 50, 66, 92, 115, 118, 127, 243–44
Gestapo, 23
Gibraltar, 56, 127, 132, 144, 146
Gilford "Tiffy" Full, 196
Glacier Bay, 146, 157–58
Glen Cove, 18, 22, 228–29, 231–43
Glen Cove's America's Sail, 229
Gloucester Massachusetts 137–38, 142, 146–47, 161, 165–66, 181, 185, 188, 190–91, 194, 242–44
Gloucester Maritime Heritage Center, 243
Godthaabfjord, 171
Gold Coast Gazette, 22, 232, 240
Good Hope, 36, 41, 67
Goteborg, 16
Gothenburg, 118
Gotland, 11
Gottfried Olsson, 246
Gotthab, Greenland 180
Graeme Ellis, 148
Gran Canarias, 35
Grand Banks, 18–19, 35, 48, 225
Gravesend Bay, 144
Greenland, 19, 163, 168–72, 174, 179-181, 188
Greenport, 5, 22, 46–47, 115–16, 166, 198–201, 202–6, 208–14, 217–19, 221–22, 225–26, 228–29, 231, 235, 237–39
Greenport Yacht and Shipbuilding, 199
Greg Cook, 91, 99, 105–6, 108, 112–13, 115–16
Gregg Swanzey, 173, 181
Greg Stone, 182
Greg Stover, 105–7
Gulf Stream, 149, 151, 162, 188
Gustaf Edvardsson, 15–18, 21, 22

H

Halifax, 145, 156, 168
Halsingborg, 11, 13, 246
Hal Whitehead, 145, 147, 156, 167, 190
Hamborgerland, 171
Hamburg, 7, 29–30, 36, 39, 66, 90
Hanis Schroybler, 38-39
Hanne Ekman, 18
Hanoa Beach, 273
Harold Selbach, 36–39
Harold Underhill, 34
Harry Hunt, 232

Harvard University Medical School, 142
Harvey Oxenhorn, 143, 147, 172, 174

Hawaii, 107, 111, 114-115, 117, 269-70, 272
Hedda Regina 86
Hellefiske Bank, 170
Hellvi Hide, 11
Hempstead Harbor, 231, 238
Henk Ahrens, 25, 32, 81–83, 92, 94–95, 97–100, 256
Henk Manussen Jr., 79, 81, 84
Henry Walters, 141
Herb Schierhorst, 232
Herman Ekman, 18
Herman Melville, 105
Hijo Knuttel, 198, 209–13, 213-217, 221

Hilo Hawaii, 89–90, 117, 272
Hitler, 17
HMS Bounty, 74
Hoivold Mekaniske Shipyard Kristiansand,15, 24-25 28, 32, 69, 79
Holger Nestorson, 9, 12, 15–17, 19–22
Holland, 41, 66, 92–93, 263
Holland Marine Design, 216
Holocaust Memorial, 228, 232, 238
Honolulu, 107, 225, 274
Hope Island, 171
Hopkins Grammar School, 147
Horseshoe reef, 163
Howard Breen, 112
Howard Swehla, 106
Howland Island area, 111
Hudson River, 145, 173
Humbolt, 256
Humpback whales, 145, 148–49, 156, 164, 177, 184
Hurricane Bob, 202–3, 212, 217–18, 224
Hurricane Cat, 270–71
Hurricane Celeste, 269–70, 272
Hurricane Diana, 269, 272–73
Hurricane Diane, 112–13

I

Icebergs, 41, 44, 160, 170–72, 186
Iceland, 18–19, 87
Indian Ocean, 67, 71, 117
International Whaling Commission (IWC), 143, 169
ISABEL MARU, 272
Isabel Wiggins, 199, 217-218
Island of Madeira, 4, 50, 52, 57
Island of Tjorn, 16
Israel, 228, 232
IUCN/SSC Marine Turtle Specialist Group, 161
IWC. *See* International Whaling Commission

J

Jacksonville, 46, 64
Jacobshavnfjord, 171
Jamaica, 96–97, 122–23, 136
James Cook, 72–73, 159
James Hall, 76
James L. Frye, 193, 196-97
James Perran Ross, 161, 167
Jamie Greens, 25
Jan Claudio, 199
Jan Davidsson, 15, 22
Jane Norton Morgan, 141
Jan Eric Nestande, 79, 84
Jan Erik, 260

Janet Blatt, 18, 22, 232, 240
Jane Tuahu, 75
Janne Hansson, 246
Janne Peter Reinhold, 246
Jean-François, 166Jeff, 116, 216
Jeff Berry, 114, 116
Jeff Gilbert, 157
Jeff Lindberg, 216
Jenni Atkinson, 129
Jennifer, 179
Jeremy Brown, 128, 137–38, 140, 280
Jeri Prince, 218
Jeri Woodhouse, 218
Jerry Brown, 152
Jill Likkel, 244, 280
Jim Goebel, 150, 153
Jim Norris, 99
Joachim Bliese, 79, 83-4
Joan Vaughn, 194
Joann Eisberg, 275
Joe Garland, 191
Joe Haberstroh, 229–30, 241
Joel Olsson, 246
Joe Tyrrell, 77–79
Joe Weiser, 231–33, 241
Johan och Reinold Moller, 246
John Adams, 75
John Bennett, 133
John Bird, 96, 98, 101–2
John Blowers, 118, 126–27, 129
John Calogero, 172, 180
John Campbell, 112
John Costello, 199, 205, 217, 221, 227, 229
John Fisher, 127
John Ford, 148
John Hart, 99
John J. McMullen Associates, 229
John L. Hall, 232
John Muir, 159
John Pasquarella, 226
John Pierpont Morgan Jr, 141
John P. Mordes M, 147
John Quackenbush, 184
John Stapley, 91
John Staply, 115
Johnston Island, 270
John T. McQuiston, 230, 240–41
John Venditto, 227
John Aage Wilson, 15, 21, 23–24, 27–32, 33–36, 38–39, 42, 44–46, 49-52, 57, 64–69, 71–73, 75– 81, 83–84, 86–89, 91–92, 97, 107, 115, 191, 242
John Wilson I, 23
John Wilson's Wooden Walls, 44, 46, 48
John Woodhouse, 218
Jolly Boat, 3, 174, 176, 240, 243, 245
Jolyon Wymhurst, 133
Jones Act, 101
Jons Peter Andersson, 246
Jorgen Ring-Andersen, 8, 15
Jorgen Ring-Andersen Shipbuilders, 15
Jorgensen, 80–81, 83, 260
Joyce Kerin, 91, 101, 108
Jubilee Sailing Trust, 127
Jude Thaddeus Marina, 231
Judith S. Perkins, 168, 181
Judy Ahrens, 203
Judy Pratt, 189
Julie Hoffman, 176
Julie Lane, 241

K

Kalapana, 272
Kapoho Beach, 272
Karen Schroeder, 218
Kathie Johnses, 69
Kelley's shipyard, 206, 208
Ken Balcomb, 157, 177, 181–82, 188–89, 191, 243–44, 280
Ken Norris, 148
Windward, 117
Kevin McLaughlin, 206, 208
King Francis I, 72
King Neptune, 33, 35, 84, 101–2, 261
King Oscar, 169
Kingston Harbor, 122
Klaus Hanusa, 28, 30-31, 36, 38, 43, 45, 54, 70, 79, 82–84, 256, 259
KNS, 50–51
Kraig R. Hankins, 171
Kristiansand, 15, 24–25, 28, 46, 65–66, 79–80, 85, 118, 235
Kristina Jonsson, 246

L

Labrador, 19, 145–46
Laguna Guerrero Negro, 158
Lake San Marcos, 95
Landing Boat School in Kennebunkport, 198
Landmark School's Watermark Program, 173
Landskrona, 13
LaPaz, 269
Larry Demmler, 232
Larry Stouffer, 77–79
Las Palmas, 32, 34–35, 65, 69, 71, 95–97
Lee Bruno, 244
Leo Goldberger, 18, 232, 240
Lettie Maistui, 75
Lindberg Marine, 209, 213, 216
Lisbon, 19, 30–32, 34–35, 92, 94–96, 100, 108
Little Lamesure Bay, 190
Lloyd of London , 18, 25–27, 32, 36, 67, 79, 85, 88, 108, 117, 125, 127, 130, 140, 190, 222
Long Beach, 4, 91, 99–101, 107, 116, 232
Long Beach California, 107
Long Cours Cap Horniers, 24, 27, 138, 140
Long Island, 142, 144, 150, 198, 200, 202, 210, 218–19, 222, 225, 227, 230, 233, 239, 241
Long Island City, 206, 216, 229
Long Island Maritime Museum in West Sayville, 237, 239
Long Island Sound, 142, 144, 238
Los Angeles, 91, 98, 103, 264–67, 272
Lotta Clark, 15, 22

M

Mae West jib, 25
Maggie Leahy, 221
Majesty King Peter, 48
Majesty's Royal Dockyard, 27
Malcolm Miller, 126
Malmo, 11, 13
Malta, 28, 48, 91, 101
Manny Grella, 238, 241
Marblehead Massachusetts, 196
Marek Kondrat, 133
Margaret O'Neil, 206-07, 216
Marianne Wilson, 23, 33
Maria Theander, 18
Marina Bay, 5, 193–94, 196–98, 193, 200, 211–12
Mari Smultea, 179, 181
Maritime Festival, 205, 221, 223
Marquesas, 101, 104–5, 109, 267, 274

Marquesas Islands, 109, 114
Marrakesh, 96
Martinez, 100
Martinique, 97, 139
Mashfords, 30
Mashomack Manor House, 47
Massachusetts Bay, 146–47
Massachusetts Environmental Protection Agency, 208
Massachusetts Historic Commission, 208
Maui, 272–73
Mayhew Folger, 75
Mazatlan, 97, 146
McAllen Air Force Base, 111
Mediterranean, 127, 132, 141, 144
Merlon Wiggin, 199-202, 204–5, 209-211, 213, 216-218, 222, 225–27, 229, 231
Miami, 115, 146
Michael Willoughby, 117, 119-20, 124, 128, 137, 222, 128, 130, 132–33, 137–41, 218–20
Miguel Evans, 109
Mike Bigg, 148
Mike Darlow, 133
Mike Kortchmar, 218–19, 229
Mike Salentino, 232
Mike White, 36, 38
Montauk Light, 47, 226
Montevideo, 29, 36–37, 41, 75, 77, 81, 257
Moorea, 107, 109
Morgan Syndicate, 141
Morton Fox, 237
Mosquito Cove, 233
Moss Landing Marine Laboratories, 179
Mount Attitash, 190
MS Atene, 15, 22
Mystic Seaport, 24, 48, 211–12, 215, 219, 239

N

Naples, 115
Nassau, 46, 146, 188
National Geographic Society, 144
National Guard, 221
National Marine Fisheries Service (NMFS), 148, 158
National Maritime Historical Society, 209, 215, 222, 229
Nature Conservancy's Mashomack Preserve, 47
Navidad Banks, 156, 177
Neil Davis, 86, 91-92, 95, 98, 101, 103, 108, 238, 262, 265, 267
Netherlands, 17, 86, 91, 99–100, 108
New England Aquarium, 176
New England Coastal News, 216
New England Deaconess, 142
Newfoundland, 18, 145–46, 168, 171
Newhaven, 93, 266
Newmarks Yacht Center, 98
Newport, 144, 150, 153, 177, 180, 183, 201, 208, 219
Newport Shipyard, 150
New York Harbor, 46-48, 238
New York Port Authority, 47
New Zealand, 187, 244, 266
Nick Calvert, 112
Nick DeSantis, 233, 236, 241
Nicola Wadsworth Bloedel, 175, 181
Nils Andersson, 246
Nils Olsson, 246
Nils P. Johansson, 246
NOAA account, 109, 112,
Noord Einde, 92
Norfolk, 46
North Atlantic, 10, 148–49, 151, 175
North Sea, 51, 85
Norway, 15, 18, 21, 23–25, 27–28, 31–32, 45–46, 64–67, 79, 85–86, 88, 90, 115, 125, 138, 243–44, 259–60
Norway's Crown Prince Harald, 51

Norway's National Day, 72
Norwegian riggers, 69, 71, 125
Nova Scotia, 145
Nuka Hiva, 101, 104–5

O

Ocean Navigator, 237, 241
Ocean Research and Education Society (ORES), 143, 148, 164, 168, 180, 184, 187, 189–90, 193, 212, 242
Ocean Transport Lines, 21, 86
Ocean-Wide Film Production Berlin-Santiago, 28, 33, 43, 45, 54, 70, 84
Oceanwide Sailing Company Ltd, 91
Ocean-Wide Steamship Company Inc., 21, 86
O'Connell Management Co, 193, 195, 197
Old Ironsides, 194
Olof Andersson, 12-14, 246
Olof Bengtsson, 7–8, 10, 12–14
ORES. *See* Ocean Research and Education Society
Oresund, 12
Orkney Islands, 118
Oxford, 72
Oyster Bay, 227

P

Palos Verdes Estates, 91, 262, 274
Panama, 23, 39, 83, 86, 95, 97, 112, 121, 125, 137, 146, 257, 259–61
Panama Bay, 122
Panama Canal, 46, 79, 84, 142, 146, 262
Papeete, 32, 73–75, 100, 105, 107, 112, 114, 267
Patch Willoughby, 119, 121–23, 128, 130-34, 137, 139
Pat Malloy, 211
Pat Quiter, 106
Patrick Wadden, 174
Pat Rogers, 230
Paul Casciotta, 204
Paul Coble survey, 223
Paul Gauguin, 74, 105
Paul Maskell, 28, 59, 68, 76–77, 79–82, 84, 91–92, 106, 108, 110, 112–13, 115–16
Paul Nelson, 95, 97, 99, 101, 108, 262
Penny Kerr, 3, 58, 213-214, 221, 223–24
Perran Ross, 183, 244
Peru, 41–42, 45–46, 79–80, 83, 257, 260, 269
Pete Jacobson, 231
Peter Bent Brigham, 142
Peter Bryant, 158–60, 167
Peter J. Bryant, 157
Peter O'Connell, 194
Peter Olley, 117
Peter Seamans, 141
Peter Stanford, 209–12, 216, 222–23, 229
Peter Wilson, 27–29, 32-33, 35–37, 40, 42–43, 46–47, 49-50, 58-59, 66, 68, 70, 76, 86–90
Petter Jacobsson, 246
Phil Clapham, 182–83, 191
Phil Colararusso, 210
Phoenicia, 87
Pierre Bowman, 107
Pipe's Cove, 201, 220
Piraeus, 136, 141, 146
Pirana II, 133
Pitcairn Island, 75–76, 80–81, 83, 256
Plum Gut, 229
Plymouth England, 27, 30, 50–51, 54, 57, 73, 115, 117–18, 123–24, 144
Point Camden, 113
Polish National Film Corporation, 130, 133–34
Polynesia, 108, 114
Port Antonio, 97
Portland, 241
Port Royal, 122–23
Portsmouth, 126–27

Port Townsend, 244, 280
Portugal, 27, 31–33, 71–72, 94, 263
Provincetown, 183
Puerto Citos, 146
Puerto Plata, 146, 164, 166, 176–77, 187–88
Puerto Rico, 97, 142, 146, 150, 152–54, 176, 181, 190–91
Puerto Vallarta, 97, 146, 264
Punta Arenas, 97, 146
Puntarenas, 263

Q

Queen Elizabeth II, 51
Quincy, 193–94, 197, 212
Quinn's Bar in Papeete, 74

R

Raa Sweden, 7–8, 10–16
Raa division of Sweden's Sailing Ship Association, 14
Radio-Televisione-Luxembourg (RTL), 50
Raiatea, 106, 109, 267
Rammon River, 118
Rand Wilson, 191
Rangiroa, 106, 109
Reginald Spinello, 238
Reinhold Olsson, 246
re-rigging, 65–67, 71, 73
Retter Hoivold, 32
Richard Perkins, 189, 191
Richard Sears, 182–83
Rich Mula, 150, 153
Ring-Andersen Shipyard, 8, 228, 231
Rio Janeiro, 33, 36–37, 90

River Plate, 37
River Taqus, 31–32
Roald Amundsen, 88
Robby Robinson, 212
Robert Eisberg, 110, 275
Robert Gearty, 241
Robert Val Rosenbaum, 198–202, 204–6, 208–9, 211–12, 215-16, 219, 221
Robin Suess, 218
Rockport, 245
Rocky Neck, 190
Rodriguez shipyard in Ensenada, 113
Roger Callan, 28, 43–45, 49-51, 57–58, 61–62, 64, 66, 68, 71, 76–80, 84, 102, 103, 108
Roger Compton, 231
Roger Payne, 160
Rolling Home, 52, 88–90
Ronnang, 16
Rostock, 11
Royal Astronomical Society, 74
Royal Dockyard, 38
Royal Navy, 27, 118, 132
Royal Norwegian Yacht Club, 50, 67
Royal Sydney Yacht Club, 51
Royal Sydney Yacht Squadron, 50
Royal Yacht Britannia, 122
Royal Yugoslav Commemorative War Cross, 23
Rudolf Ahlman, 246
Rudolph Shubert, 229
Russell H. Tripp, 206–7, 208-14, 216
Russian, 136, 138
R/V Regina Maris, 143, 188, 191

S

Sag Harbor, 199, 210–11, 213
Sag Harbor Whaling Museum, 211

Sail Boston, 245
Sailing Education Association SEA, 142
Sailing School Vessels Act, 181
SAIL Magazine, 142
Sailors House in Halsingborg, 11
Sail training, 180, 187, 242
Saint Malo, 24, 30, 45, 48
Sam Berliner III, 234, 236
San Diego, 139, 142
Sandy Hook, 144
San Francisco, 100, 107, 146, 215, 274
San Juan Puerto Rico, 97142, 146, 154, 187, 190, 245,
San Pedro, 112–13, 115, 146, 275
San Pedro News Pilot, 116
Santa Barbara, 84, 110, 275
Santa Cruz, 118
SANTA ISABEL MARU, 269
Santander, 30–31
Santiago, 28, 33, 36, 86, 121
Santo Domingo, 164
Sardinia, 132
Sarkhamn, 16–19, 21
Scheveningen Harbor, 4, 91–93, 99
Schooner America, 141
Schooner Bowdoin, 173
Schooner Dodi, 138
Schooner Jakob, 7
Schooner Mary E, 229
Schooner Rambler, 143, 187
Scientific Research in Greenland, 169
Scoresby Sund, 169
Scotland, 118
Scott Cordes MD, 144
Scott Emerich, 232
Sea Breezes, 130, 137, 139
Sea Cliff Yacht Club, 231
Sea Cloud, 139, 181
Sea Education Association, 147, 212
Sea History Gazette, 230, 240
SEA Semester, 143
Seattle, 146, 148, 159, 175
Seychelles, 139
The Shadow Line, 130
Shamrock Quay, 127
Shellbacks, 101–2
Shelter Island, New York, 15, 22, 47, 49, 99, 202, 223
Shenandoah, 90
Shep Root, 1
Sherryl Taylor, 142–43, 147
Sicily, 133
Sidney Daily Mirror, 76
Sidney Sun, 76
Sigfried Wilson, 21, 23–24, 28–31, 36, 48, 66, 73, 79, 81–83, 86, 88
Sigurd Thuvik of Sarkhamn, 21, 25
Silver Bank, 146–47, 155–56, 175–76, 178, 181, 184, 187–89
Silvia Regina 86
Singapore, 134
Sir Joseph Banks, 72
Sir Winston Churchill, 118
Skagerack, 18
Skarhamns Sjofartsmuseum, 9, 15–17, 19–22
Skeppoch Sjoman, 15, 22
Smuggler's Cove, 245
Society Islands, 74, 106
Sondre Stromfjord, 169
Soundings Magazine, 216
Southampton, 5, 7, 22, 69, 127–28, 130–31, 136, 138–39, 141, 229
Southeast Alaska, 157–59
South East Asia Command, 118
Southern Tuamoto Archipelago, 107

Indian Ocean, 67
South Kona, 270
Southold, 164, 206, 216
South Pacific, 41, 59, 74, 91, 113, 266
Sparkman & Stephens, 216
Spuyten Duyvil Bridge, 145
Squantum, 193–94
Stanislaw Tym, 133
Steam Boat Landing, 231, 233
Sterling Yachts, 211-212, 219
Steve Bovan, 98
Steve Clarke, 199–201, 215, 220, 222–23, 226, 228–29, 235
Steve Katona, 2-3, 182, 242
Steve Nelson, 3, 243–45, 280
Steven Soter, 166
St. Johns, 187, 190
Stockholm, 11, 13, 17
St. Petersburg, 13
STRM, 212–13, 215, 217–20, 222-226, 229, 231
St. Thomas, 187
Sukkertop Dyb, 169
Sukkertoppen, 171
Sundsvall, 11, 13
Sunny Seitier, 231–32, 240
Susie Lange, 15, 22
Sussex, 32, 40, 49, 58, 68, 76, 85, 90, 99
Svendborg, 8, 15, 231
Sven Olsson, 246
Sweden, 7, 11, 13–14, 16–19, 21–22, 24, 27, 118, 228, 232
Sweden's Sailing Ships Association, 14
Sydney, 50–51, 73
Sydney Harbor, 73

T

Tabor Academy, 212
Tad Pennoyer, 165
Tahiti, 32, 73–75, 81, 100–101, 107, 109–10, 112–14, 117, 267, 272, 274–75
Taiohae Bay, 105
Taipivai, 105
Talara, 79–80, 83, 259–60
Tall Ships Race, 144, 226
Tarawa Island, 269
Tasmania, 99
Ted Schmidt, 47
Ted Schroeder, 226
Tenerife, 118, 146, 190
Teodor Lindgren, 246
Terry Leggett, 27-36, 40
Thames TV, 133, 140
Thames TV/Film 130
Olympic Soling Yacht class, 50
Thomas Cook Ltd, 120, 128
Thomas Suozzi, 228, 231-237, 240–41
Thor Bie, 79–81, 85
Tiffy Full, 196
Tiger Timbs, 138
Nicola Wadsworth Bloedel, 175
Tim Kelly, 206, 216
Tim Nossiter, 29, 32, 79–80, 83–85, 92, 95–97, 99
Timor, 74
Tim Pickthall, 79–80, 83–85, 92, 97, 256
Tole Mour, 225
Tom Clawson, 92
Tom Cox, 198, 211, 196
Tom Hoffman, 231
Tom Maguire, 112, 120–21, 128, 130, 136–37, 139
Tommy Clawson, 92
Tommy Nielsen, 138

Tom Wilkinson, 133
Toni Bryant, 157-167
Tony Avanzino, 98
Tore Jongensen, 79-80
Tortuga, 97
Trade Wind Cruises (TWC), 91, 108, 113, 115, 262
Traveler-Watchman, 206
Troy Gustavson, 206
Tuamotu Archipelago, 106, 109, 267, 274
John Wannamaker tugboat, 193
Tunis, 87
TWC. *See* Trade Wind Cruises
Tyholmen Hotel, 25
Typhoon Celeste, 110
Typhoon Diana, 112-113, 272–73

U

UK, 84, 117–19, 123, 137
Uleaborg, 13
Umea, 13
University of California, 110, 148, 157
Uphams, 30
Uruguay, 36–37, 75, 225
US Coast Guard, 221
USCGC MELLON, 269, 272
USS Constitution, 145, 227
USS Forrestal, 145
Uver Helm, 35

V

Valletta, 91
Valparaiso, 78, 80
Vancouver, 65
Varna, 130–33, 135–36
Vega, 118, 125, 173–74
Venezuela, 225
Venus Point, 74
Verrazano-Narrows Bridge, 145
Viborg, 228
Village of Greenport, 208, 221, 237
Village of Sag Harbor, 210–11
Vince Mow, 211-212, 215, 221
Vincent Thomas Bridge, 101
Vinny Martinez Jr, 240
Virginia Clark, 46–47
Virgin Islands, 97, 176
VISHEA TRUTH (VWWT), 111–13, 269, 272, 275
V.Penghana, 99

W

Wade Curry, 232
Wajda, 130
Walter J. Hannon Sr, 193
Ward Murphy, 94, 99
Warnow River, 11
Washington, 65, 146, 148, 175, 181, 243–45
West Australia, 7, 72
Westbury Times, 230
West Greenland, 146, 168–69
West Sayville, 237, 239
Whale research, 141, 166, 189, 244–45
Whalewatcher, 2, 141–42, 145, 147, 155–56, 158–59, 167–68, 179, 181–82, 191
Wigglesworth, 212
Wijtola Sobolinski, 133
William Allen, 219
William Bligh, 74

William Claudio, 199–200, 204, 210, 213–14
William Dobriner, 206, 229
William O'Connell, 193
Williams College, 161
William Street, 127
Willi Prestin, 92, 105
Wilmington, 98, 100, 232
Windjammer Cruises, 115
Winston Churchill, 127
Woods Hole, 212
World Holocaust Remembrance Center, 228-230

Y

Yad Vashem, 230, 232
Yastad, 21, 24

Z

Zeas Marina, 136
Zenobe Gramme, 225
Zihuatenejo, 97, 264

Made in the USA
Lexington, KY
05 December 2017